MW00564561

MARKETING MANAGEMENT
A Strategic Framework and Tools for Success

FIRST EDITION

Dawn Edmiston, Todd Mooradian, Kurt Matzler, Lawrence Ring

cognella®

SAN DIEGO

Bassim Hamadeh, CEO and Publisher
Peaches diPierro, Associate Acquisitions Editor
Alisa Munoz, Project Editor
Susana Christie, Developmental Editor
Celeste Paed, Associate Production Editor
Emely Villavicencio, Senior Graphic Designer
Kylie Bartolome, Licensing Associate
Ursina Kilburn, Interior Designer
Stephanie Adams, Senior Marketing Program Manager
Natalie Piccotti, Director of Marketing
Kassie Graves, Senior Vice President, Editorial
Jamie Giganti, Director of Academic Publishing

3970 Sorrento Valley Blvd., Ste. 500, San Diego, CA 92121

Brief Contents

Detailed Contents

Preface

The field of marketing has seen dynamic changes during the past decade, with advanced technologies creating a world that is more connected than ever before. As marketing professors, we are constantly examining how these changes have created both challenges and opportunities for organizations and their leaders.

Our passion for teaching the discipline of marketing and our experience consulting for organizations across the globe, served as the motivation to develop this book. In an effort to quickly capitalize on market opportunities, firms often deploy a broad range of marketing tactics without a strategic plan, and then wonder why such tactics were not effective. Other organizations might understand the value of a strategic approach to marketing, but not have the tools necessary to develop such an approach. Thus, we were inspired to write a book for marketing students and professionals that not only outlines a strategic marketing framework, but also provides the tools necessary to ensure success.

Our intent for this book was to achieve a balance between academic insight and practical application. As such, we divided the book into two distinct sections to emphasize both the processes *and* the tools involved with strategic marketing.

The first section of the book is comprised of four chapters; the initial chapter introduces core concepts, and the remaining chapters examine each of the three stages in the Strategic Marketing Framework. This section allows readers to gain a comprehensive understanding of the entire process before reviewing specific tools related to each stage.

The second section of the book is comprised of "Notes" that highlight tools and concepts to support the various stages of the Strategic Marketing Framework. We recognize there are vast resources available to marketers, so we sought to feature those tools that have proven to be the most valuable to us, both inside and outside of the classroom.

Whether your work is focused on a start-up, a multinational corporation, or a nonprofit organization, we hope this book will serve as an indispensable guide for your strategic marketing efforts.

Dawn Edmiston
William & Mary, USA

Todd Mooradian
University of Louisville, USA

Kurt Matzler
University of Innsbruck, Austria

Lawrence Ring
William & Mary, USA

AN OVERVIEW—UNDERSTANDING THE ROLE OF MARKETING MANAGEMENT ACROSS THE STRATEGIC MARKETING PROCESS

At its core, strategic marketing focuses the organization on the customers it serves and their specific needs. Peter Drucker, known as the founder of the field of management, famously stated, "There is only one valid definition of business purpose: *to create a customer* [emphasis added]. … It is the customer who determines what a business is" (Drucker, 1973, p. 61, emphasis in original). Drucker's simple statement is sometimes misunderstood; it does not mean that an organization should try to meet the needs of all customers or try to meet all of the needs of any customer. It does not mean that the customer is always right or that serving a customer should be done at any cost. However, it does mean that the customer, and the customer's needs, must be the foundation upon which an organization builds its purpose and marketing strategy.

Understanding this "marketing concept" is the critical starting point for all marketing management. The marketing concept is not simply an abstract theory or altruistic philosophy—organizations should be driven by the customers they serve and the needs they meet because that is the most effective approach. **The marketing concept suggests that if we take good care of our customers, everything else, such as sales and profits, will follow**. Extensive research has linked a market orientation to higher long-term profits; however, most firms and managers are measured in the short-term, and therein lies a conflict. Balancing short-term objectives with long-term outcomes is the most common challenge faced by managers when developing a marketing strategy. Thus, in this chapter, we specify what a strategy should include—that is, what elements make up a comprehensive marketing strategy to effectively balance short-term gains with long-term sustainability.

MARKETING STRATEGY VERSUS STRATEGIC MARKETING

There are two critical concepts to understand in marketing management. They are *marketing strategy* and *strategic marketing*. Marketing strategy refers to a plan of action to serve the needs of customers. Strategic marketing refers to the act of formulating, executing, and evaluating the marketing plan. This book addresses *both*. As the title of this book implies, our primary focus will be on the active process of marketing management through a strategic framework. Before digging into that process, however, we should know where it leads. What should the outcome of the process be? What is a "marketing strategy"?

A comprehensive marketing strategy is focused on defining the *who*, *what*, *where*, *how*, *when*, and *why* of the customer value proposition.

1. *Who* will the firm serve? *Who* are the customers and the market segments?
2. *What* specific needs of the customer can the firm identify and meet?
3. *Where* will the firm do business? *Where* are the customers located?
4. *How* will the firm use their resources and distinctive competencies to serve customers and their needs better than the competition can?
5. *When* is the optimal time to deliver products and services to the customer?
6. *Why* will the firm do these things? In effect, what is the compelling business model that specifies how long-term revenues will exceed costs by a reasonable rate of return on the capital employed? (adapted from Hambrick & Fredrickson, 2005)

A comprehensive marketing strategy will stipulate each of these essential elements related to how the company goes to market. **A sound marketing strategy must eventually meet the specific needs of specific customers better than the competition, within profitable relationships.** That is, the six questions above define a customer-driven strategy and can be summarized as three high-level decisions:

- *Target segments.* Questions about *who* the firm serves, *what* needs the firm meets, *where* it does these things, and *when* the firm meets those needs are essentially about the segments the business serves. In effect, it is the role of the marketing manager to determine *"Where's the pain?"* for specific segments of customers.
- *Competitive advantages.* Questions about *how* the firm serves those target segments and meets their needs better than the competition, and *why* the firm does that (the business model or profit logic) are about what competitive advantages (resources or capabilities) the firm has or will build. In effect, *"Where's the magic?"* that the firm can deliver to delight specific segments of customers.
- *Singularity.* The idea that a strategy must specify how the firm meets a certain set of customer needs better than the competition does not mean that the firm has to be better than the competition on *all* elements of the offering. Rather, the firm's offering must, in the end, be different from the competition in a particular way that a specific segment of customers will value. The strategy must be *unique* or *singular*, and not in an inconsequential way. It does no good to be "just like" the competition—copycats may or may not survive, but they will not thrive. In addition, it also does no good to be better than the competition on attributes that customers do not value. Michael Porter, the renowned strategy expert, noted, "Competitive strategy is about being different. It means deliberately choosing a different set of activities to deliver a unique mix of value" (Porter, 1996, p. 64).

Table I-1 highlights the basic elements of marketing strategy, including what questions to ask when evaluating potential market segments and how to leverage the organization's competitive advantages to meet the needs of selected target markets.

TABLE I-1 What Is a Marketing Strategy?

BASIC ELEMENTS	QUESTIONS TO ASK	PORTER, 1996
MARKET SEGMENTS *Where's the pain?*	Who? The customers and segments the business will serve	*Strategic Target or Competitive Scope*
	What? The needs that the firm will meet	
	Where? The geographic markets the firm will serve	
	When? The occasions the firm will serve	
COMPETITIVE ADVANTAGES *Where's the magic?*	How? The resources and distinctive competencies the firm will use	*Strategic Advantage or Competitive Advantage*
	Why? The compelling business model that specifies how long-term revenues will exceed costs by a reasonable rate of return on the capital employed	

THE STRATEGIC MARKETING PROCESS: A FRAMEWORK

This book is intended to be a comprehensive guide for marketing management across the strategic marketing process. To assist with understanding this process, the authors have developed a Strategic Marketing Framework (SMF) comprised of three stages: situation analysis, strategy formulation, and marketing execution. The next three chapters of this book examine each of these stages. The remainder of this book consists of "Notes" on applied tools that are useful during each stage of the SMF.

The SMF recognizes that effective marketing strategy is all about maintaining a high-level strategic perspective, while at the same time dealing with the never-ending urgencies of day-to-day management. Making that perspective more difficult is the fact that strategic questions do not arrive neatly labeled, "this is a product development opportunity," "this is a distribution problem," or "this is a competitive threat"—marketing managers must first figure out what the question is before they can analyze it, address it, exploit it, or fix it.

A review of the various strategic planning and management practices at firms that do these tasks well suggests there are certain things that all effective approaches have in common. The Strategic Marketing Framework (SMF) presented in this book integrates and organizes those shared elements. This model is neither revolutionary nor complicated. It can be applied easily and often, and it should become second nature to successful marketers. As shown in Figure I-1, the SMF involves three stages: situation analysis, strategy formulation, and marketing execution.

The first stage of the SMF, situation analysis, emphasizes the need to monitor the environment (external forces) while also examining the organization itself (internal factors), including core competencies, resources, and strategic direction. The external and internal environments can be further organized into the "four Cs" of *customers, competition,* and *context* of the external environment, as well as the *company* internal environment. Situation analysis involves analyzing whether the firm (or business unit or product) is moving in the right

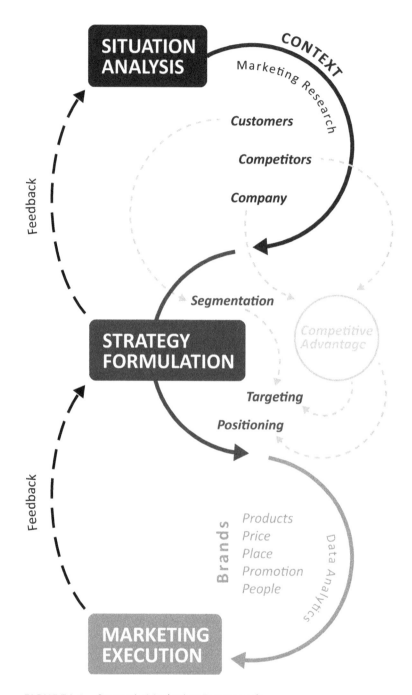

FIGURE I-1 Strategic Marketing Framework

direction; setting appropriate objectives; competing for the right customers; and developing the necessary skills, resources, and capabilities for success. Answers to the basic questions that drive a marketing strategy—what customers and customer needs should be served and how to profitably serve those needs better and differently than the competition—can result in countless, almost infinite specific strategies across industries, companies, and products. Thus, this first stage of the

SMF requires thoughtful market research to identify strategic gaps or planning gaps. The bigger the gap, the more change is needed in order to reach the objectives during the next stage of the SMF, strategy formulation.

Strategy formulation involves meeting specific needs of certain customers better than the competition within enduring, profitable relationships. Once you have gained a clear understanding of customer needs through situation analysis, then you need to consider what things your organization does, or could do, better than the competition and at a profit. In effect, what is your competitive advantage? Ultimately, your competitive advantage needs to be leveraged across the market segments that most value your products and services. Once market segments have been determined, then the firm needs to decide which of these segments to target; in effect, which specific customers and needs will be served utilizing which specific competitive advantages? Targeting is where the marketing strategy is specified and becomes concrete. The final step in strategy formulation is determining how to position your brand in the mindset of the customer so that it is distinctive from the competition. Once you have determined your intended positioning, then you need to achieve that positioning through appropriate marketing mix tactics in the third stage of the SMF.

The final stage of the SMF involves the execution of the marketing strategy. This stage focuses on the "levers" that marketing managers control, including making decisions about the product, pricing, places of distribution, promotional tactics, and people involved with selling the products and services. The best sales force in the world will have a tough time selling a product that is ill-conceived, ill-designed, or poorly manufactured, or a product with a price that is misaligned with what the customer thinks is good value, or a product that cannot be found in the places where the customer prefers to shop. These decision variables must be "mixed" correctly. We need the right product at the right price in the right place to serve our target segment in light of uncontrollable forces—the external situational factors such as the competition, political, legal and regulatory environments, economic conditions, social/cultural forces, and technological influences.

In the following chapters, we delve into each stage of the SMF, gaining a detailed understanding of how to effectively conduct a situation analysis and then formulate and execute a successful marketing strategy. Once you have gained an appreciation of the overall SMF process, then you can start to apply the various tools featured in the remainder of the book to make the SMF work for you and your organization.

REFERENCES

Drucker, P. (1973). *Management*. Harper & Row.

Hambrick, D. C., & Fredrickson, J. W. (2005). Are you sure you have a strategy? *Academy of Management Perspectives*, 19(4), 51–62.

Porter, M. E. (1996). What is strategy? *Harvard Business Review*, 74(6), 61–78.

FOCUS ON SITUATION ANALYSIS

Situation analysis involves monitoring the environment (external forces) while also examining the company itself (internal factors), including its core competencies, resources, and strategic directions. **Understanding external and internal factors at a given time, and, just as importantly, anticipating future events, trends, and conditions is critical to creating and advancing effective strategies.** Situation analysis can be divided into two basic categories—external and internal environments—which can be further organized into the "four Cs" of customers, competition, and context of the external environment, as well as the company internal environment. Note that the term *company* can refer to both profit-oriented and nonprofit organizations. As such, the terms *company* and *organization* will be used interchangeably throughout this book to reinforce that any organization, not just established business companies, can benefit from strategic marketing.

CUSTOMER ASSESSMENT

Throughout this book, the term *customers* will be used to refer to both business-to-business (B2B) transactions and business-to-consumer (B2C) transactions to the ultimate customer or consumer of a product. **Customer assessment, which is part of situation analysis, is the broadest consideration of the firm's current customers, the competitors' customers, and customers not yet in the market (potential customers).** Market research draws on both secondary and primary data to identify emerging trends in the market, understand how products deliver value and how customers consume the products, and anticipate future patterns of customer needs and consumption. Note 1 examines the importance of the market research process in greater detail.

Trends represent significant marketing opportunities that are grounded on substantive transformations such as changes in values, lifestyles, or technology, and are accessible to the *mainstream* or the majority of the market (Zandl, 2000). Monitoring the environment for trends can be highly quantitative and can include traditional, statistical methods for econometric forecasting as well as emerging methods of data mining (Han & Kamber, 2006). Data mining involves the analysis of large databases using diverse analytic methods to identify patterns, associations, and emerging

7

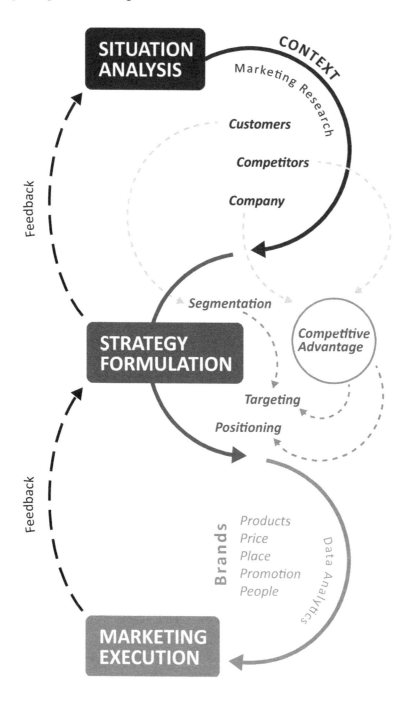

trends. Research firms such as Nielsen, IQVIA, Kantar, and Gartner, as well as mega-retailers like Walmart and Amazon, collect multi-terabytes of data across billions of transactions. These data create new opportunities for insights, but also increase the possibility that strategic marketers will be overwhelmed with information.

Finding markets that do not yet exist often begins with a customer insight. A customer insight is a penetrating, discerning understanding of customer needs, the ways that customers derive value from products, and the ways customers might derive value from products; it is an insight that unlocks an opportunity (Han & Kamber, 2006). Customer insights should be fresh, relevant, enduring, and inspiring (Taylor, 2000). Note 2 in this book further explains customer assessment and how to identify market trends and insights. Note 3 examines the role of consumer (B2C) and organizational buyer (B2B) behavior in determining important market outcomes, which is essential to strategy formulation.

CONTEXT

Understanding the context of the external environment includes analyzing the dynamics of the specific industry within which the firm operates and understanding the prominent and powerful regularities. We refer to these regularities as the *laws of marketing*, in effect the fixed patterns that are observed across situations and across time in the marketplace, such as changes in the market as it evolves, the cost benefits of economies of scale, or the profitability advantages of market share. **Before any situation analysis can be done effectively, it is crucial to carefully and strategically define the market in which the firm competes or may choose to compete**; that is, to define what situation should be assessed. As such, we will first explain the crucial step of market definition and then focus on external situation analysis. Then, we will review how to undertake an internal analysis of the situation within the company itself.

Market Definition

Before assessing the situation, it is necessary to first specify exactly what situation should be assessed.

- In what market does the firm participate?
- Who are its competitors?
- Who are its customers?

How the market or the submarket is defined is critical to all marketing activities. If we define the market too broadly, our marketing activities lose focus. If we define the market too narrowly, we risk missing opportunities. Market definition is the basis upon which we measure our participation, or market share. Even the labeling of the market tends to define the boundaries of the firm's efforts and its vision. Because all markets are constantly evolving, market definition is also important to understand the dynamics in the market. Is the market growing or declining, and how do these dynamics relate to customer needs, wants, expectations, and requirements?

Managers usually have a routine answer to the question, "In what market does your business compete?" Unfortunately, the typical answer is often narrow, reflecting the target of the latest marketing mix, rather than a strategic perspective. Often, it is backward looking and describes where the firm has been, not where it is headed. Irrespective of whether that answer is accurate or inaccurate, it is useful to periodically reexamine the boundaries of the firm's markets and to consider the ways those boundaries influence strategy. **The market definition becomes the lens through which the firm determines who its customers are and who its competitors are.**

Thus, a thorough and accurate market definition is a critical precondition to strategic thinking and strategic planning.

Markets can be thought of as having concentric boundaries (see Figure II-1), beginning at the core with product form (mid-size sedans, for example) and moving outward to product category (automobiles), generic competition (transportation), and finally, at the broadest level, to budget competition (money spent on a car could be spent on other large expenditures, from a vacation to home improvements). Traditional approaches to market definition typically focus on the *supply side* perspective, often based on the industry or product (e.g., railroads, automobiles, airlines). These definitions are limiting; while they may help identify traditional competitors, they may obscure opportunities, potential competitors, and substitutes. A second, complementary approach is to define markets from the customers' perspectives, that is, the *demand side* perspective: Which customers (segments and/or occasions) does the product serve? What needs does the product meet? Who else and what else (competitors; alternative products) could meet those same needs?

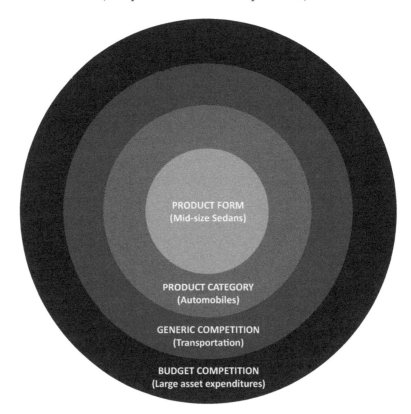

FIGURE II-1   Concentric Boundaries of Markets

When defining a market, two important premises must be considered. First, it's important to remember that customers seek the benefits that products provide, rather than simply the features or attributes of the products. Thus, the specific products that customers consider in a buying situation represent the benefits they seek. Second, it's critical to note that customers consider different alternatives in a buying situation, and these alternatives define the market. So the market also depends on what customers consider as alternatives and substitutions for their specific need (Day et al., 1979). The scope of a market definition should be flexible, adjusting to the purpose at hand. For some purposes, a relatively narrow market definition is appropriate: Who are our customers and competitors today? Other tasks require a broader view and may include nearby and potential customers or competitors: Who is likely to buy our existing offerings but is not currently buying them? For long-term planning and growth, the broadest outlook is appropriate: Where can we find long-term growth and profitability? What needs do our strengths meet? What needs could they meet? What technologies might supplant our strengths? Defining a market is a critical decision in marketing management, as it ultimately defines the boundaries of the organization's strategic marketing efforts and the horizons of its creative vision.

PESTLE Analysis

The general context or environment within which a firm, brand, or product operates has pervasive and complex effects on strategy and results. It is useful to begin with a succinct classification of the environmental factors that influence strategy. This classification imposes discipline on the assessment, stimulates brainstorming, and assures completeness. The mnemonic "PESTLE," which represents Political (regulatory), Economic, Social (cultural), Technological, Legal, and Environmental factors (see Table II-1), is an insightful partitioning of the macro level business environment.

TABLE II-1 PESTLE Analysis of External Environment

POLITICAL CONTEXT
Marketers operate in powerful, complex regulatory and legal environments that are shaped by political processes. Government policies as well as political stability can impact labor, trade and tax policies, as well as federal, state and/or local funding initiatives.
ECONOMIC CONTEXT
Economic variables such as currency exchange, inflation, interest, and unemployment rates can impact marketing strategies in substantial ways.
SOCIAL CONTEXT
Social and cultural values, attitudes, norms, manners, and tastes all affect customer needs. Demographics and lifestyles of the population (i.e., age, education, and social class) are important components of the social/cultural context that change across time.
TECHNOLOGICAL CONTEXT
Technology, innovation, and technological progress can have a critical impact on marketing strategies and tactics. New technologies can replace or become direct or indirect substitutes for a product form or product category. Technological changes can also alter the way a product is distributed and/or consumed.
LEGAL CONTEXT
Legal and regulatory requirements (current and future) can affect the development and sustainability of products and markets. Legal factors can include advertising standards, consumer protection, data privacy, intellectual property, and international and domestic trade regulations.
ENVIRONMENTAL CONTEXT
Environmental influences can include attitudes toward green products, climate change, an epidemic/pandemic, recycling, and renewable energy.

Changes in the general context are often the fundamental cause of problems and also the root of important opportunities. Failure to connect symptoms such as sales declines to underlying causes can blur strategic decision-making. For example, declining sales due to an economic recession can be expected to rebound; declining sales tied to deep-seated changes in social values or fundamental technological changes related to demand may not rebound so quickly or so surely.

Industry Analysis

An analysis of the industry or industries within which the firm operates is a more specific *micro* perspective embedded within the broader *macro* setting of situation analysis. Michael Porter (1980), a renowned strategy professor at Harvard Business School, determined there are five forces that drive industry analysis, including the bargaining power of suppliers, the bargaining power of customers, the threat of substitute products, and the threat of new entrants. The fifth force that influences industry competitiveness is the intensity of rivalry among existing competitors in the industry. The five forces together influence industry profitability and are examined further in Note 4.

Physicists know that an object will stay at rest or continue at a constant velocity unless acted upon by an external, unbalanced force, but the total energy in a system remains constant over time. These observed regularities are the laws of physics (Newton's First Law of Motion and the Law of Conservation of Energy, respectively); they're *truths* that describe underlying realities that do not change (Holzner, 2006). In strategic marketing there are similar truths—the *laws of marketing strategy*, so to speak—that describe essential regularities in the way things work and the way things relate. These generalizations include the product life cycle (product-market evolution), scale effects (cost leverage), and market share effects (share leverage). Managers may choose a strategy that builds directly on one of these generalizations or they may choose a strategy that is less directly tied to a given generalization, but they cannot change the reality. For example, Toyota builds its strategy on the benefits of scale effects; they produce more cars than anyone else in the world based on a set of common core processes. Although another car company, such as Porsche, may choose to forego scale to compete on high performance using small-scale production, it cannot change the reality of scale effects.

Product Life Cycle

All products and all markets are in a constant state of evolution. Some evolve in fairly smooth and expected patterns, while others evolve less predictably, such as when "disruptive technologies" cause unexpected, sharp declines. Nevertheless, the biological analogy of birth, growth, maturity, and decline is generally reliable. The S-shape of the product life cycle (see Figure II-2) describes this market evolution—the vertical axis is the percentage of the total market and the horizontal axis is time. Distinct life cycles exist for industries, products, and product forms. Note 5 examines the various stages of the product life cycle.

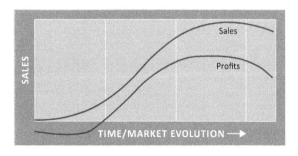

FIGURE II-2 Product Life Cycle

Markets behave differently at different stages: competitors compete differently, sales are more profitable or less profitable, and customers buy differently. Products clearly have life cycles, but markets evolve, and the life cycle depends on the definition of the market in the first place. Most major strategic gains and losses occur in the growth phase of a market. While all competitors are growing, share gains can frequently be achieved without significant competitive reaction. Share building in mature markets is tougher and frequently results in rapid competitive reaction, often in the form of price competition. Those who have achieved lower costs have an advantage at this stage.

Thus, understanding where a product and an industry are in the life cycle facilitates better prediction of competitor actions, customer responses, and sales trends that will inform considerations about what strategies are typically effective. Recognizing when the market is evolving from one stage to another—that is, anticipating inflection points—can create a significant advantage; missing such a shift can be a substantial disadvantage.

Scale Effects/Cost Leverage

Cost leverage can be achieved by both scale and experience. Scale is related to volume and time. It is axiomatic, whereby as volume in a given time period increases, fixed expenses as a percentage of sales decline. This effect is referred to as economies of scale. Similarly, the more units a company produces of anything, the lower per-unit costs will be. With each doubling of accumulated volume, costs decline by a determinable percentage. That is, experience effects are generally expressed as a percentage (e.g., 10%, 15%, 17%) decline in costs realized with every doubling of units produced (i.e., moving from 1 to 2, 2 to 4, 4 to 8 … 1.6 million to 3.2 million, etc.). That relationship between unit costs and volume produced forms the experience effects curve, as shown in Figure II-3. This percentage decline varies from industry to industry, but, regardless of the industry, significant cost advantage can be achieved by the competitor who moves down the experience curve faster. We can visualize that advantage as the distance between competitors' positions on the experience curve. The experience curve effects on cost reduction are examined in greater detail in Note 6.

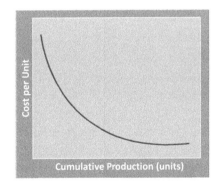

FIGURE II-3 Experience Curve

Too often, any cost reduction as units produced increases is mislabeled as an "economy of scale." In fact, at least four distinct sets of forces with differing implications for strategy can drive scale effects: learning- or experience-curve effects; economies and diseconomies of scale; economies of scope and synergies; and, network effects and virtuous circles. These distinct sources of benefits from scale are clarified in Table II-2. These different sources of scale effects are important in that they respond differently to managerial actions, and they are more or less enduring. For example, learning curve effects can contribute to both lower unit costs and higher quality (especially reliability and conformance quality). They endure across time and can be increased by enhancing institutional learning and knowledge retention. Economies of scale, on the other hand, lower costs but do not relate to quality, are less enduring, and are increased by one thing: higher units of production in a given time period. Economies and diseconomies of scale are examined in greater detail in Note 7, and economies of scope and related synergies are discussed in Note 8.

TABLE II-2 Sources of Scale Effects

LEARNING CURVE EFFECTS OR EXPERIENCE CURVE EFFECTS	The effects of the organization, its suppliers, and its employees literally *learning*—becoming more knowledgeable and more skilled and thereby doing things more *efficiently*.
ECONOMIES OF SCALE	The lowering of per-unit costs as the number of units produced increases via the spreading of fixed costs across units.
DISECONOMIES OF SCALE	Diseconomies of scale are the realization of *inefficiencies*, that is, of increases in unit costs as production increases.
ECONOMIES OF SCOPE	The lowering of unit costs realized when producing *more than one product* lowers the cost of production of all products.
SYNERGIES	Synergies are two (or more) inputs or activities (factors) coming together or acting together to result in output that is greater than the sum of the two factors taken separately.
NETWORK EFFECTS	When a product provides more value to *each customer* because more *overall customers* own it or use it.
VIRTUOUS CIRCLES	Systems of factors that provide feedback on themselves. For example, in a "virtuous" circle, the more people buy a product, the more retailers will want to stock the product, leading to higher sales. A "vicious" circle is the opposite—the feedback of negative factors exacerbating problems.

Market Share Effects/Share Leverage

One of the most widely accepted observations in the marketing strategy literature is that firms with higher market share tend to be more profitable. This share–profitability association is real; it has been replicated empirically many times in well-known business data systems, such as "PIMS" data (from the Profit Impact of Marketing Strategy database [Farris & Moore, 2004]). The share–profitability association is also logical; market share will correlate with advantages of scale, as discussed above. Scale generally leads to lower unit costs, and lower unit costs should lead to higher profits (firms with lower unit costs can lower price and gain sales volume or maintain price and realize higher per-unit margins). Nevertheless, shaping strategy around market share ignores the ambiguity in the share–ROI findings: the causal direction of the relationship is unclear and the relationship is undoubtedly complex. For example, many other factors, such as product quality and managerial skill, should lead to *both* relative market share and profitability, rendering market share a dubious starting point for strategy. Still, share-building activities in the market growth phase do pay off in superior competitive position during maturity. The concept of market share effects is examined in greater detail in Note 9.

COMPETITIVE INTELLIGENCE

Knowing the plans, intentions, and capabilities of existing and potential competitors is essential to understanding your own organization and anticipating the future of the market. Understanding your competitors is necessarily imperfect. Even the most transparent firm with inept security has activities and plans that the competition cannot detect. **Several aspects are important to understand about competitors: corporate level missions and objectives; marketing strategies; strengths and weaknesses along the value chain; current marketing tactics; and, the directions those missions, strategies, and tactics might take.** One should also try to understand how competitors act and react. For example, will they grimly defend their position, will they aggressively attack, or will they inconspicuously capture market share? Table II-3 outlines these areas of inquiry, emphasizing the need to anticipate future strategies and tactics.

TABLE II-3 Questions in Competitive Analysis

STRATEGIC QUESTIONS

- Who are the competitors?
- What are their corporate missions, goals, and strategies?
- What are their marketing strategies and objectives?
- What are their objectives at each business unit level?
- What are the firm's operational strengths and weaknesses?
- How badly do they want to play this game?

TACTICAL QUESTIONS

- What does their marketing plan look like?
- What are their attribute-level product strengths and weaknesses? What are their product line strengths and weaknesses?
- Can they execute? Do they have (or can they acquire) the skills?

In a real sense, the marketing strategist chooses the competition, deciding where to direct strategic energies and scarce marketing resources. You may choose to target alternative products or technologies early in the product life cycle, while in a mature market, competition often comes in direct, same-product forms. For example, satellite television providers such as Sky in Europe and DirecTV in America focus a large share of their strategic efforts against alternative technologies (cable television and terrestrial services). Later in the life cycle, as satellite television matures, it is likely that these firms will compete more directly and more intensely against other satellite television services (such as UPC in Europe and Dish Network in the US). The concepts of competitor analysis and competitive intelligence are examined further in Note 10.

SUMMARY OF THE CUSTOMER, CONTEXT, AND COMPETITIVE (EXTERNAL ENVIRONMENT) ANALYSIS

Marketing strategy involves developing an effective marketing mix for a given marketplace reality and then adapting that mix to changes in those environmental forces. Therefore, marketing strategy demands a thorough analysis of the external environment—in effect, the customer, context, and the competition. If marketing strategy is a marketing mix evolution in response to the environment, really *good* marketing strategy is a marketing mix evolution in *anticipation* of changes in those forces—that is, anticipating future configurations of the forces in the environment and developing effective marketing mixes in advance of those future realities. This section has organized and explained tools and frameworks for analyzing the environment—the external situation—and anticipating where it may be headed. The next section reviews analyzing the internal situation—that is, analyzing the company itself, including its mission and vision, values, strengths and weaknesses, and competitive advantages.

COMPANY (INTERNAL ENVIRONMENT) ANALYSIS

In the simplest terms, marketing strategy is about matching external opportunities with internal strengths and competitive advantages. The previous section developed ideas about analyzing the external situation, the environment within which the firm and the strategy compete. The obvious complement to that external analysis is the development of a thorough and transparent review of the firm itself. **Strategies and tactics must be developed within an understanding of the overarching organizational context and should align to the overall mission and goals.** Company analysis includes the following four related considerations:

- forming mission and vision statements;
- assessing past performance and current strategy;
- establishing preliminary objectives and targets; and
- identifying strategic gap(s) or planning gaps.

Mission and Vision Statements

Companies have unique values and cultures, as well as distinctive resources and competitive advantages. Any marketing strategy is supported by and constrained by those parameters. Most organizations begin their strategy formulation process with some sort of guidance statement— sometimes called a vision or a mission statement, although those two ideas can be separated, and some organizations have *both*. Most corporations have a mission that establishes the purpose of the firm—its reason to exist. Many now have values statements that articulate the values that shape the culture, mission, and vision of the organization. Vision statements, which are sometimes included within mission statements, are the forward-looking part of the mission, "the desired future state of the organization" (Raynor, 1998, p. 371).

Mission and vision statements clarify the firm's identity and purpose and should include at least four elements:

- the core purpose of the company,
- the core values of the company,
- the visionary goal (as noted, vision is sometimes pulled out on its own); and
- a vivid description of the envisioned future (specification of goals) (Collins & Porras, 1996, p. 65).

These various guidance statements, therefore, should be important documentation of the higher-level corporate context within which the product and business unit operate, and to which they should contribute.

Despite common poor execution, mission and vision statements should be the primary stipulations and records of what the organization is, why it exists, what its values are, how it does business, and what it intends to become. In these guidance statements the company clarifies its goals. The terms *goal* and *objective* are synonyms in the English language, but in the strategic management literature they are used to distinguish desired results that are long-term and general (goals) from desired results that are short-term and specific (objectives). Goals are specified in mission and vision statements; objectives are related to marketing plans, specified time periods, and specific marketing mixes.

Company missions and visions may, or may not, embrace purposes and goals beyond shareholder value; however, it is nevertheless important that marketing strategists at least consider the broader issues of corporate social responsibility, stakeholder theory, and the triple bottom line (i.e., the impact on profits, people and planet). To learn further about these concepts, review Note 11.

Assessing Past Performance and Current Strategy

The strategy formulation process must be grounded in a thorough analysis of past performance.

- Which objectives over the most recent period have been met?
- Which ones have been missed? Why?
- What are the firm's current strengths and weaknesses?

Challenging the present strategy, assessing its current competitiveness, and looking for areas of leverage are essential in developing the *next* strategies. Several factors are integrated into assessment of past performance. One is review of ongoing financial and operating performance. Another is review of data from marketing information systems. A third review involves the understanding of the firm's existing competitive advantages (and disadvantages) vis-à-vis the competition. Financial and operating results include firm, business-unit, product-level, and account-level data on prices realized and revenues, margins, and profitability, as well as operating results such as units shipped, costs, inventory, and defects/reworks. A value chain analysis, as described in Note 12, is a helpful tool to not only identify what activities can lead to competitive advantage, but also to identify what activities do not lead to advantages in the marketplace.

Understanding the company's strengths and weaknesses, or competitive advantages, is a crucial company-related consideration in creating and maintaining effective strategies. A company's strengths and weaknesses are only strengths or weaknesses in comparison to the competition and the perceived opportunities and threats in the marketplace. Identifying the company's strengths, weaknesses, and competitive advantages—and matching them with market opportunities while avoiding threats—is the essence of SWOT analysis as outlined in Note 13.

Establishing Preliminary Objectives and Targets

A marketing strategy without specific objectives is like a ship without a compass. It can sail, but it cannot be sure whether it sails in the right direction or whether it ever reaches its destination. Having clear marketing objectives enables a company to do the following four things: (a) focus and organize its efforts; (b) direct day-to-day activities and achieve consistency in decisions;

(c) motivate people to strive for excellence; and, (d) most importantly, provide a basis for assessment and control. A simple mnemonic for weighing effective and useful marketing objectives is "SMART," which denotes that objectives should be: specific, measurable, achievable, relevant, and time-bound, as shown in Table II-4.

TABLE II-4 SMART Marketing Plan Objectives

SMART ELEMENT	DESCRIPTION	EXAMPLE
Specific	*What exactly is to be achieved?*	Dollar sales of merchandise to new accounts in Italy
Measurable	*What quantitative or quantifiable methods and metrics will define the objective?*	Dollar sales associated with shipped merchandise as communicated to management on report 2022A
Achievable	*Is the objective realistic and demanding/ challenging?*	20% increase in sales over last year
Relevant	*Is the objective under the control of the people or unit for whom it is established?*	The sales team for this merchandise is empowered to call on new accounts in Italy
Time-bound	*When should these objectives be achieved and when will these objectives be assessed?*	During calendar year 2023

Two distinct kinds of objectives are useful and common in developing marketing strategies: market-related objectives and financial objectives. Some **typical marketing objectives**, which are often measured both at the market and the segment level, include the following:

- **sales volume and market share** (in units and/or dollars);
- **customer readiness variables** (awareness, interest);
- **customer behaviors and attitudes** (satisfaction, brand attitudes, repeat-purchase intention, recommendations/word-of-mouth, complaints); and
- **accounts and distribution** (retailers stocking, SKUs or facings, business-to-business customer accounts opened, approved-vendor lists).

These market-related objectives highlight the need, discussed earlier, to first clearly demarcate what market is being targeted and measured. Metrics like market share and customer satisfaction are meaningless unless the market to be shared and the customers to be satisfied have first been defined clearly. **Typical financial objectives** include:

- **profits** (overall profits, contribution, margins, and contributions by units, products, and lines) and return-on-investment;
- **costs of marketing** (sales costs, costs of goods sold); and
- **inventory and logistics** (inventory levels and turns, fulfillment time, stockouts).

In setting objectives there is an important tension between *investing* in long-term strengths—such as innovation and developing new products, building customer loyalty, and the like—and *harvesting* short-term profits. Whether or not the strategy is to invest or harvest, that decision must be made deliberately and in the context of a clear understanding of the business model and of consumer responses (for instance, customer stickiness, customer profitability/customer lifetime value, and purchase rates).

Identifying Strategic Gaps or Planning Gaps

One way to think about strategy is to think about the gaps that exist between where we are and where we want to be. Figure II-4 depicts what has often been referred to as the strategic gap or the planning gap. The horizontal axis represents time, divided into the past and the future. The vertical axis represents performance. As noted above, there are two types of performance measures and objectives that are important to marketing strategists: market performance and financial performance. Market performance is often measured as sales or market share. Financial performance usually relates to profitability or return on something, such as sales, assets, or capital.

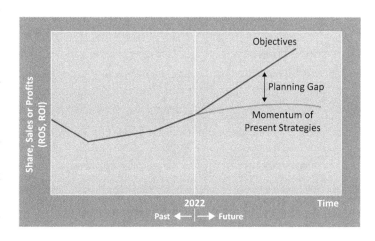

FIGURE II-4   The Strategic or Planning Gap

Figure II-4 is divided into the past and the future, where past performance is past sales or share or past profitability (return). Looking toward the future we have marketing and financial objectives (hopefully heading in an upward direction). Below the objectives, we have a momentum forecast of our current strategy; this is where our current course (strategy and programs) will take us if we just keep doing what we have been doing. If there is a difference between the objectives and the momentum of the present strategy, we have a planning or strategic gap. The bigger the gap, the more strategic change is needed in order to reach the objectives.

Closing the Gap

Let us think about the situation in which the organization has a sales gap—that is, the planning gap in Figure II-4 is between the sales objectives and the momentum of the present strategy with respect to sales. What are the possible ways to close such a sales gap? One way to think about this would be based on the relationship with existing company offerings and existing markets, as discussed earlier in Chapter I relative to product–market growth strategies. There are a limited set of possible "growth strategies." At any given time, a firm is selling its existing products to its existing markets. Logically, growth (closing the gap) can come from (a) selling more of the firm's existing products to its existing markets (market penetration); (b) selling existing products to new markets (market development); (c) selling new products to existing markets (product development); or (d) selling new products to new markets (diversification). One other possible way to increase sales would be to forward integrate—an option open to manufacturers, but not to retailers as they are already as forward integrated as possible.

If the gap is a profitability gap, that is, if the gap between objectives and momentum in Figure II-4 is between profitability objectives and the momentum of profits, then another set of generic strategies is suggested. These include the five below:

1. *Increasing the yield.* This can be done, perhaps, by improving the sales mix, increasing the price, or reducing distribution margins.
2. *Reducing costs.* This can be achieved through economies of scale, better capacity utilization, systems and process efficiencies, or direct cost cutting.
3. *Backward integration.* This implies undertaking value-added activities that had been outsourced to suppliers; that is, making or doing things within the organization that had been purchased. Backward refers to integrating toward the source in the channels of distribution.
4. *Reducing investment intensity.* This can be achieved by reducing inventories, factoring accounts receivable, or the sale and lease back of property, plant, and equipment.
5. *Selectivity and focus.* Abandoning segments where we cannot win or rationalizing the product line or the channels of distribution; "rationalizing" generally refers to narrowing the scope by concentrating on the most profitable and effective products or channels and cutting inefficient or ineffective products or channels.

Figure II-5 shows generic profitability-improvement strategies. In other words, at a high level there is a finite set of available strategies—some relate to sales or marketing improvement and some relate to profitability improvement. A company might employ several of these strategies simultaneously. For example, we might be pursuing a market penetration and product development strategy along with cost reduction at the same time.

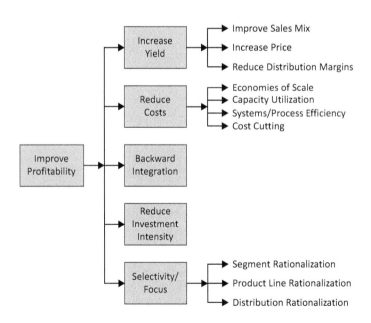

FIGURE II-5   Alternatives for Improving Profitability

INTEGRATING SITUATION ANALYSIS IN STRATEGIC MARKETING

A situation analysis should be wide-ranging and descriptive in the sense that it seeks to understand what is going on across the environment and within the firm. But situation analyses are also analytical in the sense that they assess, integrate, and organize vast and potentially overwhelming data into organized information that can be used to drive decision-making and action. Situation analysis establishes the foundation for planning and strategy formulation. There are several tools available for systematically managing and integrating the situation analysis and for structuring the outcome of that assessment in ways that facilitate strategic thinking. First, there is a pervasive *relevance test* that should be applied to all assessments. Second, *scenario analysis* is an invaluable tool for integrating situation analysis and uncertain possible future trends and events into strategic planning.

Relevance Test

It is worthwhile to highlight the fact that not everything in the environment is meaningful, at least not to every decision or strategy. To avoid "paralysis by analysis," the first job of the marketing strategist is to cull through the tremendous amount of noise to focus on substantive and important information. Because every situation is complex and there are overwhelming amounts of data that could be considered, it is important at the outset to emphasize a relevance test before assessing the situation. This is the *"so what?"* of strategic marketing analysis. The manager must constantly ask, "Is this important and relevant to this firm and to this strategy?" In fact, the first job of a manager is to filter the available data down to usable information. Time, energy, and attention should be reserved for information that directly affects strategy and ties to decisions.

Scenario Analysis

An effective tool for bringing together situation analysis and for planning for future uncertainties is scenario analysis. For example, if a regional home construction company wants to forecast interest rates, because interest rates have a strong impact on the building industry, the builder would base that prediction on trends in the economy and on inputs from economists and bankers. However, forecasting interest rates is challenging and expensive, and interest rates are not the only driver of any company's circumstances and strategic results. Other drivers for a builder might include the regulatory environment (such as local housing policies) and the competitive environment. Instead of forecasting specific variables, a marketing strategist might conduct a scenario analysis for the builder in which several levels of interest rates are incorporated (high, moderate, and low interest rates, for example), along with two levels of competition (a large, national builder enters market or no change in the competition) and a couple of possible regulatory shifts (such as continued growth versus tightened regulations/slow growth).

Scenario analysis is essentially an elaborate "if … then" planning tool—maybe more accurately described as an "if … and if … and if …, then … " tool because it considers multiple factors evolving to shape possible futures or scenarios. Scenario analysis is described further in Note 14 and is a powerful method for formalizing situation analysis, clarifying possible futures, and preparing the firm's preferred responses to those possibilities.

REFERENCES

Collins, J. C., & Porras, J. I. (1996). Building your company's vision. *Harvard Business Review, 74*(5), 65.

Day, G. S., Shocker, A. D., & Srivastava, R. K. (1979). Customer-oriented approaches to identifying product-markets. *Journal of Marketing, 43*(4), 8–19.

Farris, P. W., & Moore, M. J. (2004). *The profit impact of marketing strategy project: Retrospect and prospects.* Cambridge University Press.

Han, J., & Kamber, M. (2006). *Data mining: Concepts and techniques* (2nd ed.). Morgan Kaufmann Publishers.

Holzner, S. (2006). *Physics for dummies.* Wiley Publishing.

Porter, M. E. (1980). *Competitive strategy: Techniques for analyzing industries and competitors.* Free Press.

Raynor, M. E. (1998). That vision thing: Do we need it? *Long Range Planning, 31*(3), 368–376.

Taylor, D. (2000). *Drilling for nuggets: How to use insight to inspire innovation.* Brand Strategy.

Zandl, I. (2000). How to separate trends from fads. *Brandweek, 41*(41), 30–35.

CHAPTER III

FOCUS ON STRATEGY FORMULATION

This chapter discusses strategy formulation, the second stage of our framework and the heart of the strategic marketing process. Too often organizations move from the first stage of the framework, situation analysis, directly to the third and final stage, marketing execution. Failing to recognize the importance of intentional strategy formulation will ultimately result in a doomed marketing effort.

The overarching objective of strategic marketing is to meet specific needs of certain customers better than the competition in the context of enduring, profitable relationships. Strategy formulation consists of the following four steps:

1. *Identifying competitive advantages.* What things does the firm do or could it do better than the competition and at a profit?
2. *Segmenting the market.* What are the important differences across customers regarding their needs and their responses to the marketing mix? How attractive are the various segments?
3. *Targeting.* Which specific customers and needs (segments) will be served, utilizing which specific competitive advantages? How well do segments fit or match with the firm's competitive advantages?
4. *Positioning.* What unique position in the marketplace will the firm claim? How will the firm claim that position? Positioning is the implementation of the strategy (targeting) into specific tactics (the marketing mix—product, price, place or distribution, promotion or integrated marketing communications, and people/service).

IDENTIFYING COMPETITIVE ADVANTAGES

For long-term viability, every firm must be better than the competition at something. **Those things a firm does best are considered its *competitive advantages* (sometimes stated as *core competencies* or *sustainable competitive advantages*).** A company has a competitive advantage if it possesses resources or capabilities that are (a) valuable in the market (who wants to be best at something no one cares about?); (b) rare (competitors do not have the same resources or

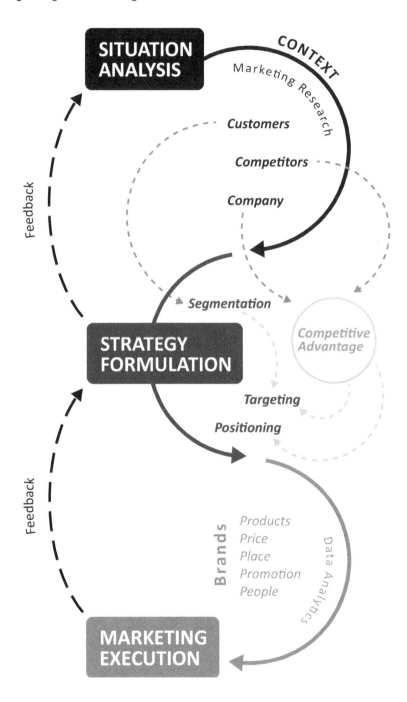

capabilities); (c) not imitable or substitutable (competitors cannot easily imitate or work-around them); and (d) transferable to other markets or products. In a strengths-and-weaknesses framework, competitive advantages are the strengths.

Note 15 expands upon two broad approaches to assessing and developing competitive strategies: the market-based view and the resource-based view. The market-based view assumes that success depends on characteristics of the market or industry the firm competes in (industry attractiveness, industry structure, and the like). The resource-based view regards a company's success as largely self-determined, dependent on its unique resources and capabilities. These two paradigms imply very different strategy formulation processes with fundamentally different starting points and identification of competitive advantages.

The following section will review a few of the most common frameworks for developing marketing strategies, including generic strategies, the value map, and product-market growth strategies, as well as how a firm's competitive advantages can be leveraged within those strategies. In addition, this section will examine two prevalent trends that should be considered when formulating marketing strategies—international market opportunities and the role of digital transformation and platform economies.

GENERIC STRATEGIES

Harvard Professor Michael Porter (1985) developed a generic strategies model that states a firm should focus on cost leadership or product differentiation (referred to as competitive advantage), within a range of segmentation alternatives from a broad, mass target market to a narrow, niche target market (referred to as competitive scope). By simplifying the two attributes of generic strategies (competitive advantage and competitive scope) to two broad market alternatives (differentiation versus cost and narrow versus broad, respectively), it is easier to consider the resulting possibilities. In effect, a firm can differentiate its offerings or compete on price, and it can do that at a broad or mass scope or at a narrow or niche scope. Note 16 expands on the high-level categorizations of generic strategies, which are a useful starting place in understanding what strategies are possible, how they differ, and how they relate to each other.

VALUE MAP

Another general framework for organizing all possible strategies is the value map or value frontier. In this instance, *value* is defined as what the customer gets (performance or quality) adjusted for what the customer gives (price). The value map framework plots performance and price as the axes of the two-dimensional space as reviewed in Note 17. Keep in mind, these are customer *perceptions* of performance and price (making this one type of perceptual map), and these are *relative* dimensions; price and performance are perceived as high or low *relative to other offerings in the marketplace*. Products in a market will tend to form a frontier within this space along which there is equilibrium between changes in performance and changes in price. People are willing to pay more for higher performance (better quality), but the market will punish firms charging more or offering less quality or services for the same price. This two-dimensional space highlights three potentially effective strategies—premium (high price/high performance), high customer value (low price/high performance), and economy (low price/low performance)—and one unsustainable strategy—inferior customer value (high price/low quality). Within this framework, successful innovations can be viewed as the creation of ways either to offer the same performance for a lower price or to offer more performance for the same price.

PRODUCT–MARKET GROWTH STRATEGIES

A third framework organizes *growth strategies*—strategies specifically seen as expanding sales—based on their relationship with existing company offerings and existing markets. At any given time, a firm is selling its existing products to its existing markets. Logically, growth can come from selling more of the firm's existing products to its existing markets (market penetration), selling existing products to new markets (market development), selling new products to existing markets (product development), or selling new products to new markets (diversification). This logic was first spelled out by Professor Igor Ansoff and is examined further in Note 18. The product–market growth framework suggests the concept of *adjacencies* and *core competencies*—the idea that strategic growth is best found by identifying new markets or new products for which the firm can parlay existing core strengths into growth.

INTERNATIONAL MARKET OPPORTUNITIES

When a company seeks to grow beyond domestic markets, it typically has four options: an international strategy; a multinational strategy; a global strategy; or a combination of a multinational and global strategies to develop a transnational strategy (Bartlett & Ghoshal, 1992). The selected strategy can also influence the entry method in a market, from the low risk and standardized approach of exporting to the high risk and market-adapted approach of direct investment. Ultimately, when pursuing internationalization, marketing managers must decide how many resources to commit and the extent of control needed over their brand and overseas operations. Note 19 further examines possibilities related to pursuing international market opportunities.

DIGITAL TRANSFORMATION AND PLATFORM ECONOMIES

Digital transformation has become a strategic imperative for most companies in the 21st century. New digital technologies (e.g. Internet of Things, artificial intelligence, 5G, robotics) change the way organizations create and deliver value for their customers and capture value for their brands. Disrupters such as Airbnb, Amazon, Bolt, and Netflix have developed new business models that fundamentally change industries like travel, retail, transportation, and entertainment. Consumer behavior is evolving as well, as customers shift their purchases to online stores, use social media to become informed, and rely on mobile and AI-powered technologies. Digital transformation has a pervasive impact on formulating strategy and should be examined relative to three distinct phases—digitization, digitalization, and digital transformation—which are explained further in Note 20.

SEGMENTING THE MARKET

Because customers within a broadly defined market almost never have the same characteristics or the same needs and requirements, there is an opportunity to subdivide or segment the market. The purpose of market segmentation is to identify subgroups (segments) of customers that are like each other and different from the rest of the market with regard to needs, wants, and responses to the marketing mix. Marketing mix response differences are not only responses to product differences; customers may respond differently to price, service levels, advertisements, and/or distribution channels. Differences in responses to any of these marketing mix elements—which correspond to differences in underlying needs or wants—are meaningful segmentation differences and an opportunity to gain advantage through targeted marketing mix development. Note 21 expands upon various approaches to market segmentation.

The primary reason to differentiate customers into segments is to capture the strategic advantage of meeting differing needs with tailored marketing mixes. The objective and the key to successful segmentation is to find differing needs that match the firm's competitive advantages and thus can be served at a profit better than the competition. If all customers respond to all elements of the marketing mix in the same way, then there is no reason to segment. The objective then would be to develop the single optimal marketing mix for all customers, and there would be only one *winner*. Finding substantial differences that others have overlooked can constitute a customer insight that creates a significant opportunity for the firm.

There are two types of variables to be distinguished in the segmentation process for both business-to-consumer (B2C) and business-to-business (B2B) markets: segmentation basis and segment descriptors. The basis of segmentation—the underlying differences that warrant targeting with distinctive marketing programs—should be differing customer needs, differences in needs that underlie differences in responses to elements of the product, and the marketing program. Table III-1 clarifies a customer *need* as well as the related ideas of customer *wants, benefits sought,* and *demand.* All of these can be legitimate segmentation factors.

Descriptors of segments are observable variables that correlate with the differences in needs/wants/benefits sought and allow the segment to be identified and targeted. Descriptor variables in B2C markets include things like demographics (age, education, income, etc.), geographics (the location of consumers), psychographics (lifestyles), and behaviors (usage rate, stage in buying process or readiness, loyalty, and profitability or customer lifetime value). In B2B markets, segments of organizations can be described on firm demographics (size, ownership), behaviors (purchasing histories) and firm psychographics including purchasing processes (buying centers, bidding), ownership, and strategies.

Although it is important to describe segments in observable and actionable ways—ways that allow the marketer to identify and address the segment—it is still true that at the root of differences in how customers respond to the marketing mix are differing customer needs. If a segment is, for example, more price conscious than other segments, that is the basis of the segmentation (the need for economy). Such a segment may be described as older, retired consumers, or busy single-income parents. But age, family status, and employment (retired or full-time homemaker) do not drive the segment differences—the need for economy is what differentiates the segment

TABLE III-1 Needs, Wants, Benefits, and Demand

DEFINITION OF TERMS	EXAMPLES
Needs: The underlying motivation or reason driving consumption. Conceptualized as the difference between customers' perceived *current* state and their *desired* state. Needs include: basic physiological needs (food, shelter), safety (security, property), social needs (belonging, affection), esteem (self-esteem, respect by others), and self-actualization (intellectual growth, self-expression) (Maslow, 1943).	Hunger
Wants: The specific form that customers may desire to address needs, influenced by culture, experiences, situations, individual factors, and marketing actions.	Filet Mignon Kung Pao Chicken Risotto al Gorgonzola
Benefits or Benefits Sought: An outcome of consuming a product that motivates purchase and consumption. Benefits are the consequences of the consumption of the product and of product attributes.	Nourishment Hunger satiation Taste sensations
Demand: A want combined with the ability (including resources such as time, money, and access) to purchase. Demand requires that consumers *want the product* and have *the ability* to buy the product	Hungry customers who want filet mignon, who can afford filet mignon, and who can access filet mignon.

from other customers. Age, family status, and employment are all demographic variables that correlate with the need for economy. They also describe the customers and the segment, and most importantly, allow the segments to be targeted with tailored offerings. Demographics are a good starting point for segmentation, but the most effective market segmentation typically includes geographic, psychographic, and behavioral factors as well.

Product-related behaviors, such as usage rate and loyalty, are important to strategic segmentation, but they are still only *correlates* of the underlying *needs* that drive the segments' behaviors. For example, it makes strategic sense to develop loyal customers and to target customers who have higher lifetime value. However, loyalty and customer lifetime value are themselves driven by underlying needs, and efforts to build loyalty or target high-value customers will be most successful if they include efforts to thoroughly understand those needs. Note 22 further examines loyalty-based marketing, customer acquisition, customer retention, and customer lifetime value.

Segmentation decisions include not only *which* segments to target but, simultaneously, the *scope* of the targeted segments; that is, decisions about the number and size of the segments and the relationship amongst the segments to be targeted. Some firms target very broad segments with relatively homogeneous offerings—marketing based on global and mass marketing strategies. Other firms target adjacent segments with somewhat differentiated offerings—a form of target marketing. Finally, some firms target smaller segments of the market with very focused offerings—niche marketing.

Segments are dynamic and preferences change—that is, a segment's ideal product can shift over time, sometimes quite rapidly. In addition, segments can split or merge. Groups of consumers that were reasonably treated as homogeneous may develop important differences, and consumers who had differing response profiles may converge around common preferences and behaviors. For example, the luxury sedan market treated affluent professional Americans as relatively homogeneous—and BMW dominated the younger luxury sedan market in the mid-1980s. By the early 1990s, Lexus and other Japanese brands had split the segment by recognizing and serving differing needs. BMW retained the performance luxury drivers, while Lexus carved out a large segment of reliability–comfort luxury drivers.

TARGETING

Targeting—matching the firm's competitive advantages with attractive market opportunities—is the crux of the strategic marketing formulation. Targeting is the critical junction in formulating strategy and translating strategy into tactics, matching external opportunities with internal strengths—strengths the firm has or strengths the firm can develop or acquire. Situation analysis and environmental scanning, scenario analysis, segmentation, and analysis of competitive advantages are all factors that drive targeting.

As the company customizes products and marketing programs to the segments, as shown in Figure III-1, it can better meet the segment-specific needs and requirements, and therefore, create superior value and demand price premiums. The downside is a higher complexity of the organization and the product portfolio, lower economies of scale (standardized products and marketing mixes optimize economies of scale, but economies of scope can still be achieved across products/programs), and, as a consequence, higher unit costs.

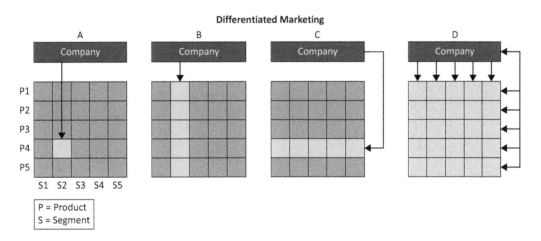

FIGURE III-1 Differentiated Marketing Approaches. Adapted from Abell, 1980.

Differentiated marketing can consist of the following:

- *Selected specialization.* The company selects and focuses on one or a few single segments (Case A in Figure III-1).
- *Segment specialization.* A producer decides to serve several different needs of one segment and develops many products and marketing programs for this segment (Case B in Figure III-1).
- *Product specialization.* Focus on one product that is tailored to all market segments (Case C in Figure III-1).
- *Full market coverage.* A company decides to address all market segments and develops all products the segment wants (Case D in Figure III-1).

In many situations it is just as important to know who the firm is *not* targeting as it is to know which segments it *is* targeting. No product offering can be right for everybody, and a common trap is that in trying to grow sales toward new customers and new segments, marketers lose their focus and their original advantage in their primary segments. This may be termed *target drift*, the loss of focus on the target segment in favor of broader or alternative segments.

Closely related to target drift is the temptation to target more than one segment with a single mix; that is, to *straddle*. That strategy may work in the short-term, particularly in the early stages of the product life cycle, but it is unlikely to succeed in the long-term. The problem with trying to serve two or more segments with a single marketing mix is that the mix is not exactly right for anyone—and a competitor will, eventually, offer a mix that is exactly right. One solution to straddling may be to revisit the segmentation scheme, looking for multiple segments where the original segmentation solution had identified just one. Another alternative to straddling is to offer more than one marketing mix. That is, to focus tailored marketing mixes for each segment. In any case, it usually turns out that the marketer who targets two segments with a single marketing mix does not effectively reach either one.

Targeting loyal customers—especially profitable loyal customers—can lead to dramatic improvements in profitability. Frederick Reichheld and W. Earl Sasser (1990) conducted numerous studies across industries and found that firms with more loyal customers were more profitable. They attributed that relationship to the related findings that longer-term customers spread acquisition costs across more purchases and continue to provide base profits while increasing their purchases, costing less to serve, referring other customers to the products/brands, and even paying a price premium. Subsequent research has augmented those findings to propose that it is not just loyalty that matters, but, rather, loyalty and profitability. The converse to targeting profitable, loyal customers is also true; although we generally think of firms as ceaselessly seeking to attract more customers, firing unprofitable and fickle customers can also improve results. The concept of targeting is examined further in Note 23.

POSITIONING

Positioning, the construction of the brand and deployment of a unique marketing mix, flows from and is determined by targeting. Targeting is where the strategy is specified and becomes concrete. The overarching objective is to identify segments that will value offerings built upon the firm's strengths; that is, to meet some specific needs of some specific customers better than the competition within enduring, profitable relationships. The concept of positioning is examined further in Note 24.

As previously discussed, a SWOT analysis (see Note 13) can be helpful to identify attractive markets. This tool summarizes the juncture of *internal* analysis (strengths and weaknesses inherent in the company) and *external* analyses (situation analysis of customers, the context, and competitors). We can think of the strengths and weaknesses as a summarization of the company's competitive position, whereas the opportunities and threats represent the market's attractiveness, as seen in Figure III-2.

We define positioning as the deployment of the entire marketing mix (products, prices, places/distribution channels, promotions/integrated marketing communications, and people/selling) to claim a unique, valued, and defensible position in the marketplace. Many experts have highlighted the fact that a product's or brand's position is really something that resides in the consumers' minds. That position is driven by the actions of the marketing firm and those actions are encapsulated in the marketing mix. The mix is the totality of tactics and offerings that the firm can use to influence consumers' perceptions of the offering's position and to thereby meet customer needs. The next chapter elaborates on executing marketing strategy through the marketing mix to claim a unique position in the consumers' mindset relative to the competition.

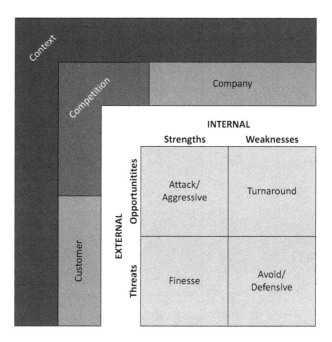

FIGURE III-2   SWOT Analysis

REFERENCES

Abell, Derek F. Defining the business: The starting point of strategic planning. Upper Saddle River, New Jersey: Prentice Hall, 1980.

Bartlett, C. A., & Ghoshal, S. (1992). *Transnational management: Text, cases and readings in cross border management.* Irwin.

Maslow, A. H. (1943). A theory of human motivation. *Psychological Review, 50*(4), 370–96.

Porter, M. E. (1985). *Competitive advantage: Creating and sustaining superior performance.* Free Press.

Reichheld, F. F., & Sasser, W. E. (1990). Zero defections: Quality comes to services. *Harvard Business Review, 68*(4), 105–111.

FOCUS ON MARKETING EXECUTION

Effective marketing execution starts with an understanding of the product or brand's position in the marketplace. **Positioning involves tailoring the marketing mix to target a specific set of customer needs in a unique way—a way that no competitor matches—and effectively communicating that position to customers.** Positioning is something that, in reality, lives in the customers' perceptions of the offering.

Customers will not see a brand manager's positioning statement or care what the marketing strategist thinks the product's position is supposed to be; they'll rely on their own perceptions to decide where it's positioned—and that will be the only product position that matters. Nevertheless, those perceptions are shaped by the marketing mix and its coherence. Thus, **the objective of positioning is to own a valued place in customers' perceptions.** Once the organization has determined which customers and which needs it is targeting with which competitive advantages, it must identify and delineate exactly what position those decisions equate to in the marketplace: In what territory does the product or brand seek to be unique? How does the marketing mix claim that territory?

Segmentation is a tough job—but, if done well, it makes positioning a simpler job. That is, if you understand the segment's needs well enough, the positioning challenge should be straightforward, if not easy. If you believe you have a positioning problem, it is probably because you are not sure which segment you are trying to serve or you are attempting to serve too many segments.

Positioning aligns the myriad tactical decisions involved in going to market. It is the implementation of strategy into specific brand-building marketing mix elements. These are all the details and specific decisions about the firm's products and services, brands, prices, places (channels and distribution), promotions (communications with customers), and people (selling). It is important to remember that **the fundamental objective of positioning is not the marketing mix activities themselves, but rather the resulting customer perceptions.**

Marketing research should lie at the heart of the marketing program and guide all the tactical elements of the marketing mix. Brands are the cumulative sum of all the marketing tactics and messages across the history of the offering. In addition, brands are the company's and the consumer's shorthand for the overall offering and its position in the market. Therefore, this section on marketing execution begins with an emphasis on marketing research and then examines the concept of brand development before considering the marketing mix and its execution.

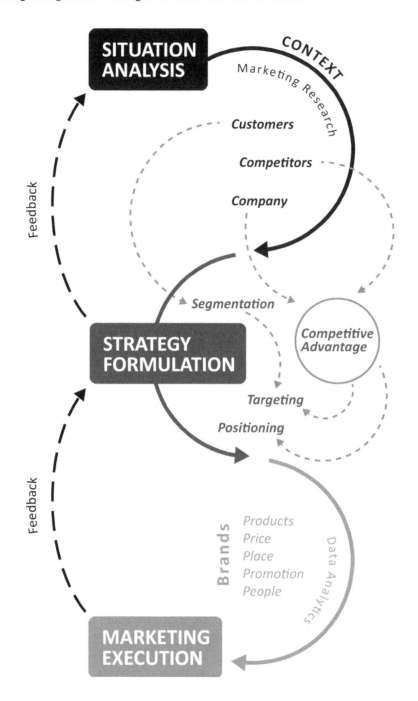

MARKETING RESEARCH

Although all marketing research is focused on understanding the customer and tying the firm's actions to a customer orientation, broad customer assessment and issue-specific market research begin with different objectives, draw on different methods, and result in different sorts of information and guidance. As mentioned in Chapter II, marketing research includes a range of activities, from exploring the environment for opportunities and insights to project-based research to hone specific elements of the marketing mix, as well as Customer Relationship Management (CRM) systems, which entail the ongoing collection of marketing metrics and customer data for program assessment and customization/targeting.

Too frequently, managers take a *more is better* approach to marketing research and data collection. They collect reams of ill-defined data and then sift through those voluminous data hoping to find usable information to support decision-making. This is dysfunctional and contributes to *paralysis by analysis*, the tendency to overanalyze and over research issues and the failure to make decisions and act. To avoid unfocused and ineffective research, **the marketing research process stipulates that the market problem or opportunity be clearly specified in detail before the research is designed and well before any data are collected.** The basic marketing research process (Kotler & Armstrong, 2010), as seen in Figure IV-1, emphasizes the necessity of early problem and objective specification. Some experts have even recommended actually outlining the "final report" *first*—before designing the study or collecting any data—in order to

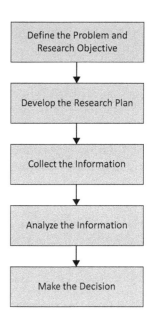

FIGURE IV-1 Marketing Research Process

engage management early in the research process and focus efforts on the right questions and on guiding managerially controllable outcomes (Johansson & Nonaka, 1987).

THE POWER OF BRANDS

As a collection of meanings, brands are represented by symbols such as names, logos, colors, and imagery; however, the power of branding extends far beyond such tangible assets. **A brand signals a product's position and its benefits in the mindset of consumers** and can have enormous value to the marketer. Facilitating choice and reducing search and evaluation demands are ways that brands can deliver value to customers as well. Brands also deliver assurance, meaning, and self-expressive value to consumers. Drinking a Coca-Cola is very different from merely drinking carbonated water and other (secret) ingredients that make up the tangible core product. Drinking a Coca-Cola is an experience and has meanings that the substance and ingredients do not have on their own. Thus, the brand can have great economic value to the firm. According to Interbrand (2021), in 2020 the Coca-Cola brand was considered the sixth most valuable brand in the world, and it was estimated to be worth nearly $57 billion. From a strategic perspective, the importance of branding is that the brand embodies the goodwill or *equity* the firm has earned and can retain with its consumers. Note 25 expands on the concept of branding.

POSITIONING STATEMENTS

Most good brand-building organizations have developed a narrative of what the brand is meant to be, what needs it is meant to serve, for which specific customers, and on what specific occasions. That is, **for positioning strategies to be clear, actionable, and enduring they should be documented in *positioning statements*.** Without working through the process of documenting the intentions of a positioning effort, members of the organization and elements of the marketing mix can drift *off strategy* or *off message*. A positioning statement makes it straightforward to go back to the statement and hold each action up against the original intent. Further, documenting the positioning in a statement facilitates getting people who join the organization up to speed, as well as retention of knowledge when people depart.

Positioning statements are not strategy statements; they are statements about how the strategy should come together and how the brand should be positioned *in the mindset of the customers*. A complete positioning statement usually specifies the following five things:

- the brand/product to be *positioned*;
- the market (the frame of *reference*);
- the target segment(s) and target needs (the *target*);
- at least *one point of difference* or brand promise; and
- the *reasons to believe* (which support those points of difference) (Tybout & Sternthal, 2005).

A positioning statement is not intended for customers to see; it is an internal record of what the brand is meant to be. It serves to keep the various tactics on strategy, and it fosters institutional memory of what the brand is and, often just as importantly, what it is *not*. The positioning of brands can change and migrate to follow customer preferences, but brands that change position too frequently rarely succeed. In any case, a strong, concise, and clear positioning statement reduces ambiguity, ensures institutional memory for positioning decisions, and focuses tactics of the marketing mix effort, which will be discussed in the next sections.

THE MARKETING MIX

As the previous section emphasized, the objective of positioning is to establish the product's place (position) in the customer's mindset. The marketer does not directly control the customer's mindset, but those perceptions are nevertheless influenced by controllable marketing actions, in effect, the marketing mix. The marketing mix includes all the things that marketers can manage and deploy to meet customer needs and to claim a place in customers' minds. **The marketing mix is often summarized as the product, price, place (or distribution of the product), promotions (or marketing communications), and the people involved with selling the product,** as shown in Table IV-1.

TABLE IV-1 The Marketing Mix

MIX ELEMENT	DEFINITION	STRATEGIC CONSIDERATIONS

Product	The need-satisfying offering of the firm, or customer solution, includes physical goods, intangible services, and myriad combinations of the tangible and intangible.	Product-level considerations
		  Features and benefits
		  Quality
		  Versions and alternatives
		  Level of technology
		  Service
		  Warranties
		  Packaging
		Branding and image
		  Assortment considerations
		  Product lines
		  Product portfolios

Price	From the firm's perspective, the money or other value received for the product in an exchange. From the customers' perspective, price can include related costs (installation, etc.) and other expenditures such as time and effort.	Objectives and time horizons Business model (Profit and loss considerations) List price(s) Flexibility Discounts and allowances Margins to intermediaries (channels) Terms and financing Bundling
Place	Distribution of the product or service and the location(s) of that distribution. How does the customer choose and receive the product?	Length of distribution channel(s) Number of distribution channels Channel members (types of intermediaries, including ownership and control) Channel control and channel conflict Functions (logistics, warranties, etc.; demands of functions and location in the channel) Distribution intensity Support and training

Promotion	All communications directed toward customers including:
	Advertising
	Direct marketing
	Digital communications
	Event marketing
	Public relations
	Sales promotions
		Objectives
		  Targets
		  Reach
		  Frequency
		Media (digital, print, etc.)
		Messages and meanings (copy)

People	Personal selling
	Consultative selling
	Trade selling
	Missionary selling
	Technical selling
	Entrepreneurial selling
	Hybrid sales force
	Retail selling
		Objectives
		  Targets
		  Desired behavior
		  Promotional emphasis
		Managerial activities
		  Coaching
		  Counseling
		  Evaluating
		  Administrating

These are referred to as the "five Ps" of marketing, meant to memorably summarize the entire range of marketing actions that an organization can direct at customers to fulfill their needs. The strategic issues related to the marketing mix, including changes in effective tactics across the product life cycle, are important to concisely summarize and connect to the strategic planning model, as shown in Table IV-2.

TABLE IV-2 The Marketing Mix Across the Product Life Cycle

Mix Element	INTRODUCTION	GROWTH	MATURITY	DECLINE
Product	Initially one; Few	Increased number; Increasing available features and alternatives	Stable number Commoditization	Fewer
Price	Skimming and Penetration	Competitive	Price competition intensifies	Deals and price cutting deepen
Place	Limited distribution; High support required	Building distribution; Moving toward intensive	Intensive	May be reduced
Communication, including both Promotion and People	Build primary demand; Information needs high	Build selective demand; Differentiation	Reminder; Communication budgets reduced	

PRODUCT

The first "P" in the marketing mix is product. A product can include tangible goods, intangible services, and all the innumerable combinations of tangible and intangible value. Strategically, products can be understood in layers (as shown in Figure IV-2) ranging from:

- The core product (the essential need-fulfilling elements);
- The expected and augmented products (the essential need-fulfilling elements augmented by the peripheral accessories, warranties, service, etc.); and
- The potential product, the factors capable of engendering "Wow!" responses from customers—the unexpected factors that delight customers and lead to satisfaction, loyalty, and positive word-of-mouth—and that command high profit margins.

When attributes of the product that once were new and unexpected become expected and even ubiquitous, and all products in a market offer those attributes, it is called *commoditization*. Commoditization in a product category often leads to price competition (what else is left to compete on?). Creative marketing strategists succeed in avoiding price competition by finding new "Wow!" attributes—exciting new options or services that augment the core product—thereby differentiating their offerings and avoiding the perils of commoditization.

A product can ultimately be a part of a product line, which is an assortment of products offered by the same business unit. Strategies related to product lines include price lining, line/brand

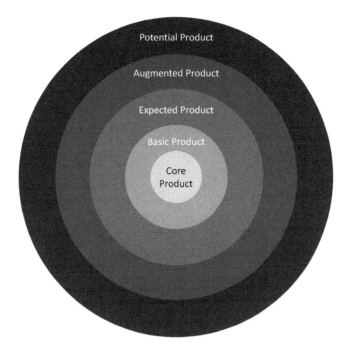

FIGURE IV-2   Product Layers

extensions, and product platforms. Product strategies include not only decisions about specific products, but also decisions about the firm's overall assortment or portfolio of products, how those multiple products relate to their markets, and how they relate to each other. Many firms manage multiple business units and products lines and must make strategic decisions about which products to invest in, which to harvest, and even whether or not to divest some products or business units. Product portfolios are examined in greater detail in Note 26.

New Product Development

New product development requires a keen focus on anticipating customer needs and even discovering unrecognized (latent) needs. Because it takes time to bring new products to market, there may be no task in the strategic planning process that requires more foresight. The consulting firm Booz Allen Hamilton developed the classic new product development model, identifying a flow of seven basic activities required for successful new product development, beginning with idea generation and culminating in commercialization (see Figure IV-3). New product development highlights the need for cross-functional as well as external input (from customers, vendors, and collaborators). Research shows that firms that build innovative cultures—cultures in which ideas are valued and failures tolerated—are more successful than their conservative competitors (Matzler et al., 2007).

A critical strategic task is planning the product pipeline; anticipating needs and preparing to meet future needs in the marketplace. In many industries, the lead time required to develop a new product is substantial. Differences across competitors in lead times required to launch new products can constitute a substantial driver of strategic success. Therefore, time-to-market and foresight are important considerations in new product development, and anticipatory customer

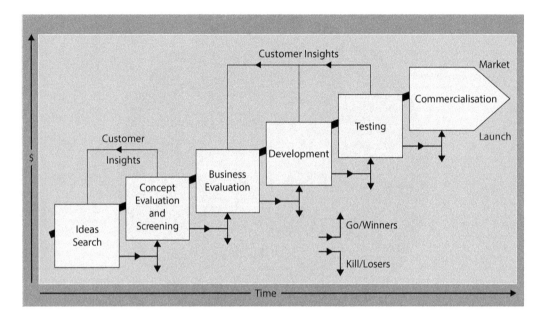

FIGURE IV-3   New Product Development Process (Adapted from Knox, 2002)

assessment, marketing research, and product planning are critical to strategic marketing success. New product development is examined in greater detail in Note 27.

Product Innovation

Innovations do not always, or even usually, entail advanced technologies or technological break-throughs. More often, innovation involves identifying latent customer needs or viewing customer needs differently than they had been understood before and drawing together existing technologies to meet those needs better than current solutions. Such market-oriented innovation entails identifying customer insights and understanding how innovations spread or *diffuse* through the market. Product innovation is examined in greater detail in Note 28.

Understanding the diffusion of innovations is important to a market strategist. Considering the following three concepts can help:

1. *Understanding differences across innovations themselves.* Innovations can be distinguished with regard to their degree of newness to the firm and their degree of newness to the customer. Innovations range from *discontinuous* (radical or truly new; changing the way customers consume and/or meet the target need) through *dynamically continuous* (noticeable but negligible changes to consumption behaviors) to *continuous* (incremental; improving on existing products with no impact or very low impact on consumption patterns and behaviors).
2. *Understanding what aspects of those innovations accelerate or slow their diffusion.* Various characteristics of those innovations predict the rapidity of their diffusion into the target markets. Things like relative advantage (How much better is the innovation than existing ways to meet the same needs?), observability (How easily can others see the innovation in use?),

and compatibility with existing lifestyles and consumption patterns all *accelerate* diffusion. On the other hand, characteristics like risk (physical risk or the risk of hurting someone, financial risk, and social risk or the risk of embarrassment) and simple cost will all *slow* the diffusion of an innovation into the market.

3. *Understanding how different consumers respond to innovations.* One well-known typology segments customers based on their propensity to adopt an innovation—innovators, early adopters, early and late majorities, and laggards.

PRICE

Viable pricing strategies are linked to the product life cycle (see Table IV-2). Early in the product life cycle, as products are being introduced, demand is driven by the value of the innovation—customers are attracted to the new benefits or relative advantage of the product in the new offerings. Pricing can take advantage of that quality-focused demand by *skimming*, charging a relatively high price to profit from the newness of that product. A skimming strategy may, however, dampen overall demand. Alternatively, the firm can charge a lower *penetration* price intended to increase volume. Penetration pricing makes the most sense when customers are at least somewhat *sticky* (i.e., can be expected to stay with their initial brand selection due to loyalty or some other source of inertia) and when certain benefits of scale can be expected as production increases. Later in the product life cycle, pricing becomes increasingly competitive. Pricing strategies are explored further in Note 29.

Profits

Strategy is not successful unless it is profitable. Too often, the terms *profit* and *revenue* are used interchangeably, but these terms are definitely not synonyms, since profit is what results after costs are deducted from sales revenue. Although sales revenue is an important objective, unless costs are controlled, there will be no profits for the organization and no sustainable business model.

Strategies can be developed with an emphasis on either short-term or long-term profitability. Profitability in the long term generally requires investment in the short term; those investments do not preclude short-term profitability, but they do rule out maximizing short-term returns. Having growth aspirations is important, but it is also wise to remember that "growth for growth's sake is the ideology of the cancer cell" (Abbey, 1990, p. 98). Growth or market share objectives should be set in the context of a specific business model with consideration given to long-term returns. Top-line growth (revenues) can come at the expense of the bottom-line (profits) and can strain the firm's cash flow and other resources. Targeting the *right* customers—customers who are profitable in the long-run, who are relatively likely to become loyal, and who will appreciate and benefit from the firm's competitive advantages (that is, take value from the firm's unique points of differentiation and competitive advantages) are all at least as important as simple *growth*, and require a keen understanding of *cost–volume–profit* logic in the context of the firm's business model.

Breakeven Analysis

Breakeven analysis is an important computation in evaluating the feasibility of an endeavor, a marketing plan, or a strategy. The breakeven point is defined as the point where the sales revenues exactly cover all the costs. Sales revenues are the unit price multiplied times the average price. Total costs can be divided into two parts: variable costs (the costs that go up with the sale of each unit) and fixed costs (overhead costs and expenses that do not change with each unit sold). This can be summarized simply in the following formulas:

$$\textbf{Revenue} = \textbf{Price} \times \textbf{Quantity}$$
$$\textbf{Total Costs} = \textbf{(Variable Costs} \times \textbf{Quantity)} + \textbf{Fixed Costs}$$

Therefore, if breakeven is where revenues exactly equal expenses, we can set the two equations as equal:

$$\textbf{Revenue} = \textbf{Expenses} \text{ or}$$
$$\textbf{(Price} \times \textbf{Quantity)} = \textbf{(Variable Costs} \times \textbf{Quantity)} + \textbf{Fixed Costs}$$

Solving that equation for breakeven quantity (that is, setting quantity on one side and all other variables on the other) yields the formula for the number of units that must be sold to exactly cover expenses:

$$\textbf{Quantity Breakeven} = \frac{\textbf{Fixed Costs}}{\textbf{(Price} - \textbf{Variable Costs)}}$$

For example, if we are going into business selling something, for example ice-cream cones, and the variable costs (the cost of the scoop of ice cream, the cone, and the napkin) are $1, the selling price is $2, and we have to pay $150 for our ice-cream cone vending cart, we would be able to figure out pretty quickly that we need to sell 150 ice-cream cones to *breakeven*. That is because we make $1 on each sale (price minus variable costs or $2–$1, which is called the *contribution margin*). We need to make $150 just to cover the cost for the vending cart. Once we've paid for the cart (sold 150 cones), we're in the black (traditionally red ink was used to indicate a loss in ledgers and accounting ledgers so *in the black* means we're profitable). In fact, we're making $1/cone; however, what the bank that lent us the money to buy the cart would want to know is "How many cones need to be sold to *breakeven* (and pay us back our money)?" Basic financial math for marketing strategy is examined further in Appendix A.

PLACE/DISTRIBUTION CHANNELS

Place, or the channel(s) of distribution, involves several categories of decisions, including selecting, motivating, and controlling channel members. These decisions should be based on some basic market-oriented considerations:

- Where, how, and when do customers shop for the product?
- What level of support (service, information and training, maintenance, etc.) do customers require for the product?

- What level of control does the distribution require to ensure quality and to satisfy customer needs?
- How do different means of distribution relate, and how might they conflict?

These considerations change across the product life cycle. Early in the life cycle, customers require more information and training, especially for technologically sophisticated products. Later in the product life cycle, customers may need less hand-holding, but they may respond more to peripheral services and almost always become more price conscious.

Distribution channels and channel intermediaries can add value for both the consumer and the marketer by performing at least three types of *channel functions*, including the following:

- transactional (buying, selling, holding inventory, and assuming inventory risks such as obsolescence and spoilage);
- logistical (shipping, breaking bulk, assorting); and
- facilitating (information gathering and conveyance, including giving information *to customers* and giving information *about customers* to the marketer, financing).

Understanding these functions, as well as how and by whom they are performed in a particular distribution system, allows for strategic thinking about how those functions may change. If channel members stop adding value or the functions become unnecessary, they will eventually be bypassed. For example, as technology changes (including Internet-based delivery of product *help* information), it is becoming possible for manufacturers to deliver information directly to customers, bypassing channel partners who specialized in facilitating/information functions. This will reduce the need for intermediaries to educate and provide information and perhaps eventually result in channel reconfiguration. The role of place and distribution channels is examined further in Note 30.

PROMOTIONS/INTEGRATED MARKETING COMMUNICATIONS

Promotions, or integrated marketing communications, include all the efforts to communicate to the customer. Traditionally, advertising was the dominant tool in the communications arsenal. Advertising effectively and efficiently reaches large numbers of consumers and is particularly effective at creating awareness and reminding large audiences about the product or brand. A focus on advertising is considered a *pull strategy*; it develops demand at the level of the ultimate consumer, and that demand *pulls* sales through the channel.

One reality of advertising in the new millennium is the *death of mass*. Media that used to reach truly mass audiences, such as television, radio, and magazines have fragmented across digital channels. This proliferation of media and technologies that allow consumers to choose what they engage with and what they bypass or ignore has created challenges and opportunities for marketers. On the one hand, it is now nearly impossible to quickly communicate with mass audiences. On the other hand, marketers can now reach more defined and refined targets with specialized messages.

Changes in owned, paid, and earned media, as well as advances in understanding how markets work, has led to an increased emphasis on other communication tools, from digital to experiential. These elements of promotion are examined further in Note 31.

PEOPLE

The fifth "P" of the marketing mix reflects people and refers to personal selling and service delivery. Personal selling is usually the most effective means of closing the deal (moving customers from consideration to purchase). Nevertheless, the cost per contact of personal selling is high and its ability to reach mass markets is limited. A communication strategy emphasizing personal selling is a *push* strategy; it develops demand at the immediate next level of the distribution system and, thereby, pushes demand through the channel. In practice, most marketing strategies employ a balance of *push* and *pull*.

Managers make a serious mistake when they refer to what salespeople do as merely *selling*, as though the salesperson's personality alone brings in the sale. Rather, the modern professional salesperson relies on analytic skills as much as on character and professionalism. Getting the order is only the final stage of a complex set of activities involving many people within the seller's firm as well as within the customer's organization. Personal selling is consultative and involves a two-step process:

1. Determine and articulate for the customer their real problem.
2. Present the product's or service's benefits as a partial or complete solution to that problem.

By helping the customer to define their own needs, the salesperson enters the sale at the very beginning and, in this way, can often place their products at a considerable advantage. The concept of people as the ultimate sales tool is examined further in Note 32.

Once the various elements of the marketing mix have been determined, an overall marketing plan needs to be established and forecasts and budgets need to be developed. Note 33 provides additional background on budgets, forecasts, and objectives. In addition, Appendix B outlines a comprehensive strategic marketing plan template.

MEASURING SUCCESS

Customer satisfaction, repeat-purchase intention, and intention to recommend are generally considered to be the three essential markers of how well customers are responding to their experiences with the firm and its offerings. Research efforts have focused on reducing various customer responses to some more parsimonious measures that can be easily collected and assessed. That is, too many customer-response metrics can be confusing, and it seems evident that all these things are basically tapping into the same underlying customer evaluations.

Frederick Reichheld, an authority on strategy, conducted research that began with roughly 20 items and examined various post-consumption responses ranging from satisfaction, loyalty, and repeat-purchase intention. The single item "How likely is it that you would recommend [company X] to a friend or colleague?" on a scale from 1 to 10 (extremely likely) was found to be the most predictive of future behaviors (actual recommendations as well as actual repeat purchase) and, at the firm level, of future growth and profitability (Reichheld, 2003; Reichheld & Covey, 2006). This concept is now known as the *Net Promoter Score* and is calculated as the sum of the number of customers who respond with a 9 or a 10 on the scale in response to the single question (labeled as *Promoters*) and subtracts the number who responded with anything from 0 to 6 (labeled as *Detractors*). Respondents who gave a 7 or an 8 are termed *passively satisfied*. It has been argued that this Net Promoter Score is the ultimate question—the one number you need to grow (Reichheld, 2003; Reichheld & Covey, 2006). Although it is a simplification of the complex array of customer responses that likely begin with some evaluation like satisfaction, it is certainly a revealing

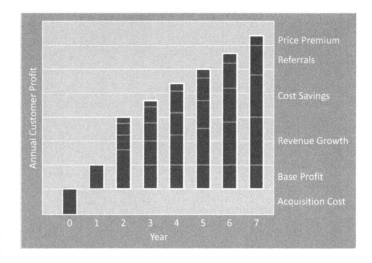

FIGURE IV-4   Breakdown of Typical Company Profit (Reichheld, 1996.)

post-consumption marker relative to customer loyalty. Figure IV-4 highlights the impact of customer loyalty on profits.

Core metrics such as customer satisfaction, customer loyalty, customer profitability, and cost to serve, are all essential in setting objectives and are a key basis of assessment and adjustment for strategic marketing planning. Some of these data come from operational data—sales and shipment records, accounting systems, and the like—and other data come from surveys of current customers. On an ongoing basis, CRM systems collect data about customers and their responses to the firm's marketing mix. Those data are used to tailor the firm's offerings and communications toward profitable customers and to evaluate and adjust ongoing efforts. In fact, market- and customer-related metrics are essential to assessing and adjusting marketing strategies.

APPLYING THE STRATEGIC MARKETING FRAMEWORK

In applying the Strategic Marketing Framework (SMF) and developing the marketing plan, the manager should strive to surface assumptions about expected responses by customers, competitors, channel partners, and other constituents. As strategy is established and its implementation begun, those parameters must be monitored, thus beginning anew the situation analysis and strategy formulation stages. Assessment and adjustment feeds back into gap analyses of *all* of the stages in the SMF—situation analysis, strategy formulation, and marketing execution—via positioning and the marketing mix.

The remaining Notes in this book highlight tools that support each of the stages in the Strategic Marketing Framework (SMF), shown again in Figure IV-5. In addition, appendices at the end of this book provide helpful resources for computing basic financial math for marketing, establishing a strategic marketing plan, and developing effective one-page memos.

FIGURE IV-5   Strategic Marketing Framework

REFERENCES

Abbey, E. (1990). *A voice crying in the wilderness.* St. Martin's Press.

Interbrand. (2021). Best global brands 2020. *Interbrand.* https://www.interbrand.com/best-global-brands/coca-cola/

Johansson, J. K., & Nonaka, I. (1987). Market research the Japanese way. *Harvard Business Review, 65*(3), 16–22.

Kotler, P., & Armstrong, G. (2010). *Principles of marketing.* Pearson Education.

Matzler, K., Bailom, F., & Tschemernjak, D. (2007). *Enduring success: What top companies do differently.* Palgrave Macmillan.

Reichheld, Frederick F. *The Loyalty Effect: The Hidden Force Behind Growth, Profits, and Lasting Value.* Boston, MA: Harvard Business School Press, 1996.

Reichheld, F. F. (2003). The one number you need to grow. *Harvard Business Review, 81*(12), 46–55.

Reichheld, F. F., & Covey, S. R. (2006). *The ultimate question: Driving good profits and true growth,* 211. Harvard Business School Press.

Simon Knox, "The Boardroom Agenda: Developing the Innovative Organization," *Corporate Governance: International Journal of Business in Society* 2, no. 1 (Emerald Group Publishing Limited, 2002): 27–36.

Tybout, A. M., & Sternthal, B. (2005). Brand positioning. In *Kellogg on branding: The marketing faculty of the Kellogg School of Management* (pp. 11–26). John Wiley & Sons.

Figure Credit

Fig. IV.3: Adapted from Dieter Tschemernjak, Franz Bailom, and Kurt Matzler, Enduring Success: What Top Companies Do Differently. Copyright © 2007 by Palgrave Macmillan.

NOTES ALIGNED WITH CHAPTER II: FOCUS ON SITUATIONAL ANALYSIS

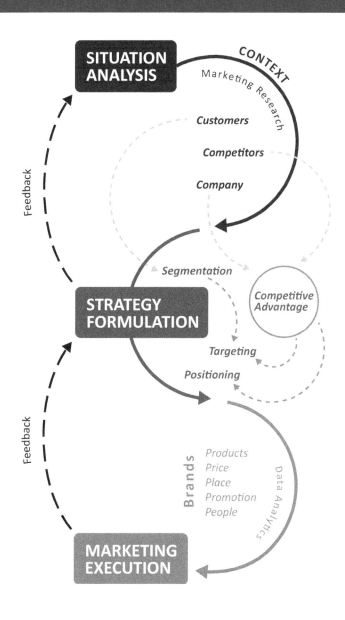

MARKETING RESEARCH

Effective strategic marketing requires persistent and thorough attention to customer needs—that's the *marketing concept*. Marketing research includes studying events and trends in the general context, as well as with regard to competitors. Marketing research can also address specific problems or guide marketing mix decisions. Various distinctions across market research activities related to the Strategic Marketing Framework are summarized in Table 1-1.

TABLE 1-1 Research Across the Stages of the Strategic Marketing Framework

Customer-Oriented Marketing Research			
	Situation Analysis	*Customer and Market Analysis*	The broad, exploratory, and inductive study of customers and markets to identify (a) customer insights, and (b) trends in needs and demand.
	Strategy Formulation	*Segmentation, Targeting and Positioning*	Identifying meaningful differences across markets with respect to needs and descriptive characteristics.
		Marketing Mix Development	Focused research to pretest and refine tactics, including new products or product modifications, price, promotions, advertising, and merchandising programs.
		Customer Relationship Management (CRM)	Ongoing data collections tied to specific accounts or customers that serve to tailor offerings (personalize or customize offerings) and direct investments and efforts toward the "right" customers and segments.
	Marketing Execution	*Customer- and Market-Oriented Metrics*	Focused and ongoing research collecting information on customer responses to the marketing mix, including measures of satisfaction, loyalty, profitability, and revenues.

Those applications of marketing research related to situation analysis and, in particular, to customer assessment are inductive, exploratory, and less structured. The advancement of digital technologies and data collection tools has enabled marketers to monitor consumer behavior on a real-time basis. However, increased analytic opportunities bring increased responsibilities for marketers to act in an ethical manner. In the U.S., the American Marketing Association (2021) has established codes of conduct that emphasize honesty, responsibility, fairness, respect, transparency, and citizenship. It is essential to consider ethical implications at every step in the strategic marketing process.

This Note links customer-oriented market research to marketing strategy; this is the issue-specific research that (a) segments and targets customers, (b) shapes specific marketing programs and tactics (positioning and marketing mix), and (c) evaluates those activities against standards and objectives for use in assessment and adjustment. This Note is not about how to *do* market research; it is about how to *manage* market research and how to integrate market research into strategic planning.

Market research is a required input to segmenting customers based on consequential differences in needs and responses to the marketing mix. Market research is similarly essential to developing marketing mixes; it tests and directs everything from new product development and pricing to advertising, sales, and distribution. The assessment and adjustment of a marketing strategy require rigorous measurement and a dashboard of marketing metrics, including outputs such as customer satisfaction, customer profitability, and customer loyalty that gauge how the firm is doing with its customers. Still, every problem or opportunity does not require formal market research. Before discussing market research from a strategic perspective, it is worthwhile to clarify when market research is required and when it may not be necessary or wise.

WHEN TO DO MARKET RESEARCH–AND WHEN *NOT* TO DO MARKET RESEARCH

Obviously, every marketing decision does not require formal market research; in fact, in many situations, traditional market research may be inaccurate and misleading. Decisions about when to undertake market research and when *not* to invest in market research should be based on considerations of whether the information can realistically be researched (for example, whether or not customers can be realistically expected to know or estimate their responses to a proposed marketing action) and whether the *benefits* outweigh the *costs* of doing the research.

When a product is truly new to the world customers may not understand it well enough to predict their responses. Apple founder, Steve Jobs, observed that "People don't know what they want until you show it to them. That's why I never rely on market research. Our task is to read things that are not yet on the page" (Smith, 2019, para. 4). There is an understanding that, in some cases, customers cannot accurately respond to new product ideas. In addition, the knowledge and the instincts of experts, including marketing managers and channel partners, may be more accurate in developing true innovations and predicting market responses.

Before investing in market research, the marketer needs to weigh the costs against the benefits of the effort. The costs of market research include financial costs—market research can be very expensive—as well as the opportunity costs and time required to conduct the research. The benefits of market research are its support for decision-making and the reduction of risk. Risk assessments should be multifaceted, taking into account both the probability of an outcome (its likelihood) and the consequences of the risk. Market research may be wasted on refining elements of a marketing program that can be easily adjusted after launch, on reducing risks of highly unlikely outcomes, or on reducing risks that will in any case have inconsequential impacts on the program or the firm. Those deliberations are especially relevant when speed to market is critical. Introducing new products into actual markets and seeing what sticks may, in many cases, be more efficient and more effective than investing in expensive and time-consuming market research and test markets.

One interesting observation in this regard is that modern business education and culture seems to teach managers not to trust their instincts or expertise. That is probably a good thing in many situations; good market research should suffer less bias than managerial judgment. Nevertheless, in certain cases managerial expertise or *instinct* is accurate, and more accurate than customers themselves can be in various situations. Further, for some decisions, managerial expertise can be close enough; more research may refine a decision but those refinements may not produce much in terms of substantive improvements or increased sales—and the time and resources involved in research may have been better spent on other marketing activities.

THE MARKET RESEARCH PROCESS

When market research *is* appropriate and needed, it should be clearly based on a specific understanding of the issue, opportunity, or problem that is to be researched and with a detailed understanding of the managerial decision(s) to be guided by the research. Figure 1-1 presents two versions of the basic market research process. The four-step process on the left, adapted from Philip Kotler and Gary Armstrong's classic *Principles of Marketing* textbook, is a traditional view of the market research flow, where the first step is to define the problem and the objectives of the research (Burns & Bush, 2000; Kotler & Armstrong, 2009). Subsequent steps plan and execute a data-driven project that addresses those problems and objectives, leading toward a summary report.

The process depicted on the right in Figure 1-1 is adapted from the article, "Backward Market Research," by Alan Andreasen (1985) in which he argued that, "Only by first thinking through the decisions to be made with the research results will the project be started with a high likelihood of action-ability" (p. 180). Andreasen argued that the manager should not only spell out the issue or problem to be addressed by the research, but should also carefully tie the research *to specific managerial actions* (the implementation or action-ability) that are possible depending on the outcomes of the research, and even go so far as to *draft the eventual report*—including the tables for presenting quantitative results—before developing

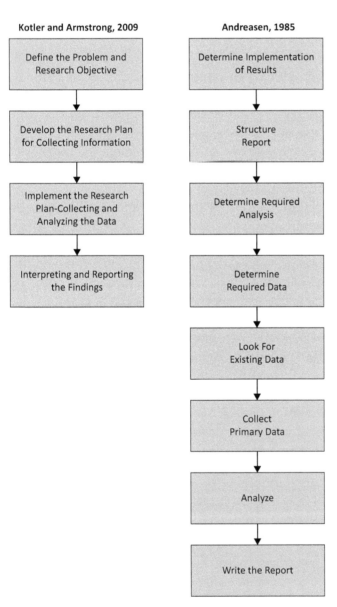

FIGURE 1-1   Market Research Process Comparisons

and executing the research plan. Andreasen's framework emphasizes the need to hone in on exactly what could be done differently, depending on the results of this research and the need to think ahead about how the research will address the issue and how the recommendations will be communicated.

Most of the remaining marketing research process steps are technical—sampling plans, collecting data, and analyzing statistics that are the purview of research staff and vendors. An appreciation of the need to link investments in research to specific issues and feasible strategic actions, as well as a broad understanding of the ways different research approaches link with different issues and produce different sorts of information, are invaluable to guide decision-making for effective and efficient strategic management.

There are at least three broad categories of questions that market research can address:

Market Questions

- Demand forecasting: What is the size of the market? What are the sizes and growth rates of the different segments? How will markets/segments respond to the offerings?
- Competitive insights: What is the nature of the competition? Which competitive brands are most recognized in the market, and why?
- Needs identification and segmentation: What do customers need and care about, and how much do they care? How do customers differ in regards to those needs and importance weightings?

Marketing Mix Questions

- The effect of various marketing mix elements: What is the best product, message, channel, or price? What is the best combination of these interdependent tactics?

Assessment and Adjustment Questions

- Market share: How are we doing vis-à-vis the competition? How are we meeting our business and marketing objectives?
- Performance: How do our customers feel about us (customer satisfaction)? How loyal are they? How profitable are they?

As marketing strategists develop research projects, they need to be sensitive to the various types of errors that can occur. In science there are two types of errors: Type I errors are when the research finds positive results for something that is, in fact, not true (*false positives*); and Type II errors are those that reject hypotheses that are actually true (*false negatives*). A third sort of error, not as often discussed in the research literature, is a Type III error, which involves *finding the right answers for the wrong questions* (Kimball, 1957). Marketers should be particularly attentive to Type III errors when structuring the parameters of a research project.

TYPES OF RESEARCH

There are several different types of research methodologies, including exploratory, descriptive, and causal. Exploratory research uses less structured and wide-ranging methods to identify issues for further research without imposing a priori structure or hypotheses on the data collection or the respondent. In market research, focus groups, depth interviews, and other methods may all be useful, especially at the start of a project, to explore customer experiences and the underlying factors driving observed phenomena and to generate specific issues for further research.

Descriptive research characterizes the who, what, when, and where of the market (but not the why—why implies causation, which is discussed below). Descriptions are most often of markets, segments, or specific customers and their size, attitudes and preferences, and behaviors or other characteristics important to strategy and marketing mix management.

Causal research is the *why* of a marketplace phenomenon. It relates two or more variables and isolates the causal factors. Causal research identifies the event (or cause) and its consequence (or effect). Experiments are the most common form of causal research. Experiments are research designs in which one group of customers or one market is exposed to one level of a variable (a promotion, a price level, or an advertisement) while another group is not (making it the *control group*), or in which different groups are given different levels of a variable (different prices, for instance, or different advertisements).

TYPES OF DATA

There are several ways to differentiate sources of data and types of data. Some data are *internal* to the firm—and most firms can find out a lot just by analyzing data they already have in house—and other data are *external* to the firm. Generally, because internal data are more readily at hand (although not necessarily easy, or free, to access), it is a good idea to start by asking "What do we already know?" and thoroughly analyze internal data first, before investing in gathering external data. It is also generally true that firms underappreciate the informational value of internal data, such as shipments, inventories, and returns. Compared to American managers, the Japanese tend to rely more on hard data along with channel partners (conversations with distributors and retailers) in making decisions (Johansson & Nonaka, 1987).

A second distinction across data is between *secondary* data, preexisting data already collected for some other purpose, and *primary* data, which is data collected specifically for the current research project. As with the internal–external distinction, there is a general rule that looking at secondary data first is a good idea. Secondary data may not be free or immediately available, but such data is generally cheaper, easier, and faster to access than primary data.

For example, a firm might want to know how much has been paid in taxes on the sale of alcohol in a certain jurisdiction in order to estimate the size of the market for adult beverages. Obtaining those secondary data may require sending a paid staff researcher to the Alcoholic Beverages Commission and could involve fees for the reports; however, those costs and the time required would be less than doing a survey to estimate the size of the market. On the other hand, primary data would be customized to the specific research issue being addressed. If the product being considered is high-end tequila, for example, a primary data collection tool such as a consumer survey could ask how much premium tequila the customer has consumed or intends to consume, providing more specifically relevant information compared to general tax receipts. In addition, secondary data can be outdated (e.g., tax receipts for the current year may not be available). Table 1-2 summarizes these basic distinctions between primary and secondary data.

TABLE 1-2 Primary Versus Secondary Data

	COST	TIME REQUIRED TO OBTAIN	TIMELINESS	CUSTOMIZATION
Secondary	Low	Quick	Can be outdated	Low to none
Primary	High*	Delayed	Current	High

*Costs of primary market research are high in both monetary terms and in terms of managerial time and effort, as well as with regard to delays in taking action.

Another distinction across data is between *qualitative* and *quantitative* data. Every marketer can appreciate that a customer's reaction to almost any consumption experience—from dining at a fine restaurant to purchasing raw materials for a plant—is going to be hard to summarize with a single, simple number. Customer satisfaction, for example, is certainly a richer experience than a single number (e.g., on a scale of 1 to 10) can possibly describe. Nevertheless, in order to test hypotheses and evaluate concepts in large, random samples, and in order to compare responses across customers, marketers frequently must use simple, forced-choice scales to gauge and analyze phenomena such as customer satisfaction.

Qualitative data methods involve observation or textual, verbal, and open-ended responses. Qualitative data tend to be subjective and imprecise and are not easily compared or generalized across customers; however, qualitative data can provide invaluable depth and vividness. Quantitative data are responses that are provided or can be summarized numerically, and are conducive to statistical analysis, enabling generalization of results across populations. The ability to compare data across customers, for example the ability to compare customers across time (e.g., last year versus this year) or across segments, and the ability to generalize to all customers in a target population (a segment or a market) support the use of quantitative data in many market research applications.

Generalizability is an important idea. Because qualitative techniques typically require significant time, thought, and energy from respondents, it is often impossible to develop qualitative data from adequate-sized, truly random samples. Only when each member of a population (the overall group the researcher is interested in) has had an equal chance of being selected for a data collection can the results of that data collection be generalized to the population. If the researcher selects and pays eight retirees that they personally know to attend a focus group, the research only reflects what those eight retirees think about the product or advertisement—they were not selected randomly and they are a very small sample so we cannot generalize to all retirees. If we randomly sample from all of the retirees in a market and survey a large enough number of people regarding their responses to a new product idea, our results will be quantitative and, although not rich (e.g., a rating of a new product might be an 8.73 versus a 7.49 for an alternative), those results will be generalizable to all retirees in the market. We would know that there is a significant probability that all retirees will prefer one product to the other.

Thus, as summarized in Table 1-3, there is an inherent trade-off between the richness of qualitative data and data collection methods and the generalizability and comparability of quantitative data.

TABLE 1-3 Qualitative Versus Quantitative Data

	RICHNESS	GENERALIZABILITY	COMPARABILITY
Qualitative	High	Low to None	Low
Quantitative	Low	High	High

Various specific types of data combine these characteristics—internal/external, secondary/primary, and qualitative/quantitative—in different ways. Some data, like syndicated data (i.e., scanner data or panel data), are external/secondary/quantitative data tied to observations of consumers' behaviors recorded electronically (in the case of scanner data) or via surveys (in the case of panels). Other data, such as sales force feedback, are internal/secondary/qualitative. Other sorts of data can combine these characteristics in innumerable ways, but all can be characterized using these three qualities. Those characterizations are useful for understanding the data's content, their applicability in strategic planning, and their limitations.

DATA ANALYSES

It is typically neither the job of the marketing strategist to design or execute the data collection in a research project, nor to analyze those data; however, it is important to understand the following analyses that are especially useful in strategic marketing planning:

- syndicated data and associated analyses, such as the Brand Development Index (BDI) and Category Development Index (CDI);
- perceptual maps, including those developed from direct items (such as, "On a scale of 1–7, how light is beer X?") or from indirect paired comparison ("How similar or dissimilar are beers X and Y?") using multidimensional scaling;
- conjoint analysis, which pulls apart customer preferences along specific attributes when customers consider those attributes in conjoint with (or "simultaneously and interdependently with") other attributes; and,
- experiments, which allow the researcher to identify with certainty which actions or other variables cause what outcomes (e.g., to determine with certainty that a change in price leads to higher sales).

Syndicated Sources

Syndicated data are collected by third parties, usually one of a very few large market research companies such as Nielsen. Syndicated data have grown dramatically with technological advances over the past few decades, and today researchers have access to zettabytes of data. These data include scanner data, the data recorded each time a UPC code (Uniformed Product Code or bar scan) is passed over a checkout scanner at a grocery store, from retailers across the country. Those scanner data are augmented with information about causes or events such as coupons, price promotions, and similar data, to allow for analysis of sales patterns across time and in correlation with price and promotion tactics. Other data offered by research syndicators include panel data, which results from a panel of consumers tracking their actual purchases, including the retailers they purchase from, across time. Single-source data combine panel data (tracked purchases and purchase venues) with surveys of things like demographics and lifestyles, and augments those data with consumer media usage (television watched, newspapers read, etc.). These syndicated data are powerful tools for understanding the links between segments, media, marketing actions (especially price and price promotions, but also advertising), and purchase behaviors, as well as describing retail coverage.

Perceptual Maps

One of the most useful ways to visualize competitive position in the marketplace is to translate positions in consumer perceptions to a two-dimensional map, with products and customer preferences graphed into that space. Perhaps the most common and basic anchors for *perceptual maps* (also known as *positioning maps*) are that of price (low to high) and quality (low to high). The usefulness of maps in understanding actual positions held in customers' minds is well-established. Although it is unlikely that many customers carry such maps in their minds, they do perceive the various products relative to each other and to some salient characteristics—and the maps capture that reality. It is, therefore, reasonable to conceptualize targeting (directing marketing programs at segments) and competitive differences (relationships amongst products and brands) within these two-dimensional representations. The application of perceptual maps for positioning purposes is examined further in Note 24.

   Joint space maps allow the researcher to also place characteristics and customers' ideal points into these maps—usefully showing how perceptions of product alternatives and attributes correspond with product attributes and customer preferences. Two commonly applied approaches to creating perceptual maps are (a) structured or semantic items mapped into Cartesian coordinates, and (b) multidimensional scaling, which derives similarities from less structured customer responses that tap into the dimensions customers perceive across the product category when they are not given dimensions but must develop their own.

Conjoint Analysis

Another valuable approach to data analysis addresses how customers evaluate and choose between products when those products are made up of multiple attributes, when those attributes must be considered together, and when preferences with regard to those attributes involve trade-offs across attributes. For example, everyone would like a car that handles really well. Everyone would also prefer a car that can carry a lot of luggage. But customers know that if they want handling, they must give up some cargo capacity (and vice versa). It is physically impossible to get a great handling car that also has the maximum cargo capacity. In other cases, those trade-offs are based on price; even if it were possible to purchase a car that could handle well and move lots of things, most customers know it would cost a substantial amount, and they are unwilling to pay it. In this way, different customers and different segments of customers have different preferences. The perfect car for one segment will embody a certain set of trade-offs. Young families frequently trade off handling and performance for cargo space and fuel economy. On the other hand, young single professionals probably will prefer handling and performance.

Conjoint analysis, which takes its name from the fact that multiple attributes are considered *in conjoint* or simultaneously and interdependently, is capable of identifying the trade-offs or value functions of different customers and different segments, gauging the importance different segments place on different attributes and identifying each segment's perfect product or ideal point. Those pieces of information can be invaluable in new product development, integrated marketing communications, and other positioning activities.

Experiments

Experiments are a powerful tool for fine-tuning marketing programs and linking specific actions (causes) with specific outcomes (effects). Managers have been encouraged to turn to experiments more as technology has allowed for easier targeting of different groups with different actions. For example, the Internet allows for quick changes in the way products are described and priced. By varying the description and price across consumers, the researcher can link specific changes in the marketing mix to specific outcomes (usually those outcomes are desired customer responses such as sales or satisfaction). If customers are assigned to different treatments randomly, then differences in their responses (higher sales, greater satisfaction) can be attributed to the treatment variable (different price, different advertisement) with confidence.

SUMMARY

The marketing strategist at most firms should not be designing research, collecting data, or analyzing results, but should be aware of what sorts of research are possible, what sorts of information those research alternatives can provide, and how market research should drive strategy development, implementation, and assessment. Having said that, managers at small firms may actually conduct research themselves, and there are many sources available to guide the details of those activities. In any case, market research should start with a clear understanding of the problem or issue to be addressed and intended managerial actions should guide the research, but may actually change as a result of the research. The marketing strategy itself should be based on and tested against data.

This Note has presented a high-level perspective on when to do research, why to do research, how to manage the research effectively and efficiently, and the critical link between research and strategy in a market-driven firm. The only way to develop, implement, monitor, and adjust the appropriate marketing mix toward achieving a desired marketing strategy is by means of rigorous marketing research.

REFERENCES

American Marketing Association. (2021). *Codes of conduct: AMA statement of ethics.* https://www.ama.org/codes-of-conduct/

Andreasen, A. R. (1985). Backward market research. *Harvard Business Review, 63*(3), 176–182.

Burns, A., & Bush, R. (2000). *Market research* (6th ed.). Pearson Prentice Hall.

Johansson, J. K., & Nonaka, I. (1987). Market research the Japanese way. *Harvard Business Review, 65*(3), 16–22.

Kimball, A. W. (1957). Errors of the third kind in statistical consulting. *Journal of the American Statistical Association, 52*(278), 133–142.

Kotler, P., & Armstrong, G. (2009). *Principles of marketing* (11th ed.). Pearson Prentice Hall.

Smith, D. (2019). What everyone gets wrong about this famous Steve Jobs quote, according to Lyft's design boss. *Business Insider.* https://www.businessinsider.com/steve-jobs-quote-misunderstood-katie-dill-2019-4

CUSTOMER ASSESSMENT

This book's pervasive emphasis on the customer and on customers' needs in the strategic marketing framework is deliberate: *effective and efficient marketing strategies begin with and are continuously aligned with customer need.* Customer assessment can be distinguished from other market research that is focused on specific customers or on particular issues or decisions. Although all of these activities are "market research," customer assessment is different in that it is best done *without* prior hypotheses and should *not* be focused on addressing specific issues. Thus, this Note focuses on that exploratory customer assessment, the broadest and most inductive form of market research; this is the wide-angle view of customers and potential customers. Customer assessment has the following two primary objectives:

1. Identifying trends in the environment that could impact customers and their needs and mining increasingly large internal and external databases for a better understanding of customer behaviors and needs.
2. Discovering customer insights by means of rich, inductive exploratory approaches. Customer insights are original understandings of the ways customers consume and take value from products connected to innovative ways of meeting those customers' needs.

Although these two objectives—identifying trends and discovering customer insights—are distinct, they are also closely related and may overlap.

IDENTIFYING TRENDS: FORECASTING, DATA MINING, AND FUTURING

Identifying marketplace trends and distinguishing trends that have deep, broad, enduring foundations from more ephemeral fads is essential to developing and sustaining effective marketing strategies. Trends are (a) broad-based changes in the marketplace that endure over time; (b) evidence of significant market opportunities; (c) grounded on substantive transformations (such as changes in demographics, values, lifestyles, or technology); and (d) accessible to the mainstream. In contrast, fads are tied to transient shifts in popular culture, in fashion, in the media, or within a subpopulation such as "the trendy crowd" (Zandl, 2000). Analyzing the environment for trends can be highly quantitative, and it frequently includes well-established trend-extrapolation techniques as well as emerging data-mining procedures. Looking for trends sometimes also involves much more subjective *futuring* or wide-ranging, multidisciplinary exploration of the environment in search of possible future events or trends and consideration of the impact of these possibilities on both customers and markets (Gladwell, 1997; Gloor & Cooper, 2007).

Forecasting

The best-known way to look for trends is to perform quantitative analysis of data on past market-place phenomena and search for patterns and relationships that can be extrapolated to the future. Similar econometric and judgment-based forecasting methods may also be used to explore trends in demographics, attitudes, and lifestyles, and cultural and social forces, as well as trends in the economy, in competitor actions and strategies, and in the technological and natural environments. Any of these elements can connect with strategy via some related change in customer behaviors or demand patterns. These quantitative forecasting tools are usually focused on projecting one to two years into the future. There are several basic categories of forecasting approaches, which subsume innumerable variations and can get somewhat complex, including trend extrapolation, causal modeling, and judgment-based forecasting. An exploration of each of these categories is below.

Trend Extrapolation

Statisticians often use trend extrapolation or "curve fitting" methods such as moving averages, exponential smoothing, and the like to identify the direction in which customer, economic, and other phenomena are headed. These analyses are relatively straightforward and require few data points, which make them attractive to managers and forecasters. However, they are also dependent on past data and past market realities, which inextricably ties them to an assumption that the future will be an extension of the past.

Curve fitting frequently involves uncomplicated straight-line extrapolations, but it can also include nonlinear extrapolation, such as geometric and exponential curves, parabolic (polynomial) curves, and even Gompertz or sigmoid (S-shaped) curves. The latter category consists of S-shaped curves common to natural growth patterns. In marketing, these sorts of curves are often seen in product life cyles, diffusions of innovations, and other phenomena in which growth is initially slow, gains momentum through some rapid growth phase, and then abates as new growth becomes harder to obtain.

Causal Modeling or Econometric Forecasting

Regression analysis, the most often used tool of causal modeling and econometric forecasting, identifies the relationships between variables that cause or at least predict some target variable. That is, regressions predict some phenomenon of interest, called the *dependent variable* and usually designated as Y. With this method, the predictors, or *independent variables*, usually designated with Xs, are the things that cause or at least correlate with Y. There may be many independent variables, and the relationship between the independent and dependent variable can be linear, or it can take on nonlinear forms (e.g., exponential curves, Gompertz functions).

The difference between causation and prediction is complex. It is usually the topic of an entire course in graduate programs, but it is not especially important to most marketing managers. Essentially, the question of causation addresses whether two things are related because one leads to the other, or whether the two things simply correlate (move together), perhaps because of some other factor that causes them both. For example, the value of customers' houses and the value of customers' cars will correlate; when one is high, the other is likely to be high, and when one is low, the other is likely to be low (with exceptions and variance, of course). In this situation, if one value is known, the other can reasonably be predicted, but neither one causes the other. In fact, it's likely that both values are caused by income and wealth. Thus, if we know that two things move together and we also know or can estimate one of the two things, then we can predict the other—and this sort of prediction is usually sufficient for managerial purposes. For example, if a car dealer would like to know what sort of car (e.g., luxury sedans versus economy compacts) to present to a certain customer, knowing the value of that customer's home is good information to have, regardless of the underlying causality or lack of causality.

Judgment-Based Forecasting

Although the idea that any single person can foresee future patterns and trends based on *gut instinct* is antithetical to the dominant analytic paradigm of contemporary management, it is nevertheless an alternative—one that is used more often than generally acknowledged, and one that may be underappreciated given emerging evidence that intuition can be a powerful decision-making tool (Duggan, 2007). One study found that 45% of the executives polled relied "more on instinct than on facts and figures in running their businesses" (Bonabeau, 2003, p. 116). These and other findings suggest that intuition can be accurate—more accurate than rigorous analysis in some contexts—and they also emphasize the role of unconscious learning and the validity of rapid-processing heuristics (Gigerenzer & Todd, 1999).

Rather than relying on a single expert's predictions, formal judgment-based approaches to forecasting typically draw on panels of diverse participants. Although individual input to consensus methods, such as surveys and Delphi panels, may itself be based on intuition, the underlying assumption is that compiling input from multiple and diverse perspectives reduces bias and gleans valid insights from the aggregated perspectives. In fact, there is voluminous evidence that supports the assumption that panels (or crowds) make better decisions and more accurate forecasts than individuals (Cook & Frigstad, 1997; Surowiecki, 2004).

Data Mining

Whereas forecasting involves looking at past and current data or behavior to identify trends that can be expected to extend into the future, data mining involves searching through available information to detect relationships among behaviors or to identify original descriptions of consumption phenomena. In particular, data mining is the extraction of knowledge from huge amounts of data (Han & Kamber, 2006). Typically, this process involves analysis of large databases using sophisticated computational and statistical methods that consider internal and/or external data to identify interesting relationships. Culling actionable knowledge from such extensive data is a challenge, but today's increasingly large databases can hold valuable information about consumption patterns and preferences.

Harrah's Casinos, for example, collected extensive data on its customers over the years, including information on their spending and gambling patterns; however, it took sophisticated data mining to identify actionable understandings in these data. It turned out that Harrah's most valuable customers—the 26% of the company's customers who generated a whopping 82% of revenues—were *not* the "gold cuff-linked, limousine-riding high rollers" the company might have assumed; instead, they were "former teachers, doctors, bankers, and machinists—middle-aged and senior adults with discretionary time and income who enjoyed playing slot machines" (Loveman, 2003). This data-mining insight was readily linked to managerial actions, including customizing offerings and communications to target those valuable customers.

Futuring

Although forecasting and data mining may seem straightforward, the assumption that the future will be an extension of the past or that relationships found in the past will hold into the future is rarely met, at least not directly. The future, it turns out, is usually a function of the past modified by unforeseen factors. In addition, everyone knows about the past—or could and should know about it. Because your competition can see the past as well as you can, forecasts based solely on past data may not yield substantial competitive advantages. Therefore, marketing strategists should not only understand how to extrapolate patterns—they should also consider what things might disrupt those patterns and explore the implications of those possible discontinuities. The essential marketing question might be reduced to the following: If these uncertain but possible things happen at some point in the future, what would we want to have done between now and then to be prepared to take advantage of (or to avoid harm from) such an eventuality?

Futuring, or "the act, art, or science of identifying and evaluating possible future events," focuses on the uncertainty of the future and on environmental changes or events that might impact customers (Cornish, 2004, p. 294). Futuring begins with traditional extrapolations from past patterns, but it goes well beyond forecasting by looking further into the future and (especially) by considering what might disrupt those patterns. Futuring adopts a broader mindset than traditional forecasting, embracing a multidisciplinary set of more qualitative and judgmental approaches and ways of understanding the world. Despite some common misperceptions, futuring is *not* mystical prophecy, prescience, or clairvoyance. Rather, futuring studies the possibilities of the future—what might happen—using a wide range of tools and a variety of perspectives. Futuring also studies ways organizations and people can prepare for these possibilities. Thus, futuring is about both anticipation and preparation.

DISCOVERING CUSTOMER INSIGHTS

Gary Hamel and C. K. Prahalad, two esteemed business academics, have argued that "to realize the potential that core competencies create, a company must also have the imagination to envision markets that do not yet exist and the ability to stake them out ahead of the competition" (Hamel & Prahalad, 1991, p. 81). The realization of exceptional returns often means disregarding mature, competitive markets for truly new ones. Finding markets that do not yet exist—that is, identifying and meeting latent needs—begins with the search for customer insights. A customer insight is a penetrating, discerning understanding of customer needs, the ways that customers derive value from products, and the ways customers might derive value from products (Kotler & Armstrong, 2009; Taylor, 2000). Good customer insights are fresh, relevant, enduring, and inspiring.

Identifying customer insights requires more than painstakingly asking customers what they *think* they want; rather, it often necessitates deep customer intimacy with an eye toward discovering solutions customers could not have envisioned or articulated themselves. In other words, customer assessment requires a *deep dive* to understand customers and to identify unmet and even unrecognized needs. An important distinction between the search for genuine customer insights and other forms of marketing research is that customer insights come from *inductive* reasoning—exploration that does not start with a theory, a hypothesis, or a specific issue to be addressed, but instead attempts to observe in as unbiased and wide-ranging a manner as possible, to *let the data speak*, and to identify unexpected insights.

Data Collection Methods for Customer Insights

Searching for customer insights requires a 360-degree view of customers—looking at the way they consume from every possible angle—and a broad description of consumption that includes not only information about the consumption itself, but also about the consumption's context. For example, if a consumer drinks a glass of wine, the meaning and significance of that consumption, the value derived from the wine, and the needs that are satisfied (and that remain unsatisfied) are dependent on the context, including the social, physical, temporal, and emotional context in which the consumption is situated. Wine consumption would, in most cases, be difficult to understand in a laboratory or simulated setting or via retrospective self-reports (Geertz, 1973). Therefore, customer assessment must draw on a variety of predominantly qualitative methods, such as total immersion, depth interviews, projective techniques, and ethnography.

Total Immersion

Through *total immersion,* corporate executives gain a deep appreciation for customers' experiences with a product. This technique involves executives, rather than researchers, immersing themselves in the customers' experience and point of view (Knapman, 2008). Sessions, which are typically *not* called "total immersion" sessions—at the BBC, for example, they're called "Meet the Audience"— include deep and rich interactions between the executives and their customers (Knapman, 2008). Some marketing research firms, such as the British firm Essential Research, specialize in facilitating meaningful immersion projects, whereas other marketing researchers criticize these projects as scientifically unsound. Stuart Knapman, a partner at Essential Research and an expert in total immersion, has observed that total immersion can be invaluable in generating customer insights.

> Immersion helps to bring consumer issues into sharp focus and undoubtedly gets consumer insight into the boardroom. ... Many researchers and senior execs alike complain that ... the company is driven by research measures rather than vice versa and that business metrics have more to do with maintaining the status quo than identifying new and exciting opportunities. ... Immersion can be the perfect antidote to this insight inertia (Knapman, 2008, p. 36).

Depth Interviews and Laddering

Depth interviewing is a technique in which one or more researchers meets with a single customer and asks that individual about his or her needs, buying behaviors, and experiences with a product category. Depth interviews are resource intensive because they require researcher time and the qualitative data they generate are difficult to manage and interpret; also, any conclusions drawn from these interviews cannot easily be generalized to larger populations. Still, depth interviews offer a deep, rich understanding into the customer's motivations, values, and experiences with a product, insights that can be worth the investment.

Projective Techniques

Projective techniques, such as word or picture association, sentence completion, and metaphor elicitation, originated in psychology and psychoanalysis and have been applied to understanding consumers since at least the mid-20th century. Some of the earliest marketing researchers, including Ernest Dichter in the well-known "motivational research" tradition of the 1940s and 1950s, used projective techniques to dig into consumers' subconscious or covert motives (Ames, 1998). By asking a decision maker (a buyer or a consumer) to look at a picture, for example, and consider what they believe is going on or what they think someone in that situation would do or want (i.e., by asking the individual to project beliefs or motives onto the picture), the researcher avoids defensive reactions and may elicit more honest, deep, and even subconscious beliefs and motives.

Ethnography

Ethnographic research methods are drawn from social anthropology—the social science focused on understanding contemporary social interactions and, especially, groups and cultures (Durante & Feehan, 2005). Ethnography emphasizes depth and context in observation. Ethnographic observation is done in the context of consumers' natural habitat; that is, where the consumers live or consume the product, rather than in a simulated consumption context, in a laboratory, or via self-reports. Ethnography also emphasizes deep, long-term and all-embracing observation, as opposed to other market research methods with narrow, reductionist scopes. Ethnographic studies can recognize realities that customers themselves may be unaware of, cannot articulate, or are unwilling to offer in interviews or surveys.

For example, Moen, a manufacturer of premium plumbing fixtures, hired QualiData, a firm specializing in ethnographic research, to study the way consumers use showers. The resulting study involved watching people take showers—and yes, in order not to bias those observations, these people were naked—and then interviewing them about their shower experiences, the way they felt about the experiences, and ways the experiences might be made better. One outcome of this study was a unique, easy-to-use dial that allows people—naked people who often cannot see well due to low light, flowing water, and the absence of corrective glasses—to adjust water flow and massaging action (El Boghdady & Staff Writer, 2002).

Interestingly, managers and entrepreneurs have always used this sort of "participant-observer learning," usually without calling it that or even knowing that it has parallels in the study of cultures. In fact, Moen itself is a brand born of customer insight and participant observation. In the 1930s, its founder, Al Moen, was scalded by a rush of hot water from a conventional, two-handled faucet. As the *Washington Post* described it, "Eureka! A flash of genius, a product is born. ... Al Moen had no research go to on, just his own intuition and life experience" (El Boghdady & Staff Writer, 2002, p. 1). Today, trained ethnographers search for these same types of eureka moments using deep, extensive observation of consumers in their natural habitats. When applied to the new product development process, ethnographic research is sometimes called "empathic research," emphasizing the fact that the researchers and the designers try to empathize with customers using the product (Leonard & Rayport, 1997).

Importantly, all of these methods (total immersion, depth interviews and laddering, projective techniques, and ethnography) intended to identify customer insights are inductive. They begin with observations that shape the eventual conclusions, rather than beginning with preconceived structures or setting out to confirm or refute a priori propositions and deductive hypotheses. As a result, one stipulation for the use of these tools is the need to be cautious in extrapolating insights from observations of convenience samples to broader populations. For instance, in the research done by Moen and QualiData on showering, the need to observe consumers showering as they normally shower (i.e., in the nude) required the recruitment of nudists as subjects. Nudists are a unique subpopulation, so generalizing understandings of showering from observations of nudists required an assumption that, although the subjects were from a particular subsegment, their visible consumption (showering) would nevertheless be like that of other consumers in important ways.

Other Sources of Insights

Other sources of insight can be customers who are lead users of a product or product category; online collaborators participating in product development via communities of enthusiasts and experts; and even the company's own executives, an often-underappreciated source of knowledge and insight into the product and its customers.

Lead Users

In the 1980s, Professor Eric von Hippel of MIT recognized that many innovations come from sophisticated, creative customers. In the manufacture of semiconductors and circuit boards, for instance, the most important innovations did not come from the developers of the relevant process technologies, but from the semiconductor manufacturers themselves. Indeed, almost 80% of innovations in scientific instruments came from customers (Von Hippel, 2006). Of course, there are innovative customers in all product areas, not just in the business-to-business sector. For example, around 20% of mountain bikers work on their own mountain bikes and have ideas for solutions that they realize themselves. This figure is almost 40% for extreme sports enthusiasts and almost 10% for users of outdoor consumer goods (Von Hippel, 2006). Von Hippel labeled such innovative customers as "lead users." Today, lead users are recognized as having the following characteristics:

- Their needs are months or even years ahead of the mass market;
- They are very demanding and have their own ideas for solutions; and
- They are often opinion leaders, using the product they developed themselves with conviction and then making a significant contribution to quickly establishing the innovation on the market.

There are many examples that illustrate how lead users can give insights into customer problems and needs and become part of the product development process. For instance, in the 1980s, Hilti, a Liechtenstein-based company providing leading-edge technology to the global construction industry, began looking into flexible and easy-to-use fastening systems. Up until that point, there were no functionally efficient systems, but some customers had developed their own solutions. Therefore, Hilti tried to integrate these customers into a development project. From a group of 150 users, 14 lead users were selected. In a workshop, these lead users then developed an innovative fastening system that formed the basis for a new business unit at Hilti (Herstatt et al., 2002).

Another example is Johnson & Johnson Medical, which brought three innovations into the market—innovations that were not developed by the company itself, but by users. In this lead-user project, the company screened the market for lead users, selected them according to well-defined criteria, and brought them together in a workshop. Then, in the two-day lead-user workshop, the users themselves developed a new film for covering robots used in surgery, an all-in-one solution for preventing particulate matter from becoming airborne during operations, and an integrated sterile system for supporting patients' legs during hip operations (Herstatt et al., 2002).

Online Communities

Today, you can find online communities for virtually every product or topic. There are online communities for coffee drinkers, outdoor enthusiasts, aspiring chefs, and so on. Consumers gather in these online communities to exchange ideas, discuss their problems, and share enthusiasm for their common interests. For example, in alt.coffee, a virtual café, coffee connoisseurs discuss how coffee machines and roasters could be improved; in the outdoorseiten.net online community, mountain hikers develop their own equipment (e.g., functional jackets and particularly light tents); and at chefkoch.de, cooking enthusiasts consider how utensils could be improved (Füller et al., 2007).

Many companies use these sorts of online communities to get customer insights. Audi, for instance, involved its customers in the conception phase during the development of a new infotainment system. Through several sites that are regularly visited by car fans, Audi reached over 1,600 auto enthusiasts who worked on the virtual development of the infotainment system. This resulted in 219 service ideas, 261 comments on the console, 728 visions of future cars, and the eventual selection of the optimal product configuration (Füller & Matzler, 2007). Similarly, during a design competition phase that lasted just four weeks, Swarovski—the Austrian manufacturer of crystal figurines and jewelry—obtained 263 usable motifs for crystal tattoos that were produced by Internet users by means of tool kits (Füller et al., 2006).

Sometimes, the company itself may simply observe online discussion without directly participating in it. Consider the example of NikeTalk, a community of more than 50,000 basketball fans that has no official connection with Nike Inc. Thousands of discussions between basketball fans take place in this virtual community every month. Basketball fanatics can be found in the community, as can sports equipment retailers, students of industrial design, and Nike fans in general. Some of the subjects these community members discuss include how to customize your basketball shoe, how to distinguish a branded shoe from a fake, what basketball shoes might look like in the year 2050, and what they think about Nike's latest products (Füller et al., 2007).

Observing discussions within these communities can provide valuable insights into customers' interests, opinions, problems, acceptance of new products, and so on. In fact, companies such as Munich's Hyve AG specialize in mediating between online innovation seekers and innovation providers in the role of *innomediator*. These companies develop tools to harness the innovative power of online communities, using *netnography*—ethnography adapted to the Internet—to identify communities, screen them for innovations, and set up a virtual dialogue with them in order to systematically open up these sources of innovation.

Executives and Channel Partners

Experts, including managers, salespeople, channel partners, and engineers, can also be an invaluable source of customer insights and creative product ideas. Although untested hunches can be dangerous, ignoring input from managers and collaborators risks missing important and worthwhile experience-based ideas. In the fast-food industry, for example, the idea for the Egg McMuffin, one of McDonald's most popular items, came from a McDonald's franchisee. As McDonald's founder Ray Kroc later wrote, "The advent of the Egg McMuffin opened up a whole new area of potential business for McDonald's, the breakfast trade." Similarly, Subway's "$5 Foot-Long" promotion, in which the sandwich chain sells 12-inch sandwiches for an even $5, was a franchisee's idea—and this promotion is credited with more than $3.8 billion in annual sales (Boyle, 2009; Kroc & Anderson, 1977).

INTEGRATING TRENDS AND CUSTOMER INSIGHTS INTO STRATEGIC PLANNING

Although following a teenager around in their daily life or videotaping people while they shower may seem impractical, significant strategic advantage goes to the firm that first recognizes and capitalizes on a true customer insight. Uncertain trends and indefinite patterns of emerging customer needs can be inputs to scenario analysis. That is, various distinct possible customer outcomes (e.g., changes in attitudes and tastes toward health or thrift) can be included in factors that define possible futures (i.e., scenarios), and contingency plans can be constructed to contend with those possible futures. Cross-impact matrices, for example, are a typical futuring and scenario planning tool. As its name indicates, a cross-impact matrix integrates multiple events to identify their joint impacts; in other words, rather than considering what might happen if one event occurs or a single trend is disrupted, cross-impact matrices consider the interaction of factors and their joint implications (or "impacts").

Cross-impact matrices are similar to scenario analysis; in fact, they are used in scenario analysis. If, for example, the economy improves dramatically, health concerns shift diets toward vegetables and seafood, lifestyles change toward smaller households, and a disruptive technology emerges that dramatically lowers the cost of electricity, then what would the future look like? What are the implications of these events on each other and on other elements of the future? What are the implications of these events on the marketing organization, and how would the organization want to be positioned to respond to this future? These possible futures do not need to be likely (or unlikely); if they are merely possible, then they are worth thinking about and planning for. However, cross-impact matrices facilitate basic stochastic analysis in which, by estimating the probability of each event and its interactions with the others, the joint probability of any specific future reality can be estimated. Thus, cross-impact matrices are a structured and rigorous examination of what might happen tied to consideration of how the organization should prepare for those possibilities.

SUMMARY

Customer insights are understandings into customer needs and how customers consume and take value from products. Robust evidence has shown that the more firms focus on their markets and their customers, the more successful they are. Trend spotting is about looking at past and current phenomena to predict the future; in comparison, searching for customer insights focuses on present (but heretofore unrecognized) customer conditions and needs. Thus, successful marketing strategy is about meeting some specific customer needs better than the competition at a profit. But, of course, those customer needs are changing. Thus, adequate marketing strategy can be viewed as marketing mix evolution (changing the "P"s) in response to changes in environmental forces, while *really good* marketing strategy is marketing mix evolution in *anticipation* of changes in those forces.

REFERENCES

Ames, L. (1998). The view from Peekskill: Tending the flame of a motivator. *The New York Times.*

Bonabeau, E. (2003). Don't trust your gut. *Harvard Business Review*, 81(5), 116–123.

Boyle, M. (2009). The accidental hero. *Business Week*, 40–46.

Cook, V., & Frigstad, D. (1997). Take it to the top: Delphi sampling is the best for supply chain research. *Marketing Research*, 9(3), 23–29.

Cornish, E. (2004). *Futuring: The exploration of the future.* World Future Society.

Duggan, W. R. (2007). *Strategic intuition: The creative spark in human achievement.* Columbia University Press.

Durante, R., & Feehan, M. (2005). Watch and learn: Leverage ethnography to improve strategic decision making. *Marketing Research*, 17(4), 10.

El Boghdady, D., & Staff Writer, W. P. (2002). Naked truth meets market research: Perfecting a new shower head? Try watching people shower. *The Washington Post*, 24.

Füller, J., Bartl, M., Ernst, H., & Mühlbacher, H. (2006). Community based innovation: How to integrate members of virtual communities into new product development. *Electronic Commerce Research*, 6(1), 57–73.

Füller, J., Jawecki, G., & Mühlbacher, H. (2007). Innovation creation by online basketball communities. *Journal of Business Research*, 60(1), 60–71.

Füller, J., & Matzler, K. (2007). Virtual product experience and customer participation—A chance for customer-centered, really new products. *Technovation*, 27(6–7), 378–387.

Geertz, C. (1973). *Thick description: Toward an interpretive theory of culture 1973.* In *The Interpretation of Culture: Selected Essays.* Basic Books.

Gigerenzer, G., & Todd, P. M. (1999). *Simple heuristics that make us smart.* Oxford University Press.

Gladwell, M. (1997). The Cool-hunt. *The New Yorker*, 78–88.

Gloor, P. A., & Cooper, S. M. (2007). *Coolhunting: Chasing down the next big thing.* AMACOM.

Hamel, G., & Prahalad, C. K. (1991). Corporate imagination and expeditionary marketing. *Harvard Business Review*, 69(4), 81–92.

Han, J., & Kamber, M. (2006). *Data mining: Concepts and techniques* (2nd ed.). Morgan Kaufmann Publishers.

Herstatt, C., Luthje, C., & Lettl, C. (2002). Wie fortschrittliche Kunden zu Innovationen stimulieren. *Harvard Business Manager*, 24(1), 60–69.

Knapman, S. (2008). Customer immersion: Total immersion. *Research*, 36–37.

Kotler, P., & Armstrong, G. (2009). *Principles of marketing* (11th ed.). Pearson Prentice Hall.

Kroc, R., & Anderson, R. (1977). Grinding it out: The making of McDonald's Henry Regnery Co. In *Chicago, Illinois*. Contemporary Books.

Leonard, D., & Rayport, J. F. (1997). Spark innovation through empathic design. *Harvard Business Review*, 75, 102–115.

Loveman, G. (2003). Diamonds in the data mine. *Harvard Business Review*, 81(5), 109–113.

Surowiecki, J. (2004). *The wisdom of crowds: Why the many are smarter than the few and how collective wisdom shapes business, economies, societies and nations.* Doubleday Random House.

Taylor, D. (2000). Drilling for nuggets: How to use insight to inspire innovation. *Brand Strategy*.

Von Hippel, E. (2006). *Democratizing innovation*. MIT Press.

Zandl, I. (2000). How to separate trends from fads. *Brandweek*, 41(41), 30–35.

CONSUMER AND ORGANIZATIONAL
BUYER BEHAVIOR

Academic researchers have spent decades studying how consumers and organizations make purchase decisions. *Consumer behavior* usually refers specifically to models of how the ultimate consumers make decisions about and consume products. *Buyer behavior* is broader; it considers organizational buyers (especially businesses, but also non-profits and government entities) as well as consumers. Consumer and buyer behavior models and frameworks are theoretical, especially in comparison to market research, which studies the firm's specific customers and specific issues. Buyer behavior looks at basic processes that are true for consumers or organizations in general. Despite the general and theoretical nature of buyer behavior, understanding this concept is a basic foundation for strategic marketing. Understanding how customers make decisions and the role of customer evaluations and behaviors in determining market outcomes is essential to segmenting, targeting, positioning, and to developing, and assessing an effective marketing mix.

CONSUMER BEHAVIOR

Consumers are the ultimate user of a product. In comparison to organizational buyers (referred to as B2B markets), consumer markets (referred to as B2C markets) are more numerous and dispersed geographically, as well as harder to address (harder to identify and therefore harder to target with personalized communications or offerings). Consumer markets may also involve many more transactions, but generally much smaller transactions (smaller in quantity and in value). Additionally, consumers use more personal and more emotional purchase criteria in comparison to organizational buyers. The following section examines the consumer decision-making process, moving from the recognition of a need through the search for information about possible ways to satisfy the need and the evaluation of those alternatives to the purchase and then post-purchase processes, as outlined in Figure 3-1. Many similar models have been proposed, some with much more detail, but this elemental flow is commonly accepted.

Consumer Decision-Making Process
The degree to which customers engage in effortful thought and search as they move through the stages in the decision-making process varies with consumers, products and product categories, and across situations. Grocery shoppers spend an average of less than 6 seconds making most purchase decisions. Although shoppers bring carefully thought-out lists to the store, more than 70% of the purchase decisions are reported to be made after the shopper has entered the store (Liljenwall, 2004).

Hierarchy of effects models in communications and advertising management are similar to the consumer decision-making process framework. However, instead of modeling the flow of a

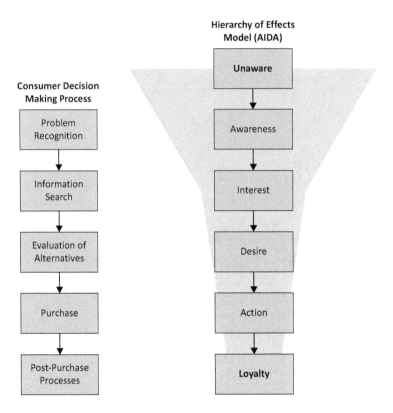

FIGURE 3-1   Consumer Decision-Making Process and Hierarchy of Effects Models

customer through a purchase decision—from the recognition of a need through to post-purchase processes—hierarchy of effects models focus on the relationship of the consumer with a specific product or brand, from unaware through degrees of awareness, liking, and bonding toward purchase and adoption or loyalty, as seen in Figure 3-1 (Barry & Howard, 1990; Lavidge & Steiner, 1961; Vakratsas & Ambler, 1999). One of the earliest hierarchy of effects models is "AIDA"—Awareness, Interest, Desire, Action (Strong, 1925, p. 76; Vakratsas & Ambler, 1999)—although a variety of more detailed models have also been proposed (Barry & Howard, 1990; Mahajan et al., 2000). For example, in the context of the diffusion of innovations, a very similar awareness-interest-evaluation-trial-adoption process is generally accepted (Robertson, 1967; Rogers, 1995). Customer loyalty, the development of long-term relationships with valuable customers who may themselves serve as promoters of the brand, was omitted from the brief AIDA summary, but it logically follows after action or trial; it is important to consider that ultimate loyalty in understanding the flow of relationship intensity. The importance of customer loyalty is examined in greater detail in Note 22.

More customers will become aware of a product than those who will become interested in it, and more customers will be interested in a product than those who will ever buy it. In addition, not all customers who buy and try a product will adopt the product or become loyal customers. Therefore, hierarchy of effects models can be viewed as funnels into which a large number of customers enter, while a smaller number, usually quite a bit smaller number, becomes the firm's loyal customer base.

Understanding where different segments of customers are in this flow is invaluable in developing communications and distribution strategies. Different tools and different tactics are more effective at different points in this flow of effects. Advertising is effective, for example, at building awareness, but less effective at moving customers to action. On the other hand, personal selling is effective at closing the sale—that is, at moving customers to purchase—but selling is less effective at generating awareness. Thus, marketing managers are often more focused on segments of customers at different stages of a familiarity/liking continuum (customer readiness) than they are on the customers' relationship with the purchase decision. Nevertheless, the consumer decision-making process framework is essential in organizing consumer-behavior theory and understandings.

Stages in the Consumer Decision-Making Process

When consumers make decisions, they move through different stages. The process starts with problem recognition and an information search, evaluating alternatives, and making the purchase decision. A marketing manager is also concerned with understanding how customers consume and take value from products, as well as post-purchase processes like customer satisfaction, loyalty, or word-of-mouth.

Problem Recognition

The consumer-decision-making or buying process is initiated by the recognition of a need or want. Needs are fundamental human requirements; everybody experiences needs. Abraham Maslow organized human needs in a hierarchical structure (see Figure 3-2) in which the most basic and compelling needs are physiological—things like food, drink, and shelter (Maslow, 1943). The next level of needs is safety needs—the need for physical safety, economic security, and protection from harm. Social needs reflect the needs to be accepted as part of a family or group. The top two categories of Maslow's hierarchy of needs are ego-driven needs, related to respect and prestige, and self-actualization. Self-actualization needs involve learning, spiritual and personal growth, and self-expression. The organization of Maslow's well-known structure indicates prioritization and urgency; lower-level needs are more compelling, and meeting those needs takes priority over meeting higher-level needs.

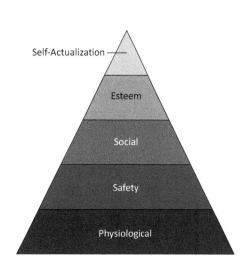

FIGURE 3-2   Maslow's Hierarchy of Needs

Needs can be distinguished from *wants* and other related constructs, including *demands* and *benefits sought*. Needs are basic human requirements and are universal—all people have needs. Wants are needs that have been shaped by the environment, including the customer's culture, personality, and situation, as well as by the actions of marketers. For example, everybody gets hungry—it is the prototypical physiological need in Maslow's framework—but everybody does not want to meet that need with filet mignon. Consumers need food; they want filet mignon because of their experiences, their culture, their individual tastes, and the actions of marketers (such as advertisements, price promotions, service personnel recommendations, menu presentation, or even restaurant signage). Demand results from the combination of wants and the ability of consumers with those wants to buy the product. Ability is a function of both resources and availability/access; that is, consumer demand is not just having the money to buy the product, but also having the opportunity and means.

Benefits or benefits sought are closely related to needs and wants. Benefits sought are what the consumer desires to get out of or gain from a purchase or consumption experience. These are not product attributes; they're outcomes of buying and consuming the product (Haley, 1968). A customer may buy a drill with an 18-volt battery and rubber-cushioned grips, but the benefit they seek is the ability to drill a hole with ease, convenience, or comfort. Different customers seek different benefits from a product category, and benefits-sought segmentation is a powerful way to distinguish groups of customers based on differing desires and differing responses to the marketing mix. Problem recognition is generally understood as a form of *gap* processing related to needs, wants, and the benefits of the product. Customers recognize a need when they recognize, consciously or subconsciously, that there is a gap between their current state (the way things are) and their desired state (the way they'd like to be). That gap can be between needs, wants, or benefits in their current state versus desired state.

Information Search

The idea that consumers search for information when making a purchase seems reasonable; in fact, we know it occurs some of the time. The idea that consumers actively search and process information is appealing to marketing managers because of the amount of time that the managers themselves spend thinking about the various attributes and trade-offs that make up their product. But the information search stage begins to highlight an important aspect of consumer behavior and of the overall decision-making process: consumers do not spend much effort on most purchases, and they spend very little effort on many purchases.

The amount of time a consumer will spend on a purchase decision, including information search and alternative evaluation, is a function of motivation and ability. The term "customer involvement" captures the degree of importance and relevance that a consumer places on a product or a purchase; that is, involvement is the consumer's motivation to analyze a purchase decision. Involvement itself is a function of inherent interest, risk (financial, social, and physical), and practical importance (importance to personal well-being or to a job; e.g., a car to a salesperson of the car-manufacturing company, whether or not the consumer is a car enthusiast). Some consumers are interested in cars, cooking, or woodworking, while others are not interested in these categories at all.

The ability to research and evaluate a purchase also influences the time and energy spent on it. Some consumers, no matter how much they'd like to shop and deliberate a decision, do not have the time or the expertise to devote to the decision. A few products almost never rise to a high-involvement status: almost no one spends much time on mundane and repeat purchases such as soda or laundry detergent. Consumers rely on habit and, especially, brands to guide routine purchase decisions. On the other hand, some product categories are almost never approached casually; choices of college, or cars, or real estate almost always involve high involvement and deliberate consideration, including extended search and careful evaluation. This should not be taken to mean that involvement is determined by product category, although product categories do have typical levels of involvement (e.g., very expensive products usually are associated with extensive decision-making); there is substantial variance across customers with regard to their involvement, depending on their personal attributes and their personal situation. In fact, although some products rarely elicit high involvement responses or decision-making, given the right circumstances—such as buying the product for one's boss—almost any product can be a high-involvement purchase on occasion.

Customer information search may tap a range of sources. Each type of source has different advantages, disadvantages, and consequent strategic implications. Customer information search can be limited and constrained to internal sources, that is, to memory. It is increasingly difficult to gain consumers' attention or to earn a place in consumers' memory because of the overwhelming amount of information in the modern environment and because of growing consumer skepticism. Other sources of information include interpersonal sources—friends, neighbors, and colleagues. Information search may also include public sources, such as online peer review sites, consumer organizations, and marketer-controlled sources—advertisements, salespeople, and published materials. Within this category, marketer-controlled sources face increasing clutter, diminishing attention, and growing skepticism.

Alternative Evaluation

As with information search, involvement levels and situational factors determine whether consumers will undertake extensive and demanding evaluations of purchase alternatives or routinely process the alternatives with what borders on no evaluation at all. Marketing researchers have proposed elaborate information processing models in which consumers gather information, weigh attributes, and determine finely grained rankings of alternatives. At the same time, research has shown that most grocery decisions are made in a matter of just a few seconds—usually between 3 and 6 seconds—and that many purchases, even big purchases such as automobiles, are driven by emotions as much as or more than by rational processes.

One fundamental tenet of consumer behavior theory is that consumers form attitudes toward products and those attitudes drive behaviors, especially purchase behavior. Attitudes are relatively enduring summary evaluations; that is, attitudes are evaluations of whether something is good or bad, pleasant or unpleasant, and so forth. We summarize and remember these evaluations across time (but not forever—attitudes do decay if consumers are not reminded of the product or brand). Elaborate models of attitude formation have been proposed and tested and those models may resemble the decision-making processes that consumers work through for some purchase decisions. For example, a well-known model of attitude formation hypothesizes that while people hold beliefs about whether or not a product has certain attributes (things like power, comfort, reliability, and high price, in case of a car) they also hold evaluations of those attributes and about whether the attribute (power, comfort, reliability, price) is a good or bad thing for the product to have (power is likely a good thing; high price is usually avoided).

This model of attitude formation is built on a view of products and alternatives as being defined by multiple attributes. That understanding of how consumers view and evaluate products is fundamental to models of consumer choice, benefits-sought segmentation, and market research methods, including perceptual mapping and conjoint analysis. Usually customers view products as bundles of attributes, but this is not always true and, even when approximately true, there may be some characteristics or specific attributes of products that customers care about that are hard to summarize in specific statements. Although attitude models are predictive, this is *not* how most consumers actually think in many situations; in fact, consumers usually do not process information with anything like this sort of computer-like precision or effort. Hence, contemporary understandings of consumer behavior have also emphasized the importance of:

- *Low-involvement decisions*, which are made with little effort or thought and which often rely on brands to cue the consumer about qualities of the product; and
- *Emotional decisions*, which are made with emotions guiding consumer preferences and behaviors.

The model of attitude formation presented above is highly rational—it assumes that consumers will think and think very hard about the purchase. This is not always true. In many instances, consumers respond with a fairly automatic feeling about the product and act on that—with very little rigorous thinking or effort. That is, emotional responses to products, brands, and consumption experiences also have powerful effects on consumer judgments and behaviors, including purchase, repeat purchase (loyalty), complaints, and recommendations. The two systems, that is, the rational thinking or cognitions and the more visceral and automatic feelings or emotions, have been considered as distinct, although they interact and influence each other, and both are essential in understanding the way that consumers respond to marketing actions. They are sometimes thought of as *the head* and *the heart* or gut instinct. In the literature on integrated marketing communications and advertising, a well-known framework is the FCB Matrix, so named because it was developed at that forerunner advertising agency by Richard Vaughn (Vaughn, 1980, 1986). That framework organizes products by their typical level of involvement (high and low involvement) and whether the typical motivation for buying and consuming the product is emotional (*feeling* products) or rational (*thinking* products). Frameworks, such as the FCB Matrix, guide the development of products and the development of communications programs to position the product and persuade consumers to think and feel about the products in desired ways.

Two additional ideas, brands and customer value, are important to understanding how consumers evaluate alternatives:

- *Brands.* Customers face an overwhelming array of information and make innumerable decisions, big and small, every day. They cannot possibly think about all that information or reevaluate each decision. Therefore, consumers establish habits and heuristics. Heuristics are shortcuts or *rules of thumb* used in decision-making (Gigerenzer & Todd, 1999). Brands are the most common rule of thumb in the marketplace. Brands tie current and future decisions to past experiences and satisfaction, simplify decision-making, and offer reassurance. Although brands have been criticized as unnecessary and exploitive, they are useful to customers and provide real value to customers (Klein, 1999; Norberg, 2003). From a buyer behavior standpoint, brands simplify purchase decisions in an extraordinarily hectic, cluttered, and demanding environment. Brands offer reassurance and communicate more complex information in simplified ways.

- *Customer Value.* We define "value" as the difference between, or ratio of, the *benefits* that the customer gets from a product (and its consumption) compared with all the *costs* of acquiring and consuming the product (including monetary costs, time, and effort). This is the balance of the *get* and the *give* from the customer's perspective (Gale, 1994; Woodruff, 1997; Zeithaml, 1988). The appraisal of value may be subjective. For example, something that is worth paying for to one consumer will be disregarded as unimportant by another. However, along with attitudes, those appraisals of value are essential in understanding consumers' decision-making. Perfectly rational consumers will often pay more to get something more or accept less in order to save money. Many rational consumers will opt for cheaper alternatives that offer the same performance (including brand image as a *get* component) or similarly priced alternatives that offer better performance. Very few consumers will knowingly pay more for the same performance or accept less performance than they could have gotten for the same price. These trade-offs and choices combine to define a value map or space and to create a balance in the marketplace, a fair value frontier along which consumers willingly make choices and trade-offs, as highlighted in Note 17.

Purchase Decision

Once the consumer has evaluated the alternatives, he or she must still decide *when to buy* and *where to buy.* That is, the purchase decision is about time and place, distinct from evaluations of alternative products (i.e., the product decision). Interestingly, although marketers spend enormous time and resources communicating with customers across settings, the time a consumer spends on any individual purchase at a grocery store is preciously short—3 to 6 seconds—but more than 75% of specific product choices are made in the store (for grocery stores and fast-moving consumer goods) (Thomassen et al., 2006). This indicates that the point-of-purchase is an important decision point, but also that those decisions are made quickly and with little effort.

More and more, consumers choose different channels for different parts of a purchase decision or process, and they move across channels several times within a single decision process. By this we mean that different channels of distribution ranging from brick-and-mortar stores to in-home repair services to online retailers can all deliver certain functional values (product information and training, financing, physical receipt or delivery, installation, user help, etc.). Consumers can use different channels to do different parts of the purchase and to access different sorts of value. They may, for example, choose one or more channels to shop and a completely different channel to buy, creating a disincentive for channels to provide high service or, especially, free advice without somehow also generating revenue or capturing the customer's loyalty (Grau, 2006). For example, when a customer can visit a full-service specialty store, use the time and expertise of the well-trained and expert service staff, and then go home and purchase the product at a deep discount online, it puts the full-service specialty store's business model at risk. That reality has ominous but still uncertain implications for the future retail landscape.

Post-Purchase Processes

Marketers that are interested in creating profitable long-term relationships with their customers need to understand post-purchase processes as well. For example, how do buyers consume or use the product, how do they form feelings of satisfaction or dissatisfaction, do they engage in word-of-mouth communications, and what makes them become loyal (or not loyal) Marketers are increasingly concerned not only with how to persuade consumers to purchase their products, but also with understanding how customers consume and take value from those products.

An important strategic consideration, especially in regards to innovations and truly *new to the world* products, is the fact that changing consumer behaviors is extremely difficult. Innovations are often classified along a continuum from continuous innovations that demand little change in the way customers consume and solve their needs through dynamically continuous innovations, all the way to discontinuous innovations, innovations that are truly new to the world and require substantial changes in consumption patterns (Robertson, 1967; Rogers, 1995). It has been shown that, even when innovations have substantial advantages over existing alternatives, consumers value existing ways of behaving and existing product alternatives over innovations that necessitate changes in behavior and require abandoning existing, comfortable, and familiar ways of meeting needs. The tendency to stick with proven solutions has been attributed to the economic costs of change (transaction costs, learning costs, and obsolescence costs or the sunk costs of equipment tied to existing solutions) and psychological costs related to a pervasive perceptual bias toward avoiding losses as opposed to seeking gains. These have been called the *endowment effect* and *status quo bias*—customers are more reluctant to give up what they have than they are eager to gain new advantages (Gourville, 2006).

Customer Satisfaction

The marketing concept asserts that a marketing strategy and, in fact the overarching strategy of the entire firm, should be built around serving—or *satisfying* customer needs. Satisfying the customer is an essential goal that should pervade strategic marketing. Extensive theory and observation across decades of research have confirmed that firms that satisfy their customers better prosper, while those that leave customers dissatisfied fall short. Those findings hold across consumer goods, services, and business-to-business markets. Customer satisfaction is the customer's evaluation (good to bad, pleasant to unpleasant) of a specific purchase or consumption experience. That is, satisfaction is how the customer feels about a specific product choice and usage. I may have an attitude toward the a certain fast-food restaurant—I like its chicken sandwich and its friendly, fast service—but when I visit that restaurant on a specific occasion I form a related but differentiable evaluation of that specific visit (the sandwich tasted great and was fresh and hot; the service was excellent; and the server remembered my last visit and gave me extra mayonnaise).

Customers evaluate purchases and consumption experiences and arrive at satisfaction judgments by comparing what they actually received or experienced with their subjective standard about what they thought they'd get or felt they should have gotten. A customer comes to every purchase with some idea about what they think they'll get. If we go to a fine-dining steak restaurant to order a cheeseburger, we expect a certain sort of product and service. Those expectations include what we think we should pay for the cheeseburger. If we go to a quick-service restaurant and order a cheeseburger, we have vastly different expectations. We might come away from a quick-service encounter with a rather unremarkable cheeseburger for less than a dollar and, nevertheless, be quite satisfied—it was, after all, less than a dollar. On the other hand, we might spend 10 times that amount on a cheeseburger at a full-service restaurant and receive a product many times the quality, with much more flavor and individual service, and nevertheless come away far less satisfied because our expectations were so much higher. This framework has been tested and retested: customers form judgments of satisfaction by comparing what they get to what they thought they would get.

This understanding of customer satisfaction creates an interesting tension for marketing strategists, whose first concern is often to attract customers via appealing offerings, which would lead to extolling the virtues and, thereby, building high expectations. On the other hand, creating high expectations creates challenges—the product has to deliver against those expectations or risk dissatisfied customers. There may be situations when the strategist chooses to *under promise and over deliver* (Peters, 1987). There are many ways that a marketer can influence expectations and enhance resulting satisfaction. It has been shown, for example, that people waiting in line who are given an expected wait time and then have a wait time that is shorter than that "expectation" are more satisfied with their experience compared to people who wait the same amount of time but were not told to expect a longer wait time (Kumar et al., 1997). In any case, regardless of how expectations are managed, the marketing strategist's challenge is almost always to somehow exceed expectations.

There may be many situations in which the marketer cannot set modest expectations and then exceed them, but there are few situations in which the marketer would ever want to *over promise*. That is a recipe for a short-term relationship with those customers because customer satisfaction drives a range of important subsequent customer behaviors. Research has shown that satisfaction is an important intervening variable that drives subsequent price sensitivity, positive word-of-mouth, and loyalty. Loyalty itself, the tendency of customers to stay with a company or a brand, has been closely related to firm profitability, especially when considered together with customer-lifetime value. Another strategic consideration is the emphasis on understanding customer satisfaction and the role it plays in delivering quality products and exceptional service.

Factors Influencing the Purchase Decision Process

Customers make purchasing decisions within specific cultural/social, personal/individual, situational and commercial (marketer influenced) contexts, as highlighted in Figure 3-3.

- *Individual.* Individuals come to purchase decisions with different personalities, such as their degree of introversion or extraversion, and motivational factors. All of these factors influence the way consumers consider options, make purchases, and use products.
- *Social/cultural.* Factors such as national culture, regional culture, social class, and reference groups influence purchase decisions, product preferences, and consumption. People from different nations and regions hold different values, different norms of behavior and manners, and different aesthetic preferences and tastes.

- *Situational.* Many factors are tied to particular situations more than to ongoing conditions or attributes of the consumer. Time pressure, resource or information availability, and immediate environmental factors (such as music, odor, or colors) all affect purchases and consumption.
- *Marketer actions.* Although all of these aforementioned factors have powerful influences on consumer decision-making and consumption patterns, the marketing strategist will recognize factors that influence decision-making that are under their most direct control. These factors are the marketing mix: the product, price, place or distribution, promotion and marketing communications, and the (sales)people. These are the *levers* under the marketer's control that influence the consumer's purchase decisions.

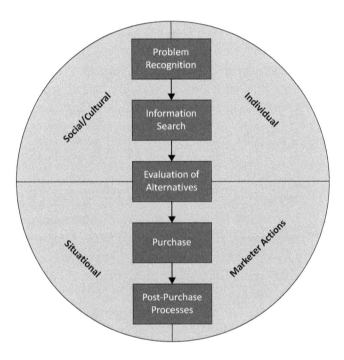

FIGURE 3-3   Consumer Decision-Making in Context

ORGANIZATIONAL BUYING

In comparison to business-to-consumer markets (B2C markets), business-to-business markets (B2B markets) are characterized by having fewer buyers and fewer transactions (but far *larger* transactions in dollar value and quantity of goods per transaction). B2B segments are easier to address (catalogue and target with customized communications). Other differences between B2C and B2B markets emphasize the differences in the way purchase decisions are made. Consumers, who as a rule make purchases as individuals, may use limited problem solving and rely on emotional responses in many situations. Businesses are generally more thorough and more analytic and often make purchases with teams or buying centers using formal procedures and approved specifications. Business-to-business frameworks on buyer behavior include distinctions across types of purchases and across stages in the decision process, as well as distinctions concerning roles in the purchase across members of the organization. As is the case with B2C markets, many of these frameworks lend themselves to graphic presentations that clarify the relationship between stages in processes.

Stages in the Buying Process and the Sales Funnel

Like consumer decision making, organizational purchase decisions can be broken into process models starting with recognizing needs and proceeding through formal need definition—something that is not necessary for consumer decision makers—and continuing through specifying the solution to be sourced, identifying viable suppliers or vendors for the purchase, proposing specification and review, and ultimately selecting a vendor and then reviewing and giving feedback

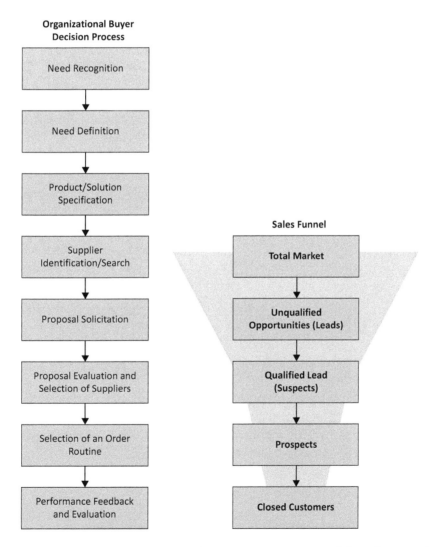

FIGURE 3-4   Organizational Purchase Decision Process and the Sales Funnel
(Donald et al. 1984)

on performance (see Figure 3-4). At the same time, and again parallel to the similar hierarchy of effects in consumer behavior, another process model can be created by organizing customers taken as segments along a continuum based on their relationship with the firm and its offerings. In business-to-business markets that process is usually called the "sales funnel" (Dalrymple et al., 2004; Robinson et al., 1967).

Personal Selling Process

Organizational buyers are generally targeted with *push* communication strategies, that is, strategies designed to create demand at the next level in the channel of distribution. These rely heavily on personnel selling and interfirm partnering. Because of that reliance on sales, a third process model also offers perspective on business-to-business buyer behavior: the "personal selling process." This framework organizes the various steps that the sales force can take, from prospecting, to assessing fit, gaining the initial order, fulfilling the initial order, to delivering value (see Figure 3-5) (Anderson et al., 2009; Spiro et al., 1976).

Personal selling reflects the fifth "P" (for people) in the marketing mix, and is further examined in Note 32. Personal selling has evolved from a transaction-focused activity toward being a solutions-focused function. That solutions focus puts the salesperson in the role of a consultant; success is viewed as long-term relationships with customers for whom the firm can deliver real value in the form of solutions and expertise.

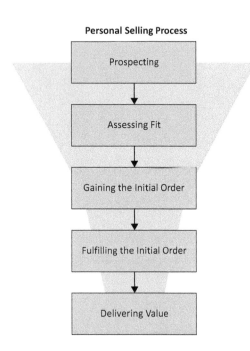

Personal Selling Process

- Prospecting
- Assessing Fit
- Gaining the Initial Order
- Fulfilling the Initial Order
- Delivering Value

FIGURE 3-5 Personal Selling Process (Anderson et al., 2009)

To review and clarify these distinctions and very similar frameworks, the buying organization moves through a series of decision stages or steps that are summarized in the organizational purchase decision process (Figure 3-4). Those buying organizations themselves can be characterized by their relationship with the selling organization, from leads to suspects to prospects to customers within the sales funnel (Figure 3-4). It is important to note that, various accounts (potential buying organizations) are categorized within the levels of the sales funnel. At the same time, the various steps that the selling organization can take to move buyers from leads to customers are organized within the personal selling process; these are the things that the salesperson, sales team, or company can do to gain new business and to turn those accounts into loyal customers (Figure 3-5).

Types of Purchases

Organizations are, generally, more involved in every purchase decision than are individual consumers. In contrast to consumers, organizations usually have someone with a *job* to make the purchase, and companies have accounting regulations and reporting obligations that require specific and explicit purchasing policies and procedures. Nevertheless, organizational buyers certainly devote varying degrees of attention and resources to different sorts of purchases. One of the best-known representations of the different sorts of organizational purchases is the distinction between straight rebuys, modified rebuys, and new tasks. For new tasks, that is for purchases that have not been made before, and especially for high cost/high risk purchases, organizations are likely to engage in all of the many steps in the purchase process with a great deal of attention. In straight rebuys, cases in which the firm buys the same item in the same quantities from the same vendor, only the essential steps are required. For modified rebuys, cases in which some element of the purchase changes (product form, quantity, or vendor), many of those steps may be reduced or even eliminated.

Buying Centers

Another perspective on organizational buying is to understand that, unlike consumer markets, buying decisions in organizations are most often made by teams. Some buying teams are formal, and some are informal and emergent. People play different roles on those teams, and the roles themselves can be formalized or left informal and may be made explicit or left implicit. These teams have been labeled "buying centers," and several categories of roles have been identified in the literature, including initiators, gatekeepers, buyers, deciders, users, and influencers (see Figure 3-6). An *initiator* recognizes the need or conceives of the purchase. The *gatekeeper* controls the flow of information within the team and access to the team from outside. A *buyer* executes the

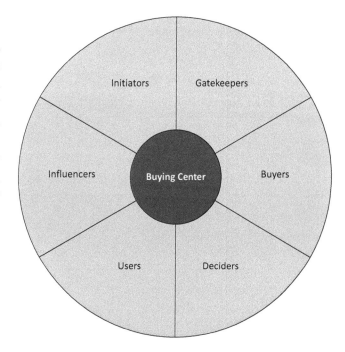

FIGURE 3-6   Buying Center Framework (Jackson Jr. et al., 1984; Johnston & Bonoma, 1981)

transaction. The *decider* holds the authority to make the purchase decision. The *user* actually uses the product once it is purchased. And an *influencer* has expertise or opinion that affects the purchase.

Sometimes the same person will perform more than one of these roles, sometimes more than one person will play any given role (e.g., there can be multiple influencers), and sometimes certain roles will not be played in a given purchase.

SUMMARY

Understanding consumer and organizational buyer behavior is the foundation for developing effective marketing strategies and valued offerings. This Note has presented an overview of the extant knowledge that has emerged from decades of academic research focused on B2C and B2B buyers, their decision processes, and their behaviors. There are parallels between the two sets of buyers and the models that attempt to clarify their decision-making. In both markets, an important factor is the degree of effort that the buyer puts into the purchase decision. In B2C markets, consumer involvement influences the amount of time and energy the consumer will spend on information search, alternative evaluation, and purchase. In B2B markets, purchases are differentiated as straight rebuys, modified rebuys, and new tasks, and the type of purchase drives the amount of effort the organization will devote to the purchase. In certain instances, the two types of buyers are quite different, and various models have been developed to respond to each of their respective needs.

REFERENCES

Anderson, J. C., Narus, J. A., & Narayandas, D. (2009). *Business market management: Understanding, creating, and delivering value* (3rd ed.). Pearson Prentice Hall.

Barry, T. E., & Howard, D. J. (1990). A review and critique of the hierarchy of effects in advertising. *International Journal of Advertising*, 9(2), 121–135.

Dalrymple, D., Cron, W., & DeCarlo, T. (2004). *Sales management*. John Wiley & Sons.

Gale, B. T. (1994). *Managing customer value*. Free Press.

Gigerenzer, G., & Todd, P. M. (1999). *Simple heuristics that make us smart*. Oxford University Press.

Gourville, J. T. (2006). Eager sellers and stony buyers: Understanding the psychology of new-product adoption. *Harvard Business Review*, 84(6), 98–106.

Grau, J. (2006). Multi-channel shopping: The rise of the retail chains. *eMarketer*. www.emarketer.com/Reports/All/Multichannel_mar06.aspx.

Haley, R. I. (1968). Benefit segmentation: A decision-oriented research tool. *Journal of Marketing*, 32(3), 30–35.

Jackson Jr, D. W., Keith, J. E., & Burdick, R. K. (1984). Purchasing agents' perceptions of industrial buying center influence: A situational approach. *Journal of Marketing*, 48(4), 75–83.

Jackson Jr, Donald W., Janet E. Keith, and Richard K. Burdick. "Purchasing agents' perceptions of industrial buying center influence: A situational approach." *Journal of Marketing* 48.4 (1984): 75–83.

Johnston, W. J., & Bonoma, T. V. (1981). The buying center: Structure and interaction patterns. *Journal of Marketing*, 45(3), 143–156.

Klein, N. (1999). *No logo: Taking aim at the brand bullies*. Picador.

Kumar, P., Kalwani, M. U., & Dada, M. (1997). The impact of waiting time guarantees on customers' waiting experiences. *Marketing Science*, 16(4), 295–314.

Lavidge, R. J., & Steiner, G. A. (1961). A model for predictive measurements of advertising effectiveness. *Journal of Marketing*, 25(6), 59–62.

Liljenwall, R. (2004). *The power of point-of-purchase advertising: Marketing at retail*. Point-of-Purchase Advertising Intl.

Mahajan, V., Muller, E., & Wind, Y. (2000). *New-Product diffusion models*. Springer Science+Business Media.

Maslow, A. H. (1943). A theory of human motivation. *Psychological Review, 50*(4), 370.

Norberg, J. (2003). *In defence of global capitalism*. Cato Institute.

Peters, T. (1987). *Thriving on chaos: Handbook for a management revolution*. Alfred A. Knopf.

Robertson, T. S. (1967). The process of innovation and the diffusion of innovation. *Journal of Marketing, 31*(1), 14–19.

Robinson, P. J., Faris, C. W., & Wind, Y. (1967). *Industrial buying and creative marketing*. Allyn & Bacon.

Rogers, E. (1995). *The diffusion of innovations* (4th ed.). The Free Press.

Spiro, R. L., Perreault Jr, W. D., & Reynolds, F. D. (1976). The personal selling process: A critical review and model. *Industrial Marketing Management, 5*(6), 351–363.

Strong, E. K. (1925). Theories of selling. *Journal of Applied Psychology, 9*, 75–86.

Thomassen, L., Lincoln, K., & Aconis, A. (2006). *Retailization: Brand survival in the age of retailer power*. Kogan Page Publishers.

Vakratsas, D., & Ambler, T. (1999). How advertising works: What do we really know? *Journal of Marketing, 63*(1), 26–43.

Vaughn, R. (1980). How advertising works: A planning model. *Journal of Advertising Research, 20*(5), 27–33.

Vaughn, R. (1986). How advertising works: A planning model revisited. *Journal of Advertising Research, 26*(1), 57–66.

Woodruff, R. B. (1997). Customer value: The next source for competitive advantage. *Journal of the Academy of Marketing Science, 25*(2), 139–153.

Zeithaml, V. A. (1988). Consumer perceptions of price, quality, and value: A means-end model and synthesis of evidence. *Journal of Marketing, 52*(3), 2–22.

Figure Credits

To understand industry competition and profitability, Michael Porter, a professor at Harvard Business School, developed an analysis framework consisting of five forces that shape industry competition: (a) bargaining power of buyers; (b) bargaining power of suppliers; (c) threat of new entrants; (d) threat of substitutes; and (e) competitive rivalry (Porter, 1980). These five forces drive the intensity of internal competition and overall industry profitability (as depicted in Figure 4-1). They provide a framework for anticipating and influencing competition over time and are essential parameters to formulate a viable strategy.

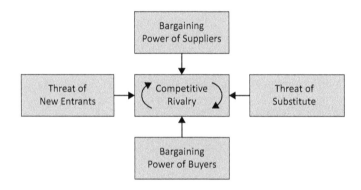

FIGURE 4-1   Porter's Five Forces Influencing Rivalry and Profitability

A thorough analysis and understanding of these five forces is of vital importance in strategy formulation. Table 4-1 outlines key questions, forces, drivers, and considerations for future development relative to each of Porter's five forces.

INDUSTRY ANALYSIS PROCESS

An industry analysis is carried out in the following steps: (1) definition of the industry; (2) identification of participants (potential entrants, buyers/customers, suppliers, competitors, substitutes); (3) assessment of the drivers of competitive forces and of overall industry structure; (4) analysis of future changes in the industry; and (5) identification of aspects of industry structure that can be influenced by the firm, existing competitors, or new entrants (Porter, 2008).

TABLE 4-1 Porter's Five Forces Analysis

PARTICIPANT	POTENTIAL ENTRANTS	BUYERS/CUSTOMERS	SUPPLIERS	COMPETITORS	SUBSTITUTES
Key questions	How likely is it that new competitors enter the industry?	How much of the value created do customers capture? How price sensitive are they?	How much of the value created do suppliers capture?	How aggressively or "friendly" do competitors act and react?	How do potential substitutes threaten sales in an industry?
Forces	Market entry barrier	Bargaining power of customers	Bargaining power of suppliers	Rivalry among competitors	Threat of substitution
Drivers	• Economies of scale • Network effects • Customer loyalty and switching costs • Capital requirements • Incumbency advantages independent of size (e.g., proprietary technology, raw material sources) • Unique access to distribution channels • Restrictive government policy	• High concentration of buyers • Undifferentiated products • Low switching costs of buyers • Easy backward integration • Product represents significant fraction of cost structure or procurement budget • Buyers earn low profits or have to cut purchasing costs • Quality of products do not affect quality of customer's offers	• High concentration of suppliers • Suppliers do not depend on customers for revenues • High switching costs of customers • Highly differentiated products of suppliers • No substitute products • Easy forward integration	• Numerous competitors of equal size • Low industry growth • High exit barriers • Undifferentiated products • Low switching costs • High fixed costs and low marginal costs • Perishable product	• Substitute offers an attractive price-performance trade-off • Low switching costs of buyers
Future development	• Do suppliers change their strategy and structure? • Does their bargaining power change?	• Do market entry barriers change? • Are new entrants attracted?	• Do customers change their strategy and structure? • Does their bargaining power change?	• Does competition change over time?	• Are new technologies arising that create new substitutes? • Do switching costs to substitute change?

Step 1: Industry Definition

Certain industries have well-defined boundaries with clearly identifiable competitors. Others have fuzzy boundaries and rivals are difficult to identify or anticipate. Therefore, the definition of the industry is a crucial, but not simple, task and should be based on these four dimensions (Day, 1997): (a) array of product or service categories (single product versus broad category); (b) customers (single versus multiple segments); (c) geographic scope (regional, countrywide, global); and (d) activities in the value chain (many versus few).

For example, is Red Bull considered an energy drink or soft drink? In the first instance, Red Bull is the clear market leader of a fast-growing market, including competitors like Monster and many smaller brands. In this case, the target market is mostly male teenagers and twentysomethings, and people interested in extreme sports. In the second instance, Red Bull is only a minor competitor of a fairly mature market, including products like carbonated beverages, fruit juices and drinks, and bottled water, competing against industry giants like Coca-Cola and Pepsi who push their offerings to all soda drinkers.

Step 2: Identification of Participants

In this step, the participants in the industry have to be identified by answering the following questions: Who are the buyers/customers? Who are the suppliers? Who are the competitors? Which products or services are substitutes for the product in this industry? Who are the potential entrants into this industry?

Step 3: Assessment of Competitive Force Drivers

Now the analysis of the underlying drivers of each competitive force and the industry structure begins. This activity is usually the most interesting part of the analysis, as it reveals the forces that shape competition and industry attractiveness, and provides a framework to anticipate and influence competition over time. Usually the analysis of the five forces is taken from the perspective of an incumbent (as in the following sections). But it can, of course, also be used to understand the challenges faced by a new entrant.

Threat of Entry

Whether existing competitors are threatened by new entrants largely depends on market entry barriers, such as economies of scale. Economies of scale exist when the unit costs of a product fall as a function of the firm's production volume. They can be achieved in most business functions (i.e., purchasing, production, marketing and sales). They accrue when fixed costs can be spread over a large sales volume, when purchasing discounts can be exploited, or when specialization advantages are present. In the pharmaceutical industry, for example, the development of a new drug costs on average $2.6 billion (Sullivan, 2019). Therefore, a market leader has a huge cost advantage over a new entrant, as it can spread the fixed costs over a larger number of units and thereby reduce unit costs.

Network effects are also an important consideration, as they constitute demand-side benefits of scale and arise when a buyers' benefit increases with the number of a company's customers. Credit card companies are more attractive the more contractual partners they have, and eBay has a competitive advantage because of its huge customer base. Limited access to distribution channels can also pose a barrier to market entry. In the beverage industry, for instance, restaurant chains usually have long-term contracts with their soft drink suppliers. As a result, it is difficult for a new entrant in this industry to get access to this distribution channel.

When customers are highly loyal to a vendor, or when they face high vendor switching costs, it is often difficult for outsiders to enter this market and attract buyers. Amazon.com, for instance, has very high brand recognition and a loyal customer base, which pose barriers for new entrants. In the enterprise resource planning software industry, customers have to invest much time to implement the software, to train the employees, and even to adapt internal processes. Hence, customers are reluctant to change suppliers after such investments.

Another market entry barrier is capital requirements. Most Internet companies face minimal capital requirements when they enter the market, whereas entry into the auto industry requires billions of investments in R&D, production facilities, and so forth. Patented technologies, managerial know-how, access to raw materials, and learning-curve cost advantages are also entry barriers independent of size that market leaders often have.

Finally, the government can impose market entry barriers. In China for instance, there are significant barriers to entry in the Internet market (Sullivan, 2019). In 2006, Google attempted to enter China but ultimately left the marketplace in 2010 amidst concerns about the Chinese government's censorship of search results (Sheehan, 2018). Thus, even a global brand leader like Google is not immune to the impact of government policies.

Bargaining Power of Buyers/Customers

Buyers of goods can capture more value when they are able to force prices down and demand better quality or service. Buyers have a higher bargaining power when they are highly concentrated; products are undifferentiated; there are low switching costs; and, backward integration is possible.

For example, the German retailer Aldi takes advantage of its size. Their relatively small outlets carry a limited assortment of products, which enables Aldi to sell more of each product and therefore to negotiate lower prices. Most Aldi stores carry between 1,300 and 1.600 items, whereas Walmart can carry as many as 120,000 items (Turner, 2017). In addition, Aldi carries few brand-name items. As a result, its suppliers are interchangeable, and Aldi exerts greater power over them as a result of that interchangeability.

Low switching costs of buyers is evident in the automotive industry, where there are many undifferentiated components. The auto manufacturers keep a handful of suppliers, playing them against each other, as they can easily switch from one supplier to another for these products. The furniture dealer IKEA (2021) uses the same strategy. It has more than 1,600 suppliers in 55 countries and a few of them sell up to 100% of their output to IKEA. As there are relatively low switching costs for IKEA to change suppliers, the Swedish furniture dealer retains enormous bargaining power as a buyer.

Buyers also have power when backward integration is easy and when they have the ability if desired to produce the product on their own. In the soft drink industry, producers have long increased their bargaining power over the packaging manufacturers by threatening to produce packaging materials themselves.

Bargaining Power of Suppliers

When suppliers have high bargaining power, they can charge higher prices, limit quality or services, and shift costs to their customers. This situation is the flip side of the customer's bargaining power. Thus, suppliers are especially powerful when the supplier group is more concentrated than the industry to which it sells or even reaches a near-monopoly position; the products are highly differentiated or specialized to the specific needs of the customer or customer groups; the suppliers do not depend on single customers; there are high switching costs for customers and no affordable substitute for the supplier's products or services; and, suppliers can threaten to integrate forward.

Threat of Substitutions

Ease of substitution strongly reduces an industry's attractiveness and profitability. The threat of substitution is high when an alternative offers an attractive price–performance trade-off and when there are low switching costs to the buyer.

Rivalry among Existing Competitors

Rivalry can take numerous forms. It can lead to price wars, increased differentiation efforts, and higher speed of innovation—all factors which lower industry profitability. Rivalry among existing competitors is particularly high when there are numerous competitors about the same size attempting to gain dominance over one another.

Another factor increasing rivalry is industry growth. When a business is mature, companies can only grow by taking market share from competitors. High exit barriers, the flip side of entry barriers, may prevent companies from leaving the business—despite low profitability. Finally, high price competition can make an industry unattractive. Price competition especially occurs when markets are highly transparent (i.e., customers and competitors can easily see price cuts), when customers are price sensitive, the products are not differentiated, and when customers have low switching costs. If these characteristics are coupled with high fixed costs in an industry and perishable products, price wars are likely to occur.

A good example is the airline industry, where fixed costs make up 60%–70% of the traditional airline's costs. This is an industry where the product tends to be undifferentiated and there are low switching costs for customers. In addition, customers are price sensitive, and, due to online booking systems, markets are highly transparent. These factors led to massive price competition in recent years and a major industry shakeout.

Step 4: Future Development

Once the industry structure and the major forces driving competition are understood, a careful look at possible future changes in the industry is in order. Several questions should be considered. These include the following:

- Do market entry barriers change? Are new entrants attracted?
- Do suppliers change their strategy and structure? Does their bargaining power change?

- Does the customer base change? Do they gain more power?
- Are any new technologies arising that create new substitutes?
- Does competition change over time?

A helpful model for this analysis is the product life cycle, as described next in Note 5, which illustrates changing competitive conditions and strategies along the distinct phases of a life cycle.

Step 5: Industry Influences

The industry analysis is a useful tool for (Johnson et al., 2008):

- identifying attractive industries in which a company can invest;
- understanding the forces that shape competition within an industry;
- better understanding and predicting changes that affect industry structure, profitability, and the strategies of competitors; and
- assessing strengths and weaknesses of competitors in relation to these forces.

It can also help managers understand how they can influence the competitive forces. For example, how can market entry barriers be built? How can bargaining power be increased? How can we react to possible substitutes?

SUMMARY

Industry analysis identifies the forces that shape industry attractiveness, especially the intensity of internal rivalry and resulting industry profitability, and the behavior of industry participants. By identifying the specific determinants of rivalry and profitability—customers' and suppliers' bargaining power, market entry barriers, substitution products, and rivalry among competitors— industry dynamics and competitive strategies can be better understood and predicted. The five forces analysis has become one of the most important tools in the strategic analysis of businesses; some businesses will have the luxury of selecting industries to enter or invest in—others will not. Regardless of whether it is being used to select industries to compete in or simply to understand existing markets and competition, industry analysis within the five forces framework is invaluable to strategy development and implementation.

REFERENCES

Day, G. S. (1997). Assessing competitive arenas: Who are your competitors. *GS Day & DJ Reibstein. Wharton on Dynamic Competitive Strategy*, 23–47.

IKEA. (2021). Let's grow together: Become an IKEA supplier. *About IKEA.* https://about.ikea.com/en/work-with-us/for-suppliers

Johnson, G., Scholes, K., & Whittington, R. (2008). *Exploring corporate strategy: Text & cases.* Prentice Hall.

Porter, M. E. (1980). *Competitive strategy: Techniques for analyzing industries and competitors.* Free Press.

Porter, M. E. (2008). The five competitive forces that shape strategy. *Harvard Business Review, 86*(1), 78.

Sheehan, M. (2018, December 19). How Google took on China—and lost. *Technology Review*. https://www.technol-ogyreview.com/2018/12/19/138307/how-google-took-on-china-and-lost/

Sullivan, T. (2019, March 21). A tough road: Cost to develop one new drug is $2.6 billion. *Policy & Medicine*. https://www.policymed.com/2014/12/a-tough-road-cost-to-develop-one-new-drug-is-26-billion-approval-rate-for-drugs-entering-clinical-de.html

Turner, Z. (2017, September 21). How grocery giant Aldi plans to conquer America: Limit choice. *The Wall Street Journal*. https://www.wsj.com/articles/how-grocery-giant-aldi-plans-to-conquer-america-limit-choice-1506004169

Figure Credit

Every market is new at some point; it has to start somewhere. After that, inevitably, it evolves, and some important aspects of that evolution are similar across all or at least most markets. Every product moves through an introduction phase, a growth phase, a maturity phase, and a decline phase. Each of these phases is characterized by changes in demand, competition, marketing tasks, and decisions. These changes during the *product life cycle* can be generalized across markets, and understanding and anticipating those changes is important for planning and for effectively adapting marketing strategies. This Note summarizes the market factors that change as markets evolve and the effects of those changes on marketing strategies and on the marketing mix.

One essential proviso is that, in order to understand the product life cycle for any market, it is essential to first define the market or the product under consideration. Understanding life cycle effects at the various coexisting levels of the industry, the market, and the product category allows for valid and valuable inferences. That is, life cycle effects underlie the evolution of an industry, a specific market, a product form, and individual products. Each of these life cycles can provide insight for marketing strategy and tactics. But it is also important to keep the level of analysis in mind in identifying and drawing conclusions from changes in the market. An industry life cycle, such as that of the telecommunication industry, is much longer than a product life cycle, such as that of a specific generation of mobile phones. And demand for a specific generation of mobile phones depends on more specific factors (e.g., technology, price, competition) than demand for telecommunication in general that depends more on need for telecommunication. It is also worth noting that not all products, and certainly not all industries, enter a decline stage in the life cycle. While industries such as beer and clothing have matured, these are really extended and perhaps eternal maturities, rather than true declines. On the other hand, product forms such as *ice* beer and *ripped* jeans have very specific life cycles (*fad* life cycles) that grow, mature, and decline toward obsolete fairly quickly.

MARKETING CHANGES ACROSS THE PRODUCT LIFE CYCLE

The single phases of a product life cycle differ in a number of important characteristics, such as competition and assortment, customer behavior, segment configuration, distribution, etc. In the following sections we describe these characteristics. A video of how the marketing mix can change across the product life cycle can be viewed at http://bit.ly/prolifecycle.

Competition and Product Assortment

Initially there are very few offerings in any market. A market must begin with a single offering—at some point, someone offers the very first version of any new product, even if other entrants follow quickly. As a market grows, more firms offer more alternatives. Because consumers tend to be price insensitive in introductory and growth stages—they're still focused on the new benefits—margins tend to be high and those high margins attract competition and investment, including investment in production capacity to meet the growing demand for high-margin sales. During the growth phase, entry of each new competitor means the expansion of available assortment, and, importantly, each competitor offers a wider and wider variety of products, creating a rapid profusion in the variety of products available and intensifying the rivalry for customers and for distribution.

Eventually growth decreases and markets enter maturity. One problem as a market enters maturity is that production forecasters often miss the *inflection point* and regularly build capacity as if markets will continue to grow, if not forever, at least beyond the point that growth actually slows. This inevitably causes *pain* in the form of excess capacity. If competitors' excess capacity cannot be converted to other uses, for example by producing other products with the same production facilities or by selling those facilities to other industries, those competitors will try to stimulate demand to maintain production, and they tend to do so by lowering prices. Thus, competitors who would not otherwise resort to price competition end up wrecking the market in order to utilize their capacity—capacity that should not have been built in the first place.

These changes in the competitive landscape lead to some predictable changes in profitability (as shown in Figure 5-1). Early in the product life cycle, firms must invest in order to develop products and to open markets. These investments represent negative profitability for the industry in the early stages. During the growth stage, firms take advantage of the investments and the product's newness to command fair margins and to reap profits. The profitability usually carries on into the early maturity stage, but later, in the maturity and decline stages, when industrywide capacity is at its peak and as customers come to expect core benefits, margins narrow, and price competition emerges to reduce profits. Nevertheless, average industry profits over any extended period should rarely be negative; that is, an industry cannot lose money for long. Although increased price-based competition is typical, almost inescapable, and margins will necessarily narrow, competitors and rivals will exit an industry characterized by losses over any extended period.

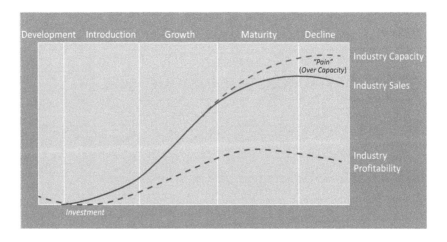

FIGURE 5-1   Product Life Cycle

Customer Behavior and Segment Configuration

Across product categories, whether they are new technologies or not, several important changes in consumer behavior emerge as the markets evolve. In markets for truly new products, that is, the markets for disruptive or discontinuous innovations, initial sales growth may be slow. Many consumers wait to see new products in use by others—that is, the majority of consumers usually prefer to imitate others rather than innovate. The rate of penetration or diffusion will accelerate as more consumers use a product and thereby create more opportunities for imitators to observe the product in use. That growth may literally be exponential in some phases for some markets; if a consumer shows the product to three others, and those three each buy it and tell three others who all tell three more, and so on. However, because markets and consumer resources are not unlimited, those periods of high growth do not last forever and, in some cases, may be very short-lived.

It is an important certainty that, as the life cycle progresses, consumers become more familiar with the product. Consumers are initially inexperienced with a product, but, as the market evolves, customers gain experience and expertise; inevitably, consumers' needs become more specific as consumers become more knowledgeable and sophisticated. Consumers who were initially satisfied by one basic offering begin to understand that they'd rather have a somewhat different version of the product or technology—something that more specifically meets *their* particular needs—and, therefore, segments emerge from what were, in the early stages, undifferentiated markets. Single segments often become two or more different segments in the growth phase of the product life cycle.

It is also true that, as some markets mature, multiple segments merge or join into one—especially as technology progresses and the need to decide between options in the product is alleviated. For example, in the late 1980s, BMW owned the high-end luxury/prestige segment of the American automobile market. "Yuppies" drove BMWs and accepted their high maintenance costs and lack of reliability as unavoidable. Then, in the early 1990s, Toyota introduced the Lexus brand of luxury sedans; Lexus's offerings were highly reliable and came with extraordinary service. The high-end luxury segment split into high-end performance (which BMW continued to dominate) and high-end reliability and comfort (won by Lexus). Lexus was positioned as a *cocoon* from the outside world (Palmer, 2002).

In the next decade, BMW and others, such as Audi and Mercedes Benz, began to match Lexus's service and reliability, and segments that had been differentiable began to blur. An assortment of manufacturers took advantage of advances in production technologies to offer similarly reliable and comfortable cars with similar performance. It might be more accurate to say that the segments reconfigured, rather than merged. Luxury car buyers in America remained heterogeneous—and are still different from European luxury car buyers—but the basis of segmentation changed toward brand image and other differences.

Later, as automobile emissions became a concern for certain car buyers, electric cars such as Tesla became popular. Tesla's Model S sedan matched many gasoline powered luxury and sports cars on performance attributes like acceleration and top speed but had zero tailpipe emissions because it was battery powered. Tesla was acclaimed for its performance and design as well. Other luxury car manufacturers such as Lexus, BMW, Mercedes, and Audi responded by offering their own electric-powered models.

Driving a shift toward price-based competition across the product life cycle (along with over capacity, as previously discussed) is the fact that the attributes of a product that began as new-to-the-world and capable of differentiating one offering from another, eventually—sometimes very quickly—become commonplace. Such benefits become expected as competition matches performance and certain benefits become must-have attributes instead of delighters—that is, product attributes that are not expected and positively surprise customers. When the core benefits have been commoditized, other benefits, augmentations, and improvements—such as additional features or convenience and packaging features—or peripheral benefits—such as service, design, environmental sustainability, and brand image/social status—begin to replace the core benefits as drivers of consumer choice. Additionally, and almost inescapably, price emerges as an important consumer choice variable and can become the dominant basis of competition.

A useful model to distinguish between types of product attributes is Kano's model of customer satisfaction, which describes three different types of product characteristics (see Figure 5-2). *Delighters* are attributes that cause satisfaction or even excitement if delivered, but that do not necessarily lead to dissatisfaction if not delivered. They are not explicitly expected and articulated. A rearview backup camera in cars is an example. *Must haves* (basic factors) are minimum requirements that a product must fulfill. They do not lead to satisfaction if fulfilled, but lead to dissatisfaction if not present. An example is the brakes of a car. *Performance factors* are those attributes that lead both to dissatisfaction or satisfaction, depending on how well they perform: the higher the product performance, the higher the satisfaction, and the lower the performance, the lower the satisfaction.

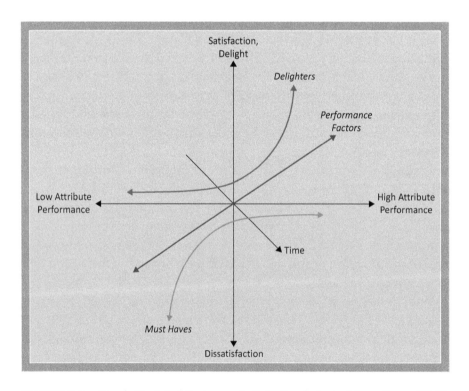

FIGURE 5-2 Kano's Model of Customer Satisfaction (adapted from Kano, 1984)

An example is fuel efficiency, battery life of an electric car, battery life of a laptop, or resolution of a digital camera. This model is dynamic, that is, the three types of attributes change over time. What delights customers today (not expected product attributes, but those that surprise customers and create a *wow effect*) become explicit expectations after some time and turn into must-haves.

These changes in the market and in consumer behavior are related to a reality about research and development investments and returns. The relationship between inputs and outputs in research and development and new product development forms an S-curve, which is a classic case of the production function relating inputs to outputs and of the law of diminishing margin returns. Small investments may be inadequate to realize *any* results, and getting started requires investment; however, a range of investments will realize substantial advances. Eventually when the *low fruit* has been harvested and the most accessible innovations discovered, the successive generations of breakthroughs become more and more difficult to realize. Thus, at the same time when customers may be taking the old technology for granted, it becomes more expensive and takes longer to bring new technologies to market, further emphasizing the migration toward noncore features and peripherals.

As product life cycles evolve, so do the drivers of consumer preferences and choice. Early in the life cycle, consumers focus on product performance and on core benefits. During growth and especially product maturity, greater consideration is given to peripheral product attributes such as service, comfort, convenience, nonfunctional design, and the like. Most importantly, price emerges as a more and more important decision criterion as the product life cycle moves forward; and price often becomes the dominant decision driver for many consumers in the later stages of the life cycle. This is especially true when core product attributes and benefits are so commoditized that they appear, largely, the same across alternatives. Attributes shift from *delighters/motivators* (things that exceed customer expectations and move consumers to action) toward *must-haves* (things that consumers expect and take for granted). The absence of a must-have can dissatisfy customers, but its presence rarely satisfies or delights. This process of commoditization denotes a competitive environment where (a) product differentiation becomes very difficult, (b) customer loyalty and brand preferences erode, (c) competition is based primarily on price, and (d) where competitive advantages come from cost leadership (Weil, 1996).

As products move into the maturity phase of the life cycle, commoditization becomes a likely threat. There are basically three ways to delay the forces of commoditization: (a) innovate—introduce a new product with new difficult-to-imitate features or upgrade existing product; (b) bundle—sell the commoditized product with a differentiated ancillary service that increases the value of the product (e.g., after-sales service) and motivates consumers to pay a price premium for more convenience; and (c) segment—further segment the mature market and address customers that are less price sensitive (Quelch, 2007).

Channels of Distribution

Gaining shelf space in traditional channels of distribution is a challenge for the most proven of brands. Getting distribution for new and unproven products that frequently require augmented customer service and *customer education* is especially challenging and creates a natural constraint on channel penetration in the introductory stages of the product life cycle. Often, new products are distributed through specialty channels, where sales staff has a particular interest and expertise in the product category; specialty sales clerks are often product enthusiasts themselves and serve as facilitators and even opinion leaders in their category. As a product gains acceptance, that acceptance and track record in the market, combined with the substantial margins realized during the growth stage, facilitate greater channel acceptance. Nevertheless, as markets grow, so does the competition and each competitors' assortment—leading to clutter and increased competition for shelf space amongst competitors, even as the shelf space grows in the overall product category. In maturity, fewer customers need the support that was necessary for early market offerings, and, as discussed previously, more competitors tend to emphasize price; therefore, mass and lower-service retailers dominate the trade, and discounters become a bigger factor. This *class-to-mass* effect across consumer-goods categories has been exacerbated and accelerated by the emergence of Walmart as the dominant retailer in America, Aldi and Lidl as similar channel captains in Central Europe, and other large-scale discounters around the world, such as Tesco in the UK and Carrefour in Western Europe. This has led to earlier and earlier emphasis on discounters. In later maturity and in decline, no-frills discounters and, more recently, direct retailers (e-tailers) dominate many channels of distribution. For example, Amazon is now the second largest retailer in the world (and the largest e-tailer) and sells just about everything on its various websites at competitive prices (Statista, 2021).

Summary of Changes in Market Characteristics

Certain basic logical and underlying realities drive a general market evolution or product life cycle (see Figure 5-1), and predictable, although not uniform, patterns provide important insight into what to expect as markets are created and as they grow, mature, and eventually decline (summarized in Table 5-1). The product life cycle forms an S-curve, demonstrating initial takeoff, leading

TABLE 5-1 Market Characteristics Across Product Life Cycle

MARKET CHARACTERISTIC	LIFE CYCLE STAGE			
COMPETITION	**INTRODUCTION**	**GROWTH**	**MATURITY**	**DECLINE**
Industry capacity	Low; building	Increasing	Over capacity	Contracting capacity
Products	One to limited	Variety increasing	Proliferation	Contraction/consolidation
Customers/Benefits Sought	Unsophisticated, un-educated, unaware	More sophisticated; greater homogeneity, more demanding	Price con-sciousness	
Segments	Gross	Emergence and clarification		Agglomeration
Customer Choice Drivers	Core product bene-fits are delighters	Differentiate by new attributes (delighters); copycats emulate	Core benefits migrate toward "must-haves"	Commoditization of core benefits; differentiate by new, noncore attributes
Channels	Limited availability; specialty	Broader distribution	Mass, discount and direct	More limited; discount and direct

towards accelerated growth, but then, eventually, to slowing, maturity, and even decline as the market becomes saturated and alternatives are introduced. These changes in the market have important implications for viable marketing strategies and for the marketing mix because things that work in one stage may not work in another, and recognizing *inflection points* can generate great strategic advantage.

STRATEGIC IMPLICATIONS

Generic strategy frameworks generally stress two dimensions of strategy—competitive scope and competitive advantage, as discussed further in Note 16. These frameworks are useful in organizing and summarizing changes in marketing strategies across the product life cycle; some strategies become more common and may generally be more effective (although it should be noted that the full range of strategies are often present in some form at most stages in the product life cycle). Those generic strategy taxonomies do *not* isolate innovation as a separate dimension of strategy—the output of innovation is subsumed by *differentiation*—but it may be useful to view innovation as a third dimension of strategy when considering changes in viable and typical strategies across the life cycle. That is, strategies can be distinguished by the (a) scope of customers/needs they target, (b) the basis of competition (differentiation versus cost/price), and also (c) the degree of innovation. These three characteristics of strategies are useful in considering what sorts of strategies are typically deployed and are most effective across the product life cycle.

Early in the product life cycle, the scope of competition is notable because the markets are small and narrow; however, the focus of most marketing programs must often be broad because consumers are unfamiliar with the product and cannot articulate the need. Marketing research, therefore, is challenging. It is difficult to focus communications and distribution even though the target segments—innovators and early adopters—are inherently narrow. As the market moves through introduction toward growth, it becomes broader and more differentiable—that is, there are more customers and they are organized into more distinct segments. As previously discussed, when markets move toward maturity these segments become dynamic, and they are likely to split into more subsegments as consumers become more familiar with their needs and with the availability of product alternatives; however, they may also merge as product features become less distinct and technology overwhelms the core needs.

Finally, in terms of competitive advantage, early stages of the product life cycle emphasize innovation. The growth stage is driven by firms attempting to differentiate their offerings in consumer perceptions. Later in the life cycle innovation becomes less salient and becomes different. Instead of searching for and exploiting fundamental breakthroughs driven by basic research, firms focus on incremental innovation—new features and the adaptation and convergence of existing technologies—improvements that result from applied research and new product development. These strategic implications are summarized in Table 5-2.

TABLE 5-2 Marketing Strategies Across Product Life Cycle

DIMENSION OF STRATEGY	LIFE CYCLE STAGE			
	INTRODUCTION	GROWTH	MATURITY	DECLINE
Scope (Who? What? Where?)	Targeting innovators and early adopters but often via "shotgun" marketing mix	Growing segments and greater heterogeneity; opportunities for niche and mass strategies	Niche opportunities remain but become limited; mass dominates	Profitable survivor (consolidation)
Differential Advantage (What? Why?)	Core benefits (performance) speed-to-market	Differentiation: core benefits	Differentiation: peripheral benefits Price	Price
Innovation	Paramount; "basic" research and discontinuous breakthroughs		Continuous innovation; incremental benefits	Innovate to extend life cycle or breakthrough to new category

TACTICAL IMPLICATIONS

The changes in the market related to life cycle and the different strategies firms pursue across the life cycle drive changes in the type of marketing mix and effective offerings of a firm. These implications are described further in this section.

Introduction

Because the product life cycle's beginning is defined by a single new and innovative product, the number of products in the early stages is necessarily limited and focused on the new technology and its core benefits. A firm may adopt two basic pricing strategies in the introductory stage: skimming and penetration pricing, as discussed in Note 29. Skimming takes advantage of the newness of the technology and the relative advantage of the innovation to demand (or *skim*) higher prices and margins. The Apple iPhone's very high introductory pricing was a good example of skimming pricing, and Apple has maintained that strategy with each new iPhone model.

Penetration pricing involves low pricing intended to gain market penetration and the ensuing benefits of scale, brand awareness, and *installed base*—that is, lower penetration prices are designed to quickly gain as much market share as possible and should be supported with some assumed benefits of early market share. The idea here is to price the new product down the experience curve and build market share. The problem with penetration pricing is that if sales and share fail to materialize, a lot of money is lost. Tata Motors (India) priced its world car, the Nano, at about $2,000—a true penetration price even in India—in order to compete with scooters and motorcycles. But sales failed to reach expectations, and the Nano ceased production in 2020 (Tata Motors, 2019).

Early in the life cycle, promotions can rely on word-of-mouth more than at other stages. Risk-averse customers are more likely to be persuaded by interpersonal communications (and observations of others adopting the product), and the early-adopters of something that is truly new are more likely to talk about it and pass along information. The channel strategy of any particular firm in a new market may be shaped by existing channel strengths and distribution coverage of similar products.

Growth

The growth stage emphasizes differentiation—as a strategy and across the elements of a marketing program. Product alternatives proliferate—new entrants bring new offerings and existing competitors offer a wider variety of products. Channels become more accessible to the category as it gains acceptance and wider market penetration, but competition within the category for space and attention within the channels becomes more intense. Prices support fair margins but increased competition prevents exorbitant returns. Gaining market share in the growth stages is paramount in preparation for maturity and price competition. Market share leads to scale effects (economies of scale and learning) and grabbing market share in the early growth stage is less difficult than later in the life cycle.

Maturity

The maturity stage in the product life cycle is marked by increasing price competition evident in increasing consumer and trade promotions (i.e., price deals for customers and volume or price deals for channel partners, especially retailers in consumer goods channels and distributors in business channels). It is also characterized by an emphasis on peripheral benefits and new features on existing core products, brand-reinforcing communications programs (image-building and reminder) along with those price promotions, and accelerating product-form cycles. Customers no longer require education or *hand-holding*, they are familiar with the product, its underlying technology, and their own preferences across configurations. Therefore, mass and discount channels as well as low- to no-touch (online) channels gain share, especially vis-à-vis high-support channels, such as specialty stores. Importantly, attention to loyalty-building tactics and customer satisfaction in this and earlier stages can drive significant competitive advantages in the maturity stage. That is, entering the maturity stage with a strong base of loyal customers or building that base in maturity can be a significant competitive advantage as markets move toward more intense rivalry with products that are inherently more difficult to differentiate.

Decline

Not all products enter a true decline stage—at least not inevitably. We have emphasized the notion that changes in underlying market realities (especially changes in the competitive landscape and in the consumers' relationship with the product) inexorably drive changes in viable marketing strategies and effective marketing tactics; however, it may be true that firm decisions and choices across marketing strategies actually accelerate the product life cycle in some instances. That is, the decline stage may be a self-fulfilling prophecy in some ways. Once the competitor(s) in an industry decide that the industry is in decline mode, a firm's actions—especially withdrawing support for innovation and initiating price competition—may actually cause or at least exacerbate the decline. Competitors *wreck the market* by moving too quickly and too willingly toward price competition, and viable entrants withdraw brand-building support in favor of harvesting profits from mature products (and shifting investment and attention toward potential stars). In the maturity and decline stages of the product life cycle, viable strategies that are too often overlooked include consolidating brands into a profitable survivor portfolio (accumulating brands and encouraging exit by acquiring the competition and seeking benefits of scale across the expanded assortment), retrenching around core profitable and loyal customers (which may move a mass or multiple segmentation scheme toward a focused or niche approach), and augmenting commoditized products with innovative new features and services, rather than succumbing to the apparent inevitability of mutually destructive price wars. The potential marketing tactics across the product life cycle are summarized in Table 5-3.

TABLE 5-3 Marketing Tactics Across Product Life Cycle

	INTRODUCTION	GROWTH	MATURITY	DECLINE
Products	Limited	Expand Assortment; Differentiated, especially by features	Full Assortment; Augmented with Service	Fewer; Technology may overwhelm and blur consumer needs
Price	Skimming or Penetration	Full (Collect margins and profits)	Increasingly Competitive	Price-based competition/Deal
Promotion	Informative; may be product category related more than specific product or brand Interpersonal communications (and observations) very important. Public relations most viable.	Differentiation; Advertising and promotions geared to distinguishing products and brands.	Reminder/Competitive; Proliferation of price promotions	Reminder/Price
Distribution	Limited; Emphasis on specialty and on high service/high customer education	Expanding	Broadest; Shifting toward discount and lower service/less to no customer education.	Contracting; low to no service/support.

RECOGNIZING INFLECTION POINTS

All of these observations about differences in markets, strategies, and tactics across the product life cycle are of no value if the manager cannot recognize the stage of the life cycle a product offering is in and, especially, if the strategist cannot anticipate and prepare for life cycle changes. Generally, the introductory stage is obvious—the new technology emerges and receives media coverage. One of the attributes of the introductory and early-growth stages is the willingness of media to respond to public relations efforts with coverage; and sales begin slowly but accelerate as channel coverage expands. The move from growth toward maturity is less obvious and often more relevant to strategy and strategic success. Besides moderating sales growth—which is the definition of the passage from growth toward maturity, but which may often be disguised as a temporary adjustment or attributed to external factors such as general economic cycles—there are several markers of maturity (Aaker, 2008), including the following:

- *Price competition.* As discussed, two phenomena that may be harbingers of market maturity are the building of too much capacity at the industry level and the commoditization of core benefits in a category. Commoditization in this case refers to the perception by customers that all products deliver the same benefits. These two phenomena lead toward price competition, and increased price competition—or signs that price competition may be looming—should be forewarnings that maturity is imminent.
- *Buyer sophistication.* Whether price competition seems imminent or not, increased buyer sophistication is an indicator of maturing markets. Sophisticated buyers tend to be better shoppers, buying what they need and unfazed by—and in fact unwilling to pay for—features or services that are not relevant to them. Knowledgeable customers need little information and less service.
- *Substitutes emerge.* Another mark of a maturing market is not only intense rivalry amongst existing competitors but also increased availability of substitutes and increased buyer willingness to consider substitutes. This buyer acceptance of substitutes is a market condition related to increased sophistication and understanding of core needs. The availability of substitutes is an external condition that may cause maturity (it is not a result of maturity).
- *Market saturation/fewer growth opportunities.* Growth markets are driven by trial—large numbers of first-time users being introduced to and then adopting the new product. In mature markets, most customers have tried the product and either adopted it or rejected it, and there are fewer opportunities to grow via first-time trial, by developing new markets, or by targeting new segments.
- *Customer disinterest.* Finally, a large segment of an active market being indifferent toward the technology or category is an indication of maturity. As discussed, it is relatively easy to gain media coverage for truly new products, and that is not only true for high-technology innovations. As markets move toward maturity, fewer mainstream media (in comparison to industry specific media) *are interested in* covering offerings and events in the sector. By the time markets reach maturity, buyer and media attention is elsewhere and the product is yesterday's news. Signs that interest is waning may be warnings of impending maturity.

SUMMARY

Product markets emerge, grow, mature, and decline over time. The product life cycle represents the typical shifts of a product through these four phases and highlights how factors related to competition and the marketing mix might evolve. Thus, understanding the product life cycle is essential. The stage of the product life cycle fundamentally determines and constrains strategic and tactical alternatives. Each phase is characterized by differences in the competitive environment, priorities in strategic objectives, and cost and profit structures. Therefore, marketing programs must be adapted to the changing characteristics and challenges of each life cycle shift. Monitoring the environment for signals that a market may be approaching an inflection point, moving from one stage to another, particularly from growth to maturity, can offer a true strategic advantage.

REFERENCES

Aaker, D. (2008). *Strategic market management* (8th ed.). John Wiley & Sons.

Kano, Noriaki. "Attractive Quality and Must Be Quality." *Hinshitsu* [Quality], 14, no. 2 (1984): 147–56 (in Japanese).

Palmer, C. (2002, May 3). Saatchis creates Lexus "cocoon." *Campaign*. https://www.campaignlive.co.uk/article/saatchis-creates-lexus-cocoon/144426

Quelch, J. (2007, December 14). When your product becomes a commodity. *Harvard Business School*. https://hbswk.hbs.edu/item/5830.html

Statista. (2021, July 30). Leading retailers worldwide in 2019, by retail revenue. *Statista Research Department*. https://www.statista.com/statistics/266595/leading-retailers-worldwide-based-on-revenue/

Tata Motors. (2019, January 24). Tata Motors to bid adieu to Nano from April 2020. *The Economic Times*. https://economictimes.indiatimes.com//industry/auto/cars-uvs/tata-motors-to-bid-adieu-to-nano-from-april-2020/articleshow/67672970.cms?utm_source=contentofinterest&utm_medium=text&utm_campaign=cppst

Weil, H. B. (1996). *Commoditization of technology-based products and services: A generic model of market dynamics* (Working Paper #144–96). The International Center for Research on the Management of Technology, Sloan School of Management, MIT.

"Any customer can have a car painted any color that he wants so long as it is black," said Henry Ford about the Model T, the most influential car of the 20th century (History.com Editors, 2019, para. 9). By standardizing the product and taking advantage of cost savings through mass production, the price dropped to $850 when it was introduced in 1909 (History.com Editors, 2019, para. 8). Looking at the prices and the cumulative number of Model T cars produced over time, one can note a remarkable relationship: Every time the cumulative output doubled, the prices of the car dropped by 15% (see Figure 6-1).

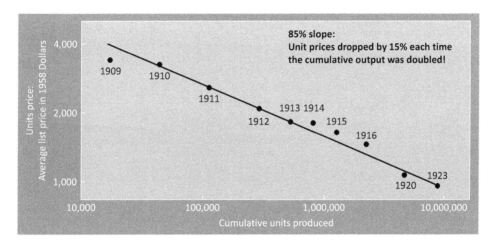

FIGURE 6-1   Price of Model T, 1909–1923 (Abernathy, 1974)

EXPERIENCE CURVE EFFECTS AND UNIT COSTS

Henry Ford took advantage of an empirical generalization, which the consulting firm Boston Consulting Group (BCG) later coined as the *experience curve*. After observing the behavior of unit costs in a number of industries like bottle caps, refrigerators, and integrated circuits, BCG generalized the regularity of reductions in unit costs with increased cumulative output in its *Law of Experience*. Costs of value added (total cost per unit of production less the cost per unit of production of bought-in components and materials) decline by a fixed percent in real terms each time accumulated experience is doubled (Henderson, 1974; Stern & Deimler, 2006).

Consider the example of the Photovoltaic (PV) technology. In the 1950s, PV technology, commonly known as *solar cells*, was developed to provide long-term power for satellites. The PV modules house an array of solar cells that deliver direct current power. In the 1970s, companies started to offer

PV technology for commercial applications (Harmon, 2000). Starting with a cumulative installed base of 15 MW$_p$ (=Megawatt peak, where "peak watt" is defined as the power of full sunlight at sea level on a clear day) in 1983, the annual average growth rate was 15%–16%. In 1995, the cumulative installed capacity reached 579 MW, which corresponded to just .02% of the global power generating capacity (Harmon, 2000), and close to 600 Gigawatts in 2019 (Bellini, 2020). In 1976, at the outset of commercialization, module costs were $106/W$_p$ (in 2019 prices) in 1986, it was $10/W$_p$, in 2010 about $2, and in 2019 it was 0.38 cents. Applying the experience curve to PV technology, it can be seen that the average learning rate (experience curve effect) is 20.2%. Thus, every time the cumulative output is doubled, unit costs are reduced 79.8%. Figure 6-2 shows the experience curve effect graphically.

The experience curve is dependent on the industry. Table 6-1 provides examples of experience curves in different industries.

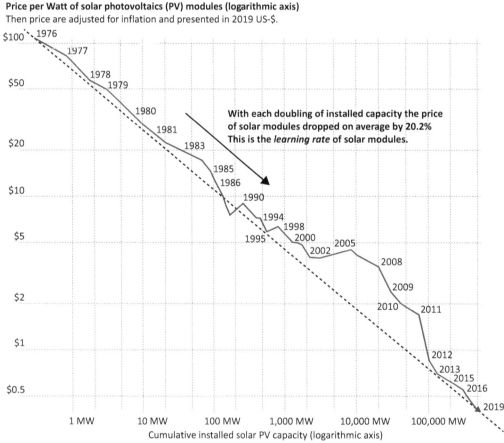

Price per Watt of solar photovoltaics (PV) modules (logarithmic axis)
Then price are adjusted for inflation and presented in 2019 US-$.

With each doubling of installed capacity the price of solar modules dropped on average by 20.2% This is the *learning rate* of solar modules.

Cumulative installed solar PV capacity (logarithmic axis)

Data: Lafond et al. (2017) and IRENA Database: the reported learning rate is an average over several studies reported by de La Tour et al (2013) in Energy. The rate has remained very similar since then. OurWorldinData.org – Research and data to make progress against the world's largest problems.

FIGURE 6-2   Experience Curve of Photovoltaic Technology (Roser, 2020)

TABLE 6-1 Experience Curves for Selected Industries

INDUSTRY	EXPERIENCE CURVE
Microprocessors	60%
LCDs	60%
Airlines	75%
Personal Computers	77%
DVD players/recorders	78%
Cars	81%
Color TVs	83%

Note. Chart source: Gottfredson, M., Schaubert, S., & Saenz, H. (2008). The new leader's guide to diagnosing the business. *Harvard Business Review, 86*(2), 62.

IMPLICATIONS FOR MARKETING

These experience curve effects occur as cost savings are gained through activities such as learning, technical progress, product and process improvement, specialization and redesign of labor, etc. It is important to note, however, that such cost reductions do not occur automatically; they require management and can be achieved only if all learning and improvement opportunities are exploited. The experience curve has a number of important implications:

- Growth is not an option in many markets. If a company grows slower than its competitors it has to expect a cost disadvantage.
- If market shares do not change over time, unit costs of competitors will remain the same.
- Profitability depends on experience curve effects; hence companies with a higher market share can expect a higher return on investment.
- The first-mover advantage can be important. Especially in industries with high experience-curve effects, first movers can try to gain market share quickly, create a cost advantage, and prevent competitors from entering the industry by reducing prices along the experience curve.
- Unit costs can be predicted. This is important for a company's competitive strategy (especially the cost–leadership strategy) and valuable for pricing decisions.

Consider this example: There were three major and one smaller producer of solar cells in 2008. The experience curve is 79.8%. Each company had unit costs of $10 when they entered the industry with a production volume of 5 MW (see Table 6-2).

Figure 6-3 shows the experience curve and the relative cost position for each competitor. Given the current industry price, Competitor A has the highest margin. Strategically, they could either take advantage of the higher return on investment and invest in further product or process improvement, or they could lower prices, for example to $3.50. In that case, they would still earn enough money and gain market share. Competitors C and D would not be able to produce and

TABLE 6-2 Cost and Volume Comparisons of Selected Levels of Competition

COMPETITOR	CUMULATED PRODUCTION VOLUME (MW)	SALES VOLUME IN 2008	MARKET SHARE (%)	UNIT COSTS	MARGIN @ UNIT PRICE $4
A	400	40	50	2.43	1.7
B	200	20	25	3.01	.99
C	100	10	12.5	3.77	.23
D	100	10	12.5	3.77	.23
Total	800	80			

to sell at a profit and might decide to go out of business. Then, if Competitor A continuously reduces their prices along the experience curve, they would prevent other competitors from entering the industry.

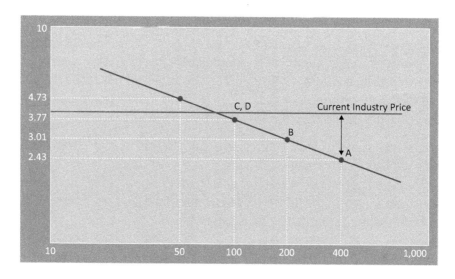

FIGURE 6-3 Experience Curve and Relative Cost Position

SUMMARY

As companies get more experienced in the production of a product (or in any task), they learn *and* become more efficient at it. The associated cost savings have been labeled experience curve effects (or learning curve effects). Every time the cumulative output is doubled, unit costs drop at a regular rate. Computing and taking advantage of experience curve effects has important strategic marketing implications. It allows for the prediction of unit costs, it grounds the formulation of pricing strategies, it helps to estimate competitor's cost advantages or disadvantages, and it provides the firm with substantial and enduring cost advantages. Those cost advantages can be passed on as savings from the customer's perspective, which should lead to higher unit sales, higher market share, and even greater experience; thus, a virtuous circle is reaped in higher margins and higher returns. The experience curve has become a critical business concept, especially for companies that pursue a cost–leadership strategy.

REFERENCES

Abernathy, W. J. (1974). Limits of the learning curve. *Harvard Business Review, 52*, 109–119.

Bellini, E. (2020). World now has 583.5 GW of operational PV. *PV Magazine.*

Gottfredson, M., Schaubert, S., & Saenz, H. (2008). The new leader's guide to diagnosing the business. *Harvard Business Review, 86*(2), 62.

Harmon, C. (2000). Experience curves of photovoltaic technology. *IIASA Interim Report. IR-00-014.* http://pure.iiasa.ac.at/6231/

Henderson, B. D. (1974). The experience curve reviewed. *Boston Consulting Group Perspectives, 128*, 1–3.

History.com Editors. (2019, May 2). Model T. *History.com*. https://www.history.com/topics/inventions/model-t

Roser, M. (2020). *Why did renewables become so cheap so fast? And what can we do to use this global opportunity for green growth?* Our World in Data. https://ourworldindata.org/cheap-renewables-growth

Stern, C. W., & Deimler, M. S. (2006). *Perspectives on strategy from the Boston Consulting Group.* John Wiley & Sons.

Figure Credits

ECONOMIES AND DISECONOMIES OF SCALE

Former CEO of General Electric Jack Welch had an iron rule: "First, second, or out!" (Krames, 2002, p. 90). Each strategic business unit was to achieve the first or the second market position—in terms of market share—or be divested or closed. Behind this dictum lay a simple observation: Return on investment is closely related to market share. In other words, size matters. Market leaders are usually more efficient than firms with lesser shares because they benefit from economies of scale.

Economies of scale exist when each 1% increase in production volume results in an increase of less than 1% in the total cost of production. Each new unit, therefore, is less expensive to produce than the previous one. Economies drive industry concentration or consolidation, causing many industries like airlines, pharmaceuticals, and telecommunications to be dominated by a few industry giants. Advertising costs in the U.S. soft drink industry is a good example of the effects of economies of scale (see Figure 7-1) (Grant, 2008).

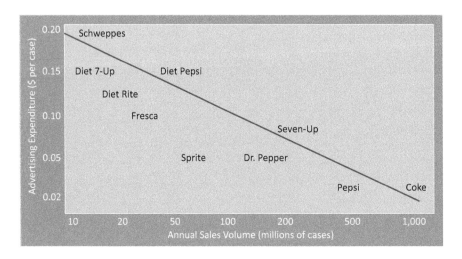

FIGURE 7-1   Economies of Scale in Advertising: U.S. Soft Drink Industry (Grant, 2008)

Economies of scale can be achieved in a number of ways (Haberberg & Rieple, 2008), such as the following:

- *Cost spreading.* This is particularly important in industries with high fixed costs. Examples of high fixed costs include research and development (R&D) costs in the pharmaceutical industry, high advertisement costs in the fast-moving consumer goods industry, and high manufacturing overhead costs (plants and equipment) in the auto industry.

- *Purchasing power.* Another source of economies of scale are the volume discounts that companies receive from vendors due to the size of their purchases and their bargaining power. Supermarket chains, fast food chains, car manufacturers, and many other big companies are able to gain price and service concessions from suppliers due to the sheer volume of their purchases in both units and in dollars. Walmart, the largest retailer in the world, is well known for using its purchasing power to achieve lower costs than many of its competitors.
- *Specialization of labor.* Economies of scale also occur because large companies with high volumes of production can divide labor into discrete activities, which are then performed more efficiently. When complex processes are broken down into a few repeatable tasks performed by specialized workers with specialized equipment, time loss due to switching from one activity to the next is avoided, making automation possible.
- *Specialized of technology.* Large companies have more capital and can more easily afford expensive machines and technology to bring costs down.

Economies of scale are especially important when companies offer standardized products or services to a mass market and aim for cost leadership. The advent of new technologies like 3D printing and the Internet of Things however may change the rules of the game in some industries as customization becomes more feasible. When customers prefer low-priced, standardized products, mass production leading to economies of scale will prevail. However, when customers favor individualized solutions and are willing to pay a higher price for them, mass production and mass marketing will be replaced by customization made possible by digital production technologies. However, 3D printing and other digital manufacturing technologies do not offer economies of scale. Economies of scale are realized when high quantities of standardized products are produced and low unit costs are important. 3D printing does not offer economies of scale but makes customization feasible.

Diseconomies of scale occur when various kinds of forces cause larger firms to produce goods and services at increased per-unit costs. In other words, each 1% increase in production volume results in an increase of greater than 1% in the total cost of production. If companies or plants exceed the optimal volume of production, costs can *increase* due to diseconomies of scale (see Figure 7-2) for the following major reasons (Barney & Hesterly, 2006):

1. *Physical limits to efficient size.* When the production volume exceeds capacity, additional investments have to be made; thus, additional fixed costs increase unit costs. Too much high-capacity utilization

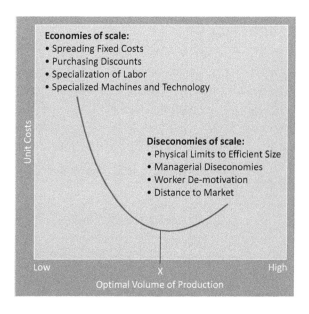

FIGURE 7-2 Economies and diseconomies of scale

can prevent workers from having the time to maintain the machines, which can result in more machine breakdowns.

2. *Managerial diseconomies.* Size can increase complexity and bureaucracy, and this can reduce the manager's ability to effectively manage an organization.

3. *Worker demotivation.* In larger companies, workers become segregated and communicate less with each other. Then the individual's contribution is diminished and increased specialization can lead to demotivation.

4. *Distance to market.* Finally, diseconomies of scale can occur because of the physical distance of larger, centralized companies from the market, leading to higher transportation costs, less direct customer contact, etc.

SUMMARY

Size can lead to cost advantages. Known as economies of scale, this important concept lies behind cost leadership strategies and mass marketing. The larger the market share and the production and sales volume, the lower the unit costs are, for example, fixed costs can be spread over a larger amount of units. However, if an optimal volume of production is exceeded, diseconomies of scale can occur. This can happen when physical limits to an efficient size are exceeded, when large organizations become complex and bureaucratic, etc. Marketing strategists need to know how costs behave depending on production volume, when they determine prices of products and contribution margins and when they formulate their strategies (e.g., cost leadership versus differentiation, mass marketing versus targeting small segments).

REFERENCES

Anderson, C. (2012). *Makers: The new industrial revolution.* Crown Business.

Barney, J. B., & Hesterly, W. S. (2006). *Strategic management and competitive advantage.* Pearson Education.

Grant, R. M. (2008). *Contemporary strategic analysis* (6th ed.). Blackwell Publishing.

Haberberg, A., & Rieple, A. (2008). *Strategic management: Theory and application.* Oxford University Press.

Krames, J. A. (2002). *The Jack Welch lexicon of leadership: Over 250 terms, concepts, strategies & initiatives of the legendary leader.* McGraw Hill.

Figure Credits

ECONOMIES OF SCOPE AND SYNERGIES

Compared to economies of scale, which are driven by producing *more of a single product*, economies of *scope* are realized when producing *more than one product* makes the production of all units in the assortment cheaper. Whereas size and volume lead to economies of scale, diversity brings economies of scope. If producing product Y makes producing product X more efficient (cheaper per unit), that is an economy of scope.

Economies of scope are a form of *synergy* (from the Greek term meaning *working together*). Synergies are realized when two (or more) inputs or activities (factors) come together or act together to result in output that is greater than the sum of the two factors taken separately (i.e., (1+1) > 2). A good example of an economy of scope and synergy is the use of by-products from the production of one product in the production of another product (i.e., by-product synergies).

Chaparral Steel, for example, realized improved efficiencies and reduced pollution by using slag *waste* from steel production in the production of Portland cement, another of its product lines. The productive use of the slag lowered the waste, and thereby the costs of steel production and the slag itself was a more efficient input than the lime it replaced. This in turn required less processing and lower energy inputs, thereby lowering the cost of cement production (Forward & Mangan, 1999). Economies of scope and synergies can be an important source of sustainable competitive advantages—and one that may be particularly difficult for competitors to replicate or substitute. Chaparral's competitors who produced only steel or only Portland cement, for example, could not easily match the new efficiencies of by-product usage.

Economies of scope exist whenever there are cost savings from using a resource in multiple activities carried out in combination, rather than carrying out those activities independently. There are basically six forms of synergies (Goold & Campbell, 1998):

1. *Shared tangible resources.* Unit costs can be reduced when tangible resources such as production plants, transportation systems, or information facilities are utilized across a range of products. The German car manufacturer Volkswagen, for example, reduced costs of the SUV Touareg by 30% by sharing resources, including production facilities with Porsche's SUV, the Cayenne. For their fleet of electric cars, Volkswagen has developed the modular electrification tool kit system, an electric-vehicle platform that will lay the foundation for affordable electro mobility in the mass market. This platform will be used by the four Group brands Volkswagen, Audi, SEAT and Skoda. By 2022, 27 models will be based on this platform and will largely benefit from the synergies of a shared platform (Volkswagen, 2021).

2. *Shared intangible resources.* Intangible resources are assets that are not physical in nature. Among them are brands, knowledge, or specific capabilities. If these are shared among products, they can constitute considerable economies of scale. When Fujifilm faced declining

sales of photographic film, it took advantage of a vast array of its original technologies to leverage them to develop skin care products. Fuji realized that the same process that prevents photographs from fading can be used to protect skin from aging. Fuji used its knowledge in antioxidants and nanotechnology to build a flourishing skincare business under the brand name Astalift. When Astalift was introduced, Fujifilm took advantage of its strong brand name and boldly appeared in the TV commercials to demonstrate that Astalift was based on advanced photographic film technology (Fujifilm, 2021).

3. *Pooled negotiating power.* By combining their purchases, different strategic business units can benefit from bulk discounts and from cost savings in transportation and logistics.
4. *Coordinated strategies.* Companies with multi-business units can coordinate market entry strategies, product development, pricing strategies, etc., to avoid duplication of efforts and to benefit from cross-selling.
5. *Vertical integration.* Vertically integrated companies can benefit from a faster flow of products through the supply chain, reduced inventory costs, and improved market access.
6. *Combined business creation.* Diversified companies can combine the know-how and technologies of each business unit to create new products or businesses.

Economies of scope is a common reason for mergers and acquisitions and for diversification strategies. Companies can benefit from synergies when they move into new products and/or markets that are related to the core businesses in one or more of the following ways (Markides & Williamson, 1996):

- *Customer assets*: Brand recognition, customer loyalty, and trust can reduce costs dramatically when new products are introduced.
- *Channel assets*: Access to distribution channels and distributor loyalty facilitates the establishment of a dealer network and can help to overcome shelf-space restrictions for new products.
- *Input assets*: Knowledge of and access to supplier markets and cheap raw materials or components can also reduce costs and time to market.
- *Process assets*: Product or market-specific experience and know-how in, for example, production and marketing processes can facilitate the development and marketing of new products.
- *Market knowledge assets*: Knowledge on competitors, customers, etc. provides valuable insights into the marketing process.

SUMMARY

While economies of scale arise when producing greater quantities of a single product, economies of scope come from selling a greater variety of products that share synergies. There are many ways to benefit from synergies, and it is important for a marketing strategist to know what types of synergies exist and to what extent they reduce costs. In practice, however, it is difficult to estimate the effect of economies of scope and to realize them. In most cases, companies tend to overestimate the potential of economies of scope.

REFERENCES

Forward, G., & Mangan, A. (1999). By-product synergy. *The Bridge 29, 1,* 12–15.

Fujifilm. (2021). Fujifilm Skincare. *Fujifilm.* https://www.fujifilm.com/jp/en/about/rd

Goold, M., & Campbell, A. (1998). Desperately seeking synergy. *Harvard Business Review,* 76(5), 131–143.

Markides, C. C., & Williamson, P. J. (1996). Corporate diversification and organizational structure: A resource-based view. *Academy of Management Journal,* 39(2), 340–367.

Volkswagen. (2021). *Volkswagen MEB.* Volkswagen AG. https://www.volkswagenag.com/en/group/fleet-customer/facts_and_figures/MEB.html

MARKET SHARE EFFECTS

Most organizations desire high market share when all else is equal, and some hold high market share as their primary objective. This may be the case because marketing managers are inherently competitive; in fact, marketing strategy is often analogized to competition in warfare and sports, with the *winner* being whichever firm has the greatest market share. Another reason for this focus may be the fact that increasing market share looks like increasing sales on a day-to-day basis. In other words, as marketers strive to improve sales, they are also working to improve market share. Thus, the processes of increasing sales and increasing market share are inextricable, especially in low- or no-growth markets.

MARKET SHARE AS A STRATEGIC OBJECTIVE

Besides its appeal as a competition-oriented yardstick for one's own performance, market share for many companies is a strategic objective. Empirical studies have demonstrated that it is related to cost advantages and profitability, and many managers incorporate market share effects into their strategic considerations. As empirical findings regarding market share are somewhat ambiguous and the use of market share comes with certain problems, a more thorough, critical look at its effects and managerial implications is necessary.

Market Share and Cost Advantages

An improvement in market share signifies more than simply a *win* or a jump in sales figures. Because market share is a relative measure—in other words, it shows a firm's success relative to the competition—an increase in this measure should also lead to certain competitive advantages. For one, the firm with higher market share has, by definition, greater *scale*, and scale leads to advantages in learning and unit costs. In particular, scale effects—experience or learning curve effects, as outlined in Note 6, and economies of scale, as outlined in Note 7—connect the number of units produced to lower per-unit costs, which offer a significant competitive advantage. The experience curve posits that the more often a task or operation is repeated, the lower the cost of completing it. Specifically, the observable relationship is that each time cumulative volume is doubled, value added costs decline by a predictable percentage.

Economies of scale, on the other hand, arise, when unit costs decrease as output increases. In practice, the experience curve and economies of scale are related and often occur together. One way to think about the difference is that experience is based on number of units produced regardless of time, and scale is based on number of units produced per period of time.

Market Share and Profits

The firm with lower costs can charge a lower price for its product (further increasing its unit sales, and thus its market share, in a virtuous cycle), or it can take higher margins at the market price. Experience curve effects also offer the benefits of higher reliability and quality. In other words, as a firm makes more units, its number of defects decreases and its conformance or uniformity increases across units. (Conformity is a dimension of quality, especially from an operations standpoint.) These basic share–profitability connections are illustrated in Figure 9-1.

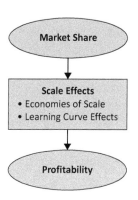

FIGURE 9-1 Market Share and Profitability

Thus, increased market share seems to be a desirable outcome that is associated with specific competitive advantages. For this reason, many firms include market share targets in their objectives and strategic planning. Extensive research has shown that market share and profitability do *correlate*—meaning that firms with higher market share are, in fact, more profitable. However, the relationship between share and profits is complex, and it is not clear whether market share actually *causes* higher profitability. It could be that the reverse relationship is true: Profitability may lead to higher market share, and other factors (such as higher quality products) may lead to the differences in *both* profits and share. Therefore, the correlation of share with profits may not be as straightforward as it first appears. For that reason, this Note will briefly describe some important findings related to market share effects and link those findings to their marketing strategy implications.

EMPIRICAL FINDINGS: THE PROFIT IMPACT OF MARKETING STRATEGY (PIMS) DATA

Research on business strategy in general and on the market share–profitability relationship in particular has been facilitated by compilation of the Profit Impact of Marketing Strategy (PIMS) database. Collection of the PIMS data was initiated by Sidney Schoeffler in the 1960s at the request of General Electric, which had begun analyzing similar information about its own business units in the 1960s. In the early 1970s, Schoeffler and the Management Science Institute at Harvard Business School extended PIMS data collection across many more companies and industries. Then, in the mid-1970s, the Strategic Planning Institute, a nonprofit organization, was created to facilitate the movement of the project from an academic to an operating system. Today, the PIMS data contain standardized information about 4,200 business units, including their market growth, market size, customer characteristics, competitive strengths, supply chain structure, and economic success factors such as return on investment and return on sales. The PIMS data have provided researchers with invaluable insight into the relationships between firm activities, strategies, and results, including the effects of market share on profitability (Buzzell, 2004; Buzzell & Gale, 1987).

The PIMS data have led to several observations that are now axiomatic in strategy literature, including the fact that market attractiveness (growth and investment intensity) and competitive position (especially market share) are strongly correlated with profitability and returns. In fact, the market share–profitability relationship is so robust and so often replicated in the PIMS database that "PIMS" was sometimes mistakenly taken to stand for "Profit Impact of Market Share" (Buzzell, 2004, p. 479). Various researchers adopting different assumptions, covariates, and statistical methods have offered different estimates of the market share–profitability relationship, but the absolute magnitude seems to be about three market-share points to one point in ROI i.e., an increase of three percentage points in market share is related to an increase of one percentage point in profitability, as shown in Figure 9-2 (Buzzell & Gale, 1987, p. 9). This figure suggests that as market share rises, pretax ROI rises as well by a fairly predictable percentage. For example, a share of 10% or less obtains an ROI of a bit more than 10%, while a share of greater than 50% obtains an ROI of around 40%.

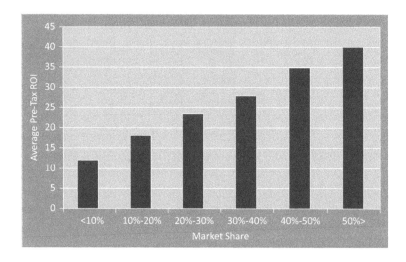

FIGURE 9-2   Market Share and ROI (From Buzzell and Gale, 1987, noting that this graph is based on 4-year average of pretax, pre-interest ROI for 2,611 business units in the PIMS database)

A review of more than 48 studies and 276 reported share–profit elasticities that have been estimated using the PIMS and other data and found that the relationship between share and ROI is still about five share points to one ROI point even with the influence of many diverse covariates taken into account (Buzzell & Gale, 1987; Szymanski et al., 1993). Nevertheless, several issues must be highlighted when considering market share, especially when considering market share as the basis of a firm's marketing strategy. These include difficulty in defining what market is being shared; ambiguity in the causal direction of the relationship and the likelihood that intangible factors (such as product quality) drive both share and profits; and the fact that market share should be approached with caution as an external, competitor-oriented objective.

STRATEGIC IMPLICATIONS OF MARKET SHARE

A number of issues emerge when companies use market share for their strategic considerations. They must be aware that market share depends on market definition, and that market definition can be a tricky task. Also, there may be an inverse causal direction between market share and profitability, and the orientation toward market share might lead to an excessive competitor orientation. Finally, market share has several strategic implications that should be considered when strategies are formulated.

Defining the Market that is Shared

Relating strategy and results to market share raises an important question: *For what market is the market share being computed?* Markets can be defined and labeled in many ways, and decisions about market definition can have powerful effects on strategic thinking and vision, objectives setting, and competitive actions. Market definition is obviously essential in the consideration of share as a means toward profits or as an evaluation metric. In fact, before computing market share, the denominator must be specified, and that specification will influence all subsequent considerations.

For example, Pepsi's Gatorade holds a dominant share of the sports drink market in the United States, and Coca-Cola's Powerade is a distant second. Meanwhile, Aquafina, another Pepsi brand, is the U.S. market-share leader in bottled water, just ahead of Coca-Cola's Dasani (although this is not true in Europe). So which *market* should Pepsi be concerned with, and under what circumstances? The Gatorade and Aquafina brand managers may argue for the *sports drink* or *bottled water* denominators, but the substantive benefits of market share—economies of scale in production and distribution, channel leverage, experience curve effects, and purchasing power—may not be achieved at the submarket or national level. Rather, they may accrue to the dominant overall U.S. beverage-category leader (Coca-Cola), or instead to the *global* beverage-category leader (also Coca-Cola). Thus, understanding the underlying drivers of share effects and the reasoning for holding share as an objective is crucial to defining the market for computing share effects. Moreover, an appropriate and clear definition of the market is essential to effective use of market share in strategy formation, implementation, and assessment.

Causation and Covariates

As previously mentioned, the causal direction of the relationship between market share and profitability is less clear than simple observations might suggest. That is, even though these two things unquestionably correlate, it is unclear whether market share *causes* profitability or vice versa. Alternatively, it is possible that this correlation could be *spurious* and explained by the fact that *both* market share and profitability are driven by other characteristics, such as product quality, management skill, organizational culture, access to scarce resources, or even luck (Aaker & Jacobson, 1994; Jacobson, 1988; Jacobson & Aaker, 1985, 1987). Figure 9-3 illustrates these alternative explanations. In this figure, market share contributes to profitability via increased scale, but, at the same time, relationships exist between other variables (especially product quality) and both share and profits. As depicted in the figure, profitability and the resources it provides can also *feed back* to increased market share.

The complex relationships between market share, profitability, and other characteristics of a firm have been examined via extensive research using sophisticated statistical techniques. The conclusion, it seems, is that all of these connections are real, at least in some degree and in some situations. Indeed, more skillfully managed firms do enjoy both higher market shares and higher profitability, and better product quality does lead to both higher margins (which contribute directly

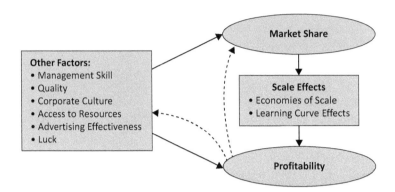

FIGURE 9-3   Possible Market Share–Profitability Relationships

to higher profitability) and higher market share. Thus, it is unsurprising that product quality, managerial skill, cost control, low-cost production, and advertising effectiveness all lead to both higher market share and higher ROI. The core connection between market share and profitability, mediated by the benefits of scale, is also real. Nevertheless, it remains unclear whether market share causes profitability or simply correlates with it, and even if one leads to the other, it may not be true that effective strategy can be developed based on the premise that increased share leads to increased profits.

Competitor-Oriented Objectives

Another problem with building strategy on market-share objectives is that market share is a competitor-oriented objective: It is inherently based on how the firm performs in comparison with the competition, rather than on how it delivers value to its customers, how it performs essential value-adding activities, or how profitable it is. That is, according to this view, market share is not itself about profitability; rather, it involves external phenomena and comparisons to others. Even more problematic is the fact that external, competitor-oriented orientations have been shown to result in worse performance across a variety of settings.

Wharton Business School Professor J. Scott Armstrong has reviewed and extended findings on the negative effects of competitor-orientated strategies. According to his results, and looking across many diverse tasks, people who adopt or who are manipulated into a competitor-oriented mindset realize inferior results compared to those who adopt internally focused objectives. Similarly, as per analysis of data from more than four decades of corporate performance by 20 Fortune 500 firms, those firms with competitor-oriented (market share) objectives fared worse than those with internal, profit-oriented objectives (Armstrong & Collopy, 1996; Armstrong & Green, 2006). Importantly, these results relate to how strategy and objectives are established, not to the basic relationship between market share and profitability. That is, the question is not whether firms would prefer higher market share (with all else being equal); after all, most firms would always choose higher market share over lower market share. Rather, the question is whether firms are wise to establish strategic objectives around market share or to undermine other objectives, such as positioning and margins, to achieve market share. Armstrong's research indicates that internally focused objectives are far more effective than competitor-oriented objectives.

Market Share and Strategy

It is a common belief that *market share leads to profits*, and behemoths like Walmart, Microsoft, Amazon, Apple, and Toyota seem to confirm that supposition. If market share does not make profits inevitable, it is certainly a powerful weapon to have in a brand's arsenal. For example, even if Coke and Pepsi fight for number 1 and number 2 in carbonated soft drink market share without gaining substantial advantage over each other in profitability, they are still the envy of Royal Crown (RC) Cola, which cannot capture shelf space or media time from the two giants ("RC," 2000, p. 14). Similarly, Walmart relies on its market dominance to apply purchasing leverage for lower costs, and its scale justifies investments, (both by it and by its vendors) in efficiencies such as RFID tag (radio frequency identification tag) inventory tracking; Walmart's purchasing leverage and investments in efficiencies then lead to even greater market share, more purchasing leverage, and yet more resources to invest in efficiencies—forming a classic virtuous cycle.

Amazon's AWS Division (Amazon Web Services) holds the dominant share of the global cloud computing market with over 30% in 2019, more than twice that of number 2, Microsoft Azure. AWS is the most profitable part of Amazon, and AWS profits have funded the growth of Amazon's online shopping business, which in 2020 held the dominant share of that market and was generating significant profits as well (Statista, 2021).

Market leaders, by definition, enjoy greater benefits of scale, including economies of scale and experience curve advantages, and they may influence category-wide price points and promotion policies. Market leaders can also invest in category expansion—advertising and promotion that grows overall category sales—and retain the benefits of this expansion, whereas *also-rans* that invest in category expansion end up contributing to other firms' sales more than to their own.

Nevertheless, other examples emphasize that high market share is not the only way to achieve returns; indeed, they suggest that market share itself may not be enough, and some recent research has concluded that setting competitor-oriented objectives in general and market-share-based objectives in particular may actually be deleterious to firm performance. It is certainly true that many firms realize high returns without high market share, and, conversely, that many firms with high market shares fail to garner high returns—or even *any* positive returns whatsoever. For example, at the same time that Toyota has succeeded as a market share leader, General Motors failed. During the 1990s and much of the 2000s, General Motors was the leading producer of automobiles in terms of units sold. Still, despite this market share, GM was leaving customers dissatisfied and losing money. By the 2020s, GM had fallen to third place among worldwide automotive manufacturers, trailing both Volkswagen and Toyota.

In the worldwide smartphone market in 2019, Samsung held the highest unit market share with 19.2%. Apple was third with 12.6%. However, Apple obtained 66% of worldwide smartphone profits compared to 17% for Samsung by achieving better design, quality, and service with lower operating expenses and a loyal customer following. In the video game market, Sony (with its PlayStation 3) and Microsoft (with its Xbox 360) struggle to realize profits even though they dominate the market in terms of share. Meanwhile, Nintendo, with the Wii system, is one of the most profitable companies in Japan.

Similarly, Silicon Valley venture capitalists have encouraged and funded many tech start-ups to race to capture market share because speed was seen as crucial in being first to market. The presumption was that share would eventually lead to profits (Timmons & Spinelli, 2004, p. 188). Unfortunately, this belief has failed to hold true for many technology-based start-ups. Billion-dollar market value start-ups (unicorns) that have never earned a profit include Uber and Lyft, Pinterest, and Slack. For them and others, share has not translated into profitability.

Given these scenarios, what conclusions can be drawn from the existing research on market share effects? Market share certainly provides some specific benefits, including economies of scale, experience curve effects, and leverage to influence marketwide norms (such as price points and discounting patterns). These benefits may lead to marketplace and financial success. However, there is also evidence that share is not the only route to profitability and that the very act of defining strategy and objectives by market share metrics may *hurt* performance. Many apparently contradictory cases—Toyota versus General Motors, Apple versus Samsung, and the unprofitable high share unicorns like Uber—underscore the need to carefully consider use of market share as a strategy objective and to carefully examine assumptions about how share might drive or impede success.

So, with all else being equal, market share indicates and correlates with profitability, as well as affording certain advantages to a firm relative to operations. However, market share is also an *outcome* of important strategic, managerial, and tactical accomplishments—that is, doing other more immediate tasks well *leads to* increased market share. Thus, market share itself may *not* be an effective means to success so much as it is a marker of success. In addition, market share can be a distracting and even misleading consideration in some instances. In particular, market share that is achieved (*bought*) with low prices, meager or nonexistent margins, and/or consequent degradation in product quality may be a Pyrrhic victory.

Some particular issues to consider when integrating market share considerations into a strategy include the following:

- *Scale effects*: The chief precondition to using market share as an objective in strategy definition should be some well-tested expectation of substantial benefits from scale. Can the firm expect to learn in important competitive areas as it gains share and experience?
- *Dissuasion of competitors*: Often, market share can serve as a barrier to entry for competing firms. Thus, companies may seek to gain market share as a way to discourage new entrants and increased rivalry.
- *Standardization*: If an industry is expected to establish standards, then the firm with the highest market share for that industry will usually earn the power to influence or even lead the process of setting standards. The ability to dictate industrywide standards is a powerful strategic advantage.
- *Ancillary sales*: Market share can establish an "installed base" of equipment and establish relationships with customers who will purchase ancillary products, supplies, or services from the firm. This is sometimes called "razor blade economics," because razor companies often give away razors (the handles) with the expectation of future, highly profitable blade sales.
- *Customer "stickiness"*: Customers gained via strategies focusing on market share must be retained as costs come down, margins go up, or competition in the market changes; otherwise, share-based strategies may be ill-advised.

SUMMARY

Market share and profits move together (correlate), but the wisdom of using market share as a dominant strategic objective, or of organizing marketing activities around gaining share, is uncertain. It may well be worth pursuing share that corresponds to other, well-thought-through strategies, especially to a strategy aimed at increasing production to realize the benefits of scale. Nevertheless, it may be wise to recall American author Edward Abbey's admonition, "Growth for growth's sake is the ideology of the cancer cell" (Abbey, 1990, p. 98). Setting market share as an objective or taking actions motivated primarily to gain share should be carefully considered and based on a solid understanding of future profits, or at least on definite and well-tested assumptions about future profits.

REFERENCES

Aaker, D. A., & Jacobson, R. (1994). The financial information content of perceived quality. *Journal of Marketing Research*, 31(2), 191–201.

Abbey, E. (1990). *Voice crying in the wilderness (vox clamantis in deserto): Notes from a secret journal.* St. Martin's Press.

Armstrong, J. S., & Collopy, F. (1996). Competitor orientation: Effects of objectives and information on managerial decisions and profitability. *Journal of Marketing Research*, 33(2), 188–199.

Armstrong, J. S., & Green, K. C. (2006). Competitor-oriented objectives: the myth of market share. *Marketing Papers*, 9.

Buzzell, R. D. (2004). The PIMS program of strategy research: A retrospective appraisal. *Journal of Business Research*, 57(5), 478–483.

Buzzell, R. D., & Gale, B. T. (1987). *The PIMS principles: Linking strategy to performance.* Free Press.

Jacobson, R. (1988). Distinguishing among competing theories of the market share effect. *Journal of Marketing*, 52(4), 68–80.

Jacobson, R., & Aaker, D. A. (1985). Is market share all that it's cracked up to be? *Journal of Marketing*, 49(4), 11–22.

Jacobson, R., & Aaker, D. A. (1987). The strategic role of product quality. *Journal of Marketing*, 51(4), 31–44.

"RC." (2000). RC Cola wins suit against Coca-Cola. *The New York Times.*

Statista. (2021, July 5). *Amazon leads $150-billion cloud market.* [Cloud infrastructure market]. https://www.statista.com/chart/18819/worldwide-market-share-of-leading-cloud-infrastructure-service-providers/

Szymanski, D. M., Bharadwaj, S. G., & Varadarajan, P. R. (1993). An analysis of the market share–profitability relationship. *Journal of Marketing*, 57(3), 1–18.

Timmons, J. A., & Spinelli, S. (2004). *New venture creation: Entrepreneurship for the 21st century.* McGraw-Hill Irwin.

Figure Credit
Fig. 9.2: Robert D. Buzzell and Bradley T. Gale, *The PIMS Principles: Linking Strategy to Performance.* Copyright © 1987 by Free Press.

COMPETITIVE INTELLIGENCE

In *The Art of War*, one of the oldest and most successful books on military strategy, Chinese general Sun Tzu declares, "If you know your enemy and know yourself, you need not fear the result of a hundred battles. If you know yourself but not the enemy, for every victory gained you will also suffer a defeat. If you know neither the enemy nor yourself, you will succumb in every battle" (Tzu, 2005, p. 13). Knowing the objectives, strategies, tactics, strengths, and weaknesses of the competitor is vital.

As an example, if you are Microsoft, producer of the market-dominating Web browser (Internet Explorer), you want to pay very close attention to what Google is doing with the development of its Chrome browser; Chrome represents an overt attack on Windows. If you are Google, you should be concerned with Microsoft's retaliatory response, Bing, intended to compete directly with Google's market-dominating search engine. Understanding the competition is vital to anticipating market actions and constructing appropriate strategies and plans to succeed against those actions. This Note on competitive intelligence will examine the following four areas of the competition: long-term objectives and motivations; strengths and weaknesses; strategies; and, marketing tactics.

LONG-TERM OBJECTIVES AND MOTIVATIONS

How competitors act and react in a market largely depends on their strategic objectives and motivations to engage in a business. Therefore, the first step of a competitive analysis should be the investigation of long-term objectives. The objectives not only determine the strategy and likely tactical moves, but they also provide insight into the motivations of your competitor in a specific business or market. For example, a competitor will defend a market or segment seen as its core business with all possible means. If the strategic goal of a company is yearly double-digit growth, and, if the company's strategic objective is to be among the top three players in terms of market share, then a business unit of that company that is in a low-growth market with a small market share will receive little attention and resources and can be more easily attacked. Market research can be used to identify the long-term objectives and motivations of a competitor to include analyzing vision and mission statements, annual reports, executive interviews, news updates, and analyst reports.

STRENGTHS AND WEAKNESSES

An analysis of a competitor's strengths and weaknesses helps you to (a) predict the competitor's actions and initiatives—as they probably want to eliminate their weak points and emphasize their advantages, and (b) to identify points of difference to position your products and services. This analysis consists of four steps:

1. success factors in a market are determined.
2. these success factors are weighted according to their importance. Usually the constant-sum scale is used: 100 points are divided among the success factors according to their importance; the higher the importance, the more points are assigned.
3. the competitor is rated on each success factor (e.g., using a 5-point scale, where 5 is excellent and 1 is very poor). Then, rate your company on each success factor.
4. multiply the rating by the importance weight. The importance weight indicates the relative advantage or disadvantage.

Figure 10-1 is an example of a strengths and weaknesses analysis. In the first column, the success factors in a particular industry are listed. The second column contains their importance. The performance of our company (We) and the competitor (Competitor A) is rated on a 5-point scale. Two weighted scores are computed: one for our company and one for the competitor. The summed weighted scores indicate the overall performance of the two companies.

Critical Success Factors	Weight	Performance					Weighted Score	
		1	2	3	4	5	We	Comp. A
Brand Image	5						10	15
Product Innovation	10						20	30
Service	20						60	100
Extensive Distribution	15						30	60
Economies of Scale	30						60	90
Logistics	20						60	100
						Sum	240	395

○------● We
●——● Competitor A

FIGURE 10-1   Strengths and Weaknesses Analysis

The best way to perform this analysis is by combining several sources of information, such as:

- customer surveys (e.g., assess brand image, service, product quality);
- sales force meetings (e.g., salespeople have close contact with customers and are confronted every day with competitors' offerings and understand their strengths and weaknesses during sales negotiations);
- analyst reports; and
- discussions with shared suppliers, distributors, etc.

It is advisable to do this analysis as teamwork with experts from several functional areas that have competitor knowledge.

STRATEGIES

The next step, the analysis of the competitor's strategies, may be the most difficult. Ideally, you can use the data you have generated for your own portfolio analysis, customer value analysis, and so on, to create the strategy profile of your competitor. The strategy profile illustrates the strategic priorities and compares them with your own company. So, you can identify the areas of strategic overlap (i.e., where you follow the same strategy) and areas of difference. Since you can also assume that your competitor uses the most essential tools for strategy formulation, you can try to decipher its strategic intent by looking through the lens of the competitor when you analyze the data. For example, a marketing strategist develops the strength and weakness analysis and then asks, "What would I do if I were Competitor A?" A comprehensive strategy assessment leads to a strategy profile containing the following analyses.

Portfolio analysis: A portfolio analysis organizes a given firms' products or strategic business units (SBUs) according to the attractiveness of the market they serve and their strength in that market; the resulting categorization prioritizes the products/SBUs and directs investment (or withdrawal of support) across the various products. It is useful to understand how the competition prioritizes its products/SBUs for investment and other efforts. Therefore, it is useful to create a portfolio analysis of your competitor. It will give you insights into its most likely strategic moves (growth, divestment, etc.). Then you will be able to tell how balanced your competitor's portfolio is, based on the positioning of the business units or products, in terms of cash flow and risk. Will your competitor have enough *cash cows* to generate financial resources for a growth strategy? Will your competitor have to invest in product development because it doesn't have enough *stars* in its portfolio? Product portfolios are examined further in Note 26.

Customer value analysis: If you create a customer value analysis, try to look at the positioning of the products from your competitor's point of view. How satisfied will it be with its positioning? Will it have to increase quality or lower prices?

Growth strategy: Try also to find out what the focus of your competitor's growth strategy is: market penetration, product development, market development, or diversification.

Marketing approach: Is your competitor's marketing approach undifferentiated or differentiated marketing? What are the target segments of your competitor?

Offensive strategy: What is the most likely *attacking* strategy of your competitor?

Defensive strategy: What is the most likely competitor response to your strategic and tactical moves?

After having analyzed these strategy dimensions, you can create the strategy profile of your competitor and compare it to your company (see Figure 10-2). Sources of competitor data for this analysis can include vision and mission statements, annual reports, press releases, newspaper articles, analyst reports, trade shows, sales force meetings, shared suppliers, shared distributors, shared customers, and shared stakeholders.

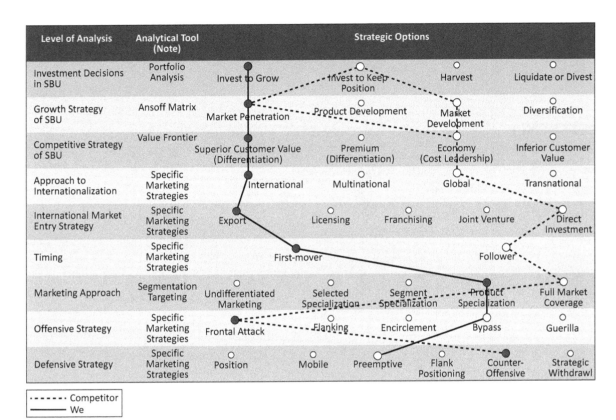

Level of Analysis	Analytical Tool (Note)	Strategic Options			
Investment Decisions in SBU	Portfolio Analysis	Invest to Grow	Invest to Keep Position	Harvest	Liquidate or Divest
Growth Strategy of SBU	Ansoff Matrix	Market Penetration	Product Development	Market Development	Diversification
Competitive Strategy of SBU	Value Frontier	Superior Customer Value (Differentiation)	Premium (Differentiation)	Economy (Cost Leadership)	Inferior Customer Value
Approach to Internationalization	Specific Marketing Strategies	International	Multinational	Global	Transnational
International Market Entry Strategy	Specific Marketing Strategies	Export	Licensing	Franchising	Joint Venture — Direct Investment
Timing	Specific Marketing Strategies	First-mover		Follower	
Marketing Approach	Segmentation Targeting	Undifferentiated Marketing	Selected Specialization — Segment Specialization	Product Specialization	Full Market Coverage
Offensive Strategy	Specific Marketing Strategies	Frontal Attack	Flanking — Encirclement	Bypass	Guerilla
Defensive Strategy	Specific Marketing Strategies	Position	Mobile — Preemptive	Flank Positioning — Counter-Offensive	Strategic Withdrawl

```
- - - - - - Competitor
———— We
```

FIGURE 10-2   Competitor Strategy Profile

MARKETING TACTICS

The final part of the competitor analysis consists of the assessment of the individual marketing decisions. They relate to positioning, product and brand decisions, pricing, distribution and sales management, and communication. Where the previous analyses should help you to *predict* what the competitor's moves most likely are, in this step you assess what the competitors *actually do*. Sources can include price lists, advertising campaigns, promotions, sales force meetings, trade shows and publications, shared customers, and shared distributors.

SUMMARY

A competitor analysis can be similar to a jigsaw puzzle. Each individual piece of data may be meaningless and pieces may be out of place, but accumulating all of the available data and organizing those data as clearly as possible will nevertheless reveal important information about the competition and the future of the marketplace. The challenge is to collect as many of the pieces as possible, to assemble them correctly, and to create an overall picture of the competitor. The objective should be to clarify the competitions' long-term objectives and motivations, strengths and weaknesses, strategies, and tactics. The broad structure and basic tools outlined in this Note will enhance those efforts.

REFERENCE

Tzu, S. (2005). *The art of war* (Special Ed). EL Paso Norte Press.

MISSION, VISION, AND SOCIAL RESPONSIBILITY

Most successful organizations are driven by a commonly shared and inspiring vision. Without such guidance, it is easy to lose direction and purpose. It is rare to find a successful company today that does not have such vision. The development of a shared vision and mission with a definition of the company's purpose, values, and long-term goals ensures all stakeholders have a common understanding of the direction in which the organization is heading (Collins & Porras, 1991). It is also important for a company to have a commitment to social responsibility and the greater society it serves.

MISSION AND VISION

The French writer Antoine de Saint-Exupéry once wrote, "If you want to build a ship, don't drum up the men to gather wood, divide the work, and give orders. Instead, teach them to yearn for the vast and endless sea" (Saint-Exupery, 1950, p. 2). This famous quote perfectly describes what a company's vision should do: it should organize and channel people's energy toward a common direction. It communicates sense and helps to actualize values, appealing to someone's heart and mind (Hinterhuber, 2004). A vision and mission statement should contain the core purpose of the company; the core values of the company; the visionary goal; and a vivid description of the envisioned future (Collins & Porras, 1996). Following are excerpts of mission statements from a few global brand leaders:

- "McDonald's mission is to make delicious feel-good moments easy for everyone ... At our best, we don't just serve food, we serve moments of feel-good, all with the lighthearted, unpretentious, welcoming, dependable personality consumers know and love" ("McDonalds," 2021).
- "Google's mission is to organize the world's information and make it universally accessible and useful" ("Google," 2021).
- "Walmart's mission is to help people save money so they can live better" ("Walmart," 2021).

Core Purpose
The core purpose of the company gives answers to questions like: What is the raison d'être of the company? Why should managers and employees put all their energy into the company and do more than the minimum required? (Campbell & Yeung, 1991).

The core purpose quickly and clearly conveys why the company exists. It is particularly motivating and inspiring if it is aimed at a higher ideal. It should be broad, fundamental, and enduring. A few examples follow:

- "We shall simplify the everyday activities of parents and children, making the most important years of life even more enjoyable" (Baby Bjorn, a Swedish baby products company).
- "We build families for children in need. We help them shape their own futures. We share in the development of their communities" (SOS Children's Villages, an international nongovernmental social-development organization).
- "To experience the emotion of competition, winning, and crushing competitors" (Nike).

Core Values

Core values are those beliefs and moral principles that shape the company's cultures and guide employees' behavior. They define what a company stands for, how business should be conducted, and what is to be held steadfast. As a small set of timeless principles that have intrinsic worth, core values need no external justification (Collins & Porras, 1996). Following are a few examples (review the websites of these organizations for how these core values drive branding efforts):

- SOS Children's Villages—Courage: We take action; Commitment: We keep our promises; Trust: We believe in each other; and, Accountability: We are reliable partners.
- IKEA—Togetherness, cost-consciousness, respect, simplicity.
- The Body Shop—Activate self-esteem; against animal testing; protect our planet; support community trade; and, defend human rights.

The core purpose and values form the fundamental ideology of the company that "provides the glue that holds an organization together through time" (Collins & Porras, 1996, p. 66). However, a company can only be sustainable in the long run if it evolves to meet the needs of the marketplace. Therefore, the second element of a vision and mission statement is concerned with progress and development. It describes the envisioned future with a visionary goal and a vivid description of what it will be like when the goal is achieved.

Visionary Goal

The visionary goal is a clear, compelling, tangible and inspiring goal with (at least) a virtual finish line. It is challenging and ambitious enough that reason says "this is impossible" and intuition says "we can do it nevertheless" (Collins & Porras, 1991). It should be set high enough that people are motivated to put the maximum effort to achieve it and do more than a required minimum, and it should be set low enough that people see a realistic chance that it can be reached. The visionary goal should be so inspiring that people say "It's worth the effort; I want to be a part of it!" Following are a few examples:

- "Every child belongs to a family and grows with love, respect and security" (SOS Children's Villages).
- "To have any book ever printed, in any language, all available in under 60 seconds" (Amazon Kindle).

Vivid Descriptions

In order to make the company's vision and mission accessible to all employees, it should be communicated through vivid pictures and words that describe the envisioned future in a way that captures the heart and soul of people. It must be authentic, passionate, and convincing (Collins & Porras, 1996). For example, from Coca-Cola ("Comparably," 2021):

> **Our Mission:** Our Roadmap starts with our mission, which is enduring. It declares our purpose as a company and serves as the standard against which we weigh our actions and decisions.
>
> - To refresh the world …
> - To inspire moments of optimism and happiness …
> - To create value and make a difference.
>
> **Our Vision:** Our vision serves as the framework for our Roadmap and guides every aspect of our business by describing what we need to accomplish in order to continue achieving sustainable, quality growth.
>
> - **People:** Be a great place to work where people are inspired to be the best they can be.
> - **Portfolio:** Bring to the world a portfolio of quality beverage brands that anticipate and satisfy people's desires and needs.
> - **Partners:** Nurture a winning network of customers and suppliers, together we create mutual, enduring value.
> - **Planet:** Be a responsible citizen that makes a difference by helping build and support sustainable communities.
> - **Profit:** Maximize long-term return to shareowners while being mindful of our overall responsibilities.
> - **Productivity:** Be a highly effective, lean and fast-moving organization.

Together, the visionary goal and the vivid prescription form that part of the vision and mission statement that stimulates and ensures progress.

Ultimately, there are several questions related to criteria that can be used to assess the company's vision and mission. Is the core purpose clear and compelling? Does the core purpose capture the heart and the soul of the organization? Is it motivating and aiming at a higher ideal? Is it broad, fundamental, and enduring? Are the values authentic and honorable?

Do executives and employees live the values of the company? Is the visionary goal long-term, inspiring, and challenging?

CORPORATE STRATEGY

In a multi-business company, strategic management encompasses four major tasks at the corporate level (Grant, 2008; Johnson et al., 2008). These include:

1. providing a clear overall vision for the single business units to exercise guidance and control over the individual businesses;
2. allocating resources to the single business units, thus managing the portfolio in a way that cash flow and risks are balanced, and sustainable long-term growth is achieved;
3. managing linkages among the business units and exploiting synergies; and
4. developing central competences and providing services and resources to the business units.

Hence, the following criteria are helpful to evaluate the corporate strategy. Does the corporate headquarters have a clear overall vision or strategic intent for its business units? Is the portfolio of business units balanced in terms of cash flow and risk? Does the portfolio assure sustainable long-term development and growth? Are synergies among the business units exploited? Does the headquarters develop core competences, and does it provide valuable services and resources to the business units?

BUSINESS LEVEL AND MARKETING STRATEGY

The business level and marketing strategy describe how a business unit competes within a market, how it creates competitive advantages, and how it achieves its goals. A comprehensive business level and marketing strategy defines:

- the customers the business will serve (who?);
- the geographic markets the business will serve (where?);
- the needs the firm will meet (what?);
- the means the firm will employ (how?);
- the business model that supports profitability (why?); and,
- the speed and sequences of actions (when?).

Each strategy is based on a thorough internal and external analysis and should withstand the following questions (Hambrick & Fredrickson, 2001): Is the strategy aligned to the vision, mission, and corporate strategy? Is the strategy built on core competences and strengths?

Are the differentiators sustainable? Are the five "Ws" and one "H" clearly addressed and internally consistent? Does the company have enough resources to pursue and implement the strategy? Does the strategy exploit opportunities in the market? Is the strategy aligned with the key success factors in the market?

CORPORATE SOCIAL RESPONSIBILITY

As noted, marketing strategies should be anchored in overarching corporate strategies, which are tied to and intended to advance, corporate-level missions and visions. Corporate missions and visions may, or may not, embrace purposes and goals beyond shareholder value and means to that end; however, it is nevertheless important that marketing strategists at least consider the broader issues of corporate social responsibility (CSR). Even if the executive and the firm reject broader obligations, that rejection should be deliberate and explicit, especially given contemporary social and regulatory scrutiny of corporate behavior.

Corporate social responsibility has been defined broadly as a firm taking "actions that appear to further some social good, beyond the interests of the firm and that which is required by law" (McWilliams et al., 2006; McWilliams & Siegel, 2001, p. 117) or as concerns about how businesses should deal with social and public policy matters (Windsor, 2006). Corporate social responsibility subsumes concerns for social and environmental outcomes. The term sustainability—"meeting the needs of the present without compromising the ability of future generations to meet their own needs"—also applies to both social and environmental matters, but is generally understood to focus on sustainable treatment of the natural environment (Brundtland, 1987).

Attitudes about the appropriate role of business in pursuing social and environmental goals have changed across time, but some broad frameworks may be valuable across trends in devising how firms, marketing strategies, and marketing strategists integrate broader social and public policy concerns into strategy formulation and daily decision making. Those include *doing well by doing good*—the idea that acting in a socially and environmentally responsible way may also enhance profitability, stakeholder theory, the triple bottom line, or the three pillars framework.

Doing well by doing good means searching for opportunities to do business in socially and environmentally responsible ways that also enhance profitability and shareholder value. An important point is that shareholder value may not be a short-term outcome, although equity markets may act as if it were. A longer-term perspective on shareholder value is more likely to recognize the merit—in tangible terms of shareholder value and profits or doing *well*—of a broad perspective on corporate responsibility or doing *good*. There is evidence that fair treatment of workers, attention to the community and society, and producing green products all contribute to increased profitability (Falck & Heblich, 2007; Hillman & Keim, 2001; Ozcelik et al., 2008). Bob Willard and John Elkington, experts on corporate sustainability strategies, have organized the various possible benefits of social and environmental responsibility into seven categories:

1. easier hiring of the best talent;
2. higher retention of top talent;
3. increasing employee productivity;
4. reduced expenses in manufacturing;
5. reduced expenses at commercial sites;
6. increased revenue/market share; and,
7. reduced risk, easier financing (Willard & Elkington, 2002).

Stakeholder Theory

Milton Friedman famously said "there is one and only one social responsibility of business—to use its resources and engage in activities designed to increase its profits so long as it stays within the rules of the game, which is to say, engages in open and free competition without deception or fraud" (Friedman, 1970, para. 33). Friedman's words have become emblematic of the extreme position that businesses need consider no consequences of their actions beyond maximizing shareholder value, although his publications are more nuanced, asserting that return maximization is moral because profits and the accompanying jobs and well-suited products are valuable contributions to society in themselves and because maximizing returns on assets is itself a moral obligation (to the equity holders).

In contrast to Friedman's narrow shareholder centered view of the firm's obligations and legitimate concerns, *stakeholder theory* broadens the understanding of the firm's legitimate audiences and responsibilities. It asks two questions: What is the firm's purpose? *And* what is the firm's obligations to its stakeholders? (Freeman, 1984; Freeman et al., 2004). Stakeholders are various groups of people or organizations that have an interest (a stake) in the actions and the success of the firm. Stakeholders can be internal (employees, managers, debt holders, and shareholders) or external (including the community and society, regulators, customers, vendors, and suppliers). Stakeholders vary in their interest in the outcomes of the firm's operations and in its success, as well as in their power or influence over the firm's actions. The fundamental premise of stakeholder analysis is a recognition that firms have always had broader groups of interested parties than just shareholders, and that those stakeholders have varying degrees of legitimate claims on the capabilities and resources of the firm and legitimate power to influence the firm's mission, vision, strategies, and actions. Stakeholder theory also asserts that firms will benefit—*do well*—by considering the interests of a broader array of stakeholders.

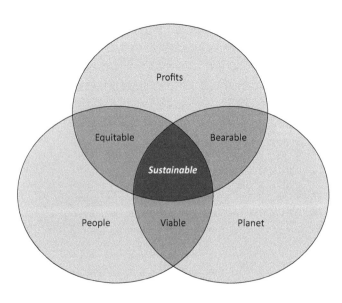

FIGURE 11-1 Triple Bottom Line (Lozano, 2008)

Triple Bottom Line

Profits, people, and the planet (or economic, social, and environmental concerns) have been integrated into "the triple bottom line," as shown in Figure 11-1. This framework highlights three clusters of legitimate concerns for any business, and it is certainly useful for sorting out and clarifying otherwise disorganized considerations and stakeholders. As originally proposed, the triple bottom line asserted that in addition to financial statements, firms should produce environmental and social impact statements. Challenges with this framework include the development of valid metrics for nonfinancial outcomes—social and environmental impact metrics—as well as the question of how performance against those diverse metrics will be motivated and regulated. That is, how will social and environmental performance be measured, and what will happen if the firm performs well or poorly on those measures?

SUMMARY

Organizations need to establish a framework to guide their operations. Such a framework should consist of the company's vision for its future and a mission statement that defines what it is doing. This Note has provided many examples of both. The vision and mission of the organization will be achieved through individual business unit and marketing strategy, and the core values of the organization should shape its culture. It is also important to consider the role of corporate social responsibility in the practices of the organization. Having a clear vision and carefully crafted, sound strategies grounded in social responsibility are critical to success in a highly competitive market environment.

REFERENCES

Brundtland, G. (1987). Our common future—Call for action. *Environmental Conservation*, 14(4), 291–294. doi:10.1017/S0376892900016805

Campbell, A., & Yeung, S. (1991). Creating a sense of mission. *Long Range Planning*, 24(4), 10–20.

Collins, J. C., & Porras, J. I. (1991). Organizational vision and visionary organizations. *California Management Review*, 30–52.

Collins, J. C., & Porras, J. I. (1996). Building your company's vision. *Harvard Business Review*, 74(5), 65.

"Comparably." (2021). *The Coca-Cola Company mission, vision & values*. Comparably. https://www.comparably.com/companies/the-coca-cola-company/mission

Falck, O., & Heblich, S. (2007). Corporate social responsibility: Doing well by doing good. *Business Horizons*, 50(3), 247–254.

Freeman, E. (1984). *Strategic management: A stakeholder approach*. Pitman.

Freeman, E., Wicks, A. C., & Parmar, B. (2004). Stakeholder theory and the corporate objective revisited. *Organization Science*, 15(3), 364–369.

Friedman, M. (1970, September 13). The social responsibility of business is to increase its profits. *The New York Times Magazine*. https://www.nytimes.com/1970/09/13/archives/a-friedman-doctrine-the-social-responsibility-of-business-is-to.html

"Google." (2021). *Google*. Google. https://about.google/intl/.

Grant, R. M. (2008). *Contemporary strategic analysis* (6th ed.). Blackwell Publishing.

Hambrick, D. C., & Fredrickson, J. W. (2001). Are you sure you have a strategy? *Academy of Management Executive*, 15(4), 48–59.

Hillman, A. J., & Keim, G. D. (2001). Shareholder value, stakeholder management, and social issues: What's the bottom line? *Strategic Management Journal*, 22(2), 125–139.

Hinterhuber, H. H. (2004). *Strategische Unternehmensführung, Band 1: Strategisches Denken* (7th ed.). De Gruyter.

Johnson, G., Scholes, K., & Whittington, R. (2008). *Exploring corporate strategy: Text & cases*. Prentice Hall.

Lozano, R. (2008). Envisioning sustainability three-dimensionally. *Journal of Cleaner Production*, 16(17), 1838–1846.

"McDonald's." (2021). *McDonald's Annual Report*. McDonald's. https://corporate.mcdonalds.com/corpmcd/our-company/who-we-are/our-values.html

McWilliams, A., & Siegel, D. (2001). Corporate social responsibility: A theory of the firm perspective. *Academy of Management Review*, 26(1), 117–127.

McWilliams, A., Siegel, D. S., & Wright, P. M. (2006). Corporate social responsibility: Strategic implications. *Journal of Management Studies*, 43(1), 1–18.

Ozcelik, H., Langton, N., & Aldrich, H. (2008). Doing well and doing good: The relationship between leadership practices that facilitate a positive emotional climate and organizational performance. *Journal of Managerial Psychology*, 186–203.

Saint-Exupery, A. de. (1950). *The wisdom of the sands* (2nd ed.). Harcourt Brace & World.

"Walmart." (2021). *Walmart*. Walmart. https://corporate.walmart.com/our-story/our-history

Willard, B., & Elkington, J. (2002). *The sustainability advantage: Seven business case benefits of a triple bottom line*. New Society Publishers.

Windsor, D. (2006). Corporate social responsibility: Three key approaches. *Journal of Management Studies*, 43(1), 93–114.

Figure Credit

A company can create competitive advantage when it is able to perform the individual activities of its *value chain* more effectively (differentiation advantage) or more efficiently (cost advantage) than its competitors. The value chain concept, developed by Harvard Business School Professor Michael Porter (1985), organizes all of the activities a company performs in bringing a product or service to the market, as shown in Figure 12-1.

FIGURE 12-1   The Value Chain

Value chain analysis has become exceedingly popular in the literature. A cursory search produces recent detailed value chain analyses of a wide variety of firms, including Apple, British Airways, IBM, Marks & Spencer, and Walmart. The value chain distinguishes strategically relevant activities that *can* lead to cost or differentiation advantages in the market, and thus influence the product's margin. In addition to identifying for the planner which activities can lead to advantage, the value chain also facilitates identification of which activities for a particular firm *do* lead to advantage—and which do not.

Primary activities are concerned with the creation or delivery of a product or service. Those activities typically include the following:

- *Inbound logistics*: Activities related to receiving, storing, and distributing internally the inputs needed to produce a product or service, including warehouse space, stock control, and internal transportation systems.

- *Operations*: Activities related to the transformation of inputs into products, including production, assembly, packaging, equipment maintenance, quality assurance, etc.
- *Outbound logistics*: Activities concerned with the distribution of the product, such as collection, storage, and delivery to the customer.
- *Marketing and sales*: Activities like market segmentation, targeting, positioning, sales management, advertising, pricing, and product and brand management.
- *Service*: Activities to enhance the value of a product, such as after-sales service, repair and maintenance, customer training, customer care, etc.

Support activities are needed to perform the primary activities and contribute to their effectiveness and efficiency. They are:

- *Firm infrastructure*: All activities and formal systems of planning, finance, quality control, accounting, information management, and so on.
- *Human resource management*: Activities related to the recruitment, training, development, and compensation of people.
- *Technology development*: All activities related to know-how, research and development, product design, process improvement, and IT development.
- *Procurement*: Activities for acquiring resources as inputs for the primary activities, such as the selection of suppliers, negotiation of quality, prices, delivery terms, etc.

The individual activities of the value chain are strategically relevant because each activity can constitute a cost advantage or differentiation advantage, and with each of these activities a company can either gain or lose money, based on how effectively and efficiently it performs compared to the competitors. Companies need to decide on how to position themselves in the industry and in which activities of the value chain they want to engage to create competitive advantages.

In the fashion clothing business, for instance, Zara has assumed a unique position (see Figure 12-2). It spends very little on advertising and has located most of its manufacturing in Spain, rather than outsourcing to low-wage countries. Through its vertically integrated supply chain, the company recognizes and reacts to new market trends quickly. All other activities of the value chain are outsourced (Grant, 2016). These make-or-buy decisions in the value chain are strategically important because they define the potential competitive advantages of the company. As for own-brand global retailers in the mass market (e.g., H&M), quality control in manufacturing is less important so this value chain step is outsourced. In contrast, quality and image are crucial for designer houses like Dior, Gucci, Armani, and therefore they tend to be highly vertically integrated and manufacture their own garments.

Hence, a value chain analyses should answer the following questions:

- *What are the activities of a company's value chain?* A generic value chain (see Figure 12-1) can be adapted to the industry and the company by adding, subtracting, or renaming activities.
- *Which of the activities are strategically important in the industry?* In this step, the strategic value of the activities is assessed. This is important, as the nature of the industry determines which activities are critical to success.

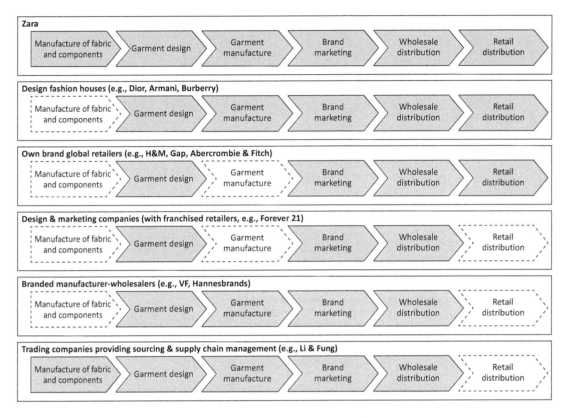

FIGURE 12-2 Value Chains in the Fashion Industry (Grant, 2016)

- *How well do we perform these activities?* By comparing the individual activities with the strongest competitor in the industry, the strengths and weaknesses of the company can be identified.
- *Which activities generate profits and which cause losses?* When costs associated with each activity are analyzed, and when the value generated in each activity can be measured, a company can determine exactly where it generates profits and incurs losses. This analysis requires detailed data that many information systems do not provide.
- *Which activities constitute competitive advantages or core competencies?* When a company shows stronger performance on an activity (more effectiveness or efficiency than a rival) that has high strategic importance, it has a significant competitive advantage. If this activity or process cannot be imitated or substituted, it is a core competence.
- *Which activities should be outsourced?* The value chain analysis can also be used to identify activities that should be outsourced, for example, if a company has little competence in this activity and an outsourcing partner could do it more efficiently or effectively.

Figure 12-3 illustrates the value chain analysis of a pharmaceutical company. This example shows the strategic importance of the primary activities, the budget share of these activities, and the relative performance (compared to the strongest competitor). It illustrates whether the amount of money a company invests in each activity and its performance are in line with the strategic value of this activity.

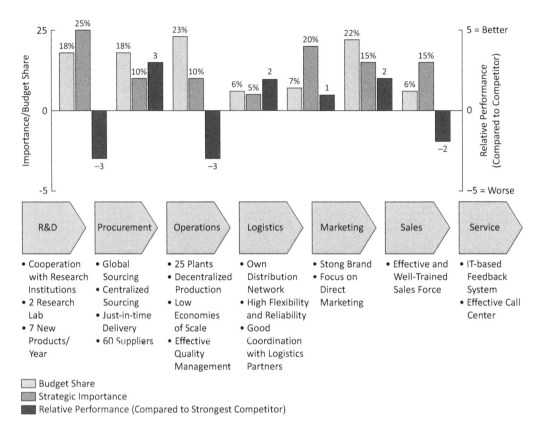

FIGURE 12-3   Analysis of the Value Chain of a Pharmaceutical Company (adapted from Müller-Stewens & Lechner, 2005)

The following major conclusions can be drawn:

- R&D has the highest strategic importance (25%), but it receives only 18% of the budget. As performance of R&D is below competition, more resources should be devoted to this activity to improve it.
- Operations constitute a major problem: It has very little strategic relevance (10%), consumes 23% of the budget, and performance is below competition. This activity obviously is a candidate for outsourcing.
- Also, marketing seems to be unbalanced: It is of central importance (20%), but it receives only 7% of the budget. As marketing, however, performs better compared to competition, no actions are necessary.

Another useful illustration of a value chain analysis is the strategic priority analysis (SPA), as seen in Figure 12-4 (Martilla & James, 1977).

Using a two-dimensional matrix, where importance of the individual value chain activities is depicted along the x-axis and performance along the y-axis, four specific recommendations can be derived:

- Quadrant I: Activities evaluated high both in performance and importance represent the company's key strengths and are opportunities for gaining or maintaining competitive

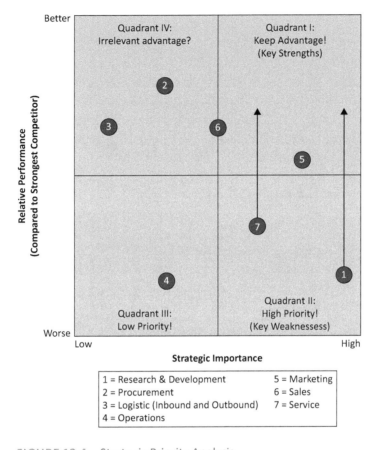

FIGURE 12-4   Strategic Priority Analysis

advantages. Only marketing (and sales) in our example is located in this quadrant. This activity should be rewarded in future strategic planning.

- Quadrant II: Low performance on highly important activities demands immediate attention. We have great risk here. To enhance competitiveness, a company should improve these activities. If these activities are ignored, a serious threat is posed to the business. In our example, research and development, as well as service, need strong efforts to be improved.
- Quadrant III: These activities are both low in performance and importance. Usually, it is not necessary to focus additional effort here. These activities of the value chain are of low priority. In the case of the pharmaceutical company, operations are positioned here. We are not very good at it, but it is not very important strategically.
- Quadrant IV: Activities located in this quadrant are rated high in performance, but low in importance. This implies that resources committed to these attributes would be better employed elsewhere. Procurement and logistics are located in this quadrant. If resources were redeployed to quadrants I and II, the company would probably be better off.

The value chain analysis is an important tool for a number of other analyses, including, for example, identifying competitive advantages.

SUMMARY

Essential to strategic management and marketing is the ability of a company to understand the critical success factors in an industry, its own capabilities and competence, and through which activities it creates competitive advantages. The value chain is a systematic and useful tool to think through the ways in which an organization delivers value to its customers, differentiates its products, and creates profits or losses. Applied in a systematic way (by answering the six questions in this Note), it leads to a profound strategic assessment of the company and to a sound basis for strategic decisions.

REFERENCES

Grant, R. M. (2016). *Contemporary strategy analysis* (9th ed.). John Wiley & Sons.

Martilla, J. A., & James, J. C. (1977). Importance–performance analysis. *Journal of Marketing*, 41(1), 77–79.

Müller-Stewens, G., & Lechner, C. (2005). *Strategisches Management—Wie Strategische Initiativen Zum Wandel Führen*, 3rd ed. Schäffer-Poeschel.

Porter, M. E. (1985). *Competitive advantage: Creating and sustaining superior performance*. Free Press.

Figure Credits

SWOT analysis—the systematic assessment of the firm's strengths, weaknesses, opportunities, and threats, and the recognition of their strategic implications—is a basic, often used tool of strategic thinking (Fehringer, 2007, p. 54). It may also be one of the most often misapplied (Hill & Westbrook, 1997). The basic process of conducting a SWOT analysis begins with the identification of the firm's strengths and weaknesses, essentially an *internal analysis*, and then the examination of opportunities and threats in the environment, or an *external analysis* (Andrews, 1971). Too often, this is where the SWOT ends—with a description of the firm's strengths and weaknesses and an organized list of trends in the environment—and too often the firm's strengths are not really *strengths*, but rather just a list of things the firm does well.

SWOT analysis is only powerful when the analysis of strengths is rigorous. Strengths are not merely things the firm does well; they are things the firm does better than the relevant competition—or could adapt to doing better. Most importantly, the outcome of a SWOT analysis is not merely descriptive—the outcome should be *prescriptive* too. That is, once the description of strengths, weaknesses, opportunities, and threats is complete, SWOT analysis should lead to actions and strategies that are derived from the analysis.

Identifying strengths and weaknesses is principally an internal analysis but involves external comparisons, as well: *Nothing is a strength or a weakness except vis-à-vis the competition.* Opportunities and threats arise from the external environment. Therefore, a full environmental analysis needs to be done before the SWOT analysis can be carried out. Figure 13-1 organizes a SWOT analysis graphically, emphasizing the role of internal and external analyses.

Identifying opportunities and threats involves analysis of many external factors, including political/regulatory factors, the economic environment, social/cultural factors, technology, legal factors, the physical environment (see PESTLE analysis in Chapter II), and the competitive environment. Still, although they may arise from many factors, those external events or

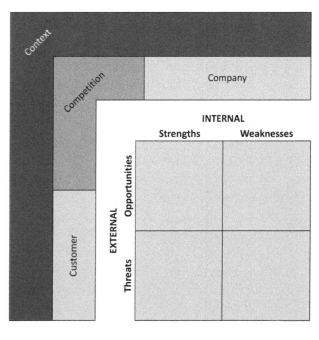

FIGURE 13-1   SWOT Analysis

trends tend to affect a marketing strategy *via their effects on customers*. That is, other external forces usually represent opportunities or threats because of the changes they produce in the way customers meet or can possibly meet a need.

For example, the emergence of computer technologies did not directly affect the typewriter industry, but rather it impacted the ways that consumers met the need to create documents and manage information. Technological change became an opportunity for IBM, a manufacturer of typewriters that developed computer technologies and competitive advantages in computers, while the same technological changes were a threat to other manufacturers of typewriters who did not have and did not develop computer technologies. Therefore, considering and continuously reconsidering customer assessment and segmentation is essential to identifying opportunities and threats.

SEGMENT CHANGES

Market segments are never static. Segments grow, shrink, and change their buying habits, preferences, and buying criterion. Importantly, segments can also split into subsegments or merge or combine into single, larger segments. For example, in many grocery markets, the dominant players were traditionally mid-sized grocers with moderately large assortments. The market entrance of a high-service player, such as Harris Teeter, created a high-service-seeking segment that had not existed before. Consumers could not have been high-service shoppers and might not even have known they valued high-service before a high-service alternative became available. The need for a high-service alternative was what would be labeled "latent"—it may have been there but it was not actively driving shopping behaviors. Low-service/low-price competitors, such as Food Lion and Walmart, did the same thing with price-conscious shoppers. By offering a price-based alternative they *created* a segment based on latent needs, that is, previously unmet needs. Thus, what had been a relatively homogeneous segment of grocery shoppers was split into subsegments based on service and price; undifferentiated stores that do not move with the market could easily be left in the unprofitable middle.

In other instances, previously different segments end up merging into larger segments based on compound benefits of product offerings. In the 1990s, for example, the computer industry differentiated products based on processor speed. Some consumers desired the latest and greatest in terms of CPU speed; others were satisfied with slower speed but required various and different accessories—audio cards, storage devices, and capacity, etc. By the early 21st century, most consumer needs for processing power were met by existing processing speed. Far fewer were demanding cutting-edge speed or even cared to improve the CPU speed. Meanwhile the cost of various accessories such as storage had come down to the point that most manufacturers provided enough memory to satisfy most users. The basis of competition shifted from processing performance to convenience and design, and segment structure shifted. Many consumer segments blurred into a single mass market, and specialty business applications were based on new competitive factors.

ENVIRONMENTAL SCANNING

Most changes in the environment manifest themselves in changes in consumer demand and consumer behavior, but many are tied to some other aspect of the environment. The competition is relevant to the assessment of both strengths and weaknesses (nothing is a strength or a weakness except as it compares with the competition). The competition is also important in identifying opportunities and threats; the competition can pose a threat and can sometimes create an opportunity (e.g., by withdrawing from a segment or market or by blundering a product offering). Whenever an opportunity or threat arises, monitoring the environment is essential to the understanding of changes, trends, and events related to SWOT analyses.

STRATEGIC IMPLICATIONS: EXPLOITING STRENGTHS AND AVOIDING WEAKNESSES

As noted above, SWOT analyses are not merely descriptions; they should direct actions and resources. One fundamental reality is that all four cells in the resulting two-by-two matrix as shown in Figure 13-2 are equally manageable or attractive. The marketing strategist is generally looking for strength–opportunity matches to exploit—that is a basic task of strategy formulation. Thus, SWOT analyses can be a very useful tool at the targeting stage. Weakness–threat fits—a threat in the environment that exposes a weakness of the firm—generally need to be addressed or at least avoided (if avoiding the threat is a viable alternative).

	Strengths	Weaknesses
Opportunities	**Exploit:** Use Strengths to Take Advantage of Opportunities. *This is the Cell to Build Strategies on—Target Opportunities That are a Good Fit with the Firm's Strengths.*	**Develop:** Invest to Improve Weaknesses into Strength to Target the Opportunity and/or Overcome Weaknesses by Taking Advantage of Opportunities.
Threats	**Contend:** Use Strengths to Avoid Threats (Reduce Exposure to Threats), Turn Threats into Neutral Factors, or Even Turn Threats into Opportunities. (Defensive Marketing)	**Address/Avoid:** Address Weaknesses and/or Avoid Threats. If a Threat puts at Risk the Core Business, Then the Weakness Requires Investment; if the Threat does not Jeopardize the Core Business, Then the Weakness-Threat Situation can be Avoided.

FIGURE 13-2   Strategic Implications of SWOT Analysis

CONDUCTING A SWOT ANALYSIS

Conducting a SWOT analysis includes these basic steps:

1. Assess the firm's competitive advantages using the competitive advantage framework and/or comparing the value chain of the firm with that of its competitors. Remember that you are not trying to discover "Is the firm good at this or that?" or "Would the firm like to be the best at this or that?"; the question to answer is "Would the firm be best at this, and how hard will it be for competitors to achieve parity?"
2. Study the environment for opportunities and threats with an emphasis on how changes will affect consumption in the relevant market and with regard to relevant consumer needs.
3. Identify strategic alternatives and imperatives from the fit or match between the strengths and weaknesses—the internal analysis, and the opportunities and threats—the situation assessment.
4. Prioritize, plan, and act.

Figure 13-3 shows a two-by-two matrix that matches strengths and weaknesses with opportunities and threats. Figure 13-4 shows the completed matrix with strengths and weaknesses and opportunities and threats driving strategy and actions. Note that, contrary to the way it is sometimes presented, the *descriptive* stages of a SWOT do *not* fill in the cells of this matrix—they

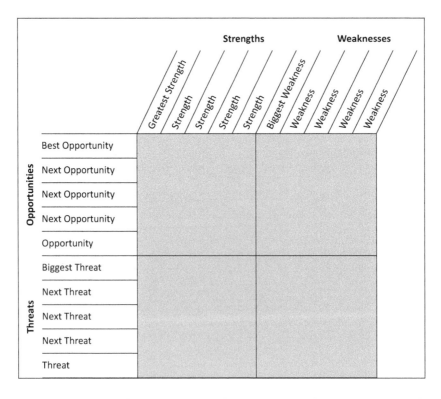

FIGURE 13-3   Matching Strengths and Weaknesses with Opportunities and Threats Matrix

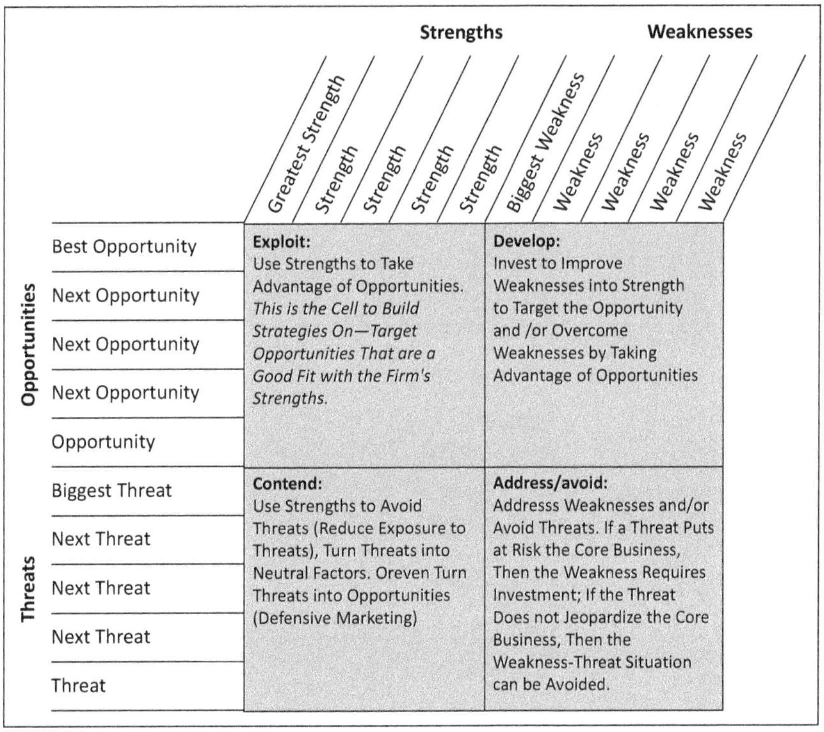

FIGURE 13-4 Matching Strengths and Weaknesses with Opportunities and Threats Example

go on the axes. Similarly, opportunities and threats are listed at the appropriate places along the OT axis. This correctly uses the SWOT framework to match and integrate external factors with internal attributes to drive strategic decisions. Strategic alternatives are listed in the cells, and then action is chosen from the list.

SUMMARY

SWOT analysis is a basic tool of strategic thinking, but it is often misunderstood and misapplied. SWOT analysis is not merely descriptive of the situation; it should be prescriptive as well, directing strategy formulation. SWOT analysis is a *matching* process, meant to find opportunities that match or fit with the firm's strengths. Further, strengths are not things the firm thinks it does well. To be effective foundations for strategy development, strengths must be things the firm does better than the competition—better than what the competition does today or what the competition can develop in the future relative to their competencies, and better than substitutes. Thus, strengths are sustainable competitive advantages—things the firm does that customers value, are rare, and do not have substitutes.

Opportunities and threats are changes in the environment that generally manifest themselves as changes in the way customers will or might meet their needs. Changes in the context (political, economic, social/cultural, or technological/natural environments) or in the competition become opportunities or threats because they impact the way customers can meet their needs. Thus, the SWOT analysis is about exploiting opportunity–strength possibilities, identifying weaknesses that require development, or avoiding a threat, and/or identifying threats to be avoided. All of those *matches* have important action-oriented strategic implications: exploit, develop, contend, or avoid.

REFERENCES

Andrews, K. (1971). *The concept of corporate strategy*. Irwin.

Fehringer, D. (2007). Six steps to better SWOTs. *Competitive Intelligence Magazine*.

Hill, T., & Westbrook, R. (1997). SWOT analysis: It's time for a product recall. *Long Range Planning*, 30(1), 46–52.

Scenario analysis is, essentially, an elaborate "if ... then ... " planning tool. It might be better described as an *"if ... and if ... and if ... and if ..."* [all at the same time], *then ... "* tool in which multiple forces ("drivers" of future conditions) are simultaneously combined to create rich "possible futures" or scenarios (Schoemaker, 1995). If forecasting asks "What will the world be like in the future?" scenario analysis asks "What *could* the world be like ... and *what will we do* if that future comes about?" Scenario analysis also asks "What should we do *now* [or between now and then] to prepare, *just in case* the future looks that way?" For example, if a car manufacturer wants to forecast the market penetration of electric cars, he would base that prediction on several trends that have an impact on the adoption of electric cars and incorporate them in a scenario analysis. Among them are drivers like total cost of ownership (e.g., battery prices), functionality (e.g., battery range), charging infrastructure, subsidies, etc.

In scenario analysis, several concurrent factors or "drivers" are combined to create descriptions of complex possible "futures"—which may not come true, *but could*. In the real world, many factors change at the same time, and many factors influence strategic results; scenario analysis captures that multifaceted nature of reality. Instead of focusing on a single factor, such as total cost of ownership or even the economy, or describing multiple factors separately, scenario analysis brings the factors together to jointly describe a complex strategic context. For example, one scenario for the car manufacturer discussed above might encompass a strong decline in battery prices, a strong increase of battery ranges, very well-developed charging infrastructure, and governments heavily subsidizing electric cars. A more pessimistic future might be modestly lower battery prices, little improvement of battery ranges, and no subsidies. These scenarios' multifaceted nature would enrich analysis in a realistic way and challenge assumptions, as well as broaden strategic thinking.

In the example of electric cars, four drivers with three levels or possible future conditions respectively, could generate 81 different scenarios. Not only would analyzing 81 scenarios be unwieldy, it would also be unnecessary. It is best to develop three or four complex scenarios for further consideration. Each plausible and internally consistent (but not real) scenario is then analyzed against the firm's strategies and possible strategies, and the most important drivers of the future and prudent actions to prepare for the future can be identified. By using scenario analysis, it becomes less important that any forecast—for battery prices or any other driver—be precisely right. Because several possible outcomes for each driver are included in the analysis, the process highlights the range of possibilities and the possible impacts of each driver, as well as helping to identify feasible strategic responses to those eventualities.

SCENARIO ANALYSIS PROCESS

As powerful as it is, scenario analysis can nevertheless be reduced to a few basic steps (Mercer, 1995):

1. Define the scope of the analysis.
2. Identify the drivers of future strategic contexts.
3. Select specific levels, changes, or events within each driver to frame the future.
4. Combine those drivers and levels/changes/events to develop comprehensive scenarios.
5. Select three or four scenarios for analysis.
6. Analyze and plan for each selected scenario.
7. Integrate results to identify near- and long-term directions, actions, and investments and to appraise strategic alternatives.

Define Scope

Most scenario analyses in marketing strategy are focused on specific product offerings and their target markets. In order to encourage deep analysis, creative thinking, and relevance, spell out at the outset the sector (markets/industries), the environmental/internal factors to be considered (at a broad level, such as economic, social, competitive, etc.), and the specific time frame. Scenario analysis can accommodate a variety of time frames, but it is most useful for longer term strategizing, and long-term horizons. Specific forecasts about various factors in the environment (interest rates, consumer preferences, attitudes, etc.) may be quite accurate in the near term, but scenario analysis is more realistic and accurate in the long-term because it accommodates the inherent uncertainty of long-term forecasts. In our case, a car manufacturer wants to create scenarios for the market penetration of electric cars (EVs) in 2030 in Germany.

Identify Drivers of Future Strategic Contexts

What factors or forces could drive the firm's future or the industry—and which of those drivers are most important? Searching for the three to five most important drivers involves consideration of the various elements of the situation (to include the PESTLE domains of political/regulatory, economic, social/cultural, technical/physical, legal, and environmental, as discussed in Chapter I) and consideration of internal factors and initiatives with uncertain outcomes, such as new product development projects and human resource training initiatives. That is, all drivers need not be external, but most uncontrollable drivers are external. In the example developed briefly above, the main drivers of market adoption are total cost of ownership (e.g., battery prices, electricity prices, maintenance costs), functionality of electric cars (e.g., battery range, product range), charging infrastructure, and regulations (e.g., subsidies, CO_2 limits).

Select Specific Levels, Changes, or Events within Each Driver

Many drivers have a continuous range of possible outcome levels—not all equally likely, but certainly a wide range of values the driver could have in the future. For example, inflation is, in reality, a continuum of percentage changes that can range from 0 (or even negative in those rare instances of deflation) to 5%, 10%, or 15%—and the reality will certainly be measurable down to the tenth or hundredth of a percentage point (e.g., 6.9% or 3.48%). Creating specific scenarios for analysis and planning requires selecting a few specific levels of each driver to represent the whole range (e.g., low inflation will be 2%, moderate inflation will be 6%, and high inflation will be 12%). The chance that the analysts will have selected the exact level that eventually occurs is very low—but the chance that scenario analysis can select a set of specific values that, taken together, represent the range of possibilities is very high. The specific levels selected for analysis are not necessarily the "most likely"; they should be the levels that insure that the planning process considers the whole range of possibilities. They should also include levels or conditions that, even if unlikely, would have extreme impacts. Examples for the levels of drivers in our case in 2030 could be battery prices of EUR 120/kWh, EUR 90/kWh, or EUR 65/kWh. The European Union could set CO_2 limits for fleets at 90g/km, 65g/km, or 49g/km.

Combine Drivers into Scenarios

The next step is to select levels from each driver and combine those into internally consistent scenarios. Levels of certain drivers may be incompatible with levels of other drivers and are thereby internally inconsistent; national competition may not enter a market during a recession or downturn in the housing market. Therefore, high interest rates would be internally inconsistent with intensification of the competitive environment—that scenario would not make sense. In our case, it would be unlikely that the EU would not subsidize electric cars, as electric cars are needed to reach the CO_2 limits. So, internally consistent scenarios would include low CO_2 limits and high subsidies or high CO_2 limits and low subsidies.

Select Scenarios for Further Analysis

A very few drivers can quickly create an unmanageable number of scenarios (two drivers with two levels each and two drivers with three levels each yield 36 scenarios). Therefore, three or four scenarios should be chosen that frame the range of possible outcomes. That is, all of the possible scenarios define the universe of possibilities—but the analysis should consider a sample from that universe. In that way, it is possible to dig deep into the selected scenarios rather than to skim a wider range. The ultimate reality will be different than *any* of those three or four fictitious scenarios—but three or four is enough to facilitate consideration of the range of possible futures and the implications of those possibilities for current and potential strategies. At this stage, it is useful to *name* each selected scenario to help organize and enliven discussions, and each scenario should be expanded into a fully-developed narrative to enrich discussions. For our example of the market penetration of electric cars, three scenarios were developed, a pessimistic one, a realistic one, and an optimistic one (see Table 14-1), resulting in different numbers of new car registrations in each of them (see Figure 14-1).

Analyze Each Scenario

"If these drivers worked out in this pattern to create this scenario, then a _____ strategy for this firm would be best, a _____ strategy will meet challenges in _____. The firm would want to have _____ between now and then." For each scenario, how would the firm answer those related questions? Essentially, the analysts (or cross-functional team of strategists) assume the scenario will come

TABLE 14-1 Scenarios for Market Penetration of Electric Cars

PESSIMISTIC SCENARIO: 450,000 NEW EV REGISTRATIONS IN 2030	REALISTIC SCENARIO: 900,000 NEW EV REGISTRATIONS IN 2030	OPTIMISTIC SCENARIO: 1,300,000 NEW EV REGISTRATIONS IN 2030
Total cost of ownership: Battery prices = EUR 120/kWh, gas prices are low, gas powered cars are an economical substitute for EVs	*Total cost of ownership:* Battery prices = EUR 90/kWh, prices of EVs and ICVs (internal combustion vehicles) at the same level, EVs have lower maintenance costs	*Total cost of ownership:* Battery prices = EUR 65/kWh, EV prices lower than ICV prices
Functionality: Battery range for most consumers too low, too small product range of EVs	*Functionality:* Battery ranges over 600km, EVs for all major market segments are offered	*Functionality:* EVs offered for all market segments and market niches, very long battery ranges
Charging infrastructure: Not enough charging stations, different EV charging standards, no user-friendly payment systems	*Charging infrastructure:* 250,000 charging stations of which 25,000 superchargers; Apps show availability of charging stations in real time and allow easy payment	*Charging infrastructure:* 500,000 charging stations of which 50,000 superchargers; Apps show availability of charging stations in real time and allow easy payment
Regulations: CO2 limits for fleets 90g/km, very few subsidies for EVs, very limited bans of internal combustion vehicles (ICV)	*Regulations:* CO2 limits for fleets 65g/km, moderate increase of mineral oil taxes, some cities ban internal combustion vehicles (ICV)	*Regulations:* CO2 limits for fleets 49g/km, most cities ban internal combustion vehicles (ICV), massive increase of mineral oil taxes

Note. Table source: Bratzel, S., Thömmes, J., & Tellermann, R. (2017). *Marktentwicklung von Elektrofahrzeugen für das Jahr 2030: Deutschland, EU, USA und China*. Gladbach: Center of Automotive Management.

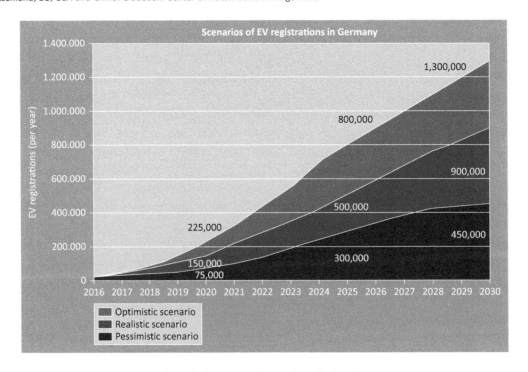

FIGURE 14-1   EV Registrations in Germany (Bratzel et al., 2017)

true and plan for it. These analyses should consider the resulting industry structure (within a fiveforces framework or otherwise), competitive actions and reactions, key uncertainties and risks, and the resulting impacts on the firm and its offerings. Existing strategies and alternative strategies should be tested within the "reality" of each scenario: How will this strategy work in the future envisioned in the scenario? What would have to be done to make the strategy work better? What alternative strategy would work well?

Integrate Results

The final step in scenario analysis is integrating the results of all of the scenarios/plans and gleaning insights from commonalities and differences across them. Some insights come from what is very likely or what is common to many results, but others may come from the anomalies—the things that are true only if a certain set of outcomes occurs—and from considering very unlikely but potentially impactful possible futures. That is, the questions facing the analysts are not only about what strategy the firm would want to have pursued if the future ended up looking like any given scenario, likely or improbable; scenario analysis also offers the chance to look at low-cost/low-risk investments to position the firm to take advantage of improbable but potentially lucrative opportunities. Furthermore, it can also enable a company to take early, cost-effective steps to address potential threats and to preclude or cope with catastrophic scenarios.

The planning against the whole set of scenarios will identify likely events that should be dealt with, as well as unlikely but potentially impactful events that should be prepared for regardless of their improbability. That is, things that are likely to occur require planning even if the impacts are not extraordinary; and unlikely events that would *change the firm's world* if they occurred also require planning because of their potential impact.

SUMMARY

Scenario analysis is a powerful framework for formalizing situation assessment, surfacing assumptions and important uncertainties, dealing with uncertainty and clarifying possible future events, and determining the firm's possible and preferred responses to those events. Analyzing across scenarios and plans allows the firm to identify near- and long-term directions, actions, and investments and to appraise strategic alternatives. Scenario analysis clarifies the forces or drivers that shape *or could shape* the future operating context, promotes creative, long-range thinking, and produces robust, action-oriented *contingency plans*.

Regardless of the industry or the times, scenario analysis has the capacity to develop effective responses to concurrently evolving forces and for unlikely but potentially debilitating disruptions. Scenario analysis is done best by diverse teams of managers and experts *brainstorming*. The more diverse the team in terms of functional area (marketing, operations, research and development, etc.), geographic location, and perspective, the broader the scope of the thinking will be—and broadening the scope of the analysis (in terms of time horizon and regarding elements of the environment considered) is critical to the quality of the outcomes.

REFERENCES

Bratzel, S., Thömmes, J., & Tellermann, R. (2017). *Marktentwicklung von Elektrofahrzeugen für das Jahr 2030: Deutschland, EU, USA und China*. Gladbach: Center of Automotive Management.

Mercer, D. (1995). Scenarios made easy. *Long Range Planning, 28*(4), 81–86.

Schoemaker, P. J. H. (1995). Scenario planning: A tool for strategic thinking. *Sloan Management Review, 36*(2), 25–50.

Figure Credit

NOTES ALIGNED WITH CHAPTER III: FOCUS ON STRATEGY FORMULATION

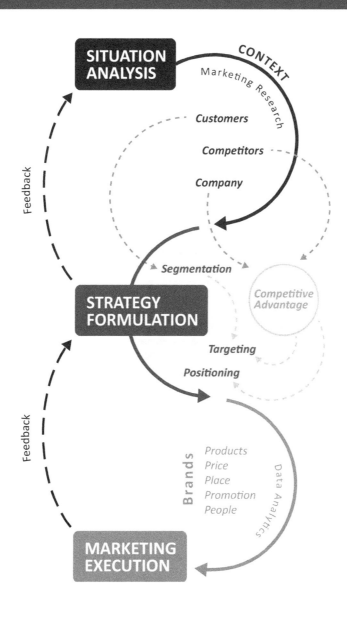

COMPETITIVE STRATEGIES

Why are certain organizations more successful than others? What is the secret of earning above-average returns? In the strategic management literature there are two broad schools of thought that attempt to address these fundamental questions: the market-based view and the resource-based view. The market-based view assumes that success depends on characteristics of the market or industry the firm competes in (industry attractiveness and industry structure). The resource-based view regards a company's success as largely self-determined, dependent on its unique resources and capabilities. These two paradigms imply very different strategy formulation processes with fundamentally different starting points, as highlighted in Figure 15-1.

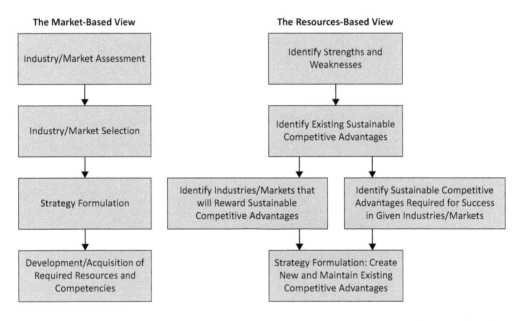

FIGURE 15-1   Distinct Strategy Formulation Processes Underlying the Market-Based and Resource-Based Views (Adapted from Hitt et al. 2005)

THE MARKET-BASED VIEW

Michael Porter's five forces analysis (see Note 4) is the seminal model of a market-based view of strategy development. In this framework, the interplay of five forces (bargaining power of suppliers, bargaining power of customers, threat of substitute products, rivalry among competing firms, and threat of new entrants) determine an industry's attractiveness, or its competitive intensity and profitability. For example, in an industry with low barriers to entry (high threat of new entrants) such as the restaurant sector, competition is intense and profit margins are generally low, making it a somewhat unattractive industry for new investment. Thus, from the market-based perspective, the firm's success depends on its abilities to position itself in an attractive industry, to adapt to industry structures, and to develop strategies accordingly. Therefore, in the market-based view, strategy development should progress through the following four steps:

1. The company's environment should be analyzed (macro environment, industry, competitors).
2. The company should select attractive industries that promise above-average returns.
3. Strategies that are aligned with the industry structure should be developed.
4. The company should develop or acquire the necessary resources and capabilities to implement those strategies.

THE RESOURCE-BASED VIEW

The resource-based view takes a very different view of strategy development and of the determinants of firm success. It argues that each company is a collection of unique resources and capabilities, and that those strategic resources of the company are the sources of above-average returns. In this framework, *unique* entails not only being different (unlike any other) but also being *valued* (being something that customers want and will pay for) and being better than the competition. Thus, a company has a sustainable competitive advantage if it has resources or capabilities that are:

- valuable in the market (i.e., create value to the customers);
- rare (no other competitor has theses resources);
- not imitable or substitutable (competitors have difficulty obtaining or developing similar/ substitute resources or capabilities); and
- transferable to other markets or products (adapted from Barney, 1991).

When a firm possesses such sustainable competitive advantages it is, in a sense, a monopolist; it owns resources or capabilities (competitive advantages) that create value to the customers and cannot be imitated or substituted for by competitors. Of course, *sustainable* is a relative and allusive quality; few advantages are truly sustainable in a long-term sense, and most are frustratingly short-lived. Within the resource-based paradigm, strategy development follows a completely different logic and process, focusing on these four steps:

1. Strengths and weaknesses of the company are analyzed.
2. Based on strengths and weaknesses, competitive advantages are identified.
3. Industries, markets, and especially market segments are targeted in which these competitive advantages can be exploited.
4. Strategies for these industries and markets are developed and implemented based on competitive advantages.

Thus, the resource-based view of the firm is less about *where* you compete and more about *how* you compete. While it is still crucial to understand the company's environment and its industry (the core of the market-based view), the resource-based view has proven to be more effective in predicting firm-level success. Further, in most strategic marketing situations, choosing the industry is not an option; the imperative is on winning in the given industry, and the resource-based view of the firm starts with this perspective.

COMPETITIVE ADVANTAGES

In the long run, a company will be successful if it is able to deliver higher customer value than its competitors. This performance can either result from bringing a product onto the market more cost efficiently, and, therefore, more cheaply, or from differentiating the product through a unique bundle of benefits for which the customer is willing to pay a price premium. A company has a sustainable competitive advantage if superior customer value is delivered more effectively and/or efficiently through a unique bundle of capabilities and resources that competitors do not have and cannot copy or substitute for with other capabilities and resources. Hence, answering the following questions is a practical three-step approach toward understanding and to identifying competitive advantages:

1. What do we do better than the competition? What are our competitive advantages?
2. Which resources or capabilities are the sources of these advantages?
3. Which of these resources or capabilities are valuable, unique, and not imitable, yet are transferable to other industries or markets?

Step 1: Determining Competitive Advantages

The first step is to identify a prioritized list of customers' buying criteria (product features, product quality, service, convenience, brand image, price, etc.). Qualitative and open-ended methods are well-suited to generating the set of criteria, and more quantitative methods, including ranking tasks and conjoint analysis, are proficient at gauging the weights customers place on the various attributes. Figure 15-2 presents a set of hypothetical attributes or criteria for costume jewelry and the accompanying weights, which total 100%. In any application of this analysis, it is likely that the strategic marketer will want to see these attributes and especially their weights by segment. That is, different customers place different importance on various attributes, and understanding those differences at the segment or individual customer level is essential.

Next, a comparison should be done from the customer's perspective. It does not matter whether the manager believes the firm is good at something; what matters is what the customers think or perceive. Therefore, gauging customer perceptions instead of accepting an expert opinion or managerial viewpoint is essential. Figure 15-3 shows a hypothetical strength-and-weaknesses profile for a costume jewelry producer. Its competitive advantages against the strongest competitors are the fashionable design, the

Buying Criteria	Weight
Fashionable Design	30
Product Quality	20
Brand Image	15
Price	25
Assortment	10

FIGURE 15-2 Possible Buying Criteria and Importance Weights for Costume Jewelry

Buying Criteria	Weight	Performance Compared to Strongest Competitor (−2 = Much Worse, 0 = About the Same, +2 = Much Better)					Weighted Score
		−2	−1	0	+1	+2	
Fashionable Design	30					●	60
Product Quality	20				●		20
Brand Image	15				●		30
Price	25		●				−25
Assortment	10		●				−10

FIGURE 15-3   Competitive Advantages from the Customer's Perspective

brand image, and the product quality; its weaknesses are the high price and (off-target or limited) assortment.

As previously discussed in Note 12, it is important to consider the sources of competitive advantages by analyzing a company's value chain (Porter, 1985). This model distinguishes *primary* value-adding activities the firm performs along the flow of goods from inputs (raw materials) to outputs (products), marketing and sales, and support services, as well as the essential *support* activities such as human resource management and research and development that facilitate those primary activities. The essential question is how well does the firm perform the various activities of the value chain vis-à-vis the competition?

A company can decide how each of the operational activities is carried out and which of these activities can be outsourced to other companies. Depending on how well a company performs on activities compared to its competitors, it can develop specific strengths and weaknesses and create and capture more value by being more effective or efficient than the competitors. The strategic importance of the activities depends on the industry. In the pharmaceutical industry, research and development are critical success factors. In retailing, procurement and inbound logistics are of strategic importance. For a consulting firm, human resource management is essential. Hence, to identify strengths and weaknesses, a company should rate the strategic importance of each activity and then examine each activity relative to the competitors' abilities (see Figure 15-4).

The company in this example has three clear competitive advantages: technology development, operations, and marketing and sales. In the next step, we analyze the resources and competencies that are the source of these advantages.

Step 2: Sources of Competitive Advantages

What leads to individual competitive advantages—from both a customer and value chain perspective? To answer this question, we try to identify those resources and skills that account for the company's strengths and competitive advantages. Step-by-step, the drivers for each competitive advantage are examined by asking questions like the following: Why do we have advantages in operations? Why are we able to continuously deliver higher product quality and more fashionable design than our competitors?

Tangible resources can be grouped into financial and physical resources (Grant, 2005). Financial resources can constitute a competitive advantage if companies have access to inexpensive capital

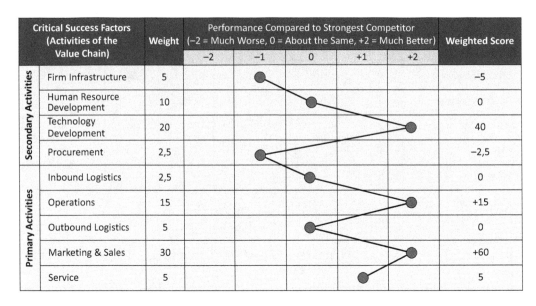

Critical Success Factors (Activities of the Value Chain)		Weight	Performance Compared to Strongest Competitor (−2 = Much Worse, 0 = About the Same, +2 = Much Better)					Weighted Score
			−2	−1	0	+1	+2	
Secondary Activities	Firm Infrastructure	5						−5
	Human Resource Development	10						0
	Technology Development	20						40
	Procurement	2,5						−2,5
Primary Activities	Inbound Logistics	2,5						0
	Operations	15						+15
	Outbound Logistics	5						0
	Marketing & Sales	30						+60
	Service	5						5

FIGURE 15-4   Value Chain Analysis

or can more easily generate funds for their investments and strategies. Physical resources (e.g., locations, plants, raw materials) can either constitute a cost advantage or access to high quality inputs. However, for many companies, intangible resources (e.g., technologies, reputation, human resources) are more important than tangible resources (Grant, 2005).

Tangible and intangible resources are not productive on their own; they only can constitute competitive advantages if companies are able to deploy them. As some companies are better able to exploit resources or are more effective in combining them, such distinctive capabilities can provide the basis of superior performance. Such distinctive capabilities can be found in each functional area, as outlined in Table 15-1.

Table 15-2 shows how sources of competitive advantages can be identified, as well as the resources and capabilities that lie behind the competitive advantages.

Competitive advantages have the following characteristics: they are valuable, rare, not imitable and not substitutable, and are transferable to other markets or applications. Therefore, each source of competitive advantage is now investigated in light of these requirements.

Step 3: Transferable Competitive Advantages

After having identified the sources of competitive advantages, that is, resources and capabilities, we take each of them and try to answer the following questions:

- Is this resource or capability valuable, that is, does it lead to a clear competitive advantage in the market?
- Is this resource or capability rare, that is, does no competitor own this resource or capability?
- Is this resource not imitable or substitutable, that is, do competitors have difficulties obtaining or developing them?
- Is this resource transferable to other markets or products, that is, can it be leveraged and constitute a competitive advantage in new markets?

TABLE 15-1 Examples of Capabilities (Adapted from Grant, 2005)

FUNCTIONAL AREA	SKILL
Corporate function	• Financial control • Strategic management of business units • Innovativeness • Multidivisional coordination • Acquisition management
Management information	• Well-functioning management information system and MIS-based decision-making
Research and development	• Research capabilities • Product development competences • Process development competences
Logistics	• Logistics competence • Process control • Interface management
Production	• Exploiting economies of scale • Continuous improvement • Flexibility
Product design	• Design skills
Marketing	• Brand management • Ability to react to market requirements • Customer relationship management
Distribution	• Efficiency in acquisition and order processing • Speed of distribution • Quality of customer service

TABLE 15-2 Competitive Advantages and Underlying Resources (Adapted from Grant, 2005)

COMPETITIVE ADVANTAGES FROM CUSTOMER'S POINT OF VIEW	RESOURCES AND CAPABILITIES BEHIND THESE ADVANTAGES
Fashionable design	• Trend competence: Ability to forecast trends in the fashion industry through a worldwide network with the leading trend researchers, designers, and artists
Product quality	• Technical sophistication of the plant and quality management system • Unique grinding technology that leads to superior quality of crystals
Brand image	• Marketing competence: Highly skilled and experienced marketing people • Decades of producing superior quality and excellent brand management skills • Customer relationship management (CRM) system
COMPETITIVE ADVANTAGES IN THE VALUE CHAIN	**RESOURCES AND CAPABILITIES BEHIND THESE ADVANTAGES**
Technology development	• First mover in the development of the grinding technology with continuous investment and improvement of the technology • Highly skilled engineers
Operations	• Technical sophistication of the plant and quality management system
Marketing and sales	• Highly skilled and experienced marketing people
Service	• Well-organized distribution and customer service department

Figure 15-5 shows a simple tool that helps to identify competitive advantages based on these four questions. If resources or capabilities are valuable but not rare, they do not constitute a competitive advantage (e.g., highly skilled and experienced marketing people in our example). If they are valuable and rare, but easy to imitate or substitute, they constitute only a short-term advantage (e.g., a sophisticated plant and quality management system). If they are valuable, rare, and difficult to imitate or substitute, these resources or capabilities are the source of a long-term competitive advantage; if they are also transferable to other markets or products they can be leveraged for a diversification strategy (e.g., grinding technology). The trend forecasting competence and the unique grinding technology are both competitive advantages, and as they can be transferred to different markets or products (e.g., crystal figurines, jewelry, accessories, or home décor), where these competences are exactly needed, they can be leveraged to build the source of sustainable competitive advantage.

Resource or Capability	Is This Resource or Capability Valuable?		Is This Resource or Capability Rare?		Is This Resource or Capability Difficult to Imitate or Substitute?		Is This Resource or Capability Transferable?		Evaluation
	YES	NO	YES	NO	YES	NO	YES	NO	
Highly Skilled and Experienced Marketing Team	[X]	[ ]	[ ]	[X]	[ ]	[X]	[X]	[ ]	No Competitive Advantage
Trend Forecasting Competence	[X]	[ ]	[X]	[ ]	[X]	[ ]	[X]	[ ]	Core Competence!
Sophisticated Plants and Quality Management System	[X]	[ ]	[X]	[ ]	[ ]	[X]	[X]	[ ]	Short-Term Advantage
Unique Grinding Technology	[X]	[ ]	[X]	[ ]	[X]	[ ]	[X]	[ ]	Core Competence!
Brand Image: Superior Quality, Brand Management Skills ...	[X]	[ ]	[X]	[ ]	[ ]	[X]	[X]	[ ]	Short-Term Advantage
Customer Relationship Management System	[X]	[ ]	[ ]	[X]	[ ]	[X]	[X]	[ ]	No Competitive Advantage
Highly Skilled Engineers	[X]	[ ]	[X]	[ ]	[ ]	[X]	[X]	[ ]	Short-Term Advantage
Excellent Distribution System and Customer Service's dpmt	[X]	[ ]	[X]	[ ]	[ ]	[X]	[X]	[ ]	Short-Term Advantage

FIGURE 15-5   Identifying Competitive Advantages

Although many management teams hold somewhat inflated views of their firm's competitive advantages, usually those views are based on, at best, casual assessment. Identifying sustainable competitive advantage is not as easy as asking "What are we good at?" First, *good at* must be a relative assessment; specifically, it is relative to the competition. In addition, it is not enough to be good at something. To qualify as an advantage, this "something" must be valuable to some set of customers and must also be unable to be matched by the competition, either by imitation or substitution. Finally, because of the imperative for growth in contemporary strategic management, the very best competitive advantages will also have *legs*; that is, they'll be exploitable in other, new markets too.

The process of identifying sustainable competitive advantages begins with the identification of strengths and weaknesses. These strengths and weaknesses must be linked with the underlying resources and capabilities that generate the advantages. Finally, the strengths must be filtered against the further criteria of being valuable, not easily imitated or substituted, and transferable. Then the firm can either find markets that will reward its current advantages or identify new advantages it should create in order to achieve success in its given markets (or, as is most often the case, do *both*). Thus, the resource-based view of strategy, and inside-out perspective, analyzes what the firm does best and what it needs to do best to target receptive industries, markets, and segments.

Once competitive advantages are established, companies need to take measures to sustain them. Competitive advantages erode because of competition, either through innovation or imitation (Grant, 2016). Companies can effectively prevent the erosion of their competitive advantages by creating isolating mechanisms (Rumelt, 1984). These isolating mechanisms can be derived from the imitation process. In order to imitate, competitors need to be aware of the advantage, they need to have enough motivation to imitate, they need to be able to identify the source of the advantage, and finally they need acquire or develop the necessary resources and capabilities. In each of these four stages, a company can create imitation barriers by answering the following questions:

- *Identification of advantage*: How can we obscure financial performance so that competitors do not become aware of my advantage?
- Can we reduce the competitor's motivation to imitate by sending aggressive signals of deterrence or by pre-emption (e.g. creating market entry barriers, securing key resources, patenting innovations, etc.)?
- Can we base our competitive advantages on a complex bundle of resources and capabilities so that competitors have difficulties identifying the sources of our advantages (causal ambiguity)?
- Can we build our advantages on resources and capabilities that are immobile, rare, and difficult to imitate?

SUMMARY

There are two broad approaches to assessing and developing strategies: the market-based view and the resource-based view. The market-based view is an "outside-in" perspective; it begins with the assessment and selection of *where to compete*. The resource-based view is an "inside-out" process that begins with the assessment of *how to compete* using the firm's strengths, weaknesses, and competitive advantages. It is important to understand the industries and markets in which the firm competes. Although at certain junctures in the firm's growth it may be possible to actually select industries and markets in which to compete, making industry/market analysis even more central to strategy formulation, by far the more common circumstances that a strategic market faces involve succeeding in pre-determined competitive contexts. Succeeding within a given competitive fray is an ongoing challenge to most marketing strategists.

Identifying sustainable competitive advantages requires understanding the firm's strengths and weaknesses and tying those strengths to the underlying resources and competencies that generate or support them. Strengths are only sustainable competitive advantages if they are valued by customers and hard or impossible to imitate or substitute by the competition. The optimal competitive advantages are extended or transferred to new industries or new markets, especially in today's growth-oriented markets.

REFERENCES

Barney, J. B., & Hesterle, W. S. (2008). *Strategic management and competitive advantage*. Pearson Publishing.

Barney, J. (1991). Firm resources and sustained competitive advantage. *Journal of Management*, 17(1), 99–120.

Grant, R. M. (2005). *Contemporary strategy analysis* (5th ed.). Blackwell Publishing.

Grant, R. M. (2016). *Contemporary strategy analysis* (9th ed.). John Wiley & Sons.

Hitt, M. A., Ireland, R. D., & Hoskisson, R. E. (2015). *Strategic management: Competitiveness & globalization concepts and cases*. Thompson South-Western.

Porter, M. E. (1985). *Competitive advantage: Creating and sustaining superior performance*. Free Press.

Rumelt, R. P. (1984). Towards a strategic theory of the firm. *Competitive Strategic Management*, 26(3), 556–570.

GENERIC STRATEGIES—ADVANTAGE AND SCOPE

Over the years, many experts have tried to summarize all possible competitive strategies within some reduced set of characteristics (dimensions) and/or types (categories). These efforts have generally converged on two fundamental characteristics of strategies that together delineate a limited number of categories of strategies. This précis of *generic* strategies has, as a rule, included a few broad types (Porter, 1985, 1996; Treacy & Wiersema, 1995). Although these characteristics and types have been labeled differently by different authors, their basic content appears robust across perspectives; the underlying logic makes it clear that, while strategies can be described in innumerable ways and countless specific strategies are feasible, these high-level characteristics and types are a useful starting place for understanding what strategies are possible, how they differ, and how they relate to each other.

COMPETITIVE ADVANTAGE

Porter (1985) offers three generic strategies for competing in an industry: cost leadership, differentiation, and focus (see Figure 16-1). Each of these strategies involves a different route relative to the type of competitive advantage desired and the scope of the strategic target segment. Ultimately, an organization must make a definitive choice about the type of competitive advantage to pursue and the intended scope. "Being 'all things to all people' is a recipe for strategic mediocrity and below-average performance, because it often means that a firm has no competitive advantage at all" (Porter, 1985, p. 12).

The first characteristic through which all strategies can be described is the *basis of competition* or competitive advantage. Strategies can either emphasize product differentiation (which can take many forms, elaborated on below) or they can pursue cost leadership (which looks like price leadership from the customers' perspective). This distinction is logical; you can either compete on cost or you can compete on something else. The other principal way strategies can be differentiated is with regard to their competitive scope—the breadth of the market and range of customer segments that the strategy intends to

FIGURE 16-1   Generic Strategies

serve. This Note describes these two dimensions and also the types of strategies that they delineate: differentiation, cost leadership, and niche strategies. These are *generic strategies* because, at this high level of description, they distinguish a few very basic strategies that encompass all possible strategies. It is worth reiterating that there are almost infinite specific forms a particular strategy can take within these broad categories.

Porter (1996) has argued that that "[a] company can outperform its rivals only if it can establish a difference that it can preserve" (p. 3). IKEA, McDonald's and Walmart have advantages because of their size and the corresponding benefits of scale that give them the lowest cost structure amongst their competitors. Proctor & Gamble has unrivaled marketing and branding skills. Apple has similarly unparalleled design capabilities. Amazon has a sophisticated value chain that yields cash flow, efficiency, and high-speed customization. *These companies are successful because they were able to create a sustainable difference.* Creating a difference means either bringing an identical or similar product or service to market more cost effectively than the competitors (and therefore being able to charge the customer less or reap higher margins) or bundling unique benefits in an offering for which customers are willing to pay a price premium. These two strategies, cost leadership and differentiation, are fundamentally different approaches to forging competitive advantage.

Cost Leadership

A cost leader typically offers a standardized, no-frills product because adding "frills" adds costs. Walmart is the classic cost leader, continuously innovating to reduce costs in its procurement, distribution, and logistics systems. The strategic objective of the cost leader is to deliver the products at lowest costs, to sell those products at the lowest prices, and to communicate that value proposition to price-sensitive markets. Such a positioning generally requires producing an undifferentiated offering (a commodity) and having a zealous focus on reducing costs. Potential sources of cost advantages are summarized in Table 16-1; many of those sources of cost advantage are tied to achieving scale advantage—that is, to being the biggest or among the biggest competitors in

TABLE 16-1 Sources of Cost Advantages (Adapted from Grant, 2005)

Economies of Scale	• Spreading fixed costs over large volume • Purchasing discounts/leverage • Specialization of labor • Specialized machines and technology
Economies of Scope	• Shared resources between products • Pooled negotiation power • Coordinated strategies between business units • Vertical integration • Combined business creation
Experience Curve Effects	• Improved skills and routines • Improved quality
Production Techniques	• Process innovation • Automation
Product Design	• Standardization of designs and components • Design to manufacture
Input Costs	• Location advantages • Access to low-cost inputs

the market. Usually there is room for only one cost leader per industry; if there is more than one, a price war is likely. Market share becomes crucial for organizations seeking to become, and remain, the cost leader because cost leadership, by definition, entails gaining competitive advantages through having the lowest costs, and low costs are related to high scale, which depends on high market share.

Cost leaders' products are highly standardized, with no-frills, and are usually produced for mass markets. Operational efficiency and process improvement are critical—the cost leader must excel in these areas. The cost-leader organization must run as a well-oiled machine to avoid inefficiencies, and its structure therefore is usually formal, standardized, and mechanistic. The dominant values are cost-consciousness, efficiency, and risk aversion. Cost leaders usually adopt a top–down approach and are authoritative to enforce smooth flowing, standardized processes, and consistency.

Differentiation

An advantage can be created when a company is able to deliver a superior product or service to the customer, for which the customer is willing to pay a premium because it better fulfills their needs. Superior value can stem from higher quality, better service, more features, more convenience, better brand image, and other distinctive qualities. Table 16-2 summarizes selected sources of differentiation, including product and service quality, image factors (such as brand personality), and distribution qualities,

TABLE 16-2 Common Basis of Differentiation

QUALITY IN GOODS[1]

- Performance
- Features
- Reliability
- Conformance
- Durability
- Serviceability
- Aesthetics
- Form
- Style
- Design
- Other Perceptions

BRAND PERSONALITY[2]

- Sincerity
- Excitement
- Competence
- Sophistication
- Ruggedness

QUALITY IN SERVICES[3]

- Reliability
- Responsiveness
- Assurance
- Empathy
- Tangibles

CHANNEL FUNCTIONS

- Transactional functions
- Logistical functions
- Facilitating functions

1 *Garvin, D. (1984). What does product quality really mean?* MIT Sloan Management Review, *25(1).*
2 *Aaker, J. L. (1997). Dimensions of brand personality.* Journal of Marketing Research, *34(3), 347–356.*
3 *Parasuraman, A., Zeithaml, V. A., & Berry, L. L. (1985). A conceptual model of service quality and its implications for future research.* Journal of Marketing, *49(4), 41–50. Parasuraman, A., Zeithaml, V. A., & Berry, L. L. (1988). SERVQUAL: A multiple-item scale for measuring consumer perceptions of service quality.* Journal of Retailing, 64(1), 12–40.

all of which can, potentially, serve as points of differentiation. This assortment of potential differentiation points emphasizes the range of ways that an offering can deliver superior satisfaction and greater value to customers.

A differentiation strategy requires almost opposite skills and organizational characteristics of a cost-leadership strategy. Differentiation requires continuous innovation and exceptional brand management; otherwise there is the chronic risk that a competitor will imitate or surpass the firm's offerings. A differentiated offering is typically highly sophisticated, depending on that technological superiority for strategic advantage, and it usually offers exceptional quality and/or a unique brand image—otherwise no customer would be willing to pay a the premium for it. To achieve and maintain these advantages, a differentiator must be customer-oriented and innovative and must have special skills in brand management. To react to changing customer needs, to be innovative and flexible, these companies must have very flexible and organic organizational structures. To ensure fast information flow and customer orientation throughout the company, these companies often work with cross-functional teams, especially in product development. Dominant values of the organizational culture are risk-taking, speed, flexibility, and experimentation—the ingredients of innovativeness. Leaders of differentiated organizations are often visionaries who involve employees in decision-making and encourage employees to innovate and generate creative ideas.

Cost Leadership Versus Differentiation

The choice of a generic strategy has long-term consequences; in fact, it is usually irreversible, at least in the near- and mid-term. Importantly, the choice must be carefully thought through and should fit the company's strengths (or with strengths the company will develop). Table 16-3 describes and compares the two alternatives. Table 16-4 lists core functions of the firm—from manufacturing through sales—that must be carried out and distinguishes approaches to those tasks within cost leader and differentiation strategies. The table highlights the fact that the two strategies require quite different strengths and emphasize different approaches, in some instances conflicting approaches.

TABLE 16-3 Comparing Cost Leadership and Differentiation

	COST LEADERSHIP (OR "EXPLOITATIVE BUSINESS")	DIFFERENTIATION (OR "EXPLORATORY BUSINESS")
Strategic Intent	Low cost, market share	Differentiation, innovation, price premium
Offering	Standardized, no-frills	Sophisticated, high quality, branded product
Critical Tasks	Operations, efficiency, process improvement	Customer orientation, product innovation, brand management
Organizing Structure	Formal, standardized, mechanistic	Flexible, organic, cross-functional product development teams
Organizational Culture	Efficiency, low risk, cost-consciousness	Risk-taking, speed, flexibility, experimentation
Leadership Role	Authoritative, top down	Visionary, involved

Note. Table source: O'Reilly III, C. A., & Tushman, M. L. (2004). The ambidextrous organization. *Harvard Business Review*.

Hybrid Strategies

Some experts have argued that, in certain instances, companies can pursue a hybrid strategy that simultaneously seeks to achieve differentiation and lower prices. IKEA is an example of having such a strategy; it has the lowest prices in the industry and is able to differentiate itself through design, image, and shopping experience. However, given the characteristics of these two strategies and their requirements (as summarized in Tables 16-3 and 16-4), it becomes clear that hybrid strategies are more the exception than the rule and that they are particularly difficult to execute. If it is not

TABLE 16-4 Generic Strategies and Related Attributes

FUNCTION	COST LEADERSHIP	DIFFERENTIATION
Manufacturing	Lean, automated, low cost, reliable quality	Flexible automation
Marketing	Emphasize value, reliability, and—above all—price	Emphasize unique product features and brand
R&D	Incremental product improvement, process innovation	New product development
Finance	Focus on low cost and stable financial structure	Enough funds for R&D
Accounting	Tight cost control, adopt conservative accounting principles	Accounting system that allows cost calculation for customized, complex products
Sales	Focus on value, reliability, low price, ubiquitous availability	Focus on uniqueness, brand, strong customer support

Note. Table source: Barney, J. B., & Hesterle, W. S. (2008). *Strategic management and competitive advantage.* Pearson Publishing.

impossible, it is certainly extremely difficult to do both of these things better than the competition because differentiation costs money, and costs necessitate higher prices. That unavoidable logic—and the contrasting, sometimes conflicting, attributes of successful cost leaders vis-à-vis differentiators—argues for treating competitive advantage as a distinction rather than as a continuum and argues against straddling a cost-leadership and differentiation strategy. Porter (1980) argued that firms that try to combine the two will end up *stuck in the middle*:

> The firm stuck in the middle is almost guaranteed low profitability. It either loses the high-volume customers who demand low prices or must bid away its profits to get this business from the low-cost firms. Yet it also loses high-margin business—the cream— to the firms who are focused on high-margin targets or have achieved differentiation overall. (Porter, 1980, pp. 41–42)

One exception to the rule of choosing one or the other may be in an offering that is distinct for its low cost (and therefore low price to the customer) as well as differentiated by its high reliability and/or conformity. This is true because reliability and conformance—two types of *quality*—are closely linked to scale though experience curve effects and economies of scale in investments in process improvement; the more units a firm makes of a standardized offering, the more reliable and invariant the units produced become. For example, Toyota produces more than 10 million vehicles every year. That industry-leading scale, along with *the Toyota Way* of continuous improvement in manufacturing, has led to Toyota and its brands (such as Lexus) leading the world not only in value pricing (not necessarily lowest price, but consistently great value for cost) as well as reliability and conformance (Liker, 2004).

COMPETITIVE SCOPE

The second dimension or characteristic of strategies that has emerged across various frameworks and been well-established by many strategy experts is competitive scope, that is, the size and breadth of the market(s) the strategy means to serve—or target(s). Competitive scope may vary in terms of the number of customers the firm targets, the number of segments the firm targets, the heterogeneity of those different customers and segments, and the variety of needs that the firm endeavors to serve. Therefore, the dimensions and decisions that structure competitive scope are the same as those that define market segmentation.

Unlike the basis of competition, which is best understood as a distinction between two mutually exclusive alternatives, competitive scope can be thought of as a continuum covering a range of viable alternatives. That is, some firms serve mass markets with standardized offerings, some firms even target the whole world as a single market (these are called *global strategies*), while others serve very small markets or *niches* with highly customized, value-added offerings, and still others carve out any number of intermediate competitive scopes.

For example, Toyota is a global brand, taking advantage of scale effects to produce 10 million low-cost, high-value vehicles a year (McFarlane, 2019). Meanwhile, Porsche is a highly focused automobile manufacturer that produces less than 300,000 vehicles a year (Porsche, 2021). These two brands represent the extremes, a global mass marketer and a focused niche brand. But between Toyota and Porsche lies an assortment of other manufacturers and brands, each defining their competitive scope differently. BMW, for instance, produces about 2.1 million vehicles a year (Best Selling Cars, 2021); BMW's scale is about 7 times that of Porsche, but still only about one fifth of Toyota's. Thus, the competitive scope of a marketing strategy can vary along a continuum and there is less chance of getting caught in the *unprofitable middle* with regard to scope than there is with regard to the basis of competition (i.e., differentiation versus cost leadership). Companies that pursue a focus strategy try to serve a well-defined and narrow market segment more effectively or efficiently than an industrywide competitor. A niche strategy is viable when segment-specific needs exist that an industrywide supplier is not able to meet or not interested in meeting.

Because of the close association between cost advantage and scale, a combination of cost leadership and a niche scope is difficult, but probably not impossible. In some markets, such as automobiles, the cost leader actually offers an augmented product. The leading *economy car* manufacturers, such as Kia and Hyundai, offer products emphasizing price with practical functionality; however, those products are also highly reliable and do offer elements of style and comfort beyond the *bare minimum*. This leaves the extreme no-frills and absolute-low-cost market space underserved. To meet this market gap in India, the automobile manufacturer Tata introduced the Nano, "the world's cheapest car." The Nano was a 35-horsepower, 2-cylinder gas engine, priced starting at 100,000 rupees (the equivalent of about $2,200) (Timmons, 2009). This vehicle was targeted to a niche of customers in developing economies who used motorcycles as basic transportation but who desired to upgrade to a (very low-cost and basic) car. Tata Motors expected to produce 250,000 units annually, but delays in production and safety and quality issues led to very low demand, resulting in a halt in production after 10 years (Buss, 2018).

The far more usual sort of niche strategy offers differentiation tailored to a small but profitable segment's needs. It is essential that segment-specific needs exist and that the focused company has the necessary skills and competences to satisfy them. Otherwise, industrywide competitors can outperform the focused, niche offering due to cost advantages.

SUMMARY

Generic strategies combine a focus on cost leadership or product differentiation, with the strategy's scope—from mass market to a narrow, niche target market. These are meant to be broad generalizations; the oversimplification is intentional, and there are countless ways in which specific strategies can be different within these rudimentary but broad categories. Nevertheless, these distinctions are useful as they create a valuable structure to initiate a high-level understanding of the breadth of strategies that are possible in a marketplace and the considerations related with certain strategic orientations.

REFERENCES

Barney, J. B., & Hesterle, W. S. (2008). *Strategic management and competitive advantage*. Pearson Publishing.

Best Selling Cars. (2021, January 12). *2020 global: BMW, Mini, and Rolls-Royce sales worldwide*. https://www.best-selling-cars.com/brands/2020-full-year-global-bmw-mini-and-rolls-royce-sales-worldwide/

Buss, D. (2018, July 27). No to the Nano: Tata phases out "World's Cheapest Car" as it failed to attract pretty much anyone. *Forbes*. https://www.forbes.com/sites/dalebuss/2018/07/27/nano-nano-tata-phases-out-worlds-cheapest-car-as-it-failed-to-attract-pretty-much-anyone/?sh=29442bb36ffc

Grant, R. M. (2005). *Contemporary strategy analysis* (5th ed.). Blackwell Publishing.

Kotler, P. (2016). *A framework for marketing management* (6th ed.). Pearson Education Limited.

Liker, J. K. (2004). *Toyota way: 14 management principles from the world's greatest manufacturer*. McGraw-Hill Education.

McFarlane, G. (2019, July 30). How Toyota makes money. *Investopedia*. https://www.investopedia.com/articles/markets/021416/how-toyota-makes-money-tm.asp

O'Reilly III, C. A., & Tushman, M. L. (2004). The ambidextrous organization. *Harvard Business Review*.

Porsche. (2021. January 12). *Porsche achieves robust level of deliveries in 2020* [Press release]. https://newsroom.porsche.com/en/2021/company/porsche-deliveries-2020-worldwide-23368.html

Porter, M. E. (1980). *Competitive strategy: Techniques for analyzing industries and competitors*. Free Press.

Porter, M. E. (1985). *Competitive advantage: Creating and sustaining superior performance*. Free Press.

Porter, M. E. (1996). What is strategy? *Harvard Business Review*, 74(6), 61–78.

Timmons, H. (2009, March 23). A tiny car is the stuff of 4-wheel dreams for millions of drivers in India. *The New York Times*. https://www.nytimes.com/2009/03/24/business/worldbusiness/24auto.html

Treacy, M., & Wiersema, F. (1995). *The discipline of market leaders: Choose your customers, narrow your focus, dominate your market*. HarperCollins Publishers.

Figure Credit

VALUE MAP

Value can be defined in many ways, but in marketing strategy it refers to what the customer *gets* (the benefits or *performance* the customer receives) adjusted for what the customer *gives* (the costs, especially price, given in exchange for those benefits). That is, it is a ratio of the benefits divided by the price:

$$\text{Value} = \frac{\text{"Get"}}{\text{"Give"}}$$

The important thing is not how the firm or the marketing manager thinks about this equation, but how the customers think about it, and how they think about it *relative to other offerings in the marketplace*. Different customers and different segments of customers will value various benefits differently; for example, families usually think safety is very important in making a car purchase while other segments, such as young professionals, may value acceleration or comfort more highly. At the same time, although what the customer *gives* may be mostly about price, there are other costs, such as time and effort (convenience or inconvenience, required assembly, expected maintenance, etc.), and those are also part of the perceived price or *give* to the customer. Thus, what *value* means in a strategic context can be elaborated to:

$$\text{Value} = \frac{\sum[(\text{Relative Benefits})^{*}(\text{Importance Weight})]}{\sum(\text{Relative Price} + \text{Other Costs})}$$

Customers understand that they can *get more* if they're willing to *give more*, and various alternatives in any market almost always offer varying degrees of benefits (performance or quality) at different price points. Customers' perceptions of value can be plotted into a two-dimensional space, give (relative price) versus get (relative performance/benefits), and there will be a segment-specific line or frontier along which customers can see fair trade-offs between give and get. Figure 17-1 is a value map defined by those two dimensions—relative price and relative performance or quality—and shows a hypothetical fair-value frontier.

For example, in the flat-screen TV market (Germany, 2015), any customer knows they can buy brands such as Philips, Sony, LG, Samsung and so on,

FIGURE 17-1 Value Map and Value Frontier/ Fair Value Zone (Gale, 1994)

as highlighted in Figure 17-2. While some customers may choose a Sony, they understand that they could pay more and get more with another alternative. Similarly, LG buyers know they could pay less and get less with either a Grundig, or a Changhong—or pay more and get a Samsung. Thus, there is a frontier or equilibrium boundary along which customers choose *fair value*; a position above or to the left of that frontier (toward the northwest) reflects an inferior value—the customer could get more performance for the same price or pay less for the given performance. Only the constrained or poorly informed customers would willingly purchase a brand in this area, and that condition may not last for long. Anything toward the southeast is a superior value—it offers more than the market had been offering

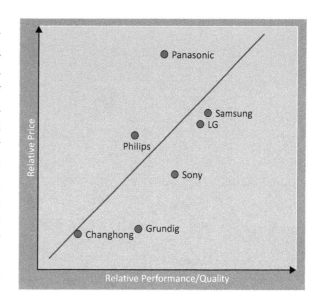

FIGURE 17-2   Value Map for Flat-Screen TVs (Based on Konsument 2015)

for the same price or charges less for the same performance. This is where innovations often enter the market, by finding a way to deliver something more or a way to charge less.

The value frontier is the maximum performance or quality currently feasible at a given cost to the customer. Southwest Airlines created a new value proposition for airline customers; Primark, an Irish fashion retailer, created a new value proposition for fashion; and Walmart did likewise for the world of retailing. Each of these companies found a way to deliver superior performance at a lower price than its competitors. Specifically, Southwest Airlines extended the value frontier at the low end of the airline industry and dramatically expanded demand for its flights. In contrast, Primark takes advantage of buying in bulk for all stores to benefit from economies of scale, relies on manufacturing in developing countries, and markets mainly by using social media and word-of-mouth, instead of expensive advertising. Finally, Walmart led mass retailers in the development of logistics, systems, and supply chain capabilities that allowed it to sell national brands for less than its competitors, thereby pushing the value frontier and eventually becoming the largest retailer in the world.

The concept of the value frontier is a powerful tool for analysis and strategy formulation. It can be used to assess the value products or services created for the customer. This analysis is of vital importance to marketing strategists because value delivered to customers directly influences market share and profitability. A customer value map is also useful in that it can assist marketers in developing clear and solid marketing strategies.

CUSTOMER VALUE ANALYSIS

The pioneers of customer value analysis—Robert Buzzell and Bradley Gale—carried out extensive research to measure the impact that customer value has on market share and profitability

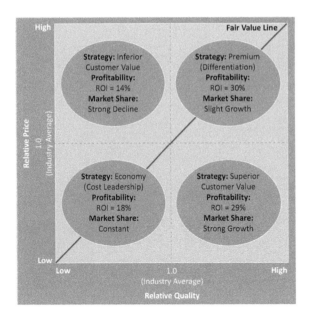

FIGURE 17-3 Strategies within the Value Map (Buzzell & Gale, 1987; Gale, 1994)

using the Profit Impact of Market Strategies (PIMS) database (Buzzell & Gale, 1987; Gale, 1994). PIMS contains data on more than 3,000 business units from about 200 companies. To analyze the role of customer value in company success, Buzzell & Gale (1987) created a two-dimensional matrix and positioned each strategic business unit on this matrix based on the dimensions of *relative price* (price compared to competitors) and *relative quality* (quality compared to competitors). They then determined the average profitability (return on investment, or ROI, before interest and taxes) of the strategic business units in the four quadrants of the matrix (see Figure 17-3).

The fair value line in Figure 17-1 indicates the points at which quality is balanced against price. Any product positioned to the left of the fair value line delivers low customer value. This product is either too expensive for its level of quality, or its quality is too low for its given price. Products positioned on this side of the line lose market share, which means that low profitability will follow. In contrast, any product on the right side of the fair value line creates high customer value. These products will gain market share and earn a high return. As shown in the Figure 17-3, four basic strategies can be derived from this customer value map: the superior customer value strategy, the premium strategy, the economy strategy, and the inferior customer value strategy.

Superior Customer Value Strategy

The superior customer value strategy is a combination of Michael Porter's cost leadership strategy and his differentiation strategy. With this strategy, the goal is to offer a product that not only performs better (i.e., offers higher quality, better brand image, better service, etc.) than those offered by competitors, but one that is also priced below the competitors' offerings. This is a particularly difficult position to achieve because it requires both a cost advantage and a differentiation advantage. However, if a company succeeds in enacting this strategy, it is rewarded with a strong increase in market share and, in turn, high profitability—on average, a 29 percent ROI (i.e., return on investment before interest and taxes).

Inditex, the parent company of highly successful apparel chain Zara, has become one of the world's largest fashion retailers by creating superior customer value. Inditex can reportedly take a new fashion idea from concept to finished garment and distribute it to over one thousand stores in about two weeks—this is truly fast fashion, as well as a significant differentiation advantage. Moreover, Inditex does this at very competitive prices due to its vertically integrated manufacturing and distribution system.

Premium Strategy

The premium strategy comes close to the differentiation strategy—with one important difference. Specifically, it requires that a company is able to differentiate itself or its products in terms of quality, innovation, service, brand image, etc., *and* that customers are willing to pay a price premium for superior product performance. Products that are sold via this strategy on average earn a 30 percent ROI and are able to slightly increase market share.

One can easily think of many luxury products that employ this strategy, including Rolex watches, Bentley automobiles, and Louis Vuitton handbags. However, this strategy is not just limited to luxury goods. Indeed, there are many other examples of both consumer and industrial goods and services for which companies offer "good," "better," and "best" products—with "the best" generally representing an exhibition of the premium strategy.

Economy Strategy

Companies that position their products using the economy strategy compete on price, primarily by focusing on cost leadership. Although the quality of these products is balanced against their price, the average ROI using this strategy is only 18 percent. The reason for this low ROI is simple—with the economy strategy, price plays a dominant role, making price wars a permanent threat to profitability. In other words, if companies want to increase market share, they usually do so by lowering the price—but their competitors often follow suit shortly thereafter. Indeed, studies show that in the long run, market shares remain unchanged because competitors respond with price reductions to recover lost market share. Walmart has successfully adopted a cost leadership strategy over the years to deliver its economy strategy to consumers and become—and remain—the largest retailer in the world.

Inferior Customer Value Strategy

Products positioned in the inferior customer value quadrant of the value frontier will be unable to contribute to a company's success unless the company has a monopoly, customers cannot switch to another product, or there is little market transparency and customers are not aware of better alternatives. This position usually is the worst in terms of market share and profitability; in fact, a strong loss of market share and a low ROI (on average, 14%) are the typical consequences of this positioning. It might be argued that the North American automobile manufacturers got in trouble by offering inferior customer value for decades and the result was a strong customer bias toward imports. Japanese brands had found ways to deliver greater reliability at the same price, and European brands were delivering higher performance and more desirable image and prestige for a higher price; the value frontier had shifted to the right, and American brands were slow to adapt.

APPLICATION OF CUSTOMER VALUE ANALYSIS

A customer value analysis serves two purposes. First, it can be useful for formulating market data-based strategies, which are preferable to vague definitions or blurry descriptions of strategies.

Second, this type of analysis helps identify clear measures to implement strategies. In other words, customer value analysis is a simple and straightforward tool to translate strategy into action. However, in order for an analysis to be successful, the marketer must have clear answers to the following questions, ideally based on market research data:

- What is our target market?
- Who are our competitors for this target market?
- What are the customers' buying criteria?
- How important is each of the customers' buying criteria?
- How do customers evaluate our product and the competitors' products on the basis of these buying criteria?
- What are our prices and those of the competitors?
- What is the customers' price sensitivity?

Strategy formulation based on the value frontier concept can be systematically accomplished using a number of analytical tools over eight distinct steps of analysis. These steps are as follows:

1. Definition of the target market
2. Identification of competitors
3. Identification of customers' buying criteria and their relative importance
4. Assessment of product performance and price
5. Calculation of relative quality and relative price
6. Estimation of customers' price sensitivity
7. Creation of the customer value map and formulation of strategies
8. Definition of an action plan using importance-performance analysis

Figure 17-4 is a worksheet that can be used for the purpose of strategy formulation based on the value frontier concept. Now let's take a closer look at what each of the eight aforementioned steps entails, referring to Figure 17-4 as we proceed.

Step 1: Defining the Target Market

A good customer value analysis begins with the definition of market segments. This is a critical step and must be done carefully because buying criteria and price sensitivity can differ significantly between segments. For instance, for sports car buyers (e.g., Porsche purchasers), characteristics such as engine power, acceleration, and brand image are typically important, whereas for family car buyers, traits like fuel consumption, space, and price are likely more important. For the purposes of this example, we'll focus on car tires, specifically on tires made for winter weather for the mass market.

Step 2: Identifying Competitors

The second step of the strategy formulation process involves identifying competitors within the market segment. For this task, the concept of strategic groups can be particularly helpful. A strategic group is a group of companies within an industry that pursue similar competitive strategies and have similar characteristics (e.g., size) and competences. These companies, therefore, offer similar products to similar customers and are in strong competition with one another. For our segment, we identified seven major competitors: Bridgestone, Michelin, Hankook, Goodyear, Pirelli, Semperit, and Dunlop (see Figure 17-4).

Customer Value Map
Product: Tires
Segment: Winter Tires 205/55

Quality Criteria	Weight	Bridgestone Perf (1-5)	WS	Michelin Perf (1-5)	WS	Hankook Perf (1-5)	WS	Goodyear Perf (1-5)	WS	Pirelli Perf (1-5)	WS	Semperit Perf (1-5)	WS	Dunlop Perf (1-5)	WS	
Dry	12,5	3,4	42,5	3	37,5	3	37,5	2,5	31,25	2,2	27,5	1,8	22,5	3	37,5	
Wet	25	4,2	105	3,5	87,5	3,5	87,5	3,5	87,5	3,3	82,5	3,4	85	3,2	80	
Snow	17,5	3,4	59,5	3,4	59,5	3,4	59,5	3,7	64,75	3,7	64,75	3,6	63	3	52,5	
Ice	7,5	3,1	23,25	3,2	24	3,1	23,25	3	22,5	3,3	24,75	3,1	23,25	3,2	24	
Noice	5	2,6	13	2,9	14,5	2,3	11,5	2,7	13,5	3	15	3	15	2	10	
Fuel efficiency	7,5	3,5	26,25	3,4	25,5	3,6	27	3,6	27	3,3	24,75	3,5	26,25	3,7	27,75	
Wear	7,5	3	22,5	4	30	3,5	26,25	3	22,5	3	22,5	3	22,5	4	30	
Brand image	17,5	4,25	74,375	4	70	0,5	8,75	2,25	39,375	1,25	21,875	0,75	13,125	1,25	30,625	
	100															
Weighted score		366,38		348,50		281,25		308,38		283,63		270,63		292,38	309,79	
Relative quality		1,18		1,12		0,91		1,00		0,92		0,87		0,94		
Price		66,00		78,00		57,00		60,00		58,00		61,00		68,00	63,33	
Relative quality		1,04		1,23		0,90		0,95		0,92		0,96		1,07		

Weight on		
Quality	40	
Price	60	
Sum	100	

	Relative Price	Relative Quality	
			Relative Quality = quality score of product X / average quality score
			Relative Price = price of product X / average price
Bridgestone Blzzak LM 005	1,04	1,18	
Michelin Alpin 6	1,23	1,12	Perf. = Performance
Hankook i* Cept RS 2	0,90	0,91	WS = Weighted Score
Goodyear UltraGrip 9+	0,95	1,00	
Pirelli Cinturato Winter	0,92	0,92	
Semperit Speed-Grip	0,96	0,87	
Dunlop Winter Sport 5	1,07	0,94	

FIGURE 17-4   Worksheet for Customer Value Analysis

Step 3: Identifying and Assessing Buying Criteria

Next comes a particularly crucial step in customer analysis: identification of the customers' buying criteria and their relative weights. This step usually requires market research in order to formulate a clear understanding what customers want, how they decide, and what is more (or less) important to them. Ideally, qualitative market research initially identifies the buying criteria (attributes). Then, by way of a subsequent quantitative, representative study, both the relative importance of these criteria and competitors' performance on these criteria are measured. There are several ways to assess the relative importance of these attributes, including:

- conjoint analysis (a research technique that identifies customer preferences when attributes are considered simultaneously and interdependently);
- rating scales (e.g., "How important is the fuel efficiency of winter tires to you?"; 1 = not at all important, 5 = very important);
- rank orders ("Please rank from 1 to 6 the following characteristics of winter tires [1 is most important and 6 is least important]"); or

- constant sum scales ("Please divide 100 points among the following characteristics so the division reflects the relative importance of each characteristic to you in the selection of winter tires.").

Step 4: Assessing Product Performance and Price

Product performance is best assessed using a rating scale (e.g., from 1 to 5, where 5 is best). In Figure 17-4, data on buying criteria and their relative weight, as well as on the performance of the single competing products, were taken from secondary market research on a European market ("ADAC," 2020; "Idealo," 2020).

The second part of Step 4 is price assessment. Prices usually are easily available. In the case of complex price structures (e.g., bank services, supermarkets) instead of using actual prices, one can also estimate price levels (e.g., our price = 100; competitor's price level = X).

Step 5: Calculating Relative Quality and Price

Next, in order to calculate the quality score of each competing product, the performance rating of each attribute must be multiplied by the relative weight of that attribute, and the resulting values must be added together. By themselves, the absolute individual quality scores and prices are not meaningful—they have to be compared to those of the competitors. Therefore, a quality ratio and a price ratio are calculated. These ratios represent a product's quality score and price compared to the average of all products' quality scores and prices. In Figure 17-4, Michelin's relative quality of 1.12 means that the quality is 12% higher than the average quality of the products, and its relative price of 1.23 means that the Michelin winter tire costs 23% more than the average cost.

Step 6: Estimating Price Sensitivity

Customers' price sensitivity can simply be measured using a constant sum scale and a question similar to the following: "Please indicate how much weight you put on quality and how much weight you put on price in the selection of winter tires. Please divide 100 points between quality and price." In our example, let's assume that the customers are rather price sensitive. Thus, they place 40% of the weight of their buying decision on quality and 60% on price. Here—and in all cases—the slope of the fair value line will be equal to the percentage of the decision based on quality divided by the percentage of the decision based on price.

Step 7: Creating the Customer Value Map and Formulating Strategies

At this point, the relative quality and relative price of each product can be used to create the customer value map (Figure 17-5). On this map, a "1" on each dimension indicates the average quality and average price of all products. As previously mentioned, the fair value line indicates the points at which quality is balanced against price. Products positioned to the left of the fair value line offer lower customer value, whereas those to the right of the line offer higher value. A flat fair-value line represents price-sensitive customers. If, for example, the price is increased by 10%, quality has to be increased by more than 10%, to, say, 20%, in order for the customer to continue to buy that product. When customers have low price sensitivity, the fair-value line is steep. Here, a low increase of quality will allow a disproportionately high increase of price.

Now the customer value map can be created and strategies can be derived. In our example, Dunlop has a clear disadvantage because its quality is too low and its price too high. In contrast, Bridgestone has the most favorable position (i.e., it offers the highest customer value), followed by Goodyear and Hankook. In this case, if, for example, Dunlop wanted to increase its market share, it would have three options: (a) lower prices, (b) increase quality, or (c) implement a combination of price reduction and quality improvement.

Step 8: Defining an Action Plan

The final step of customer value analysis involves defining an action plan. One useful tool for doing this is the importance–performance analysis method (Martilla & James, 1977). For example, if Dunlop's strategy is to increase quality and position itself as the quality leader in the industry, it must determine how to enact this strategy. To do so, Dunlop

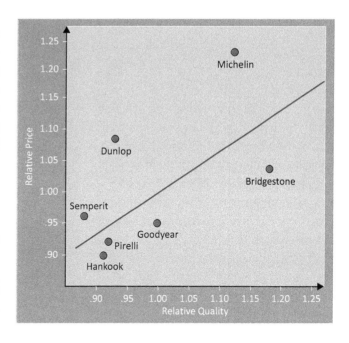

FIGURE 17-5   Customer Value Map

should compare its product's performance attribute by attribute with that of its strongest competitor (Bridgestone). Then, a matrix with attribute importance on the x-axis and attribute performance (compared to Bridgestone) on the y-axis can be created. For the y-axis in our example (Figure 17-5), we use relative performance (Dunlop's performance score minus Bridgestone's performance score). Four quadrants with the following implications are identified:

- *Quadrant 1 (high importance–high performance)*: These product characteristics or attributes (such as performance in Figure 17-6) are the competitive advantages. A company should keep up the good work here.
- *Quadrant 2 (high importance–low performance)*: These product characteristics or attributes are the "burning fires." A company should take immediate action here.
- *Quadrant 3 (low importance–high performance)*: A higher performance on unimportant attributes can represent possible overkill. If costs need to be reduced, these are the best candidates for cutting expenses.
- *Quadrant 4 (low importance–low performance)*: Actions have low priority here, as these disadvantages are not very relevant.

In our example, Dunlop's priority should be to increase its brand image, which will have the strongest effect, followed by improving its product's performance on "wet handling and breaking" and "snow handling and breaking."

After this final step, the customer value analysis is complete. Based on market research data, a strategy has been formulated and an action plan has been derived.

SUMMARY

Value mapping is a useful tool that allows marketing strategists to define the relative positions of industry competitors on performance or quality, as well as cost. The value frontier is the maximum performance or quality currently feasible at a given cost to the customer. Successful strategists attempt to find or create unique positions on the value frontier. The process by which this is achieved includes the definition of the target market; the identification of competitors; the identification of customers' buying criteria and their relative importance; an assessment of product performance and price; the calculation of relative quality and relative price; the estimation of customers' price sensitivity; the creation of the customer value map and formulation of strategies; and, the definition of an action plan using importance–performance analysis.

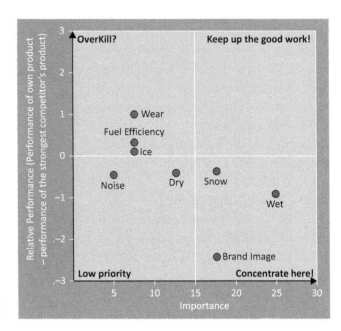

FIGURE 17-6   Importance Performance Analysis

REFERENCES

"ADAC." (2020). *ADAC Winter- und Ganzjahresreifen.* https://www.adac.de/-/media/pdf/dko/adac-broschre-winter-u-ganzjahresreifen-2020.pdf

Buzzell, R. D., & Gale, B. T. (1987). *The PIMS principles: Linking strategy to performance.* Free Press.

Gale, B. T. (1994). *Managing customer value.* Free Press.

"Idealo." (2020). *Idealo Prices.* www.idealo.at

Martilla, J. A., & James, J. C. (1977). Importance-performance analysis. *Journal of Marketing, 41*(1), 77–79.

Figure Credits

NOTE 18

Most managers are wired to pursue growth. Even if it were not part of the innate competitiveness of free-enterprise managers and markets, growth is an important strategic objective. In fact, it is an *imperative* for most firms for three reasons:

1. The only way to increase stock price, and thus shareholder value, is to grow faster in earnings and cash flows than shareholders expect. Current share prices already reflect expected growth; the only way to increase share prices is to *exceed* those growth expectations.
2. Growth equates to market share and scale; therefore, lower growth than the competition equates to exacerbating cost disadvantages as competitors gain experience and economies of scale.
3. Even firms that might choose to forego growth must, nevertheless, continuously pursue new customers and new markets for their products to simply maintain sales volume. No company retains 100% of its customer base; therefore, new customers and new products are necessary to offset customer defections and attrition.

Of course, not *all* companies are *always* growing their sales and some may choose, at least for the short term, to forego growth. Later in this Note we will briefly discuss nongrowth strategies—*maintenance* and *retrenchment*—but, for the reasons listed, those are anomalies. Most firms aspire to grow sales, revenues, and profits for growth's sake and/or in response to the pressures articulated above.

The question, then, is *how* a company or a strategic business unit can achieve that vital growth. Professor H. Igor Ansoff developed a simple, logical, and useful matrix to organize possible answers to this question, as shown in Figure 18-1. Logically, at any given time, a firm is marketing its existing products to its existing markets—that's the way it is, by definition. To grow, then, the firm must sell more of the same product to those same customers, sell its existing products to new customers, sell new products to existing customers, or sell new products to new customers. By combining those two dimensions, products (existing versus new products) and markets (existing versus new markets), the *Ansoff Matrix* defines four distinct growth strategies: (a) market penetration, (b) product development, (c) market

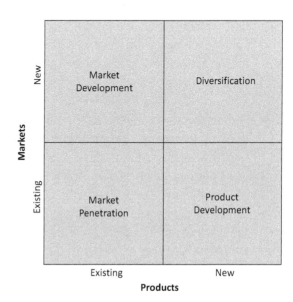

FIGURE 18-1 Ansoff Product–Market Growth Matrix (Ansoff, 1957, p. 114)

development, and (d) diversification. These four growth strategies are described in greater detail in the following sections.

MARKET PENETRATION

The easiest and most promising way to grow is to increase sales of existing products in existing markets. As long as there is still some growth potential in existing markets, a company should prioritize this strategy. The company presumably has market knowledge, a developed and proven product, the necessary resources, and access to distribution channels. Customers know the brand, are familiar with the product and are, therefore, usually easier to stimulate to purchase than new customers in a new market. Empirical studies indicate that *penetration* strategies have the highest success rate and require the lowest amount of resources and effort of the four growth strategies (Becker, 2009). There are several options to grow via market penetration:

- *Increase frequency of use.* In this case, a company tries to persuade its customers to use its products more often. Visa, for example, offers its credit card holders a rewards program. For each dollar charged, the customer earns a reward point that can be redeemed for a wide range of options, from frequent-flyer miles to brand-name merchandise. Hence, customers are motivated to use the credit card more often, instead of cash or a competitor's card.
- *Increase quantity used.* Another option to increase sales of an existing product to existing customers is to increase the quantity used. Many Internet retailers, for example, offer free shipping thresholds and remind customers of how much more they'd have to spend to get the free shipping. This policy increases sales because many customers who would have bought a single item for $85 and are reminded that they benefit from free shipping when they spend more than $100 decide to add another item to their cart to save on shipping costs.
- *Convert nonbuyers.* In any market there are customers that are nonusers of a product for one reason or another. If a company finds out the reasons for this, it can take measures to convert these customers. This is an especially important strategy for freemium business models. In a freemium business model, users get basic features for free and pay a subscription fee for additional premium features. This has become a dominant model for Internet start-ups, apps, or computer games. Skype, Dropbox, Spotify, and LinkedIn are examples of organizations that have successfully adopted this approach. But freemiums are also used for B2B companies like Yammer (Kumar, 2014). The free version of the product serves to attract new customers, which then need to be converted.
- *Show new applications.* Sales can also be increased when customers are shown new applications for existing products. Barilla, the Italian producer of pasta, offers a wide variety of recipes on the back of each package to stimulate its customers to consume more pasta. Danone increased sales of its brand *Fruchtzwerge* in Germany by demonstrating that when the popular curd cheese product with fruit was stored in the freezer, the target market of children could make their own tasty ice cream of it. Another example is the old Italian aperitif Aperol, introduced in 1911. It used to be a traditional aperitif sold mostly in northeastern Italy with a modest

market share until the Aperol Spritz was introduced. This specialty cocktail (with white wine, Aperol, and soda water) became a refreshing flavored low-alcohol drink, and sales exploded.

- *Convert lost customers.* The average customer retention rate varies across industries from a low of 63% in retail to a high of 84% in professional services (Bernazzani, 2019). It is far more profitable for companies to retain current customers than to acquire new customers; only a 5% increase in customer retention can potentially increase company revenue by 25% to 95% (Bernazzani, 2019). To bolster customer retention efforts, firms like Starbucks send customers who have not recently visited or purchased products customized messages with enticing offers built on the individual's purchase history (Marr, 2018).

- *Convert competitor's customers.* As the most difficult way for a company to grow, converting competitor's customers requires either a clear price advantage or a clear differentiation advantage. However, it can prove to be a successful strategy. A vendor of Enterprise Resource Planning (ERP) software realized that many small and medium-sized companies were dissatisfied with the competition's ERP software. Since this vendor had built deep market relationships with these companies relative to other software product offerings, it could easily determine which of these companies was dissatisfied with their current ERP software provider and why. Using this information, it could target these specific companies and could relatively easily turn these prospects into customers.

PRODUCT DEVELOPMENT

To introduce modified, improved, or new products in existing markets is the second successful growth strategy with an average success rate of 33%. However, it takes on average 8 times more resources than the market penetration strategy (Becker, 2009).

- *Product Improvements.* Adding new product features (e.g., Apple AirPod Pro's accessibility feature called "Live Listen" that can serve as a hearing aid) or improving product performance (e.g., improved camera of a smartphone) is a typical strategy in a highly competitive market in the maturity phase of the product life cycle. This way additional sales can be generated through a better differentiation of the product.

- *Product Innovations.* Synergies can be exploited when a company introduces a new product targeted to the existing customer base. In this case, the company leverages its brand equity and takes advantage of its market access and market knowledge. Stimulated by Starbucks success, McDonald's decided to add McCafe to its offerings of coffees and drinks. By simultaneously using its brand name, its experience in designing efficient processes, and its access to the existing customer base, McDonald's reduced the risk of new product development and identified a new avenue of growth.

- *Product Line Extensions.* When a company introduces new flavors, forms, colors, package sizes, etc., under its successful brand name in a given product category, it intends to grow via line extensions. Red Bull, the Austrian energy drink producer, introduced Red Bull Sugarfree to address a new market segment. In addition to the Porsche Cayenne, Cayenne S, and Cayenne

Turbo, the German car manufacturer introduced a new model, Cayenne GTS, to address the segment of SUV buyers who want to own a sporty SUV with fast acceleration and higher top-track speed, similar to the Turbo, but at a lower price.

- *Cross Selling.* Cross selling in most cases offers very attractive opportunities for growth. Cross selling involves selling new products or services to existing customers. Banks, for instance, use cross selling to increase sales by offering their customers services they have not used before. Starbucks' Digital Flywheel uses artificial intelligence in its Starbucks Rewards members' accounts to make drink and food suggestions (Johnson, 2017).

MARKET DEVELOPMENT

The third growth strategy is market development; that is, expanding sales of existing products to new geographic markets (e.g., with rapid international expansion). This strategy requires building brand awareness and brand image, accessing new distribution channels, confronting new competitors, and often formulating new marketing strategies. Data show that market development requires 4 times as much investment as market penetration, and the probability of success is only, on average, approximately 20% (Becker, 2009). The topic of market development relative to international market expansion is further addressed in Note 19.

DIVERSIFICATION

Taking a new product to a new market is the strategy with the highest risk. It has the lowest probability of success (on average 5%) and requires the highest amount of resources (12 to 14 times as much as the market penetration strategy) (Becker, 2009). There are several ways to pursue diversification.

- *Related diversification.* In a related diversification, a company enters a new market with a new product, attaining synergies by sharing assets or competencies across businesses. Synergies can be exploited by entering new markets with new products using a recognized brand name (e.g., Richard Branson's Virgin Atlantic Airline, Virgin Records, Virgin Mobile UK, Virgin Express; although not all the ventures proved to be successful), marketing skills, manufacturing skills, R&D skills, or taking advantage of economies of scale.
- *Unrelated diversification.* In an unrelated diversification, a company enters a new market with a new product unrelated to the existing product markets. In this case, synergies can be exploited, but the venture is very risky as the company has no market knowledge and no product expertise.
- *Forward and backward integration.* Vertical integration is another potential growth strategy. Forward integration occurs when a company decides to move downstream the product flow (e.g., when it acquires retailers); backward integration means that a company moves upwards (e.g., when it acquires a supplier).

The "Z" strategy is an option for small firms and companies in mature industries that often consider diversification as their only possible growth strategy. If a firm does not strategically plan its growth, it can get into a situation where it needs a new product and a new market at the same time. This, as Figure 18-2 shows, is a high-risk strategy. The risk of diversification can be reduced when a company plans its growth across time. Before entering a new market with a new product, a company can develop a new product for the existing market, which it already knows and in which it has brand equity and access to distribution channels. In the next step, it can take the product that has been successfully introduced in the existing market to a new market. Alternatively, it can introduce an existing product to a new market to gain market knowledge, create brand awareness and brand equity, gain access to distribution

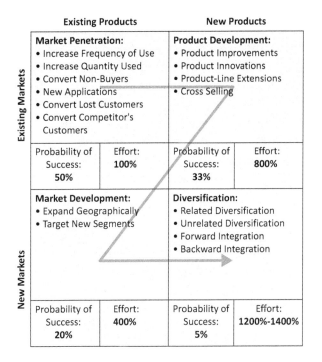

FIGURE 18-2   Strategic Planning within the Ansoff Matrix (Ansoff, 1957; Becker, 2009)

channels, and then develop a new product for this market. Thus, it does not go directly from penetration to diversification, but reduces the risk of diversification by making a detour via one or both of the other growth strategies. This "Z" strategy, however, has to be planned carefully and with a long-term perspective.

ADJACENCIES AND GROWING FROM "THE CORE"

Growth into either a new market or developing a new product is less risky than diversification, but that does not answer the question of what new market or new product to target for growth. *How should new markets or new products be selected?* A basic framework for answering that question is the notion of *adjacencies*. Prominent strategy consultant Chris Zook has elaborated on this idea, arguing that firms should identify their *core*, their essential, enduring, and defensible strengths, and grow by carefully defining that core and considering the distance or steps that any growth opportunity lies from it (Zook, 2004; Zook & Allen, 2001).

Of course, the first requirement when considering opportunities with regard to their relationship to the firm's core is to define that core rigorously and accurately. The company's core can be seen as its competitive advantages and market strengths: its most profitable customers, its key sources of differentiation, its core competencies, its most important products and sources of profits (profit pools), its relationships with channels and other collaborators, its organizational culture, and any other assets such as patents, brands, or access to scarce resources that contribute to those core strengths (Zook, 2007; Zook & Allen, 2001). Focus—that is, understanding, protecting, and nurturing a strategic core—is essential to success. Zook and his colleagues at Bain and Company studied data on more than 1,800 companies in seven countries with greater than $500 million in revenues and found that, of the companies described as "sustained value creators," those that had earned their cost of capital and realized growth of 5.5% or higher over the most recent decade, 78% had a single strong core and strong market leadership (relative market share of greater than 1.2%).

Once the firm has clarified its core strengths, it should look for opportunities that build upon those strengths (that is, opportunities that are adjacent to its core). According to Zook, adjacencies can be found along any of six paths: new geographies, new value chain activities, new channels, new customer segments, new products, or new businesses (see Figure 18-3). This six strategy scheme corresponds closely with Ansoff's original two-dimensional summary: new geographies, new channels, and new customer segments are mostly about new markets; new products is simply product development; and new businesses and new value-chain activities are diversification. Zook studied 181 randomly selected adjacency moves by major corporations and found that for growth initiatives that were one step from the core, the success rate was 37%, for two step moves it was 28%, and for three step moves it was less than 10% (Zook, 2004).

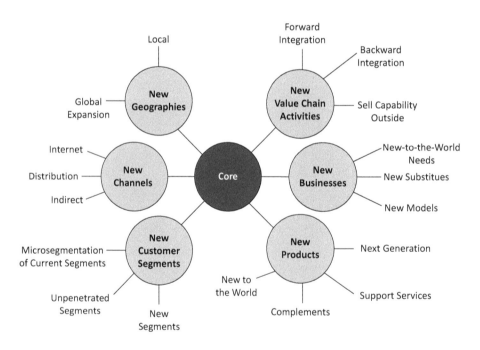

FIGURE 18-3   Building from the Core and Identifying Adjacencies (Zook & Allen, 2001)

OFFENSIVE AND DEFENSIVE STRATEGIES

Most companies adopt offensive growth strategies, both for the inherent benefits of increased revenues and profits and in response to pressures—including investor demands, the need to achieve scale and its benefits, and the need to replace defecting customers. Nevertheless, there are firms and situations for which growth is an unrealistic objective. Economic and competitive conditions may dictate, at least for certain periods, adopting a *damage control* or defensive strategy. Marketing strategy has long drawn on ideas about strategy from military and warfare strategists, and a core idea in marketing as warfare is that there are times to act defensively (Kotler & Singh, 1981; Ries & Trout, 2006). Defensive marketing strategies that are appropriate in times of low or no growth (or even decline) emphasize the need to identify the *high ground*, the place where the firm has the most strength and the most likelihood of weathering the battle (with the intention, presumably, to "live to fight again another day" or resume growth in the future).

Business strategists and marketers have developed some concepts that describe how companies can *attack* their competitors or how they can defend themselves against the *aggressor* (Kotler & Singh, 1981). Table 18-1 describes the characteristics for these strategies. Offensive or attacking strategies include the following:

- In the *frontal attack*, a challenger tries to find a way to achieve an exploitable advantage over its target competitor. The attacking company can do so by massing its forces (which may include lower prices, new features, higher quality, or superior technology) against the strengths of the competitor. For example, Walmart employed the capabilities (systems, logistics, and supply chain) it had developed serving rural USA customers to attack a leading retailer, Kmart, in the metropolitan areas of the country with "everyday low prices" and eventually won the war of the major discounters.

- The *flanking attack* is executed by attacking segments and/or by addressing needs the competitor neglects. Often, the needs of later adopting segments are different from early adopters that were targeted by the first mover. The flank attacker focuses not on the established competitor's strengths, but on their areas of weakness. Flank attacks work well when the incumbent is unwilling or unable to respond. Gillette, the long-time market leader in the razor and blade business, was surprised when Bic introduced the disposable razor, a clear flank attack that appealed to an emerging market segment and which the incumbent, Gillette, was reluctant to respond to initially.

- The aggressor can attack on several fronts simultaneously, which is known as *encirclement*. Here the plan is to surround the enemy with a variety of offerings directed at undeveloped segments of the market. Samsung has employed this strategy to become the worldwide leader in flat-screen televisions, passing Sony to become the industry leader. To achieve this competitive edge, Samsung focused on design, supplier relationships, and retail partners (Ramstad, 2010, p. 4).

- The *bypass strategy* amounts to skipping over an adversary to attack elsewhere, either through diversification into unrelated products or new geographies, or by leapfrogging into new technologies. The video game industry has been replete with technological leapfrogging, first by Nintendo leaping over Atari with next generation technology, then by Sega Genesis leapfrogging over Nintendo, then by Sony's PlayStation leapfrogging Sega, and then by Nintendo Wii leapfrogging the PlayStation ("Economist," 2003, p. 16). In each case, the new market leader used innovative technology to overtake the former market leader.

- Finally, *guerrilla warfare* means that the aggressor launches many minor attacks at multiple fronts to demoralize the competitor and eventually prepare for a massive attack. Southwest

Airlines may be the ultimate guerrilla warrior in the airline industry. Beginning in Texas with the Dallas/Houston/San Antonio markets, the low-cost carrier has slowly but surely attacked city-pair markets and entrenched airline leaders to become the most valuable U.S. airline.

TABLE 18-1 Offensive Strategies

Frontal attack Massing one's forces against the strengths of the competitor	• Must have a clear advantage (price, quality, financial strength, etc.) • Competitor should not be able to retaliate
Flanking Attacking segments or addressing needs that are neglected by the competitor	• Concentration of forces on competitor's weaknesses • Find segments that are not served well and develop them into strong segments
Encirclement Attacking at several fronts simultaneously	• Must have enough resources for a frontal attack in several segments where competitor has weaknesses • The encirclement must be comprehensive enough to overwhelm the competition
Bypass Gain strength in unserved markets to attack later	• Unserved or neglected markets must be found • They must allow to gain strength (develop and refine product, create brand awareness, gain financial strength, etc.) • These strengths must be transferable to competitor's core market for an attack
Guerrilla Minor attacks on multiple fronts to demoralize competitor	• Find several weakly defended markets • Have enough resources to attack these "blind" spots • Be able to demoralize competitor to eventually prepare for a massive attack

The attacked company has a number of options available to defend itself. Table 18-2 lists the characteristics of these strategies:

• Building a *fort* around the product (relative to positioning). Anheuser Busch (AB) dominated the U.S. beer market for decades and built a fort around its domestic position. However, it failed to see the international threat that emerged and eventually led to its acquisition by InBev, the Belgian powerhouse. AB had "all of its eggs in one basket"—the United States—when the business was becoming a global game.
• Diversifying into new products and markets to launch retaliatory strikes. This mobile defense amounts to creating a moving target that is hard for a competitor to attack. As Starbucks grew to become Europe's top coffee chain, McDonald's counterattacked by opening McCafés in existing franchises in a successful effort to gain market share with new product offerings (Liu, 2009).
• Weakening the competitor before it attacks in a preemptive strike. In effect, the aim of this strategy is to attack an aggressive competitor by blocking its anticipated move before the competitor can mount its attack. A widely known example of such preemption can be found in the software industry's practice of announcing new products well in advance of their actual (if ever) production, causing many customers of competitors' existing products to wait for the anticipated new product. This practice has been referred to as offering *vaporware*.
• Preventively developing defenders for potential attack with flank positioning. Here the idea is to protect the company by developing additional entries to cover weaknesses in the

original offering. For example, Toyota's development of the high quality and high-priced Lexus brand has often been referred to as the company's attempt to defend itself in the prestige segment—its exposed flank.

- Counterattacking is often the response of a market leader when attacked. Examples would include significant price cuts, major promotional activities, and product line improvements and extensions. Quite often the result becomes a price war. For example, Walmart could lower prices on its most popular books, which might prompt Amazon and Target to counterattack with even lower prices.
- Strategic withdrawal amounts to giving up an untenable position and freeing up the resources that had been deployed there to be used elsewhere. For example, after more than a decade of trying unsuccessfully to build a strong position in Germany, Walmart gave up and withdrew from the market. The world's largest retailer, Walmart realized that the German retail business was very established, entrenched, and already had many players such as Aldi, Lidl, and Metro that could match or beat their game of lowest prices. Walmart decided to redeploy those resources committed to Germany to other countries where its prospects appeared to be better.

TABLE 18-2 Defensive Strategies

Position Building a "fort" around the current product	All resources are used to defend the current product A "fortification" is built It is very risky to put all eggs into one basket (or behind the walls of one fort)
Mobile Diversify into new products and or markets to launch retaliatory strikes	Defend current product Exploit current strengths to diversify into new domains (products and or markets) Defend or attack out of these new domains
Preemptive Defending by attacking	Weaken competitor before he attacks
Flank positioning Develop defenders for uncertain eventualities	Identify points of weaknesses Develop defenders for potential attack
Counteroffensive Directly attacking aggressor	Use all resources and strengths to attack competitor frontally or at selected points of weaknesses
Strategic withdrawal Withdraw from unimportant segments to concentrate resources for a counterattack	Define unimportant segments and withdraw Cumulate and concentrate resources on core products or segments Counterattack out of core

SUMMARY

There are a few ways to pursue strategic growth—market penetration, product development, market development, and diversification. Each of these is described in greater detail in this Note, along with a set of specific tactics for pursuing each general growth strategy. These growth strategies are not all equally attractive or sound—the further from the firm's *core* strengths the growth initiative reaches, the less likely it is to succeed. Identifying the core strengths of an organization and building upon them is effective both in identifying opportunities for growth and in identifying defensible positions in times of retreat or retrenchment.

REFERENCES

Ansoff, H. I. (1957, September–October). Strategies for diversification. *Harvard Business Review, 35*(5), 113–124.

Becker, J. (2009). *Marketing-Konzeption: Grundlagen des ziel-strategischen und operativen Marketing-Managements.* Vahlen Verlag.

Bernazzani, S. (2019, October). Here's why customer retention is so important for ROI, customer loyalty, and growth. *HubSpot.* https://blog.hubspot.com/service/customer-retention

"Economist" (2003). Changing the game. *The Economist Technology Quarterly.*

Johnson, M. (2017, July 31). *Starbucks' digital flywheel program will use artificial intelligence. Zacks.* https://www.zacks.com/stock/news/270022/starbucks-digital-flywheel-program-will-use-artificial-intelligence

Kotler, P., & Singh, R. (1981). Marketing warfare in the 1980s. *The Journal of Business Strategy, 1*(3), 30–41.

Kumar, V. (2014). Making "freemium" work. *Harvard Business Review, 92*(5), 27–29.

Liu, L. (2009, September 28). Coffee wars: McDonald's versus Starbucks. *ABC News.* https://abcnews.go.com/Travel/mccafs-compete-starbucks-europe/story?id=8690156

Marr, B. (2018, May 28). *Starbucks: Using big data, analytics and artificial intelligence to boost performance. Forbes.* https://www.forbes.com/sites/bernardmarr/2018/05/28/starbucks-using-big-data-analytics-and-artificial-intelligence-to-boost-performance/?sh=7b024d8f65cd

Ramstad, E. (2010). Samsung edges out TV rivals. *The Wall Street Journal.*

Ries, A., & Trout, J. (2006). *Marketing warfare: 20th anniversary edition.* McGraw Hill.

Zook, C. (2004). *Beyond the core: Expand your market without abandoning your roots.* Harvard Business School Publishing.

Zook, C. (2007). Finding your next core business. *Harvard Business Review, 85*(4), 66–75.

Zook, C., & Allen, J. (2001). *Profit from the core: Growth strategy in an era of turbulence.* Harvard Business School Publishing.

Figure Credits

When a company seeks to grow beyond domestic markets, it typically has four options: (a) an international strategy; (b) a multinational strategy; (c) a global strategy; or (d) a combination of a multinational and global strategy to develop a transnational strategy (Bartlett & Ghoshal, 1992). The following sections describe each of these approaches to internationalization and highlight various advantages and disadvantages that should be considered, as shown in Table 19-1.

An *international* approach to marketing strategy takes a product developed for the home market and sells it abroad without adaptation to two or more foreign markets. This approach usually works only if foreign markets are not too different than the domestic market relative to needs, tastes, consumer behavior, and competitors. A completely standardized approach has the advantage of higher scale economies, worldwide consistent brand image, and quality. The organizational structure associated with this strategy is very simple, as all important functions are centralized. With this approach, it is easier to transfer products or technologies quickly and efficiently and to effectively control what foreign subsidiaries do and how they implement the strategy. As an example, The Body Shop grew from a single store in the United Kingdom in 1976 to distributing products in more than 3,000 stores in 69 countries (Certified B Corporation, 2021). The founder, Anita Roddick, established the company with a core value of non-animal tested cosmetic products. The marketing of that brand message and other social causes proved to have international appeal.

A second approach to internationalization is the *multinational* strategy. This approach, in which tailored strategies and marketing mixes are developed for different countries or regional markets, is appropriate if those markets are significantly different from the domestic market and/or from each other. Multinational strategies are appropriate when local conditions (context factors such as regulations, culture, or climate), competitors, or market structures (e.g., distribution systems and industry structures) require an adapted strategy and a customized marketing mix. This adaptation of strategies and marketing programs to meet local conditions is intended to maximize sales in each market, but will also increase costs, including not only the specific costs of adaptation (changes to product specifications, foregone scale effects when production runs are shortened, and the costs of adapting packaging, advertising messages, and support materials to local markets) but also the costs of redundancies in R&D, new product development, and marketing mix development as each country *reinvents the wheel*. Another risk of multinational strategies is confusion in brand building that may occur when a single brand is positioned differently or given different meanings across markets. Market boundaries are porous, and customers often purchase products and are exposed to brand messages across markets; therefore, positioning a brand differently in different markets may lead to customer confusion and consequently to dilution of the brand's equity. Nestlé is a good example of a company with a multinational strategy. Less than 2% of Nestlé's sales are in its home market of Switzerland, while it employs nearly 300,000 people and has more than 500 factories in nearly 100 countries (Nestlé, 2021). Nestlé's extremely successful multinational strategy includes developing adapted products and marketing mixes to local conditions around the world, often via the purchase of local companies and brands.

A *global* approach to marketing involves companies selling *the same thing, the same way, everywhere,* as opposed to developing products for a local market (and then adapting these products and selling them internationally) (Levitt, 1983). It is based on the observation that a global segment of customers with the same needs exists worldwide. This segment is addressed and a worldwide standardized product and marketing concept is developed. The advantage of a global approach is full exploitation of scale economies, consistent brand image and quality, and centralized control. Many companies that adopt this approach, however, quickly realize that differences in culture, consumer behavior, needs, and preferences exist, and that a completely standardized approach has a high likelihood of failure.

The *transnational* strategy has emerged in recent years because many international companies discovered that neither complete standardization nor full adaptation is successful as a strategy. Transnational strategists try to combine the benefits of a multinational and global strategy and adhere to the principle *as much standardization as possible, as much adaptation as necessary.* They develop a core product or marketing concept with standardized core components or modules, which can be adapted to local needs. This way they can exploit scale economies and customization

TABLE 19-1 Approaches to Internationalization

International	
Products are developed for the domestic market and sold abroad with no alteration	*Advantages* Scale economies Consistency in brands and offerings Ability to transfer products quickly and efficiently Simple organization Effective control
	Disadvantages Differences in customer needs, markets, and competition ignored Full potential of foreign market not exploited
Multinational	
Each foreign market develops customized strategies and offerings to fully adapt to the local requirements	*Advantages* Full adaptation to and exploitation of local market
	Disadvantages High product development and marketing costs Little economies of scale No consistent brand image, quality, etc. Duplication of efforts Little control over subsidiaries
Global	
Products are developed for the global market and companies sell "the same thing, the same way, everywhere" (Levitt, 1983)	*Advantages* Same as for international strategy, plus product developed for a global segment with the same needs everywhere Centralized control and decision-making
	Disadvantages Assumes that national tastes and preferences are similar and markets are homogenized
Transnational	
As much standardization as possible, as much adaptation as necessary	*Advantages* Combines advantages of global and multinational strategy
	Disadvantages Leads to complex organizational structures and a high need of coordination

advantages at the same time. This combination or transnational strategy, of course, requires much coordination between all the subsidiaries and the headquarters and can lead to complex and sometimes bureaucratic organizational structures. McDonald's employs a transnational strategy that allows them to simultaneously standardize their operations while adapting to local tastes and customs. For, example, a McDonald's customer can get a lobster roll in Maine, but not a Big Mac in Mumbai—instead it is a mutton substitute (lobster is readily available and a local favorite in Maine, especially with the considerable tourist trade, while the cow is considered sacred in Hinduism, the primary Indian religion). Thus, while much of McDonald's menu is standardized regardless of location, certain items are added or subtracted according to local tastes.

MARKET ENTRY STRATEGIES

When entering international markets, company executives must decide how many resources to commit, and the extent of control they need over their brand and foreign activities. Resource commitment and control are both associated with risks and profits. Basically, five international market entry modes exist: exporting, licensing, franchising, joint ventures, and direct investment (Cavusgil et al., 2008) as shown in Table 19-2.

Many companies start their first international activities with exports before they commit more resources to foreign markets. Indirect exporting through independent intermediaries and direct exporting through a home-based export department, foreign subsidiary, or sales representatives or agents entails limited risks. Limited resources are needed, and, therefore, this approach is very flexible. At any time, the company can intensify or limit its engagement without any major investments or losses. Exporting, however, is not suitable for every product, especially when high levels of service are needed. The exporter usually has no direct contact with the final customer and, therefore, will find it difficult to learn about needs and wants to adapt the product accordingly. Furthermore, the company fully bears the exchange rate risk.

Licensing is another entry strategy with limited risk and resource commitment. The licensor grants the right to use intellectual property (e.g., patents) or to manufacture and sell a company's product in a specified market against a royalty. Disney, for example, licenses its trademark and logos to manufacture apparel, toys, etc., for worldwide sales. The licensor benefits from the licensee's market knowledge and market access. As few resources are needed, this approach allows for quick entry into many foreign markets at the same time. The major drawback of this strategy is limited control over the licensor, relatively low profits (typically a 2%–10% royalty), and the risk that the licensor might become a potential competitor after termination of the licensing contract.

The difference between licensing and franchising lies in offering a complete brand concept and operating system to the franchisee. Franchising is common in the fast-food business. The franchisor provides training, marketing programs, and the whole business system against a lump-sum payment and a royalty fee. The advantages are similar to licensing. This market entry strategy usually works only for business systems and products that can be standardized. McDonald's, Domino's Pizza, and 7-Eleven stores all employ franchise models. In most franchise relationships, the franchisor and the franchisee have a contractual relationship where the franchisor provides the franchisee with certain benefits described above but also has the right to enforce certain standards on the franchisee. It could be compared to a parent–child relationship. On the other hand, a joint venture, the next concept, is more of a marriage of equals.

A joint venture with a local investor and shared ownership and control is a desirable option if the host country does not allow full ownership of a subsidiary by a foreign company. It is also desirable if competences, resources, or market access are missing and a local partner is needed. In many cases that local partner provides market access and the international partner contributes knowledge and technology resources. While this strategy allows the pooling of competencies and promotes risk sharing, many joint ventures fail because of differences in culture, strategic priorities, and conflicts regarding reinvestment or repatriation of profits. Joint ventures are often

TABLE 19-2 Comparison of International Market Entry Strategies

Exporting Indirect—through independent intermediaries Direct—through home-based export department, foreign subsidiary, sales representatives, or agents	*Advantages* Low risk Few resources needed Little organizational complexity *Disadvantages* Not suitable for complex products that need high levels of service No customer contact when indirect export Low exploitation of foreign market Exchange rate risks
Licensing Issuing a license to a foreign company to use a process, trademark, patent, or product	*Advantages* Low risk and few resources needed Allows quick entry in many markets simultaneously Licensee's knowledge of local market *Disadvantages* Little control over activities of licensor Might create and educate a future competitor Low profits
Franchising Offering a complete brand concept and operating system to a franchisee against a fee	*Advantages* Same as licensing, however higher control over franchisee Economies of scale through standardization Franchisee's knowledge of local market *Disadvantages* Only for products and concepts that can be standardized Control of franchisee necessary
Joint Ventures Joint venture with a local investor and shared ownership and control	*Advantages* Pooling of competences (e.g., market access, technology) Lower risk and capital needed as for fully owned subsidiaries In many countries, local partner required *Disadvantages* High conflict potential regarding strategy, reinvestment, etc.
Direct Investment Direct ownership of a foreign production or assembly plant	*Advantages* Full control Good relationships and better image with local authorities due to job creation *Disadvantages* Highest risks High resource commitment

common in the oil and gas industry, as well as the automotive industry. The next level in market entry is direct ownership.

Direct and full ownership of a foreign production or assembly plant implies the highest level of resource commitment, risk, control, and profit potential, but also the lowest level of flexibility. Foreign direct investment also improves relationships with local authorities and image due to the jobs created and the investments made. Japanese automakers Nissan, Toyota, and Honda have all established U.S. assembly and marketing organizations. Likewise, IBM has company-owned manufacturing facilities in a multitude of international countries.

SUMMARY

Companies can consider several approaches to internationalization, including an international strategy, a multinational strategy, a global strategy, or a transnational strategy. The decision to pursue a particular strategy depends on the extent of standardization or adaptation of products and promotions necessary in a given market. The selected strategy can also influence the entry method in a market, from the low risk and standardized approach of exporting to the high risk and adapted approach of direct investment. With the global adoption of the Internet in the 21st century, internationalization has become more attainable for companies than ever before. The related concepts of digital transformation and platform economies will be examined further in Note 20.

REFERENCES

Bartlett, C. A., & Ghoshal, S. (1992). *Transnational management: Text, cases and readings in cross border management.* Irwin.

Cavusgil, S. T., Knight, G., & Riesenberger, J. R. (2008). *International business strategy, management and the new realities.* Prentice Hall.

Certified B Corporation. (2021). *The Body Shop International.* https://bcorporation.net/directory/the-body-shop-international

Levitt, T. (1983). The globalization of markets. *Harvard Business Review,* 92–102.

Nestlé. (2021). *Is Nestlé a Swiss company?* https://www.nestle.com/ask-nestle/our-company/answers/is-nestle-a-swiss-company

DIGITAL TRANSFORMATION AND PLATFORM ECONOMIES

Digital transformation has become a top priority of almost every company. New digital technologies (e.g. Internet of Things, artificial intelligence, 5G, and robotics) change the way companies create value for their customers, deliver value, and capture value. Disruptors like Airbnb, Alibaba, Amazon, Google, Netflix, Uber, and many others have developed new business models that fundamentally change industries like travel, retail, education, media, and transportation. Consumer behavior is changing as well, e.g. they shift their purchases to online stores, use social media to be more informed, connected, and empowered, and rely more on mobile and AI-powered technologies. Digital transformation has a pervasive impact and can be divided into three different phases, digitization, digitalization, and digital transformation (Verhoef et al., 2021).

- *Digitization* encompasses the conversion of analog information into a digital format so that computers can store, process, and transmit that information. It turns atoms into bits, e.g. paper into electronic files, pictures into JPEGs, or music into MP3s. However, digitization does not necessarily change the fundamental way a company creates and delivers value (Gobble, 2018).
- *Digitalization* goes deeper. It makes use of digital technologies to change business processes such as operations, communication, distribution, and customer relationship management to increase efficiency or add customer value.
- *Digital transformation* is an enterprise-wide change of the business model. It uses new digital technologies to create, deliver, and capture value. Two examples are the move from print media to online formats or the change from video rental to video streaming.

These phases represent different degrees of change of a company and varying levels of potential to increase efficiency or to create customer value, as depicted in Figure 20-1. All of these phases also have important implications for marketing. The x-axis represents the degree of change while the y-axis represents the potential value these four types of digitalization offer.

Digitalization of products and services is the simplest form. A digitalization of products and services does not yet radically change the processes or the structure of a company, hence the required change is relatively low. A digitalization of processes goes a bit deeper as it requires more change within the company. Digitalization of the whole business model involves changes of the value created (i.e. products or services), changes of value delivery (i.e. value chain or processes), and value capture (i.e. the profit formula relative to revenue streams and cost structures). This requires a fundamental change of the company and obviously offers more profit opportunities. Finally, digitalization can go beyond a single company and involve the entire ecosystem, i.e. the company and its collaborating partners that jointly create and deliver value for the customer. The following sections describe how digitalization changes products, processes, business models, and ecosystems and emphasizes the most important implications for marketing.

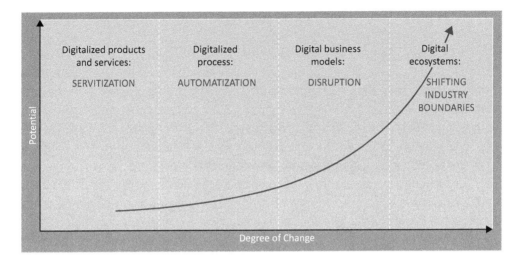

FIGURE 20-1   How Digital Transformation Changes Companies

DIGITALIZATION OF PRODUCTS AND SERVICES

A digital transformation journey often starts with the digitalization of products and services. Here the Internet of Things (IoT) has become a major trend. Products are equipped with sensors and actuators. Sensors collect data while actuators transform a signal into some form of motion. The Internet of Things very often changes the value proposition of a product, leading to what is often called servitization, i.e. a shift of revenue streams from product sales to service revenues. In simple terms, the Internet of Things (IoT) is the network of physical objects that contain embedded technology to communicate and interact with their internal or external environment ("Gartner," 2020). Ultimately, it is the connection of the physical with the virtual world.

Figure 20-2 shows a framework that demonstrates how companies can use IoT to create more value for their customers, going through a structured six-step approach (Matzler & Bailom, 2019). The award-winning digitalization project of Schindler Elevator Corporation illustrates how this IoT framework can be applied to redefine the value proposition of a product or service based on generated data and machine learning and how processes can be automatized and made more efficient (Buvat & Subrahmanyam, 2016). Following are the six steps in this process:

1. *Physical product or process.* In the first step, the physical product or service is chosen that should be digitalized. In the Schindler case, it was the elevator. The objective was to digitalize the customer experience.
2. *Sensors and actuators.* Physical objects are equipped with sensors and actuators. In the case of the Schindler Elevators, sensors in the elevator collect and transmit data on parameters such as vibration, speed, temperature, etc.
3. *Connectivity.* If the physical objects are equipped with IP-capable sensors, they can communicate with other objects or exchange data. Schindler's elevators communicate alerts

automatically to a control center in the case of an outage, and the system automatically collects 200 million data points every day.

4. *Analytics and machine learning.* The collection, storage, and evaluation of sensor data can now be used to gain valuable information that can be transformed into value-added services. Schindler applies data analytics and machine learning to detect patterns in the data. These patterns are the basis for digital services that deliver superior customer value.

5. *Digital services.* Based on big data, algorithms and machine learning are used to offer value creating services and increase efficiency of processes. Schindler uses predictive maintenance to anticipate problems and outages, automatically schedule maintenance routines and repair processes without need of customer intervention. Meanwhile, Schindler uses data analytics to reduce customers' elevator times with an intelligent destination–dispatch solution that calculates the fastest elevator to the destination.

6. *New value creation and value capture.* Finally, a new business model emerges with a new customer benefit and novel revenue logic. At Schindler, the real-time alert system makes repair services more than 20% faster, eliminates more than 40 million kilometers of driving by service technicians, and reduces by 50% the wait time for elevators in office buildings.

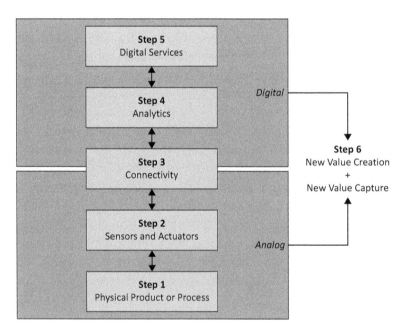

FIGURE 20-2 Value Creation Steps During Digitalization
(Fleisch et al., 2014)

IoT leads to an increasing value creation and value capture based on services. This shift from selling products to selling services, called servitization, is driven by IoT as it allows capture of in-depth information on how customers use products. This information can form the basis for four new archetypes of IoT enabled servitized business models (Suppatvech et al., 2019), which are listed below:

- *Add-ons*: Here IoT is used to offer additional functions or personalized services to the product. For example, Adidas recently introduced a smart ball. An integrated sensor captures data and provides feedback on shot strength, trajectory, and spin or speed via an accompanying app. The app provides tips for improving technique and skills. Customers can log their statistics, track their improvements, and share their success with friends (Matzler et al., 2018).
- *The sharing business model*: In this business model, the customer pays only for the use or for accessing a product for a limited amount of time. Car sharing is an example. IoT technology allows customers to locate available cars, unlock them, drive them, and return them. The fleet of cars can be used by a large pool of customers.
- *The usage-based business model*: Customers only pay for the actual usage of a product. Two forms of such business models exist. In the pay-per-use model, the customer is only charged for the actual usage or consumption. Rolls-Royce, for example, with its "Power by the Hour" program, offers a complete engine and accessory replacement service for its aircraft engines on a fixed-cost-per-flying-hour basis. In the subscription-based model, consumers pay for unlimited access to a product or service during the time span of subscription.
- *The solution-oriented business model*: Here the provider of the product or service uses IoT-technology to offer integrated solutions for uninterrupted usage to the customer. A good example is a manufacturer of machinery that uses predictive maintenance, remote support, and optimization of production based on usage data. Schindler Elevators provide an example of such a business model.

DIGITALIZATION OF PROCESSES

The digitalization of a company's processes usually leads to more efficiency through automatization, and at the same time it can create more value for the customers, very often by reducing pain points or delivering added value. For example, Schindler leveraged its IoT model to introduce an app that automatically generates job lists for its technicians based on real-time data of elevators, informs them about the tools and parts that are needed for repair, calculates the most efficient route to the customer site, and gives them access to multimedia technical information, service and safety instructions. Domino's Pizza has also used digitalization to transform its customers' journey, i.e. the steps that a customer goes through when interacting with the company (Buvat et al., 2016). Domino's has digitalized the touchpoints, delivering a seamless customer experience. To make pizza ordering as convenient as possible, Domino's invested in multiple digital platforms. Today, more than 75% of all orders come through digital channels with single-touch ordering via Apple Watch, SMS, Amazon Echo, Smart TVs, SMS, etc. As operations have been digitalized, the Domino's Pizza Tracker allows customers to seamlessly track their order from the oven to their home. With GPS technology, the customer is provided with detailed delivery information. Domino's has also been experimenting with digital delivery formats like drones and autonomous delivery vehicles.

DIGITALIZATION OF BUSINESS MODELS

A business model in simple terms describes how a company creates value for its customers, delivers this value, and captures part of the value it creates (Matzler et al., 2013). Digitalization allows companies to radically reinvent all these elements of their business model, which often leads to disruptive changes in an industry. As companies use digitalization to innovate their products and services, their processes and value chain, as well as their revenues streams, the whole business model is innovated or reinvented. Consider each part of the business model as it relates to Peloton, the technology company based in New York City that disrupted the fitness industry with its digitally connected cycles, treadmills, and subscriptions to fitness classes:

- *Value creation.* Home exercise is often boring, it lacks feedback, it is constrained by a limited range of workout options, and people have little sense of progression ("Oxygen," 2019). Peloton was designed "to bring the energy and excitement of studio-led classes … into the convenience and comfort of your home" ("Oxygen," 2019, para. 5).
- *Value delivery.* It delivers value by selling $2,000 stationary bicycles and giving access to high-energy classes. In interactive live-streamed classes, the user receives feedback from both the instructor and the bike display. Users who cannot make it to a live class have access to a large catalogue of on-demand classes. Peloton's platform also allows users to connect with other users and with friends (Iglehart, 2020).
- *Value capture.* Peloton's profit formula consists of two revenue streams. It sells the hardware (bikes and treadmills) and uses a subscription model to generate monthly recurring revenue from two million consumers.

DIGITAL ECOSYSTEMS

In many industries, digitalization has led to the emergence of giant ecosystems that radically transform industry boundaries. Ecosystems are "interdependent networks of entities that connect with one another to create and capture value" (Subramaniam et al., 2019, p. 84). While a trend towards ecosystems has been seen for many years, digital technologies have become important drivers of such ecosystems as they enable new forms of partnerships and change the nature of value creation and capture in many industries. In the car industry, for example, electrification, autonomous driving, diverse mobility, and connectivity favor software-driven innovation and a car of the future that will be a computer on four wheels (Beiker et al., 2016). As a result, a complex ecosystem of high-tech players will emerge that coordinate their activities to create value to include hardware (corner modules, advanced sensors), drivetrain (electric motors, advanced batteries), entertainment platform, autonomous drive/operating system, apps and services, alternative business models (e.g. autonomous vehicle sharing), and data analytics. Ecosystems offer a number of advantages (Williamson & De Meyer, 2012).

- First, ecosystems allow the lead firm to create customer value by offering complex, integrated solutions by coordinating diverse complementary capabilities. John Deere, for example, has developed a complex ecosystem existing of weather data systems, farm equipment systems, irrigation systems, and seed optimization systems to reposition itself as a farm management company that offers much more value than a simple producer of farm equipment (Porter & Heppelmann, 2014).

- Second, the lead firm can stay focused while its partners provide the complementary assets. This allows every partner in the ecosystem to concentrate on its core competencies and to grow faster as an ecosystem than any of the firms could if they had to invest in all the activities. In the car industry, it is likely that a handful of companies in most elements of the ecosystem will emerge as specialized and highly innovative (Beiker et al., 2016).

- Third, as the lead firm builds the ecosystem around its core competencies, it enjoys more flexibility in configuring the whole business system. Since it does not have to make heavy investments, it can more easily develop new partnerships and constantly evolve the business model.

- Finally, in an ecosystem, companies can generate more data and develop more value creating products and services based on data analytics. Ping An, for example, a global insurance and financial services company, has decided to develop a large ecosystem in the health care, automotive, real estate, smart city, and finance sectors. By offering health care consultations, auto sales, real estate listings, and banking services to more than 350 million customers through a digital platform, more customer traffic for Ping An's core services is generated, which leads to more customer touchpoints and more data ("McKinsey," 2018).

DIGITAL TRANSFORMATION SUMMARY

Digital transformation can radically change how companies create, deliver, and capture value. The digitalization of products and services, especially IoT, reinforces the trend towards servitization, i.e. a shift of value creation and capture toward services. For a marketing manager, several crucial questions emerge: How does your digitalized product or service provide value to customers? What type of useful data can be generated? How can these data be collected in real time and linked to other data? Which patterns and insights can you generate from the combined data? How can the data create new customer value? How can the created value be monetized?

The digitalization of processes leads to automatization and can dramatically change the customer's journey and its touchpoints. Some critical questions for a marketing manager include these: What is our customers' journey? What are the pain points? How can we remove those pain points through digitalization? What is the *magic* we can develop through digitalization of the processes?

The digitalization of the whole business model offers new opportunities to create, deliver, and capture value and thus change the business model of the firm. These changes can be so radical that existing business models are disrupted. The questions to consider relative to marketing strategy include these: Can we create new markets with our new business model? Can we disrupt existing industries with our new business model? Who are the other potential disruptors within our industry, and how can we counter the competition?

And finally, the emergence of large digital ecosystems can change or shift industry boundaries. Marketing managers need to consider questions such as the following: What is the new value proposition we can offer by collaborating with partners in the ecosystem? Which core competencies should we focus on, and which complementary competencies do we need for our new value proposition? Which data can we generate in our ecosystem, and how can we create and capture value based on big data and data analytics?

Now that we understand how digital transformation has the potential to change how companies create, deliver and capture value, we will examine how platform economies are changing the competitive environment.

PLATFORM ECONOMIES

In a digitalized economy, platforms provide the infrastructure to bring together producers and consumers (or consumers and consumers) and facilitate transactions among them. Amazon, Alibaba, Sony's PlayStation and SAP (which connects software developers with enterprise business clients) are examples of such platforms. Platforms differ substantially from traditional businesses (Van Alstyne et al., 2016a). *Pipeline* businesses that have dominated for decades create value by controlling a series of activities in the value chain, and economies of scale constitute important competitive advantages. In the *platform* economy, demand-side economies of scale are responsible for competitive advantages and foster the emergence of market-dominating platforms (McIntyre & Srinivasan, 2017). Platform growth and dominance are enabled by network effects, economies of scale, learning effects, and lock-in effects, as described in Figure 20-3.

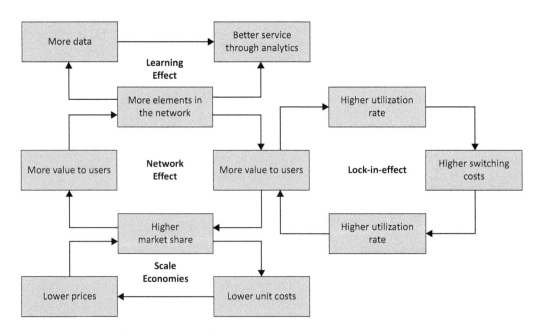

FIGURE 20-3   Platform Economies (Clement & Schreiber, 2016)

Network effects describe the increasing value of a platform as a function of the number of platform users. *Direct network effects* occur in same-sided markets when the value of the platform for a single user increases with the number of other users of the platform with whom they interact. Social networks like LinkedIn, Instagram, Facebook, or WhatsApp are examples of direct network effects. *Indirect network effects* arise in multi-sided markets where users benefit from the number of a different type of users on the other side. Airbnb, Uber, and Amazon provide examples of indirect network effects. The more customers Uber has, the more attractive the platform becomes for Uber drivers. The more Uber drivers there are, the better the service and the more attractive it becomes for customers. Platforms can also serve as building blocks on which other firms offer complements. Video game consoles (e.g. Sony's PlayStation) or mobile operating systems (e.g. Android) serve as platforms for which third-party developers develop games or apps that enhance the value of the platform. These types of platforms also benefit from network effects. The more users a platform has, the more attractive it becomes for the developers of games and apps. The more apps offered, the more value created for users.

With increasing size, platforms also enjoy *economies of scale* that lead to cost advantages. As platforms very often have to make large up-front investments (e.g. technology development) and marginal costs of serving additional customers are low, an increasing market share constitutes considerable cost advantages. Thus, economies of scale lead to cost advantages, cost advantages allow for lower prices, and lower prices increase market share. Hence, economies of scale constitute a second feedback loop for platforms.

Large platforms also benefit from *learning effects*. They process substantial amounts of data and through the use of machine learning and algorithms they are able to improve the processes and services. This, in turn, increases platform usage, and additional data improves the algorithms. At Uber Eats, data scientists develop solutions for challenges like personalized search and recommendations for restaurants, dynamic pricing, and routing optimization ("Uber," 2020). Based on large amounts of data, algorithms are developed to improve its services. The more data Uber has, the better Uber Eats' services become, and the better its services are, the more customers it will attract.

Network effects, cost advantages through economies of scale, and improved and personalized services can create considerable loyalty (through increased satisfaction) and customer switching barriers (as customers would lose advantages or would face substantial cost or inconvenience if they changed brands). The more a platform is used by the customer, the bigger the platform advantages and the customer *lock-in effect*. This not only secures constant and recurring revenues through customers but also contributes to increased usage, customer retention, and feedback to the platform economies.

While Airbnb, Alibaba, Amazon, and Google are examples of successful platforms, there are many others that failed to develop a growing and sustainable business. Thus, it is important to consider critical success factors for building and managing platforms (Van Alstyne et al., 2016a). Because of the platform economies as described here, size is crucial. The more users a platform has, the more attractive it becomes. This leads to a *winner-takes-it-all* phenomenon. Typically, only one or two platforms dominate the market so growing quickly and creating a critical mass are important.

Related to the *winner-takes-all* phenomenon is the *first mover advantage*. However, it is not necessarily the first mover that wins, but rather the first one who successfully scales its platforms to achieve market dominance. Creating superior value for the user and investing enough resources to grow are crucial. To successfully grow, the "hen-and-egg problem" needs to be solved. A platform is attractive only with enough users on both sides; to create that critical mass, it is often necessary to subsidize one side of the platform. PayPal, for instance, chose a very costly but successful tactic when it gave new users a $10 sign-up credit and $10 for referring a friend, achieving daily growth rates of 7% to 10%.

Ultimately, a platform's success depends on the value created by users and on how quickly it scales. Hence, openness regarding access (who is allowed onto the platform) and governance (what users are allowed to do there) is an important decision. If a platform is too closed, it will not attract enough users. If the platform is too open, poor quality and misbehavior of users might harm the platform. This is what happened to Myspace, a social network that was too open and lacked governance, so that "when garish advertising, spam, and pornography became the norm, users began to abandon the platform in droves" (Eastwood, 2016, para. 12). Apple in the 1980s is an example of a platform too closed. Steve Jobs decided to charge developers for tool kits, a tactic that resulted in limited software development for Apple's platform. In contrast, Bill Gates kept Windows open to software and hardware developers, growing it to become the dominant desktop platform (Van Alstyne et al., 2016b).

In the digital economy platforms are becoming an important business model. Due to network effects, economies of scale, learning effects, and customer lock-in, many platforms evolve into big market-dominating monopolies. Platforms change the rules of competition, and successfully managing these platforms requires different strategies. Creating critical mass, exploiting the first mover advantage, solving the "hen-and-egg problem," and overseeing their openness are critical success factors.

Platform economies have enabled *long tail* sales, whereby companies realize significant profits by selling low volumes of a large number of niche and hard-to-find products, instead of simply selling high volumes of a limited number of blockbuster products. The final section of this Note will examine the value of this long tail phenomenon.

THE LONG TAIL

The Pareto principle, generally known as the 80/20 rule, describes a very common principle of sales concentration. In many markets and in many firms, 20% of the products generate 80% of the sales. In other words, many markets are dominated by a few best-selling products. A relatively small number of established best-selling authors sell a big share of all books, the Billboard's "Top 40" account for the lion's share of played music in the radio and music sales, and a few blockbusters generate most box office sales (Brynjolfsson et al., 2011). The Internet, however, is changing this old principle of sales concentration, facilitating a shift from a few best-selling products to selling more hard-to-find-items; in other words it is facilitating a shift from the short tail to the long tail.

In their studies about the *long tail* in Internet markets, MIT professor Erik Brynjolfsson and his colleagues have shown that, for many products, Internet channels show less sales concentration than traditional channels (Brynjolfsson et al., 2003). Internet retailers have learned that for a wide variety of products like books, music, consumer products and apparel, relatively high sales volume and profits can be generated, even with just a few stock keeping units (SKUs) (Salvador et al., 2020). The long tail has been especially evident in digital distribution platforms like Amazon, iTunes, and Netflix. This phenomenon is illustrated in Figure 20-4. A brick-and-mortar book retailer concentrates their sales efforts on the most popular books (top 100,000), whereas Amazon generates about 40% of books sales with the long tail, i.e. products that you would not find in a brick-and-mortar store (right side).

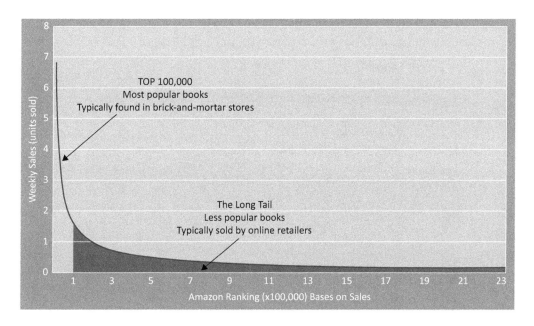

FIGURE 20-4   The Long Tail of Book Sales (Brynjolfsson et al., 2006)

There are two explanations for this shift toward the long tail. First, for an Internet retailer it is much easier and cheaper to carry an extensive product selection. A typical brick-and-mortar book retailer, for instance, has between 40,000 and 100,000 books on the shelves because of physical space restrictions, logistics and holdings costs (Brynjolfsson et al., 2006). It is not economical to carry rarely sought items or to offer out-of-print titles. Centralized inventories and drop-shipping agreements, however, allow Internet retailers to offer millions of books. Second, on the demand side, Internet retailers make it much easier and convenient for consumers to search and find niche products. Many of them have developed algorithms to recommend products based on the customers' purchase history and other data, lowering search costs for customers (Brynjolfsson et al., 2011). When there is a strong incentive for producers to focus on the mass markets because it is not economical to address very small market niches that are difficult to find and difficult to reach, only mass market products find their way to store shelves. With the Internet, however, the product portfolio of retailers can be easily expanded to include now-profitable niche products as they reach niche audiences. This provides small producers and artists new opportunities to offer their products and a greater overall choice for the consumer.

Anderson (2007) popularized the idea of the *long tail* and has described some important managerial implications. First, in most markets there are more niche products than hits. This share is growing as digital technologies lower production costs and market entry barriers for small companies or start-ups. Second, digital distribution lowers the cost of finding and of reaching niche markets for all products. This leads to a massive expansion of product variety. Third, simply offering more variety is not enough. Powerful algorithms are needed to match supply and demand. More variety can mean more choices; however, effective filters are necessary to give consumers ways to easily and conveniently find products that meet their preferences. Fourth, once there is large product variety and once there are effective matching algorithms, the demand curve flattens and sales concentration is reduced (see Figure 20-5). Fifth, the combination of all niche markets can become as big as best-selling markets.

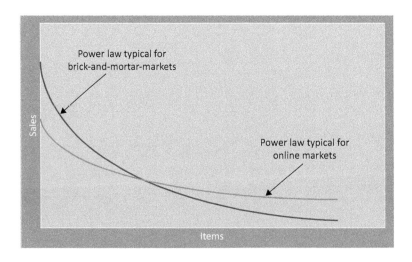

FIGURE 20-5   Power Law of Brick-and-Mortar and Online Markets

While the long tail suggests that sales concentration is reduced and more variety is offered, there is also evidence of a *superstar* effect, i.e. a skewness in market outcomes that resembles a *winner-takes-all* phenomenon. This effect is especially common on platforms that use previous selections and preferences of similar customers ("customers who bought this item also bought …") as the basis for product recommendations where self-reinforcing feedback loops (e.g. more recommendations because of popularity, and more popularity because of recommendations) favor a few stars that attract significant attention (Coelho & Mendes, 2019).

SUMMARY

Digital technologies have transformed how organizations create, deliver and capture value. The digitalization of products and services is typically the starting point for the process of digital transformation. The advent of the Internet of Things (IoT) has enabled the connection of the physical with the virtual world. IoT can be applied to redefine the value proposition of a product or service based on generated data and machine learning. IoT has also driven the shift from selling products to selling services (i.e., servitization) as it allows for the capture of in-depth information on how customers use products. The digitalization of processes and business models further extends the application of IoT for improved efficiency and profitability of a company. In many industries, digitalization has led to the emergence of new ecosystems that radically transform the boundaries of business.

In a digitalized economy, digital platforms provide the infrastructure to bring together stakeholders and facilitate transactions among them. Platform growth and dominance are increased by network effects, economies of scale, learning effects, and lock-in-effects. Platform economies have also enabled managers to consider new opportunities, such as long tail sales, whereby companies realize significant profits by selling low volumes of a large number of niche products rather than simply selling high volumes of blockbuster products. For managers to be successful in the 21st century, they must constantly consider how to leverage digital technologies and platforms to strengthen their operations and strategic marketing efforts.

REFERENCES

Anderson, C. (2007). *The long tail: How endless choice is creating unlimited demand*. Random House.

Beiker, S., Hansson, F., Suneson, A., & Uhl, M. (2016). *How the convergence of automotive and tech will create a new ecosystem*. McKinsey & Company, Automotive & Assembly.

Brynjolfsson, E., Hu, Y. J., & Smith, M. D. (2006). From niches to riches: Anatomy of the long tail. *Sloan Management Review*, 47(4), 67–71.

Brynjolfsson, E., Hu, Y., & Smith, M. D. (2003). Consumer surplus in the digital economy: Estimating the value of increased product variety at online booksellers. *Management Science*, 49(11), 1580–1596.

Buvat, J., & Subrahmanyam K. (2016). Going Up @ Schindler: How the elevator and escalator giant rose to digital excellence. https://capgemini.com/consulting/wp content/uploads/sites/30/2017/07/schindler_digital_masters_series_final.pdf

Buvat, J., Subrahmanyam K., & Cherian S. (2016). Domino's Pizza: Writing the recipe for digital mastery. https://www.capgemini.com/wp-content/uploads/2017/12/dti_dominos_pizza_masters_series_final.pdf

Clement, R., & Schreiber, D. (2016). *Internet-Ökonomie*. Springer Gabler.

Coelho, M. P., & Mendes, J. Z. (2019). Digital music and the "death of the long tail." *Journal of Business Research*, 101, 454–460.

Eastwood, B. (2016, May 3). *The return of platforms (and how to not fail at building one*. MIT Management Sloan School. https://mitsloan.mit.edu/ideas-made-to-matter/return-platforms-and-how-to-not-fail-building-one

Fleisch, E., Weinberger, M., & Wortmann, F. (2014). Geschäftsmodelle im Internet der Dinge. *HMD Praxis Der Wirtschaftsinformatik*, 51(6), 812–826.

"Gartner." (2020). Gartner Internet of Things. https://www.gartner.com/en/information-technology/glossary/internet-of-things

Gobble, M. M. (2018). Digitalization, digitization, and innovation. *Research-Technology Management*, 61(4), 56–59.

Iglehart, A. (2020). *Peloton: Riding quarantine into a demand boom*. Harvard Business School Digital Initiative. https://digital.hbs.edu/platform-digit/submission/peloton-riding-quarantine-into-a-demand-boom/

Matzler, K., & Bailom, F. (2019). Fit für die digitale Disruption werden. *Organisationsberatung, Supervision, Coaching*, 26(2), 257–265.

Matzler, K., Bailom, F., von den Eichen, S. F., & Kohler, T. (2013). Business model innovation: Coffee triumphs for Nespresso. *Journal of Business Strategy*, 34(2), 30–37. https://doi.org/10.1108/02756661311310431

Matzler, K., von den Eichen, S. F., Anschober, M., & Kohler, T. (2018). The crusade of digital disruption. *Journal of Business Strategy*.

McIntyre, D. P., & Srinivasan, A. (2017). Networks, platforms, and strategy: Emerging views and next steps. *Strategic Management Journal*, 38(1), 141–160.

"McKinsey." (2018). *Digital insurance in 2018: Driving real impact with digital analytics*. McKinsey. https://www.mckinsey.com/~/media/McKinsey/Industries/Financial Services/Our Insights/Digital insurance in 2018 Driving real impact with digital and analytics/Digital-insurance-in-2018.ashx

"Oxygen." (2019, July 29). *How Peloton has redesigned the in-home fitness experience.* Oxygen Consulting. https://www.oxygen-consulting.co.uk/how-peloton-has-redesigned-the-in-home-fitness-experience/

Porter, M. E., & Heppelmann, J. E. (2014). How smart, connected products are transforming competition. *Harvard Business Review*, 92(11), 64–88.

Salvador, F., Piller, F. T., & Aggarwal, S. (2020). Surviving on the long tail: An empirical investigation of business model elements for mass customization. *Long Range Planning*, 53(4), 101886.

Subramaniam, M., Iyer, B., & Venkatraman, V. (2019). Competing in digital ecosystems. *Business Horizons*, 62(1), 83–94.

Suppatvech, C., Godsell, J., & Day, S. (2019). The roles of internet of things technology in enabling servitized business models: A systematic literature review. *Industrial Marketing Management*, 82, 70–86.

"Uber." (2020). Uber Information.

Van Alstyne, M. W., Parker, G. G., & Choudary, S. P. (2016a). Pipelines, platforms, and the new rules of strategy. *Harvard Business Review*, 94(4), 54–62.

Van Alstyne, M. W., Parker, G. G., & Choudary, S. P. (2016b). Reasons platforms fail. *Harvard Business Review*, 31(6), 2–6.

Verhoef, P. C., Broekhuizen, T., Bart, Y., Bhattacharya, A., Dong, J. Q., Fabian, N., & Haenlein, M. (2021). Digital transformation: A multidisciplinary reflection and research agenda. *Journal of Business Research*, 122, 889–901.

Williamson, P. J., & De Meyer, A. (2012). Ecosystem advantage: How to successfully harness the power of partners. *California Management Review*, 55(1), 24–46.

Figure Credits

MARKET SEGMENTATION

When determining which consumers to target, a company has basically two options: mass marketing or segmented marketing. Mass marketing is a strategy that treats all consumers as if they are the same—or at least treats all consumers very similarly—with a standardized marketing mix. This is a *one-size-fits-all* approach with the same product, same price, same distribution, same communications, and same sales efforts in all markets. Mass marketing reflects the desire to achieve scale effects (i.e., economies of scale, learning curve effects, and synergies) and preserve organizational simplicity and control. Within domestic markets, such as the United States or the European Union, many companies pursue mass market strategies. Coca-Cola, for example, is often the exemplar for mass marketing: Everybody drinks Coke, everybody sees the same brand messages for Coke, and everybody finds Coke in the same places.

Nevertheless, for most organizations, the world is not so simple. In fact, in the majority of markets, there are opportunities to gain advantage by adapting offerings to customer differences. Customers vary in their needs, tastes, preferences, and buying behavior. As a consequence, markets can be divided into homogeneous segments of customers with similar needs and behavior, with each segment clearly differing from the others. Adopting this approach allows a company to focus on the most promising market segments, tailor its offers to their needs and preferences, and more effectively design and coordinate individual marketing activities to a specific target group.

In fact, even Coca-Cola's mass marketing strategy is more complex than it seems on first review. At one time, the company's standardized offering was simple: Coke came only in six-ounce bottles with fountain syrup, and there were no alternative formulations. Over time, however, Coke's product lines proliferated, and now customers can choose from not only traditional Coke but also Diet Coke, Coke Zero, Caffeine-free Coke, Caffeine-free Diet Coke, Cherry Coke, and Vanilla Coke in a variety of sizes and packaging. When you consider Coke's international markets, adaptations in the company's "standardized" marketing mix becomes even more striking. For example, there is a small group of enthusiastic consumers in the United States who covet Mexican Coca-Cola. The Mexican version of Coke is made with sugar instead of corn syrup and, therefore, tastes different. Thus, for a variety of reasons, including differing national commercial conditions, regulations, cultures, and available ingredients, even iconic Coca-Cola has adapted its flagship product to local contexts.

The Coca-Cola example highlights the fact that in almost every market and for almost any marketer, there are substantial opportunities to be uncovered by segmenting markets and developing tailored marketing mixes for distinct segments.

APPROACHES TO MARKET SEGMENTATION

Today, strategists rely upon one of two basic approaches when they want to segment a market: either segmentation based on observable customer characteristics or segmentation based on underlying needs and benefits sought (Dubois et al., 2007). No matter which method is used, however, the process of segmenting, targeting, and positioning (also known as "the STP process") entails the following six essential steps:

1. Identify effective segmentation variables.
2. Group customers into homogeneous segments.
3. Create a detailed profile/persona of the individual segments.
4. Select the target segment.
5. Create a sustainable positioning for the target segment.
6. Develop a tailored marketing mix to reach the target segment.

This Note addresses only the first three steps. Targeting, positioning, and the marketing mix are described in Notes 23 to 32.

FACTORS IN MARKET SEGMENTATION

The overall objective of market segmentation is to tailor products and services (and the overall marketing program) to the needs of individual segments. To do that profitably, all identified segments should possess the following factors (Kotler & Keller, 2009):

- *The segment should be internally homogeneous.* In other words, all customers within a particular segment must have similar needs and behaviors.
- *The segment should be externally heterogeneous.* This means that the members of one segment must differ in some way from the members of all other segments.
- *The segment should be accessible.* Accessibility is critical because without it an organization cannot effectively address, reach, and serve the members of a segment.
- *The segment should be measurable.* This means that marketers must be able to identify and measure the segment's size, needs, and other characteristics.
- *The segment should be substantial.* Here, the segment must be large enough to be served at a profit.
- *The segment should be actionable.* Finally, if a segment is actionable, then marketers can tailor programs that serve it both effectively and efficiently.

SEGMENTATION BASED ON OBSERVABLE VARIABLES

Markets can be segmented based on any number of observable variables. Tables 21-1 and 21-2 provide examples of variables typically used to segment consumer and business markets, respectively.

TABLE 21-1 Consumer Segmentation Variables

SEGMENTATION FACTOR	EXAMPLES OF VARIABLES USED	EXAMPLE OF APPLICATION
Geographic	• Geographic region • City size or density (e.g., urban, suburban, rural)	In Austria, a major European tourist destination, vacationers are often segmented according to their country of origin (e.g., Italians, Germans, Scandinavians, Russians) because their needs, vacation styles, behavior, and so forth strongly correlate with their nationality.
Demographic	• Age • Gender • Family life cycle • Income • Occupation • Education • Social status	Many banks use income and occupation to segment their customers for private banking services. Many producers of baby products segment the market according to age for products such as baby food and toys.
Psychographic	• Personality traits • Lifestyle • Attitudes about factors such as self, family, and society	Certain tourist destinations segment markets according to the lifestyle orientation of guests (e.g., culture, family, outdoor, relaxation, or sports).
Behavioral	• User status (nonuser, ex-user, potential user, first-time user, regular user) • Intensity of use (heavy versus light users) • Urgency, reason, cycle of demand • Attitude (enthusiastic to hostile) • Innovativeness (innovators, early adopters, early majority, late majority, laggards)	Mobile phone service providers segment the market using behavioral variables and create plans for frequency and intensity of services as well as domestic or international usage.

As demonstrated in Table 21-1, consumer segmentation variables can be broadly classified as geographic, demographic, psychographic, and behavioral.

Geographic variables (e.g., region, city size, population density) are the most basic descriptors of segments. Due to the increasing mobility of consumers and globalization of markets (which leads to stronger availability of global brands and diminishing cultural differences in many international markets or regions), this category has lost a great deal of its importance in market segmentation. In many cases, geographic variables are, therefore, combined with other variables to arrive at more meaningful market segmentation.

Demographic variables (e.g., age, gender, family life cycle, income) are more powerful in predicting behavior than geographic variables and are included in most market segmentations. However, like geographic variables, they have declined in importance during the last few decades because, in most cases, they merely *describe* segments and do not actually *cause* differences in needs and behavior. Especially in developed countries, individuals have needs and adopt behavior independent of their demographic characteristics, and this has led to an increasing standardization of consumption modes across social classes, age groups, and so forth.

Psychographic variables (e.g., personality traits, lifestyle) are often used when geographic and demographic variables fail to predict needs and behavior. Psychographic variables are tied more directly to attitudes, motivations, and behavior than the aforementioned categories of variables. However, their use is more difficult because it requires sophisticated market research techniques.

Behavioral variables (e.g., user status, intensity of use) divide customers into homogeneous segments based on their consumer behavior, or their attitudes toward the use of, and response to, a product. These variables are directly related to purchase and consumption behavior and are therefore well suited to use in marketing strategy.

When segmenting business markets, organizations consider both macro and micro variables, as shown in Table 21-2. Macro variables can include the size of the market, purchasing approaches, and situational factors. Micro variables can include characteristics specific to the target organization, such as their motivations for purchasing and their willingness to assume risk.

TABLE 21-2 Organizational Segmentation Variables

SEGMENTATION FACTOR	EXAMPLES OF VARIABLES USED	EXAMPLE OF APPLICATION
Macro variables	• Demographics (size, industry, location) • Operating variables (technology, user/non-user status, capabilities) • Purchasing approaches (single versus multiple sourcing, centralized versus decentralized purchasing, purchasing criteria) • Situational factors (urgency, order sizes, product application)	Enterprise Resource Planning (ERP) software market is segmented primarily based on company size as it influences: Number of users IT skills Propensity to use ERP Buying criteria Customization Another frequently used segmentation variable for ERP software is industry, because industry type influences product requirements.
Micro variables	• Personal characteristics (motives, risk-taking tendencies, loyalty)	Certain banks segment the market of corporate clients based on their risk-taking attitude and tailor financial products to either risk-taking or risk-avoiding customers.

Table 21-3 gives an example of market segmentation in skiing tourism based on customer lifestyles. For each segment, there is a detailed profile of the customer with socio-demographic descriptors, preferred vacation style, preferred activities, and so on. These types of segment profiles are important to marketers when identifying target markets and tailoring the marketing mix to those target markets.

Conceptually, there is no difference between segmentation in business-to-business markets (B2B) and in business-to-consumer (B2C) markets; in both cases, the logic is the same. However, the criteria that are used can differ greatly. One especially useful approach to segmenting B2B markets is the nested approach developed by Bonoma and Shapiro (1983). This approach is based on the premise that marketers should start with macro variables (e.g., demographics, operating variables, purchasing approaches, and situational factors) to find differences, and if no differences are found, they should move on to consideration of personal characteristics.

TABLE 21-3 Lifestyle Market Segmentation in Skiing Tourism

	SEGMENT 1 "PLEASURE SEEKER"	SEGMENT 2 "WORK ORIENTED"	SEGMENT 3 "COUCH POTATO"	SEGMENT 4 "FAMILY ORIENTED"	SEGMENT 5 "COMMITTED HELPER"	SEGMENT 6 "THE INCONSPICUOUS"	SEGMENT 7 "CULTURE INTERESTED"
Segment size	12.2%	13.9%	13.5%	14.9%	13.7%	13.3%	18.4%
Lifestyle	Enjoying life, fun, variety seeking	Fulfillment in occupation, self-centered	No pleasure seeker, frugal	Family is the center of interest	Socially and politically active and helping others	Living a simple and frugal life	Furthering knowledge, intellectual, culture interested
Socio-demographics	15 to 24 years, single, high school and trainees	24 to 44 years, high education, self-employed or executive	35 to 44 years major part, but also 44 and up, married with children	35 to 44 years, married with children, high education	55 to 65 years, all types of employment	24 to 35 years, low education, skilled worker and employees	15 to 24 and 55 to 64 years, students and pensioners
Winter vacation style	fun and entertainment	emphasis on sports and relaxation	relaxation, gain new strength	relaxation	cultural experience, staying at home	no clear preferred vacation style	no clear preferred vacation style
Vacation activities	going out, attending local events, skiing, snowboarding	skiing, snowboarding, saunas, eating out	skiing, going for walks	saunas, thermal spas, skiing, going for walks	cross country skiing, ski touring	not very active in general	going for walks, relaxing
Top five satisfaction drivers (correlation with overall satisfaction)	Ski resort (.501) Shopping (.454) Cityscape (.407) Entertainment (.373) Landscape (.284)	Ski resort (.644) Cityscape (.437) Bad weather program (.388) Comfort of accommodation (.358) Peacefulness of destination (.343)	Ski resort (.601) Cityscape (.489) Bad weather program (.434) Landscape (.46) Gastronomic quality (.393)	Ski resort (.515) Gastronomic quality (.301) Shopping (.283) Landscape (.259) Cityscape (.223)	Ski resort (.518) Comfort of accommodation (.457) Gastronomic quality (.427) Cityscape (.398) Bad weather program (.396)	Ski resort (.668) Cityscape (.423) Entertainment (.404) Bad weather program (.312) Landscape (.294)	Ski resort (.511) Cityscape (.425) Gastronomic quality (.382) Shopping (.322) Comfort of accommodation (.313)

Note. From Matzler, K., Pechlaner, H., & Hattenberger, G. (2004). *Lifestyle-typologies and market segmentation: The case of Alpine skiing tourism, 45.* Bolzano: EURAC.

Let's consider this approach using Table 21-4, which describes the market segments for ERP software. Here, firm size explains most differences between the segments and is the most appropriate variable. In a subsequent step, however, one might look at a second variable—such as industry—to refine the market segments even further.

TABLE 21-4 Segmentation of the European ERP Software Market

	SMALL BUSINESS MARKET	MID-MARKET	MID-ENTERPRISE	LARGE ENTERPRISE
Size	1–49 employees, < $25m revenue	50–499 employees, $25–250m revenue	500–5,000 employees, $250–500m revenue	>5,000 employees, >$500m revenue
Number of companies (Europe)	8.7m businesses	1.3m businesses	30,000 businesses	1,000 businesses
IT staff	One or a few, mostly single persons with multiple responsibilities	Small group of people, usually not involved in strategic decisions, no long term IT strategy	Full line of IT staff	CIO with board participation, full line of IT staff
IT skills	Modest, learning on the job	Generalists, usually lack of specialization	Specialists	Highly skilled IT-staff
Buying criteria	Ease of use, price	Software depth, functionality, total cost of ownership	Software depth, functionality, total cost of ownership	Security, Software breadth and depth, functionality, total cost of ownership
Customization preference	Generic and less customized ERP system	High degree of integration	High degree of integration and customization	High degree of integration and customization, ERP important for competitive advantage

Note. Adapted from SG Cowen Research, *European Observatory for SME*, 2002, No. 2, IDC, Small Business Survey, 2002. www.erpsoftware360.com

SEGMENTATION BASED ON BENEFITS SOUGHT

As illustrated in the previous section, geographic and demographic variables are widely used for market segmentation because they are easy to identify. Psychographic and behavioral variables are more relevant to needs and behavior, but they are more challenging to measure, and segments based on these variables are also more difficult to address. Thus, an alternative approach is that of *benefit* or *benefits-sought segmentation*. Benefits sought segmentation begins with the *needs* and *wants* that are responsible for and explain differences in consumers' responses to the marketing mix. Because this approach uses causal instead of descriptive variables, benefit segmentation identifies more homogeneous segments. For instance, Table 21-5 presents a well-known example of benefits-sought segmentation of toothpaste consumers. The first three steps of the benefits-sought segmentation process are as follows:

1. Identification of the benefits sought and assessment of the importance of primary benefit(s) to the individual segments.

TABLE 21-5 An Example of Benefit Segmentation

	WORRIERS	HEALTH CONSCIOUS	SOCIABLES	SENSORY SEGMENT	INDIFFERENT
Primary benefit sought	Decay prevention, sensitive teeth	Decay prevention	Cosmetic, brightness of teeth	Sensory, flavor	Economy, all-in-one
Demographics	Higher education, higher income	Families	Young people	Children, young people	Men
Price sensitivity	Low	Medium	Low–medium	Medium	High
Brand loyalty	High	High–medium	High–medium	Medium	Low
Behavior	Heavy users	Heavy users	Smokers, coffee and tea drinkers	Prefer spearmint toothpaste	Heavy user
Preferred outlet	Pharmacy, dentist	Drug store, super-market	Drug store, supermarket	Supermarket	Supermarket, discounter
Typical brand	Rembrandt, Parodontax Med, Sensodyne Med	Aronal and Elmex, Parodontax, Sensodyne	Macleans, Perlweiss	Colgate, Crest	Brands on sale
Lifestyle charac-teristic	Living a conscious life	Conservative	Active	Hedonistic	Value-oriented

Note. Based on Haley, 1968, and Lambin, 2007.

2. Building of segments based on the primary benefits.
3. Creation of a detailed customer profile of each segment based on observable variables (e.g., demographics, behavioral variables).

As previously mentioned, steps 4 to 6 (targeting, positioning, and the marketing mix) are discussed in Notes 23 to 32.

SUMMARY

Markets are almost never truly homogeneous; customers have differing needs and wants and will respond differently to the elements of the marketing mix. A basic assumption of marketing is that customers will gravitate toward offerings that best suit their own needs and wants. However, customizing the marketing mix toward distinct needs and wants has inherent costs—including the cost of adapting the mix and the opportunity cost of foregone economies of scale, to name just a few. Still, the benefits of customization often outweigh the costs, and this is where segmentation becomes important. Segmentation is the essential first step in strategy formulation—it entails differentiating relatively homogeneous groups of customers (segments) within otherwise relatively heterogeneous markets based on their needs and wants, on the benefits they seek from a product, and on observable characteristics such as geographic location, demographic attributes, and lifestyles. The most widely used segmentation schemes are based on observable customer characteristics, underlying needs, and benefits sought. Regardless of how it is done, segmentation describes individual segments and allows organizations to target them with adapted marketing mixes.

REFERENCES

Bonoma, T. V, & Shapiro, B. P. (1983). *Segmenting the industrial market*. D. C. Heath and Co.

Dubois, P. L., Jolibert, A., & Mühlbacher, H. (2007). *Marketing management: A value-creation process*. Palgrave MacMillan.

"European Observatory." (2002). SG Cowen Research: Small business survey. *European Observatory for SME*. www.erpsoftware360.com

Haley, R. J. (1968). Benefit segmentation: A decision oriented research tool. *Journal of Marketing*, 30–35.

Kotler, P., & Keller, K. (2009). *Marketing management* (13th ed.). Pearson Education.

Lambin, J. (2007). *Market-driven management*. Palgrave Macmillan.

Matzler, K., Pechlaner, H., & Hattenberger, G. (2004). *Lifestyle-typologies and market segmentation: The case of Alpine skiing tourism, 45*. Bolzano: EURAC.

At any given time, a company has a specific number of active customers—its pool of customers or customer base. To understand loyalty-based marketing strategies, it is useful to think of that pool of customers as an actual pool or tub of water with an inflow (a faucet) and a few outflows (the drain and leaks in the tub). Logically, there are two ways to increase the amount of water in the tub: increase the inflow (turn up the faucet) or decrease the outflow (slow the drain and fix the leaks). In the same way, to increase customer base and thereby sales, a firm has two basic tools: it can invest in customer *acquisition* and it can invest in customer *retention*.

Most firms are constantly trying to both attract new customers *and* keep existing customers at the same time, so this is a matter of strategic emphasis and determining the most efficient and effective balance of investments. Studies show that it can cost as much as 10 times more to attract a new customer than to keep an existing customer and that a 5% increase in customer retention can lead to a 25% to 90% increase in profitability (Reichheld, 1996; Reichheld, 2001; Reichheld, 1993). Despite these findings, research has also shown that firms regularly overinvest in customer attraction and underinvest in customer retention.

The overemphasis on customer acquisition at the expense of customer retention was, for many decades, also true in the marketing management literature; much of the research and most textbooks focused on tools, tactics, and strategies for acquiring new customers, and too little attention has focused on customer retention or allocation of resources (marketing budgets) toward that end. Over the past few decades, however, increased attention has improved managing customer loyalty and making strategic decisions that balance investments across these two fundamental marketing tasks. Still, the tendency for marketers and students of marketing to think first and foremost about customer acquisition—advertising, sales and the like—remains an impediment in formulating effective marketing strategies and allocating marketing budgets efficiently.

Frederick Reichheld, author and consultant at Bain & Company, has been an influential advocate for increased emphasis on customer-retention strategies. Reichheld's seminal book *The Loyalty Effect* (1996) articulated the logic of focusing on customer retention, which goes well beyond the water-in-the-tub analogy. As Reichheld observed, reducing customer defections is often cheaper than attracting new customers, and, just as importantly, loyal customers may actually be *better customers* than new customers or customers who must constantly be re-earned. In order to understand these relationships between loyalty and firm success, it is important to understand how loyal customers may behave differently than others, as well as to distinguish two types of loyalty—attitudinal versus behavioral loyalty—and to add other, related considerations to the analysis, especially customer profitability across time, or "Customer Lifetime Value" (CLV).

LOYAL CUSTOMERS ARE BETTER CUSTOMERS

Reichheld showed that customer loyalty predicts profitability—generally, the higher the percentage of overall sales attributed to loyal customers, the more profitable the firm will be. He asserted that loyal customers not only provide the base profit that all customers deliver (the transaction margin), they also buy more (larger transactions and increasing purchases across time), cost less to serve, provide referrals (recommendations and positive word-of-mouth that attract other customers), and pay a price premium. Furthermore, the acquisition costs per customer (the one-time costs occurring before the customer engages with the firm and not recurring while the customer is with the firm) are, in the case of loyal customers, spread across or attributed to more occasions, lowering the per-transaction acquisition cost (see Figure 22-1).

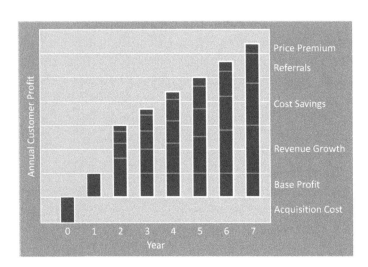

FIGURE 22-1 Why Loyal Customers are More Profitable (Reichheld, 1996, p. 39)

Subsequent research has confirmed the fundamental relationship between a firms' proportion of loyal customers and its profitability: *the more loyal customers a firm has as a proportion of its sales, the more profitable it tends to be* (Reinartz & Kumar, 2002; Reinartz & Kumar, 2000; see also Selden & Colvin, 2003 and Watson et al., 2015). As empirical research has tested Reichheld's specific hypotheses in larger samples across more industries and in more settings, it is unclear whether loyal customers are cheaper to serve or whether loyal customers pay higher prices for a given assortment of products. Similarly, accumulating research shows that although some loyal customers make frequent referrals (positive word of mouth), other loyal customers do not (Wieseke et al., 2014).

It turns out that, in order to understand loyalty and its impact on firm success, it is necessary to augment the analysis with a richer understanding of loyalty itself, distinguishing *attitudinal loyalty* from simple *behavioral loyalty*, and to add at least one other variable to the analysis. Specifically, to drive firm success through loyalty, it is necessary to also consider customer *profitability* or customer lifetime value (CLV). These considerations—adding an understanding of different types of loyalty and CLV to the analysis—can support identifying and targeting the right customers and avoiding the wrong ones.

IDENTIFYING THE RIGHT CUSTOMERS

Believe it or not, there are certain customers that a firm does not want to attract, retain, or do business with at all. One such set of "wrong" customers consists of price shoppers. These customers are attracted by discounts (coupons, rebates, volume discounts, or the like) or lowest price offers. Such characteristic usually makes these *price-sensitive* customers less attractive—although that reality is not always recognized by strategic marketers.

Unless a firm has consciously decided that its strategy is cost/price-based differentiation (such as Walmart with its impressive logistics and buying power cost advantages), those customers who are attracted by a price deal are unlikely to serve the firm's objectives well or for long. One competitor in every sector or product category has cost advantage, and a few may be close enough in their cost structure to compete successfully and profitably based on price. Only those competitors should target price-sensitive customers. All others should avoid price competition—including avoiding discounting and short-term price-based promotions—and strive to compete on differentiating attributes that attract certain customers. That is how they will command margin and profitability.

The exceptions to the general rule that only firms with the lowest cost operations (*cost leadership*) should compete on price are generally limited to specific efforts to attract customers to *try* a product. That is, some price deals are strategically shaped to induce customers to give the brand or product a trial based on the belief that trial will lead to adoption and long-term consumption. Price deals intended to induce trial need to be well thought through and impermanent, but they do represent an exception to the general warning against competing on price and hoping for loyalty and profitability.

Behavioral Loyalty Versus Attitudinal Loyalty

The relationships proposed by Reichheld linking loyalty to profits via cost-to-serve, price sensitivity, and referrals/word-of-mouth are clarified when *attitudinal* loyalty (or *psychological* loyalty) is differentiated from *behavioral* loyalty. Customers may purchase from a company, product or brand repeatedly across time (the simplest and most observable definition of loyalty is repeated purchase or patronage across time) because of attitudinal loyalty—*they really like the product*—or for some other, less flattering reasons such as high switching costs, volume discounts, or another source of inertia. Customers who are attitudinally loyal are those who like, maybe even *love* the firm, product, or brand. The brand satisfies these consumers' needs well and they perceive compelling value in their purchases. They will buy it again and again because of that affection and satisfaction, and those attitudinally loyal customers are in fact less expensive to serve, less price sensitive (although they may expect discounts in return for their loyalty), more resilient to service failures, more likely to increase their purchases across time, and more likely to recommend the product or service to others. *These attitudinally loyal customers are the most valuable.*

On the other hand, consumers can feel trapped with a product; they repurchase it for whatever reason, but they are not well satisfied with the product or service. Customers who demonstrate behavioral loyalty but feel no real satisfaction or liking for the brand may have various reasons for such behavior, including procurement policies; contractual obligations; overwhelming convenience (for example, shopping at an otherwise unsatisfactory grocery store due to geographic proximity and time constraints); or, high switching costs (for example, copying machines that require purchasing consumable supplies from the original equipment manufacturer and, at the consumer level, capsule coffee machines that require capsules from the company or licensed partners).

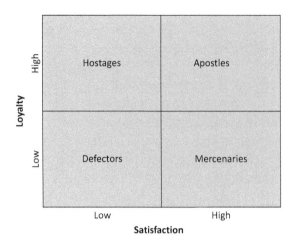

FIGURE 22-2 Apostle Model of Satisfaction and Loyalty (Jones and Sasser, 1995)

This distinction between attitudinal and behavioral loyalty is important. Building attitudinal loyalty is invaluable; trapping customers can, on the other hand, be tremendously damaging. Attitudinal loyalty results from commitment, trust, and satisfaction. Research has shown that attitudinal loyalty has much stronger positive consequences for the firm than behavioral loyalty (Watson, et al., 2015) Jones and Sasser (1995) distinguished attitudinal loyalty (highly satisfied customers who repeat purchases across time) from what they labeled *false loyalty* or behavioral loyalty (those with no underlying preference or satisfaction). They identified four types of customers who may repeat purchase across time (Figure 22-2) (Jones & Sasser, 1995):

- *Loyalists or Apostles* (high satisfaction, high loyalty). These are the most attractive customers as they are completely satisfied and loyal. These customers are highly profitable and engage in positive word-of-mouth.
- *Mercenaries* (high satisfaction, low loyalty). These customers are challenging. They are often variety seekers, and it may take a lot of effort to please them. As they are difficult to keep, these customer relationships are rarely profitable, despite the fact that the brand satisfies their needs well.
- *Defectors* (low satisfaction, low loyalty). These customers had bad experiences and will share their experiences with others. A company should try to minimize harm from defectors by listening, responding, and correcting problems—and by avoiding customer acquisition activities that draw these customers to the brand in the first place.
- *Hostages* (low satisfaction, high loyalty). Very often in a monopolistic environment or when there are high switching barriers, these customers have to accept what the company offers; they have no choice. If the situation changes, these customers will defect quickly. If attitudinally loyal customers are apostles, then these hostages may be labeled terrorists—they're likely to spread negative word-of-mouth and they can be terribly destructive to the brand and its profits.

Thus, it is important to understand both customer loyalty and customer satisfaction. Applying these dimensions to analyze the customer base creates valuable, actionable information for targeting segments, for grouping and analyzing customers, and for managing customer relationships.

Figure 22.3 shows the example of two Alpine ski resorts, one with a more favorable portfolio of customers and one with a very high share of defectors. The differences are striking and explain the key challenges of one of the resorts: low satisfaction and low loyalty, coupled with negative word-of-mouth. Data for this matrix were taken from a large-scale customer satisfaction survey (Matzler, 2014).

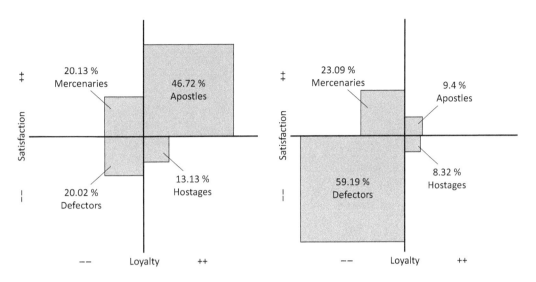

FIGURE 22-3   Apostle Model of Customer Loyalty Example

How is the ski resort shown on the left different from the one on the right? The graph on the left shows a firm that has many (46.72%) satisfied customers who return often. The resort on the right has many dissatisfied customers, including more than one in ten who revisit the resort but are dissatisfied. Strategies for the firm on the right should focus on increasing customer satisfaction, exploring why so many loyal (at least behaviorally loyal) customers are nevertheless dissatisfied, and also targeting the mercenaries with tactics to increase patronage (data collection and reminder messaging, for example, can improve repeat visits from satisfied customers who do not visit regularly).

CUSTOMER LOYALTY AND CUSTOMER PROFITABILITY

Customer loyalty is clearly a desirable and strategic objective, but it is not enough on its own to drive long-term success. Rather, identifying and attracting customers who are both loyal *and* profitable is the key to long-term profitability and sustained success. In other words, loyalty is part of the picture, but it's not the whole picture. This logic is directly related to customer lifetime value (CLV), the data-driven estimation of how much different customers, and different segments of customers, are worth across their lifetime with the firm.

CLV is an essential customer- and segment-related parameter that strategic marketers must understand and analyze to target the right customers and to gauge appropriate, efficient, effective, and strategic marketing investments across alternative activities. CLV is the present value of the contribution margins received from a customer. It is important to think of the time value of money and discounted present value in estimating CLV because it is *not* the simple sum of the future contribution. It is also important to understand that a customer's value is not the total sale but rather the contribution margin of that sale. So, customer lifetime value is the present value of the stream of contribution margins across time.

Professors Werner Reinartz and V. Kumar developed an insightful two-by-two categorization of customers based on profitability and loyalty. Shown in Figure 22-4, each type of customer has a different type of relationship with the product and, most importantly, requires different strategic actions (Kumar, 2013).

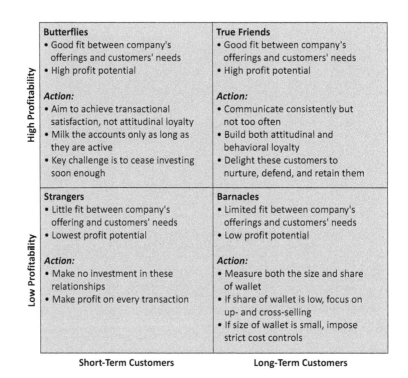

FIGURE 22-4   Customers Differentiated by Loyalty and Profitability (Reinartz and Kumar, 2002)

- *Strangers* are low-loyalty/low-profitability customers, and the firm should avoid offering loss leader products to them. Loss leaders are items priced at or below costs in an effort to build traffic and draw customers to the company's stores or website. If loss leaders are not also leading customers into profitable shopping baskets of products (i.e., if the customers are just cherry-picking the loss leaders and not buying any other, higher-margin products), then the firm should eliminate the loss leader product offerings to these customers.
- *Barnacles* are high-loyalty/low-profitability customers that present marketers with a trickier situation. Here, the first question is whether the low profitability is the result of *small wallets* (customers with little to spend) or low *share of wallet* (customers who spend on more profitable items elsewhere). In the first instance, small wallets, the appropriate strategy recognizes that customers are purchasing the precise assortment of products they need, which is likely *all* they'll ever purchase. Two viable strategies with these barnacles are to lower costs and sell the given, limited assortment profitably or avoid these customers altogether. On the other hand, if the issue is share of wallet, the firm is looking at customers who are loyal, which should make them attractive if not ideal, even if they are currently

spreading their purchases across vendors. The best strategy in this case is to target a greater share of wallet via cross-selling and to ensure that the increased share of wallet is in more profitable items (upselling).

- *Butterflies* are low-loyalty/high-profitability customers that buy full-margin items but, for some reason, are not loyal. A lack of loyalty can be due to inherent attributes of the customers—for some reason their need for the firm's products is irregular—or their lack of loyalty can be due to the manner in which the firm meets their needs. That is, some customers may only experience the need for a company's products on an infrequent basis. In those cases, there is little the firm can do (except enjoy the infrequent but profitable sales). On the other hand, some customers may have continuing needs for the products, but, upon meeting those needs from the given firm, they may either take their needs elsewhere or forego meeting the needs altogether for longer periods. That is, if butterflies are dissatisfied when dealing with the firm, they may go to the competition or exit the market. In those latter cases, the butterflies represent an opportunity to improve the offering—either by improving the core product or by improving the surrounding service and customer experience—in order to develop those customers into *true friends*.

- *True Friends* are high-loyalty, high-profitability customers and are the most attractive segment in this taxonomy. These customers should compel the greatest investment in communications, customer relationship management (CRM, discussed later in this Note), and service. A great example of a strategy that focuses on this customer segment is the shift of resources in grocery stores from express lanes (where customers with small purchases get the fastest service) toward better service (more registers, more clerks, and more baggers) for customers in the regular checkout lanes. One grocery store chain identified three large segments of shoppers: those who spent about $20 a week; those who spent about $75 a week; and, those who spent about $150 a week. It actually *cost* the grocer $3 every time the $25 shoppers visited the store; the grocer made about $6 for every $75 shopper visit, and the grocer made, on average, $30 for every visit by a big spender. However, the best and fastest checkout service was reserved for the light spenders, implying that future investments in service enhancement should be targeted at the *best customers*, in effect those customers with full shopping carts (Tompkins, 2004).

BALANCING ACQUISITION AND RETENTION SPENDING

As argued above, there is evidence that many marketers focus disproportionate levels of their resources on acquiring customers at the expense of investments in retaining customers. In fact, one study found that 95% of marketing expenditures are focused on traditional customer acquisition activities, whereas only 5% are focused on customer retention (Christopher et al., 2001, p. 58). This suggests that firms are putting too much emphasis on attracting new customers, especially in light of the aforementioned logic of customer loyalty. The solution, however, is not to refocus *all* marketing dollars on loyalty/retention. Instead, strategic marketing requires that firms systematically and analytically balance acquisition and retention investments. These decisions should be, as much as possible, data driven based on an understanding of which investments will bring in the highest long-term returns.

To understand why this balance is important, it is necessary to recognize that some customers will be easier and therefore cheaper to retain. A campaign to move a firm's retention rate by 10% from 30% to 40% will be cheaper per customer than a similar effort to go from 85% to 95%. This is a basic *production function* with diminishing marginal returns (outputs; retained customers, in this case) on marginal inputs (marketing budgets and resources). Although a firm may continue to spend on customer retention and continue to increase loyalty as it spends those marginal dollars, its returns on that spending will inevitably diminish as customer loyalty approaches some upper limit. The cost of the *next retained customer*, or the marginal cost of keeping the next customer, will go up as the firm strives to achieve ever greater retention.

There is a logical consequence of the increasing marginal cost of retention: if the value (profits from) all customers is the same (if the CLV of each customer is assumed to be constant), at some point the increasing cost of retention will reach and then *exceed* the marginal benefit (profits) from keeping that next customer. If the only marketing tools available to the firm were customer retention investments, then the firm would rationally stop investing at the point that costs reach returns.

But this analysis is about making choices between two sorts of investments—investments in retention and investments in acquisition—not simply deciding the upper limit of retention spending. As with customer retention, when the firm tries to acquire new customers, the first customers are relatively easy to attract. Some customers are predisposed to buy the firm's products for some reason. It might be said that, for those great-fit customers, all the firm had to do was *open its doors*. But, as the firm tries to attract more and more customers, each marginal new customer will cost more to acquire. The same relationships hold for acquisition as for retention: if there was only the one place to invest—customer acquisition—the firm would want to stop investing when the marginal cost reaches the marginal benefit. A rational marketing strategist will spend up to, but not past, the point where the costs of acquiring the customer are only equal to the profits that the customer will generate.

But the marketing strategist is *not* limited to just investing in customer retention or just investing in customer attraction—they are balancing opportunities to invest in *either* retention or acquisition, and they are allocating their marketing budget and resources across the two sorts of investments. Any funds invested in customer retention have an opportunity cost, a foregone investment in customer acquisition, and vice versa. The heart of the matter is making efficient and effective choices between investments.

Figure 22-5a shows that, for a hypothetical firm, increasing retention spending from €150 to €200 increases customer retention from about 67% to 70%. The key question, then, is how profitable are those 3% of customers who were retained by spending the marginal €50? The answer to this question requires more than just a cost-benefit analysis of the marginal retained customers—it also requires consideration of whether the return on those 3% of customers is worth more than the profitability of the new customers that could have been acquired with the €50 if those funds had been shifted to customer acquisition.

In Figure 22-5b, the balance of customer lifetime value against the cost of retention appears to turn (become negative for margin-retained customers) at about €75 in retention spending; after that, the marginal benefits (contribution margins) are less than the marginal costs (retention

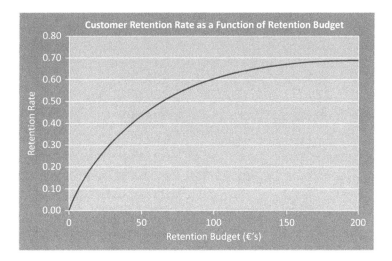

FIGURE 22-5A Return on Investment in Customer Retention
(Adapted from Blattberg and Deighton, 2010)

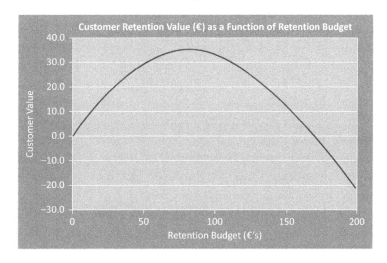

FIGURE 22-5B Profit from Investments in Customer Retention
(Adapted from Blattberg and Deighton, 1996)

spending). Of course, the converse question can and should be applied to resources spent on customer acquisition: Are the new customers acquired with this expenditure more valuable than the old customers who would have been retained if these funds had been spent on customer retention?

This system of interdependent calculations is dependent on estimating CLV reasonably accurately and on understanding the yield of various investments in terms of either new customers acquired or current customers retained. Those parameters then support a straightforward comparison of marginal investments in either retention or acquisition.

When investing in retention, the next requirement for loyalty-based marketing strategies is to understand what drives customer loyalty and what fundamental tools can be deployed to increase customer loyalty. The specific tools for building customer loyalty are idiosyncratic to the industry, the customers, the firm, and its products, but several tactics, including service recovery policies, loyalty programs, and especially Customer Relationship Management (CRM) systems are robust tools for loyalty-based marketing and for retaining the right customers.

DRIVERS OF CUSTOMER LOYALTY: CUSTOMER SATISFACTION

Customer acquisition activities include almost all advertising, most personal selling (although salespeople often service accounts as well as close deals), and traditional marketing communications, such as public relations. In contrast, customer retention tends to involve initiatives that focus on improved service and follow-up, service recovery, product quality, and especially customer relationship management (CRM). One key to choosing from this range of potential loyalty tactics is to think about the influence various actions will have on customer satisfaction. The fundamental way to gain customers' affection or attitudinal loyalty is to deliver unique value—something they cannot get elsewhere—and exceed their expectations.

Indeed, customer satisfaction is a central idea in marketing. According to this view, the purpose of a firm is to serve the customer and engender customer satisfaction. Customer satisfaction results in customer *attitudinal* loyalty. Customers form their satisfaction based on evaluation of how well a product—whether it is a good or a service—meets their expectations. If the product fails to meet expectations, customers will be dissatisfied, and, depending on their degree of displeasure, dissatisfied customers can "exit" (switch to an alternative brand) or even actively denigrate the brand or firm. If the product just meets expectations, customers will be minimally satisfied—but minimally satisfied customers are footloose customers, still shopping for a better experience. Finally, if the product exceeds expectations, customers will be satisfied and perhaps delighted—and delighted customers stay with the firm and sometimes even become *brand evangelists*.

One interesting issue to consider is the interrelationship between the details of customer acquisition—who the firm targets—and the loyalty of the resulting customer pool. Smart companies target customers who are likely to become loyal from the outset. They seek out customers likely to end up staying with the firm. Past experience with similar customers is probably the best predictor of future results with various sorts of customers. Demographics can also predict future loyalty; older customers, rural customers, customers who are not well-educated, and women are all more likely to be loyal to a brand.

The media through which customer-acquisition messages are communicated can also predict loyalty. Customers acquired through price deals are least likely to be loyal, as discussed earlier, but there are other cross-media differences that predict loyalty as well. For example, a major insurance company analyzed its customers based on which media they had responded to when acquired by the company. It turned out that direct mail customers (i.e., customers acquired via direct mail offering) were least loyal in the long term; customers who first saw an ad on television were more likely to become loyal; and customers acquired through word-of-mouth referrals from other customers were the most likely to be loyal in the long run (Verhoef & Donkers, 2005; O'Brien & Jones, 1995).

TOOLS OF CUSTOMER LOYALTY: SERVICE RECOVERY

The most robust predictor of customer satisfaction is not the absolute level of perceived quality or value but, rather, the confirmation or denial of the customer's expectations. That is, if you go to a fast-food restaurant and get a burger that tastes great for a relatively low price, you are not less satisfied than you would have been going to a white-tablecloth restaurant and getting a somewhat better burger. More important than whether the burger was high quality is what you expected prior to the purchase/consumption experience and how your actual experience compared with that expectation. But every company has failures; products and services are not always going to be of the intended quality, and they will not always meet the customer's expectations. How a firm handles these product defects or service failures is critical to managing customer loyalty.

It turns out that prompt, forthright (acknowledging the failure), and equitable efforts to remedy failures can not only restore the customer's satisfaction—that is, bring them back to the level of attitudinal loyalty they felt prior to the failure—but prompt *service recovery* can actually engender greater satisfaction and greater customer loyalty than previous to the incident. This is often called the *service recovery paradox* (McCollough & Bharadwaj, 1992; Hart et al., 1990).

All service recovery tactics do not need to include refunds or replacement products. It has been shown that simply acknowledging the service failure, demonstrating a commitment to the customer and an appreciation for their patronage, and apologizing can significantly ameliorate dissatisfaction and restore or even enhance loyalty (Roschk & Kaiser, 2013).

TOOLS OF CUSTOMER LOYALTY: LOYALTY PROGRAMS

Managing customer loyalty is a key concern of most marketing managers. When American Airlines' launch of its AAdvantage loyalty program in 1981—offering loyalty fares, free first-class tickets, upgrades, and discounts—it caused a boom in reward programs that endures to this day (Berry, 2015). Since 2000, the number of loyalty program memberships in the U.S. has increased by 400%, and the average U.S. household belongs to more than 30 loyalty programs (Kim et al., 2021). A KPMG study found that, for most mature brands, 85% of the growth comes from loyal customers (KPMG, 2016). Loyalty programs have proven to influence consumer behavior considerably. About two thirds of consumers make special trips to stores in order to earn awards in a loyalty program, 75% would give "rave reviews" to at least one of their loyalty programs, and about 60% say that they would pay slightly higher prices at a store to earn a loyalty program award (KPMG, 2016).

Loyalty programs are designed to offer rewards for customers based on repeat purchases or engagement with the brand (Kumar & Reinartz, 2018). The Volkswagen Club allows customers to collect points when VW services their car or when they buy VW accessories or products from their partners (e.g. car rental companies). These points can be redeemed for services or discounts (Kumar & Reinartz, 2018). Payback, a leading multipartner loyalty program and multichannel marketing platform in Europe, has introduced a mobile payment app with a digital loyalty card. Members can collect points from thousands of companies and marketplaces to redeem these for vouchers, rewards, frequent flyer miles, or donations to charity projects. It allows companies to upsell, cross-sell, acquire new customers, reactivate inactive customers, and build brand image (Payback Group, n.d.). Loyalty programs have become very popular and are a *sine qua non* (necessary and essential condition) for any competitive entrant in some segments, including hotels and airlines. They offer many benefits to customers and companies. Nevertheless, they are not all financially successful. Their management can be quite complex and costly (Kumar & Reinartz, 2018).

Successful loyalty programs are designed to identify prospective members, new members, active members, and dormant or lost members that offer certain benefits depending on the stage of the customer relationship (Kim et al., 2021). In the acquisition phase, prospective members need information about the future benefits. In the onboarding stage, members expect quick value deliveries. In the expansion stage, loyalty programs should focus on upgrading and cross-selling, especially for customers who want to achieve an elevated status. Finally, in the retention stage, loyalty programs should prevent status demotion, e.g. rewarding also based on social media engagement rather than only purchases (Kim et al., 2021). Advances in information technology and social media offer many new opportunities for loyalty programs, such as gathering more customer data, interacting with customers in real time, and offering personalized information and services (Kim et al., 2021). Starbucks, for example, has integrated its loyalty program into its app, helping customers to find a store, access the menu, and place orders before they even get to the café. The app also sends push notifications informing customers about special promotions.

TOOLS OF CUSTOMER LOYALTY: CUSTOMER RELATIONSHIP MANAGEMENT

Another tool—more accurately another *category* of tools—focused on enhancing customer loyalty and profitability is Customer Relationship Management (CRM). This begins with collecting data on customer behaviors across various touchpoints with the company. *Touchpoints* are the many and diverse places, ways, and times that customers interact with the company, from contact with a salesperson to a visit to the website or physical location. CRM also encompasses integrating and analyzing those data to derive actionable information or *customer insights*. Those CRM analyses can include basic statistical analyses—correlations and cross tabs, for example—to identify relationships or to describe segments. However, CRM can also involve advanced and complex data mining and machine learning analyses usually done by sophisticated experts. A marketing strategist need not become an expert in data mining to understand its results and appreciate the value of the insights it generates in guiding marketing actions.

The actions that can be guided by CRM range from choosing target segments and levels of investment across segments to customizing offerings for specific chosen segments and even for specific customers. In the past (and still today in too many organizations), a customer might talk with an executive, talk with a salesperson, call a support desk, take delivery from a route driver, and have a repair or installation person on site—all with the same vendor, but without those various contacts ever being integrated into a single understanding of that customer or that customer's needs. The repair person might observe that the customer uses certain products more than others but needs specific add-on options to use them better and with fewer breakdowns.

The executive might know that the customer is planning geographic expansion. The salesperson might know that the purchasing agent makes decisions in isolation and with little feedback from users. If all of those insights remain detached, the company may be missing an opportunity to customize a solution that will help the customer grow, reduce frustrating breakdowns and downtime in their operations, and improve their purchasing processes to optimize their buying power and operational efficiency. That is, those disconnected understandings and insights represent lost opportunities.

Customer data are valuable in adapting and driving the marketing mix—what prices, products, communications, and distribution points should be targeted at which customers and when—and such data are invaluable in analyzing customers and segments with regard to profitability and loyalty and also in understanding how to target the right segments with the right offerings. CRM uses advanced information management and communication technologies to track customer information across touchpoints, to systematically tailor new offers to individual customers, and to provide accurate and timely information on customer behavior, reactions to marketing campaigns, profitability, and so on to marketing strategists. These enhanced relationships should increase profitability and loyalty among the customers the firm wants. The accumulated data on customers' needs and profiles become a competitive asset or resource—something the competition does not have and is hard for the competition to recreate quickly. Thus, capturing data across customer touchpoints and mining those data for valuable (profitable to the firm) and valued (appreciated by the customer) insights tend to capture the customer (i.e., leads to durable and enduring customer relationships).

One essential truth about CRM and any other database or data-driven analysis is that the results are only as good as the inputs. The old adage "garbage in, garbage out" is still absolutely true. The marketing strategist need not become a data scientist and perform the advanced math and data mining that a CRM facilitates, but the marketing strategist must insist on collecting copious data throughout the customer experience. That is especially true for customer satisfaction metrics. Whether it be the Net Promoter Score (a single item measuring likelihood of the customer recommending the product, service, or firm to a friend or colleague) (Reichheld, 2003), or other measure of satisfaction (including indirect metrics like defections and complaints), managing customer loyalty demands that the firm understand how it is satisfying customers, as well as how profitable the customers are across the life of the relationships (in effect, their CLV).

Despite CRM's promise and undeniable logic of capturing and analyzing data on all the various ways customers interact with the firm across the breadth and duration of their experience with the firm, early efforts to build CRM databases (data warehouses) and to cull those data for useful insights were expensive and frustrating. This may be partly due to the fact that early CRM initiatives were focused on the technology—the hardware and software required to capture information about contacts and to build the large databases describing those contacts—and also because those data and the insights they produce were not distributed to all parts of the organization. That is, early CRM systems focused on the technology and not on getting the information into the right hands at the right time. More recent CRM investments have been more productive, and CRM is now a fundamental part of action-oriented marketing research and loyalty-based marketing strategies.

SUMMARY

The idea that it is often more effective and more efficient to invest in retaining current customers rather than investing those same resources in trying to acquire new customers is not revolutionary, but it has been underappreciated. Extensive research has revealed that firms with more loyal customers tend to be more profitable than those with fewer, and analyses have shown that loyal customers are more valuable than short-term, transitory customers. This loyalty-profitability relationship is especially true for attitudinal loyalty; it may be less true or untrue for behaviorally loyal customers lacking attitudinal loyalty. It has also been shown that most firms overinvest in customer acquisition activities and underinvest in customer retention. Still, investments in customer retention, like investments in customer acquisition, tend to produce diminishing marginal returns, and at some point, investments in retaining the marginal customer will exceed the value of (profits expected from) that customer.

Customer retention tools include enhanced ancillary services—improvements to the services that surround the core product often differentiate the offering and engender the greatest loyalty—and also include CRM systems. CRM allows for improved targeting of the right customers (picking who to serve) and the customization of offerings (tailoring or personalizing the marketing mix) to maximize customer satisfaction, customer loyalty, and firm profitability.

REFERENCES

Berry, J. (2015, February). The 2015 COLLOQUY loyalty census big numbers, big hurdles. *COLLOQUY.* https://www.petrosoftinc.com/wp-content/uploads/2018/03/2015-loyalty-census.pdf

Blattberg, R. C., & Deighton, J. (1996, July–August). Manage marketing by the customer equity test. *Harvard Business Review* 74, 136–44.

Christopher, M., Payne, A., & Ballantyne, D. (2001). *Relationship marketing.* Butterworth-Heinemann.

Hart, C. W., Heskett, J. L., & Sasser Jr., W. E. (1990). The profitable art of service recovery. *Harvard Business Review* 68(4), 148–156.

Jones, T. O., & Sasser, W. E. (1995). Why satisfied customers defect. *Harvard Business Review,* 73(6), 88–99.

Kim, J. J., Steinhoff, L., & Palmatier, R. W. (2021). An emerging theory of loyalty program dynamics. *Journal of the Academy of Marketing Science,* 49(1), 71–95.

KPMG. (2016). Is it time to rethink loyalty programs?

Kumar, V. (2013). *Profitable customer engagement: Concept, metrics, and strategies.* Sage Publications.

Kumar, V., & Reinartz, W. (2018). *Customer relationship management.* Springer-Verlag GmbH Germany, part of Springer Nature.

Matzler, K. (2014, November 6). Presentation at the Best Ski Resort Conference, Zurich, Switzerland.

McCollough, M. A., & Bharadwaj, S. G. (1992). The recovery paradox: an examination of consumer satisfaction in relation to disconfirmation, service quality, and attribution based theories. *Marketing Theory and Applications,* 119.

O'Brien, L. & Jones, C. (1995). Do rewards really create loyalty? *Harvard Business Review* 73(3), 75–82.

Payback Group. (n.d.). Marketing Services for Business & Industry. https://www.payback.group/de/en/payback-group/payback/performance/

Reichheld, F. F. (1993, March–April). Loyalty-based management. *Harvard Business Review* 71(2), 64–73.

Reichheld, F. F. (1996). *The loyalty effect*. Harvard Business School Press.

Reichheld, F. F. (2001). *Loyalty rules!* Harvard Business School Press.

Reichheld, F. F. (2003). The one number you need to grow. *Harvard Business Review*, 81, 46–54.

Reinartz, Werner J., & Kumar, V. (2000, October). On the profitability of long-life customers in a noncontractual setting: An empirical investigation and implications for marketing. *Journal of Marketing* 64(4), 17–35.

Reinartz, Werner J., & Kumar, V. (2002). The mismanagement of customer loyalty. *Harvard Business Review* 80(7), 86–94.

Roschk, H., & Kaiser, S. (2013). The nature of an apology: An experimental study on how to apologize after a service failure. *Marketing Letters* 24(3), 293–309.

Selden, L. & Colvin, G. (2003). *Angel customers and demon customers: Discover which is which and turbo-charge your stock*. Portfolio, Penguin.

Thomas, J. (2010, March 8). Personal communication. Graphic summary of Blattenberg and Deighton's ideas in Figure 22-5a was created by Thomas, a professor at Southern Methodist University.

Tompkins, J. A. (2004). Customer satisfaction and the supply chain. In *The Supply Chain Handbook*, James A. Tompkins & Dale Harmelink (Ed.). Tompkins Press.

Verhoef, P. C., & Donkers, B. (2005). The effect of acquisition channels on customer loyalty and cross-buying. *Journal of Interactive Marketing* 19(2), 31–43.

Watson, G. F., Beck, J. T., Henderson, C. M., & Palmatier, R. W. (2015). Building, measuring, and profiting from customer loyalty. *Journal of the Academy of Marketing Science*, 43(6), 790–825.

Wieseke, J., Alavi, S., & Habel, J. (2014). Willing to pay more, eager to pay less: The role of customer loyalty in price negotiations. *Journal of Marketing* 78(6), 17–37.

Figure Credits

The selection of the appropriate marketing approach and the decision about the target segment(s) requires a thorough analysis of the market and the segmentation of customers (e.g., using demographic, psychographic, or behavioral characteristics). To make targeting decisions, a detailed evaluation of segment attractiveness and competitive advantages in those segments is required. After an organization has segmented its markets and developed detailed segment profiles, two important decisions have to be made:

1. Should the organization adopt an undifferentiated or differentiated marketing approach?
2. If it adopts a differentiated marketing approach, which segments should be targeted?

UNDIFFERENTIATED VERSUS DIFFERENTIATED MARKETING APPROACHES

The two basic strategies an organization can adopt are undifferentiated and differentiated marketing (Kotler & Keller, 2009). Undifferentiated marketing ignores segment differences and applies a *one-size-fits-all* approach: one product and one marketing program for all customers regardless of segment differences. This leads to benefits from scale, especially economies of scale in research and development, production, advertising, distribution, and other overhead expenditures. Undifferentiated marketing also simplifies organizational structures. Coca-Cola once used this strategy, offering one single product and a single size—the famous original green glass bottle—to the mass market. Increasing competition against differentiated products and the emergence of more idiosyncratic needs (such as family-size bottles, sugar-free drinks, caffeine-free drinks) has led Coca-Cola to adopt a differentiated marketing approach.

Differentiated marketing means that a company develops adapted or customized marketing mixes for different target market segments. As products and programs are tailored to the segments, the company can better meet the segment-specific needs and requirements and can, therefore, create superior value and demand price premiums. The downside of differentiated programs includes the higher complexity of the organization and the product portfolio, the diluted benefits of scale, and, as a consequence, the higher per-unit costs. Differentiated marketing can consist of the following:

- *Selected specialization.* In this scenario, the company selects and focuses on one or a few single segments. The Austrian company Emporia Telecom adopted this strategy when it developed a cell phone for elderly people without digital camera, Internet access, or instant messaging capabilities. However, the cell phone did include a button to call relatives or friends in an emergency, was compatible with hearing aids, and ran on regular batteries. It had big easy-to-use buttons, intuitive dialing, and large fonts. Thus, the product perfectly fit the needs of elderly people, a segment that had been previously ignored when smartphones were initially launched.

- *Segment specialization.* In this scenario, the producer decides to serve several different needs of one segment and develops many products and marketing programs for this segment. Dr. Schär, an Italian company in the food industry, provides a good example of this approach. The company develops products for people with celiac disease that need a gluten-free diet and offers a comprehensive product portfolio, including gluten-free flours, an extensive range of pasta and bread and a variety of bread substitute products, biscuits, snacks, pizza, and prepared cookies, as well as mixes to prepare delicious recipes at home. The specialization for this segment of people with celiac condition in the food market has been Schär's strategy for decades and has led to its market leadership in Europe.
- *Product specialization.* In this scenario, the focus is one product that is tailored to all market segments. Trek, one of the world-leading producers of bicycles, is an ideal example for this approach. It offers bikes for virtually all market segments: road bikes, mountain bikes, triathlon bikes, urban bikes, electric bikes, and cruisers; bikes for men, women, and kids; and bikes in several price ranges.
- *Full market coverage.* In this scenario, the company decides to address all market segments and develops all products the segment wants. This is Volkswagen's approach to targeting. With its brands (e.g., Volkswagen, Audi, Bentley, Bugatti, Lamborghini, Porsche) it serves practically all market segments with a full range of products.

TARGET MARKET SELECTION

To identify the segments that should be targeted, two questions are of central importance:

1. How attractive are the individual segments to the company?
2. Does the company have competitive advantages in these segments?

These are the same questions that essentially shape the core idea of portfolio analysis: How attractive is a target, and how strong is the company vis-à-vis the requirements of that target? Hence, similar methodologies can be used for portfolio analysis and targeting.

In the first step, criteria for segment attractiveness are defined (e.g., segment size, segment growth rate, segment profitability, rivalry within the segment) and they are weighted and evaluated. A hypothetical example is shown in Table 23-1, with the criteria weight ranging from low = 1 to high = 5. Then, each segment is evaluated on an individual basis and scored from low = 1 to high = 5. The criteria weight is then multiplied by the segment evaluation score to calculate the weighted score, which indicates the overall attractiveness of each particular segment in a given marketplace.

The next step is to analyze whether a company has competitive advantages in the individual segments, as shown in Table 23-2. To do this, first the success factors are defined (the customers' buying criteria). Then, for each segment, an importance weight is estimated. This is a meaningful step, as the importance weights will vary greatly between segments. Finally, the company compares

TABLE 23-1 Evaluation of Segment Attractiveness

CRITERIA	WEIGHT	SEGMENT 1	SEGMENT 2	SEGMENT 3	SEGMENT 4	SEGMENT 5	SEGMENT 6
Size	3	3	2	4	1	3	3
Growth	2	2	2	4	1	5	5
Profitability	5	1	2	3	2	4	2
Competition	3	4	1	5	1	5	3
Weighted score		30	23	50	18	54	38

itself against the strongest competitor on these success factors to find out whether it performs better or worse on each buying criterion. This can be done per segment (if there are different competitors in each segment) or against one competitor (if a single competitor is competing for all the segments). Multiplying the weights with the scores and adding these numbers together gives an overall score that indicates the degree of competitive superiority or inferiority in each single segment. For example, in Table 23-2, the "Performance" factor would be multiplied by the "Segment #" score and the scores in the segment column would be added to achieve a "Weighted Score."

TABLE 23-2 Competitive Advantage Analysis per Segment

SUCCESS FACTORS		IMPORTANCE OF SUCCESS FACTOR PER SEGMENT					
(BUYING CRITERIA)	PERFORMANCE	SEGMENT 1	SEGMENT 2	SEGMENT 3	SEGMENT 4	SEGMENT 5	SEGMENT 6
Product quality	2	4	1	3	1	4	2
Brand	−1	3	3	5	2	1	1
Price	−2	2	5	1	4	2	5
Technology	3	2	1	3	3	5	2
Service	0	2	1	2	2	2	3
Weighted Score		7	−8	8	1	18	−1

Note. Company "Performance" compared to strongest competitor (−3 = much worse; 0 = equal; 3 = much better). The "Importance of success factor per segment" (0 = not at all; 5 = very important).

Finally, the weighted scores of segment attractiveness and competitive advantages are used to position each segment in a portfolio using a modified GE/McKinsey Matrix (McKinsey & Company, 2008), as shown in Figure 23-1. The segments in the upper right quadrants are the most interesting candidates for target markets, as they are highly attractive and the company performs better on the success factors than the competitors.

For the target market selection, the following additional criteria can be used:

- Are there any synergies (economies of scope) between the segments?
- Do the segments fit the company's core competences and core businesses?
- Do the segments fit the strategic objectives of the company?

The final step in the segmenting, targeting, and positioning (STP) process is the development of a unique *position* in the minds of customers. The goal of positioning, which will be examined in Note 24, is to establish a difference the company can preserve. The outcome is a customer-focused unique value proposition. Targeting is a critical task in this process; it matches the capabilities of a company with the needs of an attractive market and, therefore, requires careful attention.

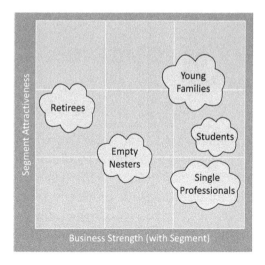

FIGURE 23-1 Hypothetical Segment Portfolio within GE/McKinsey Matrix

SUMMARY

Targeting involves dividing the overall market into smaller, more homogeneous segments. A comprehensive profile of the segments is needed to determine the attractiveness and competitive position of such segments. Segment attractiveness and competitive position can then be used to determine the target market(s) for which a sustainable value proposition is created that guides the development of the marketing mix.

REFERENCES

Kotler, P., & Keller, K. (2009). *Marketing management* (13th ed.). Pearson Education.

McKinsey & Company. (2008, September 1). Enduring ideas: The GE–McKinsey nine-box matrix. *McKinsey Quarterly*. https://www.mckinsey.com/business-functions/strategy-and-corporate-finance/our-insights/enduring-ideas-the-ge-and-mckinsey-nine-box-matrix

Figure Credit

NOTE 24 | POSITIONING

Positioning spans and organizes all of the tactical elements of the marketing mix, including product, price, place, and promotion. The purpose of positioning is to claim a unique and valued position *in the mindset of the consumer*. It answers the question, "How do we want to be perceived by our target market?" Generally, product positioning assumes that the consumer's complex perceptions of products can be thought of as an actual, physical *space*—a two-dimensional or multidimensional space in which product locations and proximities depict the way consumers think about product characteristics and perceive products relative to each other. This is why product positioning is often captured in perceptual maps and terms such as *white space* (unserved or underserved markets) and even the word *position* itself to analogize perceptions of products to actual spatial representations. Sometimes the characteristics that define a space (that is, the axes of the maps) are *real*, tangible attributes of the products (such as price or screen resolution), but consumers normally translate actual attributes into their essential benefits (such as quality or picture clarity); that is, consumers usually think in terms of how the attributes meet certain needs, not the actual attributes.

Positioning requires a thorough understanding of:

- The *needs and mindset* of the target market;
- *Competitors' positions* in the target market; and
- The firm's own *competitive advantages* and points of differentiation.

TOOLS FOR POSITIONING

Positioning relies on thorough customer analysis and marketing research, competitor analysis, and understandings of the firm's own strengths and competitive advantages. As noted, successful positioning claims a unique and valued place in consumers' perceptions. The firm retains that position by *branding*—marking or holding that position with a brand (a name, a logo, trademark, or other signals, and a meaning that consumers retain across occasions).

There are four tools specifically related to, and especially important in, positioning products and brands in the market:

- Semantic scales;
- Customer value maps;
- Perceptual maps; and
- Positioning statements.

Semantic Scales

A very useful tool for brand positioning is semantic scaling. In a semantic-scale survey, customers are asked to rate alternatives with regard to a number of specific attributes. Those questions are usually formulated as bipolar items—that is, as questions with alternative words (such as hot versus cold, or powerful versus weak, at each end of the spectrum), and customers are asked to rate each alternative (each product) on a given scale. For example, "How would you rate the style of this furniture dealer on a scale of 1 to 5, where 1 means exclusive and 5 means mundane?"

The attributes selected are intended to capture brand perceptions, and they do. However, these attributes must be selected in advance by the researcher and may not capture the manner in which consumers combine attributes into perceptions. In particular, consumers often act on their perceptions of product benefits, but semantic scales are best in order to address perceptions of attributes. Data collected via semantic items can be used to create perceptual maps, to plot attributes into perceptual maps created via multidimensional scaling (MDS), or to compare alternatives along the selected attributes. Figure 24-1 shows the positioning of a producer of premium furniture and its competitor. The dotted line represents the ideal and intended position.

FIGURE 24-1 Semantic Scale Comparison of Premium Furniture Manufacturers

Customer Value Maps

A basic positioning decision every company makes or should make is how to locate the product in the consumer mindset regarding the two traditional buying criteria of overall quality and price. A company has the option of positioning their product as the price leader, the quality leader, or as some combination of those two high-level attributes. Figure 24-2 shows the price/quality position of flat-screen television producers within a value map.

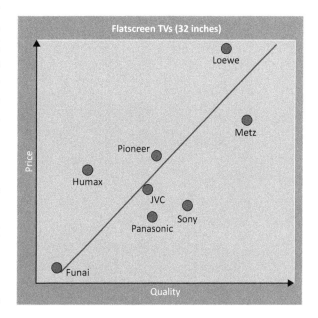

FIGURE 24-2 Price/Quality Positioning (i.e., Value Map) for Flat-Screen TVs (Based on N. N. "TV-Geräte im Test," *Konsument* 6 (2009)).

Lowe's position is unfavorable; it has the highest price but not the highest quality. Metz and Sony are much better positioned compared to their competitors' quality, with relatively low prices.

Perceptual Maps

Perceptual maps are graphical visualizations of customer's perceptions of products or brands. The Value Frontier (as discussed in Note 17) is, in fact, a specific case of a perceptual map (with the axes stipulated as overall quality and price). A more complex way to position brands is multidimensional scaling (MDS). It allows the analyst to assess the similarity between brands in a multidimensional space and, instead of being specified by theory, it allows consumers to choose the dimensions upon which they evaluate the alternatives (and identifies those dimensions for the strategic manager). The principle of MDS is simple: the positions of the brands represent their similarity; brands that are closer together are more similar and brands farther away are less similar.

Figure 24-3 is an example using major European Alpine ski resorts (Faullant et al., 2008). Based on customers' evaluations of the resorts on a number of specific attributes (e.g., entertainment and nightlife, price, quality of the slopes), a perceptual map was created for two segments (skiers aged 50 years and above on the left, and skiers aged 25 years or less on the right). The horizontal axis separates the two ski resorts and places St. Moritz (Switzerland) on the left and Toggenburg (Switzerland) on the right, indicating that these two ski resorts are perceived as the most dissimilar. St. Moritz and Dolomiti Superski (Italy) are positioned very closely to each other. Mayrhofen (Austria) and Lech/Zürs (Austria) are also perceived to be very similar.

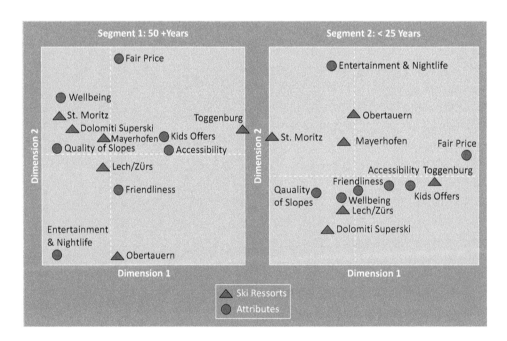

FIGURE 24-3 Perceptual Maps of European Alpine Ski Resorts in Two Market Segments (Faullant et al., 2008)

The distance of a ski resort from the attributes, which have also been plotted into the maps, indicates the strength of the perceptions on that attribute. St. Moritz shows very strong associations with well-being and quality of slopes, and weak associations with entertainment and nightlife. Toggenburg is perceived as a child-friendly ski resort and also as easily accessible. The segment of young skiers (under 25 years of age) shows quite a different perceptual map. Again, St. Moritz and Toggenburg are the most dissimilar ski resorts, but their relationships with the attributes differ from the corresponding perceptions in the above 50 years segment. St. Moritz has strong associations with well-being and quality of slopes, but is also seen as very expensive. Among skiers under 25 years of age, Lech/Zürs has a very strong position regarding well-being, quality of slopes, and friendliness. These differences show how important it is to analyze brand perceptions of specific market segments. Not only do the segments differ regarding their needs (their *ideal* products are discussed below), they may also differ regarding their basic perceptions of the assortment and the important dimensions.

Consumers' ideal products can also be understood via the perceptual mapping techniques described here. The statistical analyses underlying the identification of consumers' ideal products (or ideal points in the perceptual maps) are beyond the scope of this book and beyond the concern of most marketing strategists. It can, nevertheless, be invaluable to plot ideal products into these same product spaces or perceptual maps. The ideal point is not the consumers' *favorite* from among the offered assortment (products already in the market); in fact, there does not have to be any offered product that meets the consumers' ideal preferences. The ideal point is the product that, if it were offered, would be the favorite of the consumers of a particular segment; in fact, their *perfect* product.

Positioning Statements

The analytical tools associated with positioning—perceptual maps, semantic scales, and multidimensional scaling—reveal the current positions of products offered in a market as perceived by customers. Once a strategy has been chosen to target a position—that is, once the target position has been established—the marketing plan or strategy should generate a written statement of that intended position. These codifications of intended product positions are called *positioning statements*.

A positioning statement expresses the singular characteristic of a product or a brand aiming at establishing unique, sustainable, and positive associations in the minds of the customers. A positioning statement should be (Kotler & Keller, 2009):

- relevant—it must emphasize attributes that are important to the customer;
- distinctive—it must emphasize attributes that are superior to competitors;
- believable—the brand must provide a compelling reason for being superior;
- feasible—the positioning must be backed by superior product attributes or capabilities;
- communicable—the superiority must be easy to explain; and
- sustainable—the position must be easy to sustain and difficult to imitate.

Most positioning statements specify the target market, the brand being positioned, the product category within which it is being positioned, the point of difference or *unique selling proposition*, and the reason to believe. For example, many experts and firms use some version of a generic statement such as the following:

> For *(definition of target consumers/segments)*, *(Brand X)* is *(definition of frame of reference and subjective category)*, which gives the most… *(promise or consumer benefit/point of difference)* because only *(Brand X)* is *(reason to believe)* (Kapferer, 2008, p. 178; Tybout & Sternthal, 2005).

Key elements in these statements are the promise and the reason to believe. These specify and substantiate the intended position of Brand X in this market, specified as the *frame of reference*, for these consumers/segments. Positioning statements may also specify the *brand meaning or brand personality* of the intended positioning.

SUMMARY

Positioning represents the sum total of the marketer's actions on each of the 5Ps of the marketing mix. If there is a well-defined target market with well-defined needs and wants, then getting the Ps right—the right product at right price in right place, with the right amount of promotion and personal selling—should be relatively easy. On the other hand, if the marketer does not understand the segmentation and market structure, then getting the Ps right—and the positioning—is just a guessing game. While there are many tools available for use in positioning, marketing strategists should remember this basic rule: we position to a particular target market, not the other way around. In other words, the strategic marketing process involves segmenting, then targeting, and finally positioning.

REFERENCES

Faullant, R., Matzler, K., & Füller, J. (2008). A positioning map of skiing areas using customer satisfaction scores. *Journal of Hospitality & Leisure Marketing*, 16(3), 230–245.

Kapferer, J.-N. (2008). *The new strategic brand management* (4th ed.). Kogan Page.

Kotler, P., & Keller, K. (2009). *Marketing management* (13th ed.). Pearson Education.

N. N. "TV-Geräte im Test," *Konsument* 6 (2009).

Tybout, A. M., & Sternthal, B. (2005). Brand Positioning. In *Kellogg on Branding* (pp. 12–13). John Wiley & Sons.

NOTES ALIGNED WITH CHAPTER IV: FOCUS ON MARKETING EXECUTION

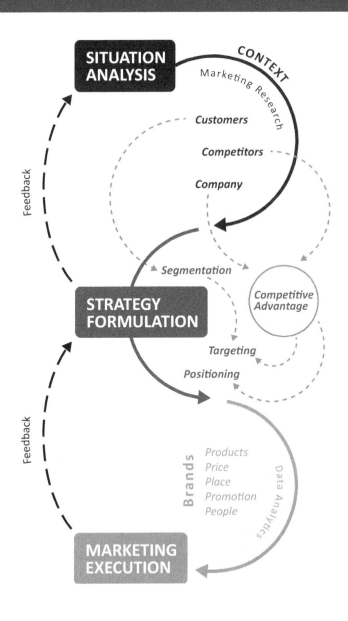

BRAND DEVELOPMENT

According to the American Marketing Association (2021), a brand is, "A name, term, design, symbol or any other feature that identifies one seller's goods or service as distinct from those of other sellers" (p. 15). This useful but narrow definition focuses on the specific indicators of brands (name, term, etc.) and the functions of brands in the marketplace. Brands are also complex social phenomena. As concepts in customers' minds (and hearts), brands have rich symbolism and meanings that extend beyond their identifying function. To varying degrees, that social symbolism and meaning is outside the marketing strategist's or the brand manager's control. Nevertheless, the essential strategic roles of a brand are to identify the product and its producer to consumers, to differentiate the offering, and to command value—roles that the marketing manager must shape and control.

FUNCTIONS OF BRANDS

Brands are manifested in an offering's characteristics that identify it in the mindset of the consumer and that distinguish it from competitive offerings. A brand's identifying characteristics usually include the brand name (or *trade name*), logos and marks (*trademarks*), and distinguishing features such as packaging, colors, and even sounds. That commercial identity is not dissimilar to an individual's personal identity; we know a person by their name, but we may also recognize them by their physical appearance, voice, experiences, etc. In fact, the concept of personal branding has become a powerful concept in the past decade, with the advent of social media allowing individuals to quickly build and share their personal brands with others (Edmiston, 2019). Both individuals and institutions have learned that brands serve as an essential cue for markets to understand and value their products and services.

Coca-Cola, for example, is a trade name—as is Coke—but Coca-Cola is also identified by the distinctive red, Spencerian cursive logo, by its packaging (especially the contour bottle), and by slogans such as "Have a Coke and a smile" and "Open Happiness." Intellectual property law not only protects trademarks and trade names, it protects trade dress—the distinctive configuration of nonfunctional elements such as package shapes, designs, colors, materials, and sounds. Thus, a straightforward way to understand what a brand is and what can be protected as a trademark, trade name, service mark, or trade dress is to understand that a brand is the producer's and the product's commercial identity (Brown, 1948).

Table 25-1 summarizes several benefits of brands to both customers and marketers. For customers, brands offer efficiency and assurance in overwhelmingly complex lives. Brands may also offer abstract benefits, including comfort, risk reduction, and self-expression. To the marketing strategist, brands embody and retain the benefits, including loyalty and margins, from a job well

TABLE 25-1 Benefits of Brands

BENEFITS TO CUSTOMERS	BENEFITS TO MARKETS/ORGANIZATIONS
• Efficiency: Reduce demands on information search/cognitive processing • Assurance: Trust and comfort in purchase • Social signals and symbolic value • Personal identity and self-image	• Responses to marketing mix • Loyalty • Prices and margins • New product launches and brand extensions • Effectiveness and efficiency of distribution/trade programs

Note. Table source: Aaker, D. (1991). *Managing brand equity*. Free Press.

done, and they can serve to facilitate distribution and accelerate new product launches (brand extensions). This information-value or commercial-identity role of brands is a good foundation for understanding brands, but it is narrow and legalistic; brands also serve to deliver value to consumers in and of themselves as they hold rich and influential meanings of their own.

BRAND MEANING AND BRAND EQUITY

The functional or information-value view of brands is useful, as explicated above, but it leaves out some important roles that brands play in the modern marketplace and in contemporary culture. Brands hold *meaning* that can encompass a variety of aspects from functional and hedonic benefits to social significance and symbolism, and those meanings reside in the minds of consumers.

Professor David Aaker, a leading authority on branding, defines brand equity as the "set of brand assets and liabilities linked to a brand name and symbol, which add to or subtract from the value provided by a product or service" (Aaker, 2013, para. 1). Thus, brand equity is a summary of brand meaning/associations along with brand awareness, brand loyalty, brand quality, and other *brand assets*, ranging from protected trademarks and proprietary technology to the strength of long-term relationships with distribution partners (channel presence). Brands have become the most valuable assets many companies own, and they account for more than 30% of the stock market value of companies in the S&P 500 index ("Brands," 2014). Aaker (1991) also distinguishes four aspects of a brand's identity or *brand meaning*. These include:

- the brand *as a product* (attributes and benefits such as hard-disc memory, taste, or reliability);
- the brand *as an organization* (ties to the identity and heritage of the parent organization);
- the brand *as a person* (includes the brand personality; for example, *rugged* as well as the brand-customer relationship such as *friend*); and,
- the brand *as a symbol* (brand meaning and the connection of that meaning to the customer's self-image; for example, youthful, prestigious, practical).

All these potential aspects of brand identity may not be relevant to every brand. The roles of brand identity and brand equity in driving desirable responses to the marketing mix, including especially purchase behavior, are shown in Figure 25-1.

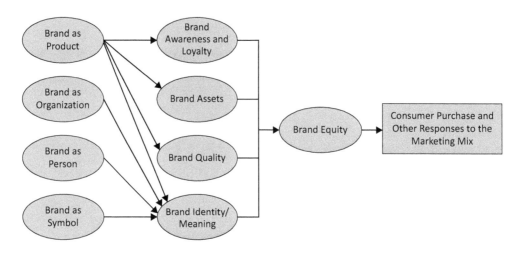

FIGURE 25-1   Brand Meaning and Brand Equity

These definitions and the graphic organization of these variables impose specific labels and roles on things that, in reality, have overlapping and blurred meanings. For example, the brand as product includes product quality, which also contributes to brand loyalty and brand equity. Differentiating these abstract ideas too narrowly could reduce to a semantic muddle: is there really a difference between *identity*, *meaning*, and *equity*? The answer is that, although some of these may be fine lines to draw, the higher-level ideas are substantive and important for marketing strategists to understand: consumers *do* hold in their minds different perceptions like awareness, beliefs about quality, feelings of attachment and loyalty, and diverse associations ranging from *prestigious* and *traditional* to *cool* or *stylish*. Those perceptions and predispositions are not only real, they are *invaluable* to the firm—they drive differences in responses to the marketing mix, in purchase behaviors, and in margins.

Brands as products delivering functional and hedonic (emotional) benefits are, in general, things that a marketer can influence, if not control. Brand *meanings*, brands as *symbols*, and brands as *means of self-expression* all begin to suggest richer cultural roles for brands. In fact, brands may begin with producers and marketers, and brand managers may influence the brand's meaning, but brands belong to the consumers who use them and who assign meaning to them. Major brands, including Timberland boots, the Cadillac Escalade SUV, and Pabst Blue Ribbon beer have all taken on meanings and gained traction in segments the branding organization never imagined or targeted. Timberland's CEO Jeffrey Swartz once acknowledged, "Timberland is being adopted by a consumer that we didn't know existed relative to our target audience" (Marriott, 1993, p. 1). He meant that Timberland had become a fashion brand for many consumers, as opposed to the functional footwear product that it was intended to be.

Some brands have become the focal point of *brand communities* that deliver complex personal, psychological, and social benefits to their members. Owning a Harley Davidson, for example, has utilitarian value (a Harley Davidson takes its owner from point A to point B), hedonic value (riding a Harley Davidson evokes feelings of joy and freedom), and self-expressive benefits (owning a Harley Davidson may tell others the rider is a *rugged individualist*). Further, Harley Davidson riders are a community of people who identify with the brand and with each other and who take value from their membership in the "HOG" (Harley Owners Group) community. The brand has even become so intertwined with some consumers' self-concepts that they tattoo the brand logo on their bodies. These consumer-centered aspects of brand meanings are more difficult to manage; in a sense, brands can take on *lives of their own* with consumers. Nevertheless, from a marketing strategist's perspective, there are marketing tools that influence consumers' perceptions of brands, that connect brands to purchase and loyalty, and that build strong, enduring brands. The next section clarifies the tools the marketing organization and strategist can use to build, shape, and profit from strong brands.

BUILDING BRANDS

The marketing strategist has numerous tools to build a brand—but building or maintaining a brand must begin with a clear understanding of what the brand is meant to be in consumer perceptions. That is, before developing any clever advertising copy or creative sponsorships for a brand, before hiring a spokesperson or choosing a promotion, the strategic position that the brand intends to claim in the marketplace must be determined, based on customer and competitive analyses, and should be recorded in a *positioning statement* (as discussed in Note 24).

A complete positioning statement usually specifies the brand/product to be positioned, the market, the target segment(s) and target needs, at least one point of difference or *brand promise*, and the reason to believe that supports those points of difference (Tybout & Sternthal, 2005). A positioning statement is not necessarily intended for customers to see—although it may be distributed to vendors such as advertising agencies and channel partners—rather, it is intended as an internal reflection of what the brand is meant to be. It serves to keep the various tactics *on strategy*, and it fosters institutional memory of what the brand is and, often just as importantly, what it is *not*.

Once the desired position has been determined and spelled out in a positioning statement, the marketing strategist has a variety of tools to use in claiming and reinforcing the brand's position. The product itself has an enormous impact on the brand in customer perceptions. Additionally, brand managers generally emphasize the promotion mix or *integrated marketing communications* to build and hone brand image. Figure 25-2 organizes the many controllable factors that can influence brand identity/meaning, brand equity, and brand strength. Let's look at some examples of those factors.

Product/Design

There is no evidence as convincing to the customer as their experience with the brand itself. In order to be credible, the core product must live up to the brand promise. Consequently, the primary and essential element in brand building is the product itself, and the surest way to dilute brand equity is for the product to fail to live up to the brand promise. Design encompasses both form and function—how the product works (functional benefits), how it is experienced (i.e., aesthetically and emotionally via its look, feel, touch), and how the two work together.

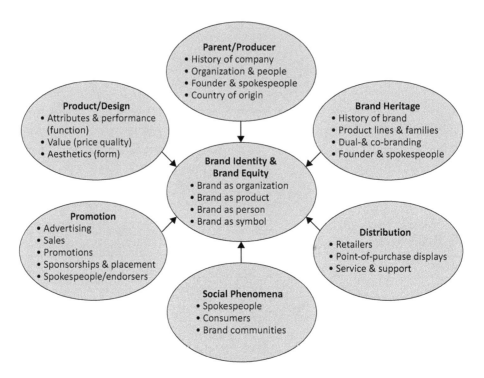

FIGURE 25-2   Building Brand Identity and Brand Equity

Promotion/Integrated Marketing Communications

One overarching, organizing principle of marketing strategy is that promotion/integrated marketing communications should contribute to building the brand and to claiming a unique and valued place in consumers' perceptions (see Note 31). The key to that investment is a unified voice; a consistent, compelling, and focused message repeated and reinforced at every point of contact. Within the promotions mix, price promotions have been contrasted with *brand building* investments, such as advertising, because some marketers have argued that price promotions may damage brand image and brand equity. Brand building, positioning, and integrated marketing communications strategies are inseparable. For example, McDonald's presents across all of its integrated marketing communications an unchanging and focused message that it delivers consistency at a great value.

Social Phenomena

Other consumers of the brand, the brand in popular art, and affiliated spokespeople all influence brand meaning and brand associations. For example, despite the fact that Cadillac's traditional target markets are older and suburban and that the company's car is perceived as *your grandfather's car* (Menzies, 2003), the brand's Escalade SUV has become popular with highly-successful athletes and celebrities, and that has fed broader popularity with young, urban consumers. The Escalade brand manager conceded, "It has been the vehicle of choice among some Hollywood folks and athletes, even though we've never particularly marketed it that way" (Strauss, 2003, p. 37).

Distribution

An underappreciated element in brand building and also a potential trap toward brand destruction is the selection, affiliation with, and control of channel partners. Especially in instances of products requiring knowledgeable sales support, products augmented by high levels of service, and products pursuing prestige positions in the marketplace, channel partners can be a powerful means for building and reinforcing the brand's promise. Stihl, the premium chain saw brand, has always insisted that its channel partners provide significant after-sale service and support.

Brand Heritage

Many brands build on strong brand heritages—they have a history of sustained and consistent presence in the market. That heritage was perhaps best illustrated in the failed product launch of New Coke; although consumers supposedly preferred the taste of Pepsi to (old) Coke, the heritage of the brand and its assimilation into American culture had secured a place in the hearts of consumers. Coca-Cola was deeply ingrained in American culture. Coke had appeared in popular media from Andy Warhol lithographs to Bob Dylan songs, and when Coca-Cola tried to adjust the taste, it found out quickly that customers wanted their familiar Coke. In fact, the Coke consumers bombarded Coca-Cola's headquarters in Atlanta with their complaints about the change in the product. Clearly, some brands have heritages that have integrated them into the common vernacular, and others have shorter histories that, nevertheless, carry over into every new endeavor.

Parent/Producer Organization

Apple makes well-designed, user-friendly products with creative cachet. *Anheuser-Busch* is the classic American brewer. BMW makes high-performance cars. These are just a few examples of companies that have well-established reputations tied to their histories and core competencies. Those corporate reputations can be advantages, or in certain cases, they can also be detriments for subordinate products and brands. Table 25-2 presents various aspects of corporate image that can influence product brand images. The country of origin will also contribute to product brand equity and is an element of parent organization reputation and legacy; country of origin can be a positive influence on the brand's meaning, as in the case of Italian shoes or French wines, but it can also be a detriment, as has become the case for American automakers.

TABLE 25-2 Dimensions of Corporate Image

Common Product Attributes, Benefits, or Attitudes
• Quality
• Innovativeness
People and Relationships
Customer Orientation
Values and Programs
• Concern with the Environment
• Social Responsibility
Corporate Credibility
• Expertise
• Trustworthiness
• Likability

Note. Table information from Keller, K. (2003). *Strategic brand management* (2nd ed.). Prentice-Hall.

MEASURING BRANDS

Like most things in strategic marketing planning, brands can be and should be measured and monitored rigorously. Measuring brands can be approached in at least two basic ways: through consumer-level brand meaning, brand equity, and brand strength; or firm- or brand-level value. Consumer-level brand meaning and brand equity focuses on the beliefs, attitudes, and behavioral tendencies that exist in consumers' minds. Firm- or brand-level value deals with the financial impacts of the brand on the financial performance and the value of the firm.

Brand equity is complex—it includes basic brand awareness but also brand associations and the meanings that a brand holds in consumers' minds, and it includes consumers' loyalty to the brand and their perceptions of the brand's quality or objective attributes. Various measurement approaches gauge these different and disparate aspects of brand equity. As each brand is unique and as not all aspects of brand equity are relevant to every brand, the measurement of brand equity should be tailored to the individual brand.

Nevertheless, there are some well-accepted measures of various aspects of brand equity. Things like awareness, quality, and loyalty are basic concepts in marketing research. For example, brand awareness is often measured as *unaided recall* and *aided recall*, that is, the proportion of consumers who mention the brand without being prompted and those who recognize it when prompted. Quality is a belief system related to product-category-specific attributes and performance. For example, how reliable is Brand X? Or how well does Brand Y remove dirt? (Buttle, 1996; Parasuraman et al., 1985).

Well-established measures are available for brand meaning, especially for *brand personality*. Jennifer Aaker's Brand Personality Scale (see Table 25-3) illuminates the measurement of brand meaning and highlights the breadth of humanlike qualities a brand can hold. The five factors—sincerity, excitement, competence, sophistication, and ruggedness—are the highest-level structure. Facets and traits expand those factors into greater detail. While any brand can be described with these traits, not all these traits are relevant to every brand.

TABLE 25-3 Brand Personality

FACTORS	FACETS	TRAITS
Sincerity	Down-to-earth Honest Wholesome Cheerful	Down-to-earth, family-oriented, small-town Honest, sincere, real Wholesome, original Cheerful, sentimental, friendly
Excitement	Daring Spirited Imaginative Up-to-date	Daring, trendy, exciting Spirited, cool, young Imaginative, unique Up-to-date, independent, contemporary
Competence	Reliable Intelligent Successful	Reliable, Hard-working, secure Intelligent, technical, corporate Successful, leader, confident
Sophistication	Upper class Charming	Upper class, glamorous, good looking Charming, feminine, smooth
Ruggedness	Outdoorsy Tough	Outdoorsy, masculine, western, tough, rugged

Note. The Brand Personality Scale consists of these 42 traits rated as to "How well does this describe [Brand]?" Traits can then be summed to facets and factors. Table source: Aaker, J. (1997). Dimensions of brand personality. *Journal of Marketing Research*, 34(3), 347–356.

Brand Valuation

While brand strength is important for building brands, and measures of brand strength are indispensable in comparing competitive brands and in evaluating specific marketing investments, another perspective on measuring brands approaches the issue from a very different angle: *What is a brand worth taken as a whole? What does a brand contribute to the firm's financial value?* This is referred to as *brand valuation*. Of course, what a brand is worth to the firm is in reality—and recognizable by a marketing strategist—the sum total of all the consumer perceptions. All of that brand strength manifests in thousands, even millions, of consumer behaviors. That is, although it is a different measurement approach, the brand is valuable to the firm because it can be expected to generate sales and command margin in the future, and those sales and margins are the product of cumulative individual feelings about the brand (Ailawadi et al., 2003; Srinivasan et al., 2005).

The strongest global brands are worth billions of dollars to their parent corporations. The global brand consultancy Interbrand, for example, values the Coca-Cola brand at nearly $57 billion (Interbrand, 2021). Brand valuation can be approached in many ways, and several agencies like Interbrand generate slightly different but similar annual rankings in an effort to measure the perceived financial value of the brand to the company. It is typical for brand valuation methods to view the brand as a source of revenue spread out across time in an effort to estimate what future flows of revenue are worth in current terms. Appendix A, "Basic Financial Math for Marketing," includes a detailed discussion of discounting future revenue to its net present value. Distinguishing future revenues attributable to the brand from proprietary technology and other tangible and intangible assets is inherently subjective but, in any case, these brand valuation efforts tend to triangulate on which brands are the most valuable, which emphasizes another approach to understanding how important brands are to the firm's success and wealth creation.

SUMMARY

Brands serve as identities that retain the value of marketing investments across time; brands that delight customers are rewarded and those that disappoint are avoided. Brand value can be a substantial asset to companies, and brand meaning can deliver real benefits to consumers beyond core product attributes or performance. A variety of tools are available to the marketing strategist to shape and maintain the value of the brand—the most prominent are encompassed in the marketing mix of product, price, place, and promotion. Brands also have social and cultural roles that are somewhat beyond the control of the parent organization. In general, brands are derived from decisions about positioning—brands are the place holders that embody the position the strategy targets in the market—and brands are shaped by and should direct all of the tactical elements of the marketing mix.

REFERENCES

Aaker, D. (1991). *Managing brand equity.* Free Press.

Aaker, D. (2013). What is brand equity? *Prophet.* https://www.prophet.com/2013/09/156-what-is-brand-equity-and-why-is-it-valuable/

Aaker, J. (1997). Dimensions of brand personality. *Journal of Marketing Research*, 34(3), 347–356.

Ailawadi, K. L., Lehmann, D. R., & Neslin, S. A. (2003). Revenue premium as an outcome measure of brand equity. *Journal of Marketing*, 67(4), 1–17.

American Marketing Association. (2021). *Branding.* https://www.ama.org/topics/branding/

"Brands." (2014). What are brands for? *The Economist.* https://www.economist.com/business/2014/08/30/what-are-brands-for

Brown, R. S. (1948). Advertising and the public interest: Legal protection of trade symbols. *Yale Law Journal*, 57, 1165–1167.

Buttle, F. (1996). SERVQUAL: Review, critique, research agenda. *European Journal of Marketing.*

Edmiston, D. (2019). Brand matters: Leveraging the power of personal branding to achieve professional success. In *Go-to-market strategies for women entrepreneurs* (pp. 161–270). Emerald Publishing Limited. https://doi.org/10.1108/978-1-78973-289-420191030

Interbrand. (2021). *"Best global brands 2020."* Interbrand. https://interbrand.com/best-global-brands/coca-cola/

Keller, K. (2003). *Strategic brand management* (2nd ed.). Prentice-Hall.

Marriott, M. (1993). Out of the woods. *New York Times.*

Menzies, D. (2003, October 24). It don't mean a thing if it ain't got that bling. *National Post.*

Parasuraman, A., Zeithaml, V. A., & Berry, L. L. (1985). A conceptual model of service quality and its implications for future research. *Journal of Marketing*, 49(4), 41–50.

Srinivasan, V., Park, C. S., & Chang, D. R. (2005). An approach to the measurement, analysis, and prediction of brand equity and its sources. *Management Science*, 51(9), 1433–1448.

Strauss, R. (2003, October 22). Marketing: Appealing to youth, selling to the not-so-young. *New York Times.*

Tybout, A. M., & Sternthal, B. (2005). Brand positioning. In *Kellogg on branding* (pp. 12–13). John Wiley & Sons.

Most companies produce and sell more than one product or service, and many companies have more than one business unit. Those collections of products and businesses are referred to as *product portfolios.* Marketing strategists must make important and inevitable decisions about how to allocate cash, expertise, time, and other scarce resources across individual products and business units. Different products and different strategic business units (SBUs) require and justify different levels of investment. In addition, those investment priorities change across time as markets, products, industries, and customers evolve. Marketing strategists need ways to decide which products justify more resources to grow, which products should merely hold their market position, and even which products should be withdrawn from the market.

When facing these decisions about investments and withdrawal of investments across the product portfolio, it is useful for managers to consider two fundamental questions: "How strong is the product/SBU in its market?" and "How attractive is the market?" (or "How likely are we to win at this game?" and "How nice would it be to win at this game?"). These two considerations—the product or SBU's *strength* in the market and the market's *attractiveness*—are, of course, complex questions, especially if a company has dozens of products or business units to manage. Fortunately, there are several straightforward models managers can use to address these questions. Two of the most widely used and well-tested models are the Boston Consulting Group (BCG) Matrix and the GE (General Electric)/McKinsey Portfolio Planning Grid. Both models hold the following two questions as central to decisions about whether to grow a business, maintain it, or withdraw: How attractive is the market? How strong is the product/SBU in the market? These frameworks differ in their complexity or *granularity* of the analyses and the resulting strategic recommendation.

THE BCG MATRIX

One of the earliest portfolio models was the BCG Matrix, developed by the Boston Consulting Group in the 1960. It remains the best known and most often applied portfolio model in business. It uses just one variable, *market growth rate,* to summarize attractiveness (Hedley, 1977). Using growth rate as the single characteristic that makes a market attractive can be justified because growing markets offer opportunities for investments that promise higher returns than low-growth markets.

During the growth phases of the product life cycle, market share can be gained by expanding capacities earlier than competitors, ensuring product availability, and managing sales effectively—all reasons to increase investments in higher-growth markets. Further, in high-growth markets, competitors may not react as intensely when they lose market share because even if their sales increase below market growth, the sales do increase. In a no-growth market, increases in sales

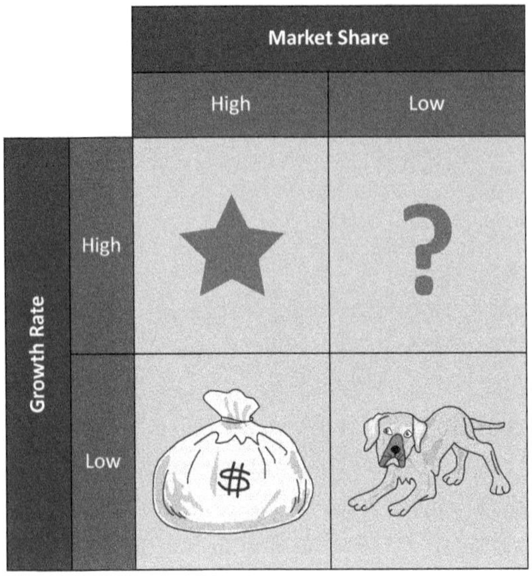

FIGURE 26-1   BCG Matrix (1970)

can only be achieved by reducing the competitors' sales—and competitors are likely to feel the losses more acutely and respond to actual losses in sales more intensely.

The BCG Matrix uses *relative market share* as the single marker of the product or SBU's strength. This is also true as far as it goes. Relative market share corresponds to relatively greater scale (production volume). That is, the greater a product or business unit's relative market share, the lesser its relative unit costs and the greater its relative margins. All of these things are *relative* in that they're specific to the comparison with the competition. The original BCG framework defines relative market share as the sales volume of an SBU divided by the sales volume of the largest competitor. Therefore, the largest firm in a market will have a relative share greater than one, and all the other entrants will have a relative market share of less than one. The BCG model combines the two questions—attractiveness and relative strength as indicated by market growth and relative market share—into a two-by-two matrix (shown as Figure 26-1). Products or SBUs in

TABLE 26-1 Growth Rates and Market Share for Selected Units of a Consumer Electronics Company (adapted from several publications of BITCOM and Statista, as well as estimates of the authors)

BUSINESS UNIT	MARKET VOLUME (IN EURO)						CAGR** 2023/2019
	2018	2019	2020*	2021*	2022*	2023*	
Notebooks	4840,00	4809,00	4792,00	4783,00	4780,00	4776,00	−0,17
Desktop PCs	862,00	846,00	837,00	831,00	828,00	827,00	−0,57
PC Monitors	595,00	589,00	585,00	581,00	578,00	576,00	−0,56
Printers and Copiers	399,00	338,00	329,00	322,00	317,00	313,00	−1,90
TV	6534,00	6515,00	6278,00	6471,00	6619,00	6734,00	0,83
Smart remotes	4,00	5,00	6,00	6,00	7,00	7,00	8,78
DVD player/recorder	169,00	146,00	123,00	100,00	76,00	53,00	−22,38
Digital Cameras	1090,00	1060,00	1040,00	1030,00	1020,00	1020,00	−0,96
Speaker	1002,00	1156,00	1288,00	1488,00	1669,00	1815,00	11,94
Headphones	407,00	426,00	428,00	447,00	461,00	471,00	2,54
Data storage	904,00	914,00	923,00	930,00	936,00	942,00	0,76
Wearables	361,00	374,00	474,00	437,00	417,00	412,00	2,45
Game Consoles	1370,00	1410,00	1460,00	1500,00	1550,00	1590,00	3,05

Note. *Forecast; **CAGR (compound annual growth rate)

BUSINESS UNIT	SALES 2019 (IN EURO)		
	SALES 2019	SALES 2019 STRONG. COMP.	PROFIT
Notebooks	1100	640	45
Desktop PCs	250	295	−17
PC Monitors	260	200	12
Printers and Copiers	180	150	8
TV	980	2120	−188
Smart remotes	0,9	0,8	0,1
DVD player/recorder	117	75	4
Digital Cameras	235	333	−48
Speaker	112	58	−18
Headphones	99	112	1,2
Data storage	306	162	18
Wearables	40	155	−5,2
Game Consoles	412	312	38
	4091.9		−152.3

each quadrant necessitate different strategic orientations, have investment requirements, and present different cash-flow challenges and opportunities.

To better understand the strategic and investment implications of the BCG Matrix, we may start by considering the information in Table 26-1, which describes the growth rates and market shares for various SBUs and their respective markets within a single consumer electronics company.

Figure 26-2 displays that product portfolio within the BCG Matrix. The size of each circle in the matrix represents that business unit's share of the company's overall sales volume.

The following strategic implications emerge for each quadrant:

Question marks (low market share/high market growth): Business units in this quadrant are usually in the early phase of the product life cycle. *In the above electronics company example, these are wearables and headphones.* As the market grows, investments in capacity expansion, marketing, distribution, and related activities are required. Cash flow is usually negative. It is vital to grow faster than the market; otherwise, the market leader cannot be caught. As their name indicates, *question mark* business units have an unsure and risky future. If they are able to build market share, they become the stars and, eventually, the cash cows of the future; if not, they become dogs and cash drains.

Stars (high market share/high market growth): These strategic business units are the market leaders in high-growth markets. *In the above electronics company example, these include smart remotes, game consoles, speakers, and data storage.* As the market

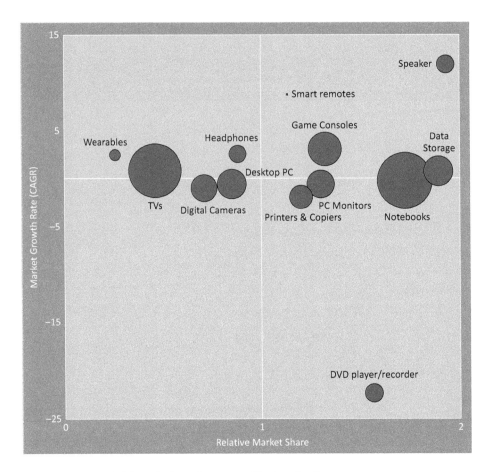

FIGURE 26-2   BCG Matrix for a Consumer Electronics Company

continues to grow strongly, they need high investments. Cash flow is usually balanced or slightly positive. The strategy should emphasize maintaining market position into the next phase of the product life cycle. If this occurs—if the star can strengthen its market-share leadership—these products/SBUs become cash cows as market growth rate inevitably declines.

Cash cows (high market share/low market growth): These products/SBUs need little investment because the market is mature, but that does not mean they require no investment at all. *In the above electronics company example, these include notebooks, PC monitors, printers and copiers, and DVD player/recorder.* These products should have a cost advantage based on their greater scale, and, therefore, they should generate a large cash surplus that can be invested in question marks and stars (even after receiving the level of investment required to maintain the cash cow).

Dogs (low market share/low market growth): Holding a weak position in an unattractive market should be a sure warning against further investment (i.e., throwing good money after bad). *In the above electronics example, these include digital cameras,* *desktop PCs, and TVs.* Dogs are candidates for withdrawal and divestment, especially if a product is at the end of its life cycle (e.g., digital cameras). Still, divestment decisions are more complex than simply sell or not sell. A well-managed portfolio is characterized by balanced cash flow and balanced risk, and it has business units in each quadrant (including dogs, as long as they are profitable).

Thus, for the company in this example, portfolio analysis suggests adopting the following strategies:

- withdrawing from the TV, desktop PC, and digital camera markets
- keeping the notebook, PC monitor, printer and copier, and DVD player/recorder units as long as they are profitable
- investing in wearable and headphone units (question marks) and investing in smart remotes, speakers, game consoles, as well as data storage (stars) because the long-term perspective is attractive; also, this company needs to develop additional products or business units as there are only two "question marks" in the portfolio
- using funds generated by cash cows to increase market share of the headphones and wearables and to maintain the leading position of smart remotes, game consoles, data storage, and speakers units

Limitations of the BCG Matrix

The BCG Matrix is widely known and often applied; it has added to the common business vernacular and it is a basic concept in strategic management. Nevertheless, it has certain limitations that managers should be aware of, including the following (Haberberg & Rieple, 2008):

- The use of market growth rate and relative market share may be oversimplifications. In reality, whether a market is attractive can depend on many factors, such as market size, competitive intensity, and average profitability, as well as growth rate. Furthermore, competitive advantages (relative strength) may not depend only on relative market share, but may also result from distinctive R&D capabilities, marketing capabilities and relationships, loyal customer bases, and other attributes. The BCG framework assumes that market growth rate and relative market share are enough, or that they, in fact, capture the effects of these other sources of attractiveness and strength. Either of these assumptions may not always be true.
- The BCG Matrix treats relative market share as a proxy for cash generation. It also treats market growth rate as a proxy for cash usage, because slow-growth markets are mature and presumably do not require much investment. Unfortunately, this is a problematic assumption, because mature markets are often competitive and, therefore, require cash. For instance, airlines and car manufacturers (combustion engines) immediately come to mind. These businesses can be said to be quite mature, but they also require huge capital investments—to replenish airlines and invest in the latest technology to manufacture cars.
- Using relative market share only makes sense when economies of scale and experience curve effects play a major role. In industries in which size does not lead to cost advantages, relative market share is not a good indicator for competitive advantages.

- Not only the variables, but also the specific values or along the axes of the matrix, are somewhat arbitrary.
    a. *Relative Market Share.* Defining market shares and splitting the *y*-axis of the matrix into high and low growth can present problems. First, for many companies, reliable market share data is not available, and second, markets can be defined broadly or narrowly (e.g., beverages, soft drinks, or energy drinks in the case of Red Bull). Market share can be high or low depending on this definition of the market, and that adds an element of subjectivity to the BCG framework, which has not always been adequately appreciated.
    b. *Market Growth Rate.* The original BCG framework suggested a 10% market growth rate as a threshold to differentiate between *high* and *low* growth markets, and that criterion is better understood as dependent upon the market and the times: a 5% growth rate may be high in the food industry but low in the consumer electronics industry, and a flat growth rate might be an achievement in a major recession but a setback in a high-growth economic cycle.
- The BCG portfolio framework ignores synergies between business units or products. Hence, it does not consider the ways in which divesting one business unit can affect other business units if those units share fixed costs or produce products that complement each other.
- Finally, the BCG Matrix is a *snapshot*; it captures the state of market growth and market share *at a specific time*, and it does not take into consideration changes or trends in the market or in the product/SBU's strength.

These cautions indicate that the BCG Matrix should not be solely used for making decisions, but instead as a guide to discussions that will lead to decisions. In any case, the BCG Matrix remains one of the most durable, well-known, and functional frameworks in the strategy literature.

GE/MCKINSEY PORTFOLIO PLANNING GRID

A second framework for managing and prioritizing multiple products or SBUs within the single firm's assortment is the GE/McKinsey Portfolio Planning Grid (also referred to as the GE Business Screen Matrix or the *Stoplight Grid* due to its adoption of green, yellow, and red to emphasize its strategic implications; henceforth in this Note, it will be abridged to the GE/McKinsey Grid). This framework was developed subsequent to the BCG Matrix, and it follows from that now-classic scheme.

The GE/McKinsey Grid, as shown in Figure 26-3 (Allen, 1977; Hax & Majluf, 1983; Rigby, 2003; Robinson et al., 1978), is a somewhat more complex matrix that addresses the *reductionist* nature of the BCG Matrix (which reduces business strength of relative market share and market attractiveness to just market growth rate). It was developed by McKinsey, the international strategic consulting firm for General Electric, in order to evaluate business units, to analyze the balance and allocation of resources across the overall portfolio of business units, and to assist in setting appropriate performance targets across products and units. The GE/McKinsey Grid is based on some of the same assumptions as the BCG Matrix—especially the assumption that investment levels across products

Industry Attractiveness

	High	Medium	Low
High	• Grow • Seek dominance • Maximize investment	• Identify growth segments • Invest strongly • Maintain position elsewhere	• Maintain overall position • Seek cash flow • Invest at maintenance level
Medium	• Evaluate potential for leadership via segmentation • Identify weaknesses • Build strengths	• Identify growth segments • Specialize • Invest selectively	• Prune lines • Minimize investment • Position to divest
Low	• Specialize • Seek niches • Consider acquisitions	• Specialize • Seek niches • Consider exit	• Trust leader's statesmanship • Sic on competitor's cash generators • Time exit and divest

(Business Strength on vertical axis)

FIGURE 26-3   GE/McKinsey Portfolio Planning Grid (Adapted from Haberberg and Rieple, 2008)

or SBUs should be a function of business strength and market attractiveness—but it incorporates more variables into the two main axes (business strength and market attractiveness) and it offers more granular distinctions across product/SBU positions within the resulting space.

Applying the GE/McKinsey Grid

To compile the GE/McKinsey Grid, six steps are necessary:

1. Define and weight *market attractiveness* markers.
2. Define and weight *business strength* markers.
3. Evaluate each product's or SBU's market attractiveness and business strength.
4. Compute weighted scores for market attractiveness and relative competitive position.
5. Position business units in the portfolio.
6. Derive strategic implications of positions within the matrix.

There are a number of variables than can be used to mark or assess market attractiveness and relative business strength (we'll refer to these as *markers*). The BCG Matrix incorporates just one of those variables for each of the two axes, and while those may be the most powerful variables in explaining strength and attractiveness, they are certainly not the only variables that lead to strength or attractiveness, and, in fact, it is likely that the *best* variables depend upon the industry, the firm, and the situation. Table 26-2 lists common indicators of business strength and industry attractiveness.

As noted, the variables chosen in any particular analysis and the relative weights put on those variables vary across different types of industries and should be selected carefully, customized

TABLE 26-2 Common Markers of Market Attractiveness and Business Strength

MARKET ATTRACTIVENESS	RELATIVE COMPETITIVE POSITION
• Market growth • Market size • Profit margins • Competitive intensity • Market entry barriers • Cyclicality of life cycle • Environmental impact	• Market share • Product quality • R&D capabilities • Marketing capabilities • Brand awareness and image • Production capabilities • Cost efficiency

to the particular firm and its circumstances. Each of the chosen markers of market strength and business attractiveness may not be equally important. Variables should be assigned different *importance weights* based on the degree to which they determine or influence the superordinate variable (market attractiveness or business strength).

After choosing the markers and assigning each marker an importance weight, each product or SBU should be evaluated on those factors (e.g., with a 0–100 score), and given a weighted score computed by multiplying the evaluation score by its weight, as in Table 26-3.

TABLE 26-3 Assessment of Market Attractiveness and Relative Competitive Position

BUSINESS UNIT: FLAT-SCREEN TVS				
ASSESSMENT OF MARKET ATTRACTIVENESS				
CRITERIA	WEIGHT (%)	EVALUATION/REMARKS	SCORE (0–100)	WEIGHTED SCORE
Market growth	30	Highly growing market in growth phase of the life cycle: CAGR 2002–2006 = 87%; 2006–2007 = 13%; Projected CAGR 2007–2011 = 3.1%; growth is going to slow down in the coming years (CAGR = Compound Annual Growth Rate)	90	27
Market size	25	Market size in 2006 = €4,000; only 15% of households own flat-screen TVs; still very high potential	100	25
Competitive intensity	10	Strong, suppliers of CRT TVs have already switched to flat-screen	30	3
Profit margins	20	Price wars not yet to be expected, high growth rate in Euro sales volume due to higher prices for high-end products: unit increase 2002–2006 = 5%, increase of Euro sales volume = 54%	80	16
Market entry barriers	15	Medium to high, biggest market entry barriers are access to distribution channels, economies of scale, and brand name	60	9
	100			80

BUSINESS UNIT: FLAT-SCREEN TVS				
ASSESSMENT OF RELATIVE COMPETITIVE POSITION				
CRITERIA	WEIGHT (%)	EVALUATION/REMARKS	SCORE (0–100)	WEIGHTED SCORE
Relative market share	30	Low relative market share (.36); strong cost disadvantages due to lower economies of scale and experience curve effects	10	3
R&D strengths	15	Low, behind competition in introducing new technologies or upgrading technologies, R&D budget only 1/3 of strongest competitor	10	1.5
Marketing capabilities	20	Brand awareness and brand image according to market research clearly below competition, lower marketing budget than strongest competitors	15	3
Distribution and sales	25	Limited access to distribution channels, listed in only 3 of 7 major distributors of consumer electronics	10	2.5
Production capabilities	10	Medium, high investments in capacity enlargement, production technologies	50	5
	100			15

As illustrated by the example, the GE/McKinsey Grid is more comprehensive and more detailed than the BCG Matrix. It has the advantage of considering more market and company information and it leads to more specific strategic recommendations. Furthermore, the GE framework can be applied at the level of business units, product lines, or single products, and it can even be adapted to a number of other applications, such as customer portfolios (by considering customer attractiveness and relative competitive position); segment portfolios (by considering segment attractiveness and relative competitive position); and, country portfolios (by considering market attractiveness and relative competitive position).

In such applications, customers, segments, or countries are rated on attractiveness and business strength. Ultimately, a company needs to ask "How much would we like to succeed with this customer (with this segment or in this country)?" And "How likely are we to succeed with this customer (with this segment or in this country)?" Companies will, generally, want to balance these two considerations when targeting customers, segments, or countries and when deciding investments relative to business strengths (competitive advantages).

For example, in Figure 26-4, segments are arrayed by their attractiveness and the strength of the business in that segment. Segment attractiveness might be a

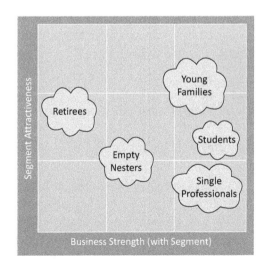

FIGURE 26-4 GE/McKinsey Grid for Hypothetical Segments of Customers

function of size, price insensitivity, lack of appropriate offerings in the marketplace, or a number of other qualities. Business strength might be a function of such things as current market penetration (market share), fit between competitive advantages and the segment's needs, proximity or access to the segment, and the like.

In this example, the company would assess the array to choose target markets and to prioritize the development of new or future strengths. This firm should likely target the "Retirees," if it has not already. The firm should avoid allocating resources toward attracting the "Single Professionals"; they are a bad fit with the firm's strengths and are, in any case, an unattractive target market. The firm might be well-advised to develop strengths that would fit well with the "Young Families" or "Students" because, although the firm's strengths and offerings are not currently well-suited to those segments, those segments are the most attractive in the market (maybe they are growing, have more money to spend, are less price sensitive, tend to be more loyal, or somehow are attractive in an important way). Very similar analyses could assort specific customers or entire countries with regard to their attractiveness and the firm's strengths to serve them, aiding in everything from account selection in sales force management to planning for international expansion.

Limitations of the GE/McKinsey Grid

The GE/McKinsey Grid also has some important limitations. In particular, because the assessment factors have to be selected, weighted, and evaluated by managers, there is greater subjectivity in this model at each step in the process than in the BCG Matrix (note that the subjectivity of distinguishing the distinct products or strategic business units and defining the market for each product/SBU is an issue in both analytic frameworks). This subjectivity is especially problematic when planners are inexperienced and when they evaluate *their own* business units. Unsurprisingly, when these analyses are done by product or SBU managers, their evaluations commonly avoid placing business units in a weak competitive position and/or unattractive markets. Finally, like the BCG Matrix, the GE/McKinsey Grid is most often a snapshot of strength and attractiveness at a particular time, unless trends are specifically incorporated into the summary variables (i.e., unless trends in business strength variables or market attractiveness variables are specifically incorporated into the analysis).

SUMMARY

Portfolio logic arrays competitive position against market attractiveness in matrix form. The growth/share matrix (a crossing of the concepts of product/market evolution and cost and share leverage) offers generic strategies for four (BCG) to nine (GE) polar product/market positions. Whereas the BCG Matrix is based on two dimensions—market growth rate and relative market share—the GE/McKinsey Grid is based on multiple dimensions relative to market attractiveness and competitive position. However, market growth rate is but one measure of market attractiveness—there are many others. Likewise, relative market share is just one measure of competitive position, and other metrics should be considered as well.

REFERENCES

Allen, M. (1977). Diagramming GE's planning for What's Watt. *Strategy & Planning, 5*(5), 3–9.

BCG. (1970). The BCG Portfolio Matrix from the Product Portfolio Matrix. *The Boston Consulting Group.*

Haberberg, A., & Rieple, A. (2008). *Strategic management: Theory and application.* Oxford University Press.

Hax, A. C., & Majluf, N. S. (1983). The use of the industry attractiveness–business strength matrix in strategic planning. *Interfaces, 13*(2), 54–71.

Hedley, B. (1977). Strategy and the "business portfolio." *Long Range Planning, 10*(1), 9–15.

Rigby, D. (2003). *Management tools 2003: An executive's guide.* Bain & Company.

Robinson, S., Hitch, R., & Wade, D. (1978). The directional policy matrix—Tool for strategic planning. *Long Range Planning, 11*(3), 8–15.

Figure Credits

NOTE 27

NEW PRODUCT DEVELOPMENT

New products make up an increasingly large share of sales across companies and industries. In many firms, new products contribute more than 50% of overall sales volume whereby the best firms commercialize about 4 times as many products as the rest. New product development, however, is a risky process. Studies show that for every seven new product ideas, on average not more than four enter the development stage, one and one half are launched, and only one succeeds. Others speak of a failure rate up to 60% (Cooper, 2019). However, only 10% of all new products are truly innovative (Trott, 2008). Most new products that are called an innovation are, in point of fact, merely line extensions, continuous improvements, or revisions of existing products.

As product life cycles become shorter and rivals are increasingly faster to copy new products, time to market becomes crucial. This implies that companies have less time for extensive market research or concept testing. Striving for higher customer value often means higher development and production costs. And if a company wants to keep development costs down, it has less time and resources to design new products in a way that they can be produced at low costs. The majority of large companies have introduced systematic processes for new product development. As found in a study on best practices in product innovation, about 90% of the best performers use a systematic blueprint or road map for moving a new product project through the various stages of new product development (Cooper & Edgett, 2012). Through systematic new product development processes, companies want to ensure that:

- there is a steady stream of new and promising ideas into the pipeline of the product development process;
- these ideas are screened for customer benefit, feasibility, and market potential systematically and early enough (before resources are committed to poor ideas);
- the product concept is market oriented and has a unique selling proposition;
- the selling price, production costs, and market demand are such that the product can be sold at a profit; and
- the concept is extensively tested before market introduction to be sure that it is accepted by the customers and that the marketing plan works.

NEW PRODUCT DEVELOPMENT PROCESS

A systematic product development process consists of several phases: idea generation, idea selection, concept development and testing, business analysis, prototype and market testing, and product launch. Each phase has important tasks to fulfill and is also characterized by critical challenges (see Table 27-1).

260

TABLE 27-1 Phases in the New Product Development Process

PHASE	TASK	CHALLENGE
Idea generation	This phase aims at collecting as many promising ideas for a new product or service as possible. The starting point is unsolved customer needs.	• Generate as many good ideas as possible • Unleash creativity • Use all internal and external sources for new product ideas (customers, suppliers, distributors, technology, R&D, marketing)
Idea selection	In the idea selection phase, ideas are eliminated that do not deserve additional resources, and the most promising ideas are selected for the next phases of the development process	Identify ideas: • that create customer value (address a real unsolved need) • that have a substantial market (size and growth of the market) • that can be profitably produced and marketed (competitive situation) • that fit the vision and strategy of the firm
Concept development and testing	Develop the marketing and engineering details	Specify: • the target market and product positioning • product attributes • unique selling proposition • prove feasibility • estimate production and marketing costs • test product idea with customers, distributors, experts, etc.
Business analysis	Create a business plan Estimate resources needed and profitability	Determine: • selling price • costs • sales volume • breakeven and profitability
Prototype and market testing	Develop a physical prototype and test it in a typical usage situation	Gain feedback: • on market acceptance • for necessary adjustments • on marketing concept in a test market Refine: • product • marketing campaign
Product launch	Launch product and marketing campaign	Execute marketing campaign React to competitor moves, changing market conditions and needs

Idea Generation

The front-end of innovation (all activities from the search of new opportunities until the development of a product concept) usually is not very capital intensive, but it can consume up to 50% of the development time. In this phase, ideas are developed and it is decided whether further resources are invested in the further development of these ideas (Trott, 2008). Therefore, this phase can be crucial for the success of the entire process. Ideas for new products can come from many sources inside or outside the company—engineers, suppliers, scientists, distributors, or customers. To get ideas for new products companies use creativity-generating techniques with internal and external groups and focus groups, conduct in-depth interviews with customers, analyze customers' problems and complaints, use surveys, engage with online communities and brand communities, integrate lead users (highly innovative customers that have their own ideas for new products), and observe competitors.

A logical starting point for the idea generation phase is unsolved customer needs. In this context, the Kano model of customer satisfaction can help to identify promising ideas (Figure 27-1). It distinguishes the following three types of product attributes:

- *Basic factors* (must haves) are minimum requirements. The fulfillment of basic requirements is a necessity, but an insufficient condition for customer satisfaction. Basic factors are entirely expected. The customer regards them as prerequisites; they are taken for granted. If basic factors are already fulfilled, an increase of their performance usually does not increase customer benefit. However, if basic factors are not yet fulfilled, this offers great opportunities for product innovation. Battery range of electric vehicles (EVs) and charging stations are examples of basic factors for potential buyers of EVs. Tesla's superior battery technology and its supercharger network and destination chargers are two of their key success factors.

- *Excitement factors* (delighters) are the factors that increase customer satisfaction if delivered but do not cause dissatisfaction if they are not delivered. Excitement factors are not expected; they surprise the customer and generate *delight*. Delighters typically are latent, not articulated, customer needs, and they add value to the core product. In the car industry, delighters play an important role in differentiating the product. Tesla's over-the-air software updates

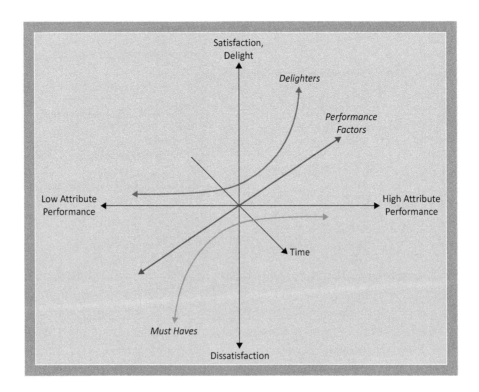

FIGURE 27-1   The Kano Model (Adapted from Kano, 1984)

create excitement among Tesla owners as their cars get new and unexpected features every few weeks.

- *Performance factors* (the more, the better) lead to satisfaction if performance is high and to dissatisfaction if performance is low. In this case, the performance–overall satisfaction relationship is linear and symmetric. These attributes usually are explicitly expected, such as driving performance of a car, battery life of a mobile phone, and the weight of a mountain bike.

For product development, the following implications emerge from Kano's model: basic factors establish a market entry *threshold*. If they are delivered at a satisfactory level, an increase in performance does not lead to an increase in customer satisfaction. Typically, performance factors are directly connected to customers' explicit needs and desires. Therefore, a company should be competitive with regard to performance factors. Excitement factors are unexpected and surprise the customer. As they generate *delight*, a company should try to stand out from the rest with regard to these attributes (Matzler et al., 1996). It is important to emphasize the dynamic nature of these product requirements. What delights customers today might become explicit expectation after some time, and eventually turn into basic factors. Free Internet service in hotels is a good example. When select hotels introduced this service, it delighted customers; however, this service soon became an explicit expectation, and now hotel guests consider it a basic required feature.

For many companies, crowdsourcing has become an effective tool to develop ideas and solutions for new products (Matzler, 2020). In a crowdsourcing project, users, innovators, problem solvers, and gifted inventors are invited and motivated to contribute their ideas and their knowledge to the innovation projects via *broadcast search*. Crowdsourcing is defined as "the act of a company or institution taking a function once performed by employees and outsourcing it to an undefined (and generally large) network of people in the form of an open call. This can take the form of peer-production (when the job is performed collaboratively), but is also often undertaken by sole individuals. The crucial prerequisite is the use of the open call format and the large network of potential laborers" ("Crowdsourcing," 2006, para. 7).

Companies and all kind of organizations can tap into a crowd to find individuals who can help them solve problems and develop innovations. According to eYeka, one of the largest crowdsourcing and co-creation platforms, 85% of the 2014 Best Global Brands have used crowdsourcing in the last 10 years, whereby of all crowdsourcing contests the quest for innovative ideas is the most frequent application (59%), followed by marketing and communication ideas (34%) and design solutions (7%) ("eYeka," 2015; "eYaka," 2017).

Crowdsourcing can take different forms (Boudreau & Lakhani, 2013). In the context of innovation, a contest is the most common way to tap into the creativity and expertise of large crowds. A company offers a cash prize for anybody who can submit an innovation idea, solve a challenging problem, or submit a creative solution. The challenge is broadcast to as many individuals as possible and is open for a specific amount of time. Some of the toughest scientific and technological challenges have been solved through contests. However, contests are also used for topics like developing new product designs (e.g. Swarovski gemstone design competition), algorithms (e.g. Netflix collaborative filtering algorithm), or commercials (e.g. Crash the Super Bowl contest by

Frito-Lay). A contest is particularly well-suited when the problem is complex or novel, and when it is not obvious who might have the best solution or idea. While contests seek the best individual solution for the problem, crowd collaboration projects try to tap into the collective wisdom of the crowd and aggregate "the outputs of multiple contributors … into a coherent and value-creating whole" (Boudreau & Lakhani, 2013, p. 66). Wikipedia is probably the best-known example of crowd collaboration.

Another common form of crowdsourcing for innovation is crowd complementors. With this approach, a product or platform owner invites the crowd to develop innovative solutions that create value through complementary innovations (Bjelland & Wood, 2008). In contrast to the other two forms, a company does not seek the solution to a defined and specific problem, but new applications for many different problems. Amazon, for example, allows the crowd to develop skills for their virtual assistant Alexa. Using the Alexa Skills Kit almost 60,000 skills had been developed by the crowd through the end of 2018 (Perez, 2019). In 2019, Amazon went even further by allowing every single user to develop skills with templates and publish them. Table 27-2 summarizes the various forms of crowdsourcing for innovation.

TABLE 27-2 Forms of Crowdsourcing for Innovation

	CROWD CONTEST	CROWD COLLABORATION	CROWD COMPLEMENTORS
Description	The sponsor (organization) broadcasts a problem and offers a prize for the contributor of the best solution	A large community works together to jointly achieve something that individuals could hardly do	The crowd develops a wide variety of solutions that enhance the value of a product or a platform
Best used for …	• Challenging technical, analytical, and scientific problems • Development of new designs • Creative or aesthetic challenges	• Tasks that can be modularized and have standardized routines • Accumulating and recombining ideas of a large crowd	• New solutions for open platforms • New solutions that complement and increase value of the core product
Principle	Diversity: Use of a large number of different approaches, ideas, or perspectives to solve a problem	Collective intelligence: Cross-fertilization, aggregating decentralized knowledge, tapping into the wisdom of the crowd	Differentiation: Create a large diversity of innovative solutions for product or platform users
Examples	NASA tournament lab, idea contests on InnoCentive	Wikipedia, OpenIDEO, IBM InnovationJam	Smartphone operating systems and apps, such as Amazon Alexa skills; Lego ideas platform

Note. Table source: Matzler, K. (2020). Crowd innovation: The philosopher's stone, a silver bullet, or Pandora's box? *NIM Marketing Intelligence Review, 12(1),* 10–17.

While these are the most relevant types of crowdsourcing for innovation, crowdsourcing has been extended to many tasks like performing micro jobs (e.g. TaskRabbit, Amazon's Mechanical Turk), crowdfunding to raise funds for start-ups (e.g., Kickstarter), or user generated content (e.g. iStock photos, YouTube).

Idea Selection

Once ideas have been generated, the next phase of the new product development process is to select ideas that are promising enough to be pursued and to eliminate those that do not deserve additional resource commitment. This is a critical task because if not done carefully, good ideas might be killed or poor ideas might enter the next phase—concept development—and waste resources. Therefore, a systematic approach to a preliminary assessment of an idea's potential is advisable. Many companies use an idea rating matrix as shown in Table 27-3. Success criteria are defined, weighted, and each idea is evaluated. A weighted score is computed, and a minimum threshold that must be met to enter the next phase of product development is defined (e.g., a weighted score above 6 in the example below).

TABLE 27-3 Idea Rating Scheme

SUCCESS CRITERIA	WEIGHT	SCORE (0–10)				
		IDEA 1	IDEA 2	IDEA 3	IDEA 4	...
Superior customer benefit	0.4	4	7	2	8	...
Potential market size	0.3	5	4	5	5	...
Competitive situation	0.1	8	3	4	6	...
Fit to vision and strategy	0.2	2	6	3	7	...
	Weighted Score	4.3	5.5	3.3	6.7	...

Concept Development and Testing

For the remaining ideas, product concepts are developed and preliminarily tested. The target market has to be clearly defined; product attributes must be specified to achieve a unique selling proposition, technical and economic feasibility must be proved, and the prototype should be tested with customers. In this phase, trade-offs among needs and features have to be made. Usually not all needs can be addressed economically, and sometimes needs contradict each other (e.g. weight and battery life of a laptop). An important principle in this phase is: *Every product feature has associated costs, but not every product feature generates value to the customer.* Hence, a careful examination of the cost–utility relationship of features is important. Conjoint-analysis is a widely used tool in this phase since it helps to measure the utility a customer attaches to varying levels of product attributes.

Business Analysis

For product ideas that *survive* the concept and testing phase, a detailed business analysis must be carried out. The exact price must be determined so the sales volume as well as costs and profits have to be estimated. A particular challenge in this phase is the estimation of demand. Not all customers react to innovation with the same speed; some need years until they take an interest in it. Innovators are adventurous and prepared to take risks, and they are the first to buy an innovation. Early adopters accept new ideas early, but they are more careful and also are frequently opinion leaders. And the mass market often reacts with an enormous time lag to innovations. Therefore, quantitative and representative market research studies cannot really help in the innovation process. On the contrary, if one tries to interview a representative cross section of customers about their desires or tries to test the potential of an innovation on them, the results can be misleading (Matzler et al., 2007).

Prototype and Market Testing

For those products that prove to be promising after a thorough business analysis, a physical prototype is developed and tested in the typical usage situation. Before the product is introduced, customer feedback is sought to make final adjustments to the product and marketing plan. This can be done by bringing customers into laboratories where they test a prototype. Other companies give the prototype to customers to test it at home. Often, test markets are used. These are representative cities or regions where the product is introduced, accompanied with all marketing activities that are planned for this product. This way trials, repeat purchases, purchase frequency, etc., can be tested.

Many companies use the idea of minimal viable products (MVP) and A/B testing in this phase. The idea of an MVP is grounded in the fact that the planning approach in new product development often does not work. Steve Blank, a Silicon Valley entrepreneur, surmised, "Business plans rarely survive the first contact with customers … No one besides venture capitalists and the late Soviet Union require 5-year plans to forecast complete unknowns. These plans are generally fiction, and dreaming them up is almost always a waste of time" (Blank, 2013, p. 65). Instead of developing the perfect version of a product and introducing it after months or years to learn that many customers do not need or want many of the features, MVPs are minimum configurations of new product ideas that are introduced very quickly to get feedback from customers and to adjust the core idea of the product.

Dropbox is an example of an organization that leveraged the MVP concept. To avoid the risk that the final product was not accepted or needed, Drew Houston, the cofounder of Dropbox, developed a banal, 3-minute video that demonstrated how the product should work after he realized that potential customers had a hard time understanding Dropbox when it was explained in focus group interviews. Thus, Houston narrated the video personally so viewers could see the proposed product screen and understand how to move around the interface. This video was an MVP to test the basic assumptions of the software and whether potential customers would sign up. Ultimately, the MVP generated significant interest that resulted in thousands of prospects visiting the Dropbox website (Ries, 2011).

The concept of MVPs is usually complemented with A/B testing, a systematic approach of online experiments. Two versions of the same experience (e.g. product, website) are set up, with only one difference. "A" is usually the current version and "B" the treatment, i.e. a modification that should improve the current solution. Users are then randomly assigned to one of the two experiences to measure their reaction. As version "B" is identical to version "A" with the exception of only one feature, differences in customers' reactions (e.g. buying decision, likes) can be attributed to this feature. This is a cheap and effective method used by companies like Amazon, Facebook, and Microsoft that allows for fast customer feedback and product improvements (Kohavi & Thomke, 2017).

Product Launch

The product launch phase is usually the most expensive phase. Advertising, promotion, and other communications of major new consumer packaged goods can cost up to $100 million in the first year;

marketing expenditures of new food products represent up to roughly 60% of the first year's sales volume (Kotler & Keller, 2009). Timing is of particular importance in the product launch decision. As a first entrant, a company can benefit from the first-mover advantages (e.g. acquiring the most attractive customer segments, locking up key distributors and suppliers, gaining market share, and benefiting from scale economies). As a follower, one can learn from a competitor's mistakes, with lower risks and costs involved to enter the marketplace.

Another critical question to be addressed during the product launch phase is internal cannibalization. When a new generation of products is introduced, they can replace old products. If the new product *only* substitutes for the old product and does not increase sales or generate marginal profits, then the company is no better off; this is called *cannibalization.* New product launches often involve some degree of cannibalization with the critical question being whether or not that cannibalization is strategically justified by marginal (i.e., new) sales and profits. GM's Chevrolet Traverse crossover, for instance, competed with other larger crossovers such as the Mazda CX-9 and Toyota Highlander. Under the skin, the seven-passenger crossover wagon Traverse was nearly identical to other GM vehicles and it could be expected to cannibalize sales and marketing budgets from these cars that are made on the same platform.

Earlier, Table 27-1 summarized the new product development process; keep in mind that the individual steps in this process may be reiterated as needed. If, for example, the physical prototype turns out to be technically unfeasible or is not accepted by the customers, a new concept needs to be developed. Also, some steps might be eliminated to reduce time to market. Some companies try to reduce development time by overlapping several activities of the process and completing them at the same time (concurrent engineering).

RESEARCH AND DEVELOPMENT

The two terms *research* and *development* are almost always used together in the everyday business lexicon to refer to a single undifferentiated set of activities. In fact, these terms are regularly shortened to *R&D* with little thought about the differences inherent in these two terms, which can have significant strategic implications. *Research* refers to more basic explorations, while *development* refers to more applied incremental and tactical new product development and design (Annacchino, 2003). Research and development ranges from basic research exploring fundamental ideas and advancing theory to applied development that takes known technologies and applies them to specific problems or products. Basic research is often conducted at universities or in very specialized laboratories. Applied research is usually done by corporate departments or teams and even by managers and entrepreneurs in commercial settings.

This distinction between theoretical research and applied and incremental development has strategic implications. Different mixtures or *R&D orientations* are appropriate for different strategies and are more effective or less effective depending on the product's stage in the product life cycle. Most new industries emerge from breakthroughs gleaned from basic research. If a firm wants to be a *pioneer* or *first mover*, it must invest in basic research to ensure that it is the one to develop the basic technology or it is not far behind. *Fast followers* and *late movers* let others do the basic research; they focus on adapting and improving those breakthroughs and on taking advantage of earlier entrants' mistakes and learning. More mature markets generally compete by incremental improvements and product augmentations anchored in development or design.

Nevertheless, firms in mature industries may invest in basic research to shift the product life cycle curve, to extend the product life cycle, or to *change the game* by forging new markets or *blue oceans*. The most important aspect of integrating this continuum from basic theoretical research to applied incremental development is to understand exactly what the investments are meant to contribute to the strategy and then shape the activities to conform to that purpose. Firms that need product modifications but that invest in abstract experiments or, conversely, that need the *next big idea* but that study mundane and well-known technologies, are likely to fail.

DESIGN

In the past, *design* meant different things to different people (and it often meant different things to different people in the same firm): industrial designers typically focused on the form in the form-versus-function distinction (Bloch, 1995), whereas engineering designers focused on function and the practical issues such as design for manufacturability (Bralla, 1998). The newer, integrated view looks at both and, importantly, does so from a customers' point of view while also considering the firm's strategy. That is, the term *design* has been broadened to recognize the essential process of integrating *both* nonfunctional and aesthetic elements of the product (i.e., the form) with the functional elements to create enhanced customer experiences and customer value.

Thus, design or *product design* as a process is a broad, holistic, and integrative set of activities linking the new product development process to the customers and to the firm's strategy from the onset. The outcome, or product, of design may be a tangible good and/or service or the combination of goods and services, and the design elements include its form, its function, and the vital interactive effect of both. These elements include, among other things, usability, ergonomics and haptics, form and aesthetics, packaging, materials, and other elements of sustainability, as well as core technology and functionality. Because customers engage with the whole product, not its parts, the holistic perspective on design is invaluable to enhancing the customer's experience and to creating customer value. Therefore, the product design process is broader than mere new product development as it has traditionally been understood; it extends backward into strategy formulation and forward into marketing research and methods for understanding how customers use and take value from the product and even how customers dispose of the product.

DIMINISHING MARGINAL RETURNS IN R&D

Research and development efforts, like many investments, conform to the law of diminishing marginal returns, which holds that, "As successive equal increases in a variable factor of production, such as labor, are added to other fixed factors of production, such as capital, there will be a point beyond which the extra, or marginal, product that can be attributed to each additional unit of the variable factor or production will decline" (Miller, 2010, p. 588). That is, there is a range of inputs to R&D that achieve a certain level of outputs, and then the output from each marginal input begins to diminish. In practice, there is often a converse relationship too—some minimal investment is required to get any benefits. To even *begin* doing research in areas like genetic therapy or nuclear power generation, investments below that threshold will likely be ineffective or wasted entirely. These realities produce an S-shaped relationship between inputs and outputs (shown in Figure 27-2) with

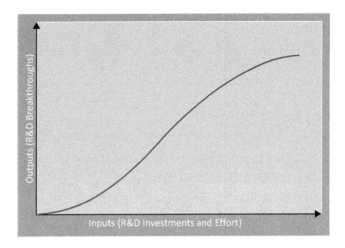

FIGURE 27-2 Diminishing Returns on R&D Investments

the inputs along the horizontal and outputs on the vertical axis. As inputs initially increase, the outputs produced are low; but once some threshold is reached, outputs rise dramatically across a range of inputs. Then, a second inflection point is reached and marginal returns diminish in accordance with the law of diminishing marginal returns.

In the strategic management of research and development, this means that if the firm cannot afford the minimum threshold amount to do R&D well, it should not do it at all. It also means that some breakthroughs will be achieved more easily than others and that a strategy grounded on breakthrough research and development may have its limits. At some point, the next breakthrough will be much more expensive to achieve than the earlier breakthroughs—if it is achievable at all. This problem of diminishing returns on R&D investments is exacerbated by the reality that early breakthroughs are more likely to meet pent-up customer demand but later, incremental advances do not enjoy that eager customer reception because the basic need has already been met.

SUMMARY

The new product development process has traditionally been organized into several phases: idea generation, idea selection, concept development and testing, business analysis, prototype and market testing, and product launch. Each of these phases has an important role in delivering successful new products to market that are consistent with the firm's strategy and with customers' needs. "Research and development," which is intended to create new products, is often reduced to a simple, undifferentiated idea within the organization. However, a continuum can be drawn between basic theoretical research and applied development, and different orientations along that continuum are appropriate and effective for different strategies. Choices of R&D emphasis have important implications for marketing strategy and the success of the firm. New product development and research and development have traditionally been set aside as distinct functional areas within the firm. However, a more integrative and broader view of product development has emerged under the rubric of product design that promises to integrate new product development into every step of strategy formulation, from situation assessment to market research and operations.

REFERENCES

Annacchino, M. (2003). *New product development: From initial idea to product management*. Elsevier.

Bjelland, O. M., & Wood, R. C. (2008). An inside view of IBM's 'Innovation Jam.' *MIT Sloan Management Review*, *50*(1), 32.

Blank, S. (2013). Why the lean start-up changes everything. *Harvard Business Review*, 91(5), 63–72.

Bloch, P. H. (1995). Seeking the ideal form: Product design and consumer response. *Journal of Marketing*, 59(3), 16–29.

Boudreau, K. J., & Lakhani, K. R. (2013). Using the crowd as an innovation partner. *Harvard Business Review*, 91(4), 60–69.

Bralla, J. (1998). *Design for manufacturability handbook* (2nd ed.). McGraw-Hill.

Cooper, R. G. (2019, January). The drivers of success in new-product development. *Industrial Marketing Management*, 76, 36–47. https://doi.org/https://doi.org/10.1016/j.indmarman.2018.07.005

Cooper, R. G., & Edgett, S. J. (2012). Best practices in the idea-to-launch process and its governance. *Research Technology Management*, 55(2), 43–54.

"Crowdsourcing." (2006). Crowdsourcing. *Crowdsourcing blog*. https://crowdsourcing.typepad.com/cs/2006/06/crowdsourcing_a.html

"eYeka." (2015, April 9). eYeka releases "The state of crowdsourcing in 2015" trend report. *eYeka*. https://eyeka.pr.co/99215-eyeka-releases-the-state-of-crowdsourcing-in-2015-trend-report

"eYeka." (2017). eYeka releases: "The state of crowdsourcing in 2017." *eYeka*. https://de.eyeka.com/resources/reports?download=cs_report_2017.pdf

Kano, Noriaki. "Attractive Quality and Must Be Quality." *Hinshitsu* [Quality], 14, no. 2 (1984): 147–56 (in Japanese).

Kohavi, R., & Thomke, S. (2017). The surprising power of online experiments. *Harvard Business Review*, 95(5), 74–82.

Kotler, P., & Keller, K. (2009). *Marketing management* (13th ed.). Pearson Education.

Matzler, K. (2020). Crowd innovation: The philosopher's stone, a silver bullet, or Pandora's box? *NIM Marketing Intelligence Review*, 12(1), 10–17.

Matzler, K., Bailom, F., & Tschemernjak, D. (2007). *Enduring success: What top companies do differently*. Palgrave Macmillan.

Matzler, K., Hinterhuber, H. H., Bailom, F., & Sauerwein, E. (1996). How to delight your customers. *Journal of Product & Brand Management*.

Miller, R. L. (2010). *Economics today* (15th ed.). Addison-Wesley.

Perez, S. (2019). The number of Alexa skills in the U.S. more than doubled in 2018. *TechCrunch*.

Ries, E. (2011). How Dropbox started as a minimal viable product. *TechCrunch*. https://techcrunch.com/2011/10/19/dropbox-minimal-viable-product/

Trott, P. (2008). *Innovation management and new product development*. Pearson Education.

When marketing strategists talk about *innovations*, they're usually referring to *discontinuous innovations*—products that are truly new to the world and that change the way a customer need is met. In marketing strategy, the degree of innovation is not generally thought of in terms of underlying technology. Although products such as hybrid-powered cars are generally viewed as very innovative and the underlying technology may be groundbreaking, the marketing of a product like hybrid cars is not necessarily *innovation marketing*. People buy and consume hybrid cars in much the same way that they bought and consumed their previous internal combustion engine cars. Even if they stop at gas stations less often with hybrid cars, owners of such vehicles bought the car from the same sort of dealer and serviced the car in a similar way, and they drive it to places in almost the same manner as they did their previous cars.

DEGREES OF NEW PRODUCT INNOVATION

For marketing strategy, an *innovation* is defined by the degree of change in consumer behavior or consumption patterns required to adopt it, consume it and meet a need with it. Consumption patterns include the actual behaviors required to use the product as well as the knowledge required and the ancillary equipment and installations required. *Discontinuous innovations* or *disruptive technologies* require substantial changes in consumption patterns (they disrupt consumption patterns and they disrupt industries and markets). Tesla's electric vehicles (EVs) for instance, are disruptive as the new technology and the new business model substantially changes consumption patterns and has disrupted the market for internal combustion engine (ICE) vehicles. Tesla sells its cars online and through exclusive distribution channels instead of through established car dealers. Owners of electric cars charge them at home or at superchargers instead of going to gas stations. Electric cars require almost no maintenance and, as computers on four wheels, software becomes a substantial value driver.

Continuous innovations offer incremental value without major or sometimes even noticeable changes in consumption patterns, and *dynamically discontinuous innovations* fall in between (they change consumption behaviors and change the way the need is met, but only to a limited degree). This may seem like a semantic exercise, assigning labels and definitions to ranges along a continuum; however, it is strategically important to consider the degree of change in consumption patterns that an innovation requires of the customers. This attribute of an innovation—required changes in consumption patterns and behaviors—determines important aspects of the marketing programs and strategies that will be effective or ineffective in supporting it. The *diffusion of innovations* framework, presented in this Note, is most relevant to marketing discontinuous innovations.

Strategies for incremental, continuous innovations are less likely to be effectively based on the diffusion-of-innovation dynamics.

CUSTOMER VALUE AND PRODUCT INNOVATION

A useful framework for understanding new product innovation in strategic marketing is the *customer value frontier*, as examined previously in Note 17. Value is defined as *relative performance* adjusted for *relative price.* In most markets, there are offerings that are low in price but also low in relative performance/quality, other offerings that deliver more performance features at a higher price, and then certain offerings that offer very high performance for quite a higher price. These two aspects of the offerings in any market can be used to create a two-dimensional space or map, as shown in Figure 28-1, in which the axes are relative price (on the vertical) and relative performance/quality (on the horizontal). In that space there are trade-offs that customers understand and are willing to make—that is, there is an equilibrium frontier or zone in which customers and marketers understand that the trade-offs are *fair.*

There are also regions in that *value map* within which the trade-offs are not sustainable. Products in the upper-left (the northwest) quadrant are charging more than products in the lower left (the southwest) quadrant but are offering only the same performance/quality. This is not viable in the long term; customers will find the offerings in the lower left and choose to save and/or find offerings in the upper right and choose to pay the same but get more.

On the other hand, products in the lower right (the southeast) are offering more performance than products in the southwest but at the same relative price; they can also be seen as offering the same quality as products in the northeast but at a lower price—either way, more-for-the-same or the-same-for-less, these products have found a way to dominate their competition. *These are innovations!* They will draw sales and gain market share until the competition catches up.

Of course, it is not easy to offer more for less, but that is what entrepreneurship and innovation require. If the firm itself is not innovating, it can be sure that the competition is or will be soon. When Walmart

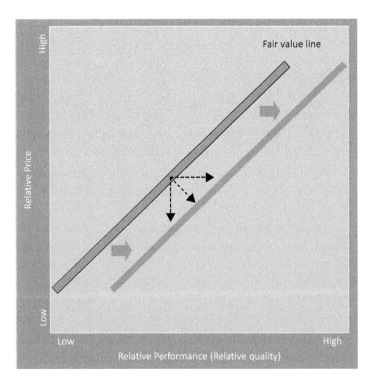

FIGURE 28-1   The Value Frontier and Innovation

introduced electronic inventory tracking systems enabled by RFID tags (radio-frequency identification tags) on pallets of merchandise, or when Apple added features, style, and convenience to its iPhone, iPad, and AirPod product lines, they delivered the same goods for a lower price or something more than the competition offered for a fair price. Walmart's extraordinary logistics backbone delivers the same products at lower prices than customers could buy elsewhere. Apple's intuitive interfaces and distinctive designs offer *much more for a little more*—that is, something customers perceive as unique and valuable at a price they are willing to pay. Such features attract customers and, eventually and inevitably, they also attract competition—which should lead to further innovation. The competition *catching up* can be understood as the fair value zone shifting to the right; as the market adjusts to new offerings that appear to the southeast of the frontier, what is considered *fair* shifts to the right to establish a new equilibrium.

DIFFUSION OF INNOVATIONS

The *diffusion of innovations* refers to the speed at which a truly new product (or an idea, for that matter) spreads through or *diffuses* into a market. Much of what is known about the diffusion of innovations comes from studies of the agricultural sector. The basic ideas and much of the early research was done by rural sociologists studying patterns of adoption for new farming methods and technologies such as weed sprays and crop varieties. Because innovations diffuse through markets much like diseases like the flu spread through populations (including the reliance on interpersonal contact), marketing has also adopted knowledge from epidemiology. Epidemiology uses sophisticated mathematical models to forecast the rate and severity of the spread of diseases through populations of people, and marketing has borrowed some of that math. Although many of those models go beyond the scope of this Note and are beyond the needs of most marketing strategists, one basic framework, the "Bass Model," emphasizes the underlying mechanisms of diffusion and is invaluable in forecasting.

Adoption Process

The adoption process of an innovation includes stages that a consumer moves through on their way from unaware of a new product to eventual (hoped for) adoption and loyalty. The consumer must start out unaware of the product, and therefore the first objective of the marketing program for innovations must be to gain awareness in target markets. Consumers then move from susceptible—that is, having the need and in the target market but unaware—through awareness, interest or understanding toward an evaluation (an attitude) eventually to trial and adoption (see Figure 28-2). It is important for the marketing strategist to recognize where consumers are in that process and to recognize that different consumers, different proportions of consumers, and different segments of consumers will be in

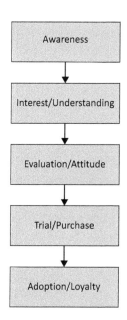

FIGURE 28-2 The Adoption Process of an Innovation

differing stages at any given time. Different tools and messages are required for consumers who are in differing stages of the adoption process.

Not all consumers are equally likely to adopt a new technology, and certainly not at the same time. Some consumers are more likely to adopt; they will buy the new product when it is very new. Others will wait for another period of time. Much of the study of the diffusion of innovations has been the study of who will adopt when and, importantly, what a marketing strategist can and should do differently when dealing with different types of adopters at different times in the diffusion of an innovation.

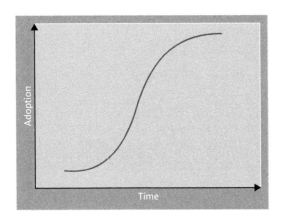

FIGURE 28-3   The Diffusion S-Curve

In general, the diffusion of an innovation into the market across time forms an S-shaped curve (Figure 28-3). At first only a few consumers will buy the product—it is untried and they cannot see anyone else using it, but someone has to be the first to buy. As more people try a product and adopt it, the speed of that adoption increases—the curve turns more sharply upward because as more people adopt the product, others see it in use, distribution broadens (it is easier to get), and perceptions of risk diminish (it's been tested by others). Eventually, diffusion starts to *max out*; most of the people who have the need and the means have purchased the product. Then more of the product's sales become repurchases, and the rate of new adoption inevitably flattens. At some point, everyone in the market who was ever going to try the product has tried it, and the only new customers are new to the market.

Types of Consumers

One of the most important understandings to come out of the study of farmers' adoption of new agricultural methods was the recognition that markets can be segmented into groups of consumers (farmers) who will adopt new technologies at different stages in the diffusion life cycle. Some consumers are inherently more likely to adopt a new technology, and some are very unlikely to be *innovative*. Some of those differences are general—they're true across product categories and across innovations—and some are product category specific.

The most basic segmentation scheme regarding adoption of a new product presents five types of consumers: innovators, early adopters, early majority, late majority, and laggards (see Figure 28-4; Table 28-1). In general, and unsurprisingly, innovators and early adopters tend to be younger, better educated, more affluent, and more open-minded. Innovators and early adopters for any particular product category tend to be more involved in the product and attuned to media that is specific to a product category.

There are some important strategic differences between these segments. Innovators typically do not influence as many other consumers—certainly not as many as the early majority influence; because they are so involved in the product category and have such a specialized knowledge, their

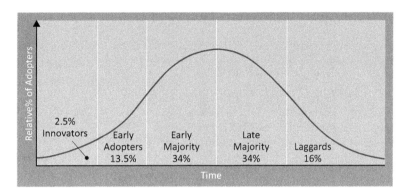

FIGURE 28-4   Segments Based on Propensity to Adopt Across Time
(adapted from Rogers, 2003)

TABLE 28-1 Characteristics of Adoption Segments

ADOPTION SEGMENT	BASS MODEL LABEL	GENERAL CHARACTERISTICS	STRATEGIC IMPLICATIONS
Innovators	Innovators	Younger, highly involved in the product category. Less socially connected than early adopters. Individualistic.	Great source of new product ideas—less important to accelerating the diffusion of the product.
Early Adopters (Opinion Leaders or Gatekeepers)		Young, better educated, more affluent, socially connected. Extraverted. Moderate-to high-category involvement.	Critical to gaining market foothold and to influencing later adopters.
Early Majority	Imitators	Deliberate but open-minded. Moderately interested in the product category.	
Late Majority		Conservative and skeptical. Low product category involvement. Risk averse.	
Laggards		Older, less well-educated, lower income, risk-averse, low interest in product category.	

needs are simply different. They also do not tend to be as well connected to broader social networks. Innovators *can* provide important design feedback and can even cocreate and collaborate in new product development, but they're less influential on other adopter segments.

Early adopters are sometimes referred to as *opinion leaders* or *gatekeepers*. Those labels emphasize the important role this segment plays in marketing and in the success or failure of truly new products. Like innovators, these consumers are younger, better educated, more affluent, more open-minded, and more highly involved in the product category. Unlike innovators, these consumers are also well connected in social networks and tend to talk with *and influence* many other consumers.

The bell-shaped curve is simply the S-curve—not coincidently exactly the shape of the product life cycle—but instead of graphing cumulative sales, it graphs trial by period. Figure 28-5 shows

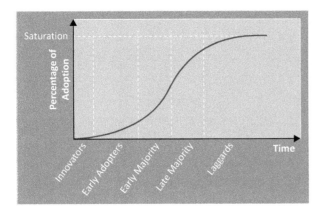

FIGURE 28-5 Cumulative Adoption and Adoption Segments

the same phenomenon with the vertical axis capturing cumulative (percent of total) trial. We highlight that relationship to emphasize the relationship between diffusion and the product life cycle. The product life cycle graphs cumulative total sales—the diffusion process addresses cumulative trial. By adding adopters or repeat sales, the diffusion curve maps directly to the product life cycle. By graphing trial as period specific rather than cumulative, the five adopter categories can be connected to the product life cycle in the same way.

Importance of Two-Step Communications

When thinking about marketing communications related to product innovations, the tendency is to think first about marketer-controlled communications—messages created by the marketing organization to send to consumers and potential consumers via media channels. Nevertheless, the most important and persuasive information that consumers receive about a product, especially a truly new innovation, is received from other consumers. Often, the most important information that consumers use in decision-making is from observing other consumers using a product (rather than from overt, explicit communications or traditional word-of-mouth communications). That is, some information consumers transmit overtly—by telling others about the product—but another influential source of information is simply observing the product being used or seeing another consumer with the product. This process is called *two-step communications*. The first step is the marketing effort—traditional elements of communications such as sales, advertising, and public relations—that results in some customers responding to marketer-controlled communications and trying the product. The second step, and the communications process that actually drives most customer behavior, is the processing of the information via other customers (as shown in Figure 28-6).

Both explicit inter-consumer communications (consumers telling other consumers something or sending a message to other consumers) and observations of other consumers' behaviors are

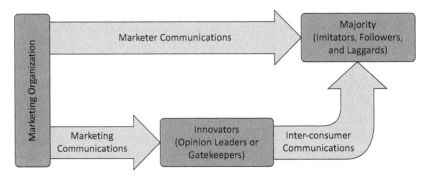

FIGURE 28-6 "Two-Step" Communications

especially powerful mechanisms via which truly innovative new products gain acceptance and thereby diffuse into the market. Social media channels such as Facebook and YouTube enable such communications to quickly proliferate, and they have proven to be a powerful factor in the success of product innovations. It can be difficult to motivate consumers to talk about older technology and familiar brands, and, although it is still possible to observe the product in use, these observations are less important. Older product categories such as fashion and clothing defy that general rule—purchases are still strongly influenced by opinion leaders within a mediated, two-step process even though fashion is not a new or technologically sophisticated category.

Nevertheless, for truly new products, inter-consumer communications are especially persuasive and, conversely, marketer-controlled communications (ads, sales messages, etc.) are not particularly persuasive. Communications mediated by third party news organizations, that is, news reports that result from public relations efforts, are more persuasive than paid-for communications such as advertisements, but they are still less influential than inter-consumer communications and observed behaviors. It is important to recognize that not all inter-consumer communication is positive—in fact, negative word-of-mouth is considered to be more influential than recommendations and dissatisfied consumers are far more likely to talk about their experience than satisfied customers.

Attributes of the Product/Innovation

Various characteristics of the product or the innovation influence the rate at which that innovation diffuses through the market. Some of these attributes can be addressed or changed by the marketing strategist to increase the rate at which consumers adopt the new product—and it should be remembered that, while we talk about the *rate of adoption*, marketers should equate that diffusion with rate of *sales growth*. Each trial is viewed as a sale and every adopter as a loyal customer. While some attributes of an innovation cannot be changed—a new medicine, for example, may be inherently risky and there is nothing anyone can do about that riskiness—other attributes of an innovation may be manageable, such as the financial risk (which can be mitigated by lowering the price or offering guarantees or warranties). So, although discussed as a separate topic here, it is important for the marketing strategist to understand that some of these *attributes of the product* that drive the rate of diffusion are under the influence of the marketing manager and are therefore part of the marketing program. Some of these attributes will be explored below.

Relative Advantage

The first and most obvious attribute of an innovation itself that is related to its speed of diffusion is the *relative advantage* the new technology offers over existing, older technologies. This is not surprising but is important to consider. The enhancement in the way consumers meet a need and the significance of the met need to the consumers will, in large part, drive acceptance of the innovation, and these two attributes (advantage over existing technologies in meeting a need and the salience of the need to consumer) equate to *relative advantage*.

Trialability

If consumers can try a product without committing to adopting it or committing to a large purchase or effort to try it, they will be more willing to sample and evaluate the product. Innovations that require complete conversion or even large purchases will diffuse more slowly due to the increased price, the increased risk, and the increased effort required for trying without perfect knowledge.

Complexity/Ease of Use

The more complex an innovation, the slower and less willing customers will be to try the innovation. The simple and easier the technology is to use, the more readily customers will try it. This may seem obvious, but in too many instances, marketers have adopted the attitude that "customers should just know how to use the product," instead of recognizing that it is the marketer's job to ensure that the product is easy for customers to understand and to use.

Observability

Innovations that can be seen in use will diffuse into a market more quickly than products that are not visible. The logic underlying the two-step process of communications and the effect it has on diffusion is that in many markets for disruptive technologies most consumers will use other consumers as *testers* for the innovation. Either deliberately or unconsciously, customers will think, *I do not want to be the first to try that innovation.* However, once they have seen someone else trying the product, they will perceive the risk to be lower and may also believe that others can give information and assistance if needed.

Compatibility

The less the degree of change, and the lower the price of change required to try a product, the more likely customers and consumers will be to try it. Innovations that require major changes—either to behaviors or to other systems—will be less readily tried.

Risk

Many forms of risk are perceived by customers—financial risk, physical (heath and welfare) risk, social risk, etc. The greater the risk of any sort, the less likely customers are to try the innovation. As previously noted, inter-consumer communications can be an important tool to mitigate such perceived risks.

Network Effects

Some of the substantive, core benefits of an innovation may also increase with wider market adoption via "network effects." For example, owning the first fax machine had few benefits to the innovative firm that bought it—until others bought fax machines. The utility of owning a fax machine was greatest when, eventually, fax machines became pervasive.

ATTRIBUTES OF THE MARKETING PROGRAM AND LINKS TO MARKETING STRATEGIES

All of the elements of a marketing strategy and the tactics of a marketing offering can influence the pace of product diffusion and the resulting realized market size. Most of those relationships can be understood as influencing that diffusion via the reality of and/or consumers' perceptions of the characteristics of the innovation, as described above. That is, changing the actual relative advantage, trialability, complexity/ease of use, observability, compatibility, risk, and network effects or changing consumers' perceptions of those things will speed diffusion. Marketers can change the size of product packages or offer smaller minimum order quantities to create easier trialability. Product names can be displayed more prominently to enhance observability. Lower prices for first-time buyers and money-back guarantees increase trialability and decrease risk. Increased channel support and training for sales clerks improves understanding (i.e., reduced perceived complexity).

Another way to think about the influence of mix decisions on the diffusion of innovation is to consider the two segments modeled in the Bass Model: marketing mix elements can influence innovation or affect imitation (or might augment both). Some elements may be specifically developed, for example, to facilitate word-of-mouth and observability. Agricultural supply companies develop programs in which farmers that are opinion leaders host events to display innovations. These companies also offer discounts to farmers who will post signage in their fields to make otherwise unobservable choices visible to passersby—choices about things such as fertilizers and seeds. Some of these mix decisions are tactical, while others may demand distinct strategies. For example, pricing to accelerate diffusion precludes skimming strategies in pricing and developing knowledgeable sales support from channel partners precludes intensive, mass distribution.

SUMMARY

Innovation involves the creation of something new that customers will value more than previous alternatives. As such, marketing strategists must understand how different customers react to innovations, including the adoption process at the individual customer level, differentiable segments of customers based on their propensity to adopt, and the essential role of inter-customer communications in driving adoption. Strategists should also understand how different attributes of the innovation and different elements of the marketing mix, such as price and integrated communications, can influence the adoption and diffusion of innovations. That is, although the diffusion of innovations into a market is influenced by some factors largely outside the marketers' direct control, there are tools available that influence customer and market reactions, and the successful strategist will have a keen appreciation of those tools.

REFERENCES

Rogers, Everett M. *Diffusion of innovations*, 5th ed. New York: The Free Press, 2003.

Moore, Geoffery A. *Crossing the Chasm: Marketing and Selling High-Tech Products to Mainstream*. New York: Harper Business, 1991.

Mohr, Jakki J., Sanjit Sengupta, and Stanley Slater.*Marketing of High-Technology Products and Innovations*. Upper Saddle River, NJ: Pearson/Prentice Hall, 2010.

PRICING STRATEGIES

Of all the marketing mix elements, price is the only one that generates revenue. Price is usually the easiest element of the mix to set and adjust—and is the easiest competitive action to imitate. A company's pricing policy can make or break the bottom line (Dolan & Simon, 1996). Pricing changes have a stronger impact on profits than revenue increases or reductions in the costs of goods sold. On average, a 5% increase in selling price increases earnings before interest and taxes (EBIT) by 22%, whereas increasing sales (revenue) by 5% increases EBIT by 12%, and a 5% reduction in costs of goods sold increases EBIT by just 10% (Hinterhuber, 2004).

As a complement to other marketing mix elements, price is also important in shaping customers' perceptions of the offering, its quality, and its value. Thus, setting pricing objectives must be done within the context of the intended positioning and the overall strategy. Four steps are central to effectively developing pricing strategies and tactics: define price objectives; analyze key elements of pricing situation; define pricing strategy; and set the price and the pricing tactics. Each of these steps will be examined in greater detail.

PRICE OBJECTIVES

Price objectives are derived from the marketing strategy and the positioning decisions the firm has made. Pricing decisions can have short-term or long-term objectives. Two common short-term objectives are *survival* or *maximum current profit* (Kotler & Keller, 2009). In the short run, sales contribute to survival as long as all variable costs are covered. That is, if price is at least as much as the marginal cost of creating each additional unit, then the sale of any additional unit contributes something toward overhead. Therefore, the *minimum* price (the floor price) is the amount of direct variable costs. In the long run, however, prices must be set in such a way that, in aggregate across the assortment, all the fixed costs are covered and the company earns a profit.

When a company knows the precise cost and demand functions for its products and markets, it is possible to set the price to ensure *maximum current profit*. In reality, however, these parameters are very difficult to gauge precisely. Furthermore, a company that maximizes current profits might sacrifice long-term profits by, for example, ignoring competitor actions. The following section will examine four long-term objectives, including building and protecting market share, market skimming, market penetration, and product positioning.

Building and Protecting Market Share

Low prices can serve to build and to protect market share. By increasing market share, companies expect to lower unit costs due to economies of scale and experience curve effects. A market leader can discourage competitors to enter the industry by cutting prices further as costs fall with increasing experience.

Market Skimming

Customers' price sensitivity depends on the product life cycle and varies across market segments. Many companies *skim* the market by setting high prices for an innovation at the beginning of the life cycle and targeting price insensitive segments. Later they lower prices step-by-step to target other customer segments' willingness to pay. A skimming strategy foregoes volume for margin.

Luxury cars and fashion apparel are good examples of the use of price skimming. In each case, prices are set high at the beginning of the *selling season* and progressively reduced as the markets near the end of the peak sales season. The consumer electronics industry is replete with examples of price skimming as well. Apple is perhaps one of the most well-known companies to employ price skimming techniques. For example, in June 2007, Apple introduced the original 8GB version of the iPhone priced at $599. Customers lined up for an opportunity to buy the new product. By September 2007, Apple had sold over 1,000,000 iPhones, but sales were beginning to slow. Apple then reduced the price of the 8GB iPhone to $399, and sales took off again. Now Apple yearly introduces a new generation of the iPhone with more features and memory at a high price, while reducing the price of existing models.

Market Penetration

The converse of a market skimming strategy, which forgoes sales volume to skim high prices from price-insensitive customers, is a market penetration strategy, which entails setting a relatively low price and accepting that lower unit margin in order to quickly gain market share. This strategy is based on the recognition that volume leads to benefits of scale, including economies of scale and learning curve or experience effects, and that those benefits of scale include lower unit costs. Further, the first brand to penetrate a market enjoys primacy effects, including brand equity and customer stickiness (customers who have purchased a product and tend to stay with the brand, sometimes due to inertia and other times due to the installed base of ancillary or support equipment).

Penetration pricing is widely used in the hotel and airline industries, as well as among Internet providers. Netflix is widely cited as an example of penetration pricing and has acquired a high share of the global streaming market through its low-penetration pricing. In another example, Android smartphones are generally available at a steep discount compared to Apple smartphones, allowing Android to build market share. Apple makes the profits with its skim prices, but Android (and particularly Samsung) takes a market share with penetration prices. Table 29-1 outlines how price skimming and penetration strategies have differing impacts relative to the costs, customers, competitors, and company.

Product Positioning

The price of a product is an important positioning variable. A premium price can serve to position the product as the quality leader in the category. In many categories, especially those in which intrinsic quality is difficult to judge, price is an important quality cue; customers may not only infer quality during shopping but may also actually perceive more expensive alternatives as actually

TABLE 29-1 Skimming Versus Penetration Strategy

	SKIMMING	PENETRATION
Costs	• Economies of scale and experience curve effects unimportant	• High economies of scale • High experience-curve effects
Customer	• Low price sensitivity • Price is indicator for quality • Early adopter of innovations	• Very price sensitive • Innovation aversive • Trial purchase should be stimulated
Competition	• High prices of competitors • Low risk of imitation • Low risk of substitution • Short product life cycle (risk of obsolescence before breakeven) • High market-entry barriers	• Low prices of competitors • High risk of imitation • High risk of substitution • Long product life cycle • Low market-entry barriers
Company	• Highly innovative product • Differentiation strategy • High quality and premium brands • Small capacities	• Large capacities • Strong distribution network • Financially strong (low contribution margins, high investments in capacity)

being of higher quality or greater prestige while consuming the product. A low price, on the other hand, can increase brand awareness and product visibility.

ELEMENTS OF PRICING DECISIONS

After the objectives have been formulated, at least four key elements of a pricing strategy should be analyzed (Cravens & Nigel, 2006; Hinterhuber, 2004): the firm's costs and cost structure; its customers; its competition; and legal and ethical implications of the decision and strategy.

Firm's Costs and Cost Structure
In the first step, fixed and variable costs are determined. Next, given a certain selling price, the contribution margin (selling price, less variable costs) and the breakeven-volume (fixed costs divided by contribution margin) can be calculated. A company can also set a profit goal. In this case, the target profit is added to the fixed costs to calculate the breakeven volume.

In a second step, cost–volume–profit (CVP) analysis can be used to answer questions like the following: If prices are raised by 10%, how much sales volume can the company afford to lose, if overall profits are at least to be maintained?; If prices are reduced by 10%, to what extent does the sales volume need to be increased if overall profits are at least to be maintained? CVP analysis builds on some basic, immutable accounting relationships between price, sales and production in units, and costs. For example, total sales revenue is equal to price (per-unit revenue) times the number of units sold. Total variable cost (the total of those costs that vary directly with units produced) is equal to variable costs per unit times the number of units sold. Overhead is equal to both marketing overhead (advertising costs, sales force expenses, etc.) and general administrative overhead. Figure 29-1 organizes these relationships graphically. These basic relationships allow for accurate

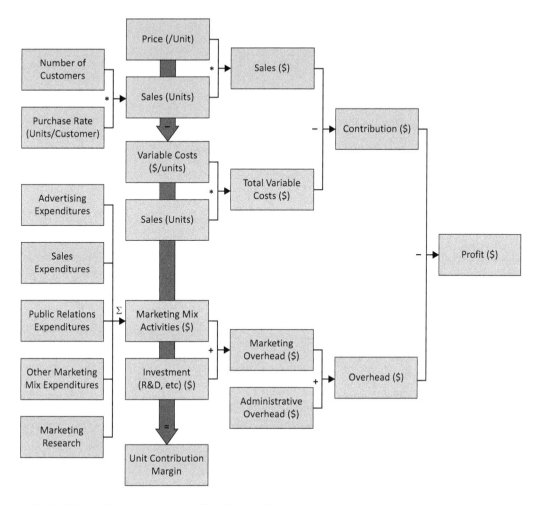

FIGURE 29-1   Cost–Volume–Profit Relationships

assessment objectives, such as breakeven and target profits, and the effects of proposed changes in price on changes in units sold (demand) and on profitability.

In the following example that illustrates a cost–volume–profit analysis, a mechanical engineering company has developed a new device to test the crashworthiness of car components using simulation software. The marketing strategy is to sell this device to auto manufacturers. The CVP parameters are shown in Table 29-2.

TABLE 29-2 Cost–Volume–Profit Parameters for a Sample Analysis

Fixed costs (e.g., R&D, production facilities, overhead)	$4,100,000	
Target profit	$2,000,000	
Variable costs (e.g., variable manufacturing and marketing costs)	$77,000	
Selling price	$120,000	
Contribution margin	$43,000	(35.8%)

Management would first want to ask "How many units of the software need to be sold to breakeven?" In effect, how many units need to be sold so that revenues equal total costs (variable costs per unit multiplied by units produced plus fixed costs):

$$(\bar{p}*Q)=(VC/u*Q)+FC$$

We can solve this equation for Q (the breakeven quantity in units) by subtracting (VC/u * Q) from both sides and then dividing by (P – VC/u), leading to the breakeven formula:

$$Q_{be}=\frac{FC}{\left(\bar{P}-\dfrac{VC}{u}\right)}$$

If management wanted to change that analysis slightly to include target profit—that is, to ask how many units sold would cover all costs plus contribute the target profit—the breakeven formula could be adjusted to include target profit with the fixed costs (π denotes "profit" or, in this case, target profit):

$$Q_{\pi}=\frac{FC+\text{Target Profit}}{\left(\bar{P}-\dfrac{VC}{u}\right)}$$

Plugging in the data from the example presented in Table 29-2, the mechanical engineering company would compute:

$$Q_{be}=\frac{\$4,100,000}{\$120,000-\$77,000}=96$$

To calculate the level of sales/production required to breakeven and make the desired target profit ($2,000,000) the formula is adjusted to:

$$Q_{\pi}=\frac{\$4,100,000+\$2,000,000}{\$120,000-\$77,000}=142$$

These illustrative calculations assume that variable costs per unit and overhead stay the same across levels of production. Variable costs are usually static across only some specific range of production; those costs will go down with increasing production or scale due to economies of scale and learning or experience curve effects. Likewise, the costs of many elements of overhead will, in reality, look like steps across levels of production; a certain investment in overhead is able to support certain levels of sales and production and then must be expanded in increments or steps.

Cost–volume–profit analysis is also invaluable in evaluating the effects of price changes. Any change in price is likely to have a direct effect on demand. A price increase will increase revenue and margin per unit and, as a rule, lower demand. A price decrease will lower revenues per unit but increase demand. The trade-offs in price changes and consequent changes in demand can also be evaluated directly using basic CVP logic (Guidry et al., 1998).

Customers

Many companies use markup pricing to determine the selling price; whatever the costs of the product are, they mark that amount up a set percentage to arrive at the list price. Others use market pricing, charging a traditional or *everybody's doing it* price. These are simple and low-risk methods to pricing, but because they do not consider the customers' perceived value or willingness to pay from the customers' perspective, they may miss opportunities. More sophisticated considerations are not based on the product's cost but begin, instead, with the customers' willingness to pay and the customers' perceived value and value function to determine prices.

Table 29-3 presents real data from the automobile industry, showing that costs associated with the car features do not correspond to customers' willingness to pay. For example, customers are willing to pay €340 for the metallic color option, which costs just €20 to add to the vehicle. However, they are only willing to pay €260 for a sunroof, even though a sunroof costs the manufacturer €350. If the manufacturer charged a fixed percentage markup on the color and the sunroof, they would be leaving a lot of money on the table when selling the metallic color and likely dissuading customers from purchasing the sunroof option altogether.

Margin is the difference between costs and price; in Table 29-3, margins are shown as percentages of selling price. For example, customers are willing to pay €340 for the metallic color option. If the pricing manager used willingness to pay instead of some predetermined markup, the price for the color would be €340. The metallic color costs just €20 to add to the vehicle. Thus, the margin is €320, a 94% margin (320 margin/340 price = 94% margin).

TABLE 29-3 Product's Cost Versus Willingness to Pay for Car Components

PRODUCT FEATURE	CUSTOMER'S WILLINGNESS TO PAY (€)	PRODUCT COSTS (€)	MARGIN
Metallic color	340	20	94%
Light-alloy wheels	220	140	36%
Air conditioning	750	550	27%
Sunroof	260	350	−35%
Navigation system	310	450	−45%

This same logic can be used in new product development to set target costs for alternatives; when developing a new product, target costs are often an important starting point. For example, if the marketer has determined that customers are willing to pay €310 for a navigation system but the current alternatives cost €450 to add to a vehicle, as shown in Table 29-3, the new product development project might focus on developing a bare-bones navigation system that satisfies customer needs but that also costs less than €310 to produce.

Competitors

The third element of a pricing decision is competition. Important questions include: What are the competitors' prices? What are competitors' costs and, therefore, their floor prices? What are their pricing strategies, tactics, and intentions? Although price-setting *collusion* is illegal, price *signaling* is an important reality in interpreting competitive strategies and intentions and in setting prices. The various rivals in a market signal their pricing policies and intentions to customers and to competitors via statements and actions. If a company advertises "We match all competitors' prices," for example, that may signal to customers that a retailer is the low-price alternative. However, that policy signals to competitors that dropping price will not lead to sustainable advantage. The expectation is that everyone will therefore maintain pricing norms.

Unfortunately, an insidious pattern in many competitive markets is the tendency to follow the competition into price wars. During a recent holiday season, for example, Walmart.com marked down the 10 best-selling books in its assortment to $10. Amazon.com responded to this promotion and matched Walmart's prices on the same 10 titles. Walmart then dropped the price to $8.99 on these books, which Amazon again matched. Target.com decided to match the $8.99 price point on these books as well. Walmart then dropped its price to $8.98 (a penny below Target's price). Of course, none of these competitors made any money on sales at such a low price point. Nevertheless, Walmart succeeded in signaling to customers and competitors that it was a serious player in the online book sector. Amazon succeeded in signaling that it would respond to any competitive price threat. Target stayed in the game. Who lost this price war? In the long run, small book retailers lost to the large online players, and consumers may have lost too. The online price competitors signaled to each other and the world that they would not be beaten on price—and all entrants are now, it seems likely, preparing to compete on something else (Stone & Rosenbloom, 2009; Surowiecki, 2009).

Legal and Ethical Considerations

Legal constraints prohibit overt price collusion between competitors, predatory pricing, deceptive pricing, price fixing in channels of distribution, and price discrimination across customers or channels. These myriad laws and regulations are complex and dynamic. For example, in the United States *any* price fixing between vertical channel members, most commonly a manufacturer setting a minimum price for its distributors or retailers, was illegal *per se* for almost a century. Recently, however, the United States Supreme Court changed its interpretation of those laws, allowing manufacturers to implement pricing policies on its resellers in some cases. ("LawSchool," 2007). In Europe, on the other hand, many countries still prohibit "sales" (temporary price reductions on items or on entire assortments) and presale price announcements, a regulation that dampens price competition among retailers ("Economist," 2008).

Ethical standards should shape *all* managerial and strategic decision-making, as they should all personal decision-making, and that includes pricing decisions. One of the most notorious cases of unethical and ill-advised strategic decision-making relates to the earlier example of customers' willingness to pay and the cost of automobile options. In the early 1970s, Ford Motor Company recognized there might be safety issues with the subcompact Pinto's gas tank rupturing in relatively low-speed collisions (Downie, 1977; Lee, 1998). Ford executives made the cost–benefit calculation that the cost of adding safety features, which was at most $11 per car and likely a lot less, outweighed the benefits of saving the victims' lives and well-being, which were callously appraised at a little more than $200,000 per life and $67,000 per burn victim. Ford argued that car buyers were not interested in paying more for safety features; CEO Lee Iacocca was quoted as saying "Safety doesn't sell" (Downie, 1977; Lee, 1998).

In hindsight, it is clearly appropriate to criticize Ford and Iacocca—the company and its executives failed to apply the same standards to their professional decision-making that they would, presumably, have applied instinctively to their personal behaviors. However, in the context of the commercial, legal, and regulatory environments of the time, their decisions seemed prudent. Nevertheless, all marketing strategy decisions, as well as professional behavior, should be ruled by ethical standards over cost–benefit analyses, worries about retooling costs, prevailing regulatory standards, or perceptions of customers' willingness to pay. Ford's analyses and rationale were documented in a memorandum that laid out the cost–benefit analysis, and when it was revealed in a prominent expose by Mark Downie in *Mother Jones*, it triggered an embarrassing and expensive public furor, a costly recall, and extended legal difficulties (Downie, 1977; Lee, 1998). The Pinto brand was destroyed; it was soon withdrawn from the market by Ford. The Ford brand itself was damaged. Even without those fiscal and brand losses, Ford, the Pinto, and the decisions made with regard to safety of the gas tank remain emblematic of shortsighted overemphasis on analysis and underappreciation of the role of managerial and personal ethics in price and strategy setting.

DEFINING THE PRICING STRATEGY

The company's pricing strategy has to be aligned with the core strategy of the business unit. A differentiation strategy, for example, implicates a premium price strategy; a cost leadership strategy usually means low prices. Hence, the core strategy defines the pricing objectives, and the pricing objectives together with customer, cost, competitor, and legal and ethical aspects set the framework for the pricing strategy. Several important concepts can shape the pricing strategy, including skimming and penetration pricing (discussed earlier in this Note) as well as the value map (discussed in Note 17). Additional strategies, which will be discussed in the following section, include razor blade pricing, price promotions versus brand building, and prestige pricing.

"Razor Blade" Pricing

Another strategic pricing idea that can be powerful in certain industries and for certain products is *razor blade* or *razor-and-blade* pricing. Economists consider this pricing strategy to be a *subsidy* since in effect the discount or freebie is subsidized by the margins on required supplies. Traditionally, dating back to King Gillette, the inventor of the safety razor, manufacturers have discounted or given away the razors (the handles) with the expectation that those handles would lead to future, plentiful, and profitable sales of the full-margin blades (razor handles are usually cheap, relatively simple to manufacture, and durable, while blades are more expensive, precision manufactured from higher-value materials, and need to be replaced frequently) (McKibben, 1998). Today, mobile phones, water purification systems, and single-serve "pod" coffee brewing machines are all discounted below costs (and are sometimes free) in strategies designed to lock in a stream of subscription revenues from monthly calling plans for those mobile phones, filters for water purification systems, and coffee pods for the brewing machines.

Some contemporary strategies are variations of that basic razor blade pricing model. For example, Zoom gives away its basic videoconferencing software and service, anticipating that sufficient customers will upgrade to its premium, for-fee versions to create overall profitability, but there is no requirement that any customer upgrade to take full value from its basic product. Ryanair, the European discount airline, charges below-cost fares—many flights are essentially *free* except for required taxes—but also charges for almost every additional service from baggage check-in to snacks and bombards passengers with offers and advertisements throughout their travel experience. Nevertheless, the traveler who does not require checked baggage service, who is not hungry, and who ignores the sales pitches and promotions can take advantage of the travel service itself at the low fare.

Price Promotions Versus Brand Building

An important tension that must be considered relates to the short-term benefits of price-based promotions—things like price-off specials at the point of purchase, coupons, and volume deals (buy-one-get-one-free deals or BOGOs, extra-volume packs, and the like)—and weighing those benefits against their costs and their long-term effects and against alternative investments in promotions that may have more muted but more enduring positive effects. Price-based promotions do have an immediate and often dramatic effect on customer behaviors—*stuff moves off the shelf on discount*—but those are short-term effects. Unfortunately, those short-term effects are made more attractive because of the incentive and evaluation systems within which many product managers work, which are often tied to quarterly or annual sales rather than to longer-term brand building.

Nevertheless, price-based promotions deteriorate more quickly than investments in brand-building tools like advertising, public relations, experiential promotions, and even sampling. Price-based promotions have certain obvious short-term costs—lost revenue and margins—and the sales lift of price-based promotions are short lived compared to other investments. Price-based promotions can even have negative effects on sales in the long term. These potentially harmful long-term effects of price-based promotions on sales and the brand include:

- *Price–quality relationship*—Customers often use price as a signal of quality, so discounting the product lowers their perceptions of the product's value and, therefore, its quality.
- *Resentment*—Customers come to expect the reduced price and may resent the price increase to what the manufacturer believes is the *regular* price.
- *Accelerating/waiting*—Customers learn to buy ahead when a product is on discount and to wait when it is not. That is, they shift purchases across time in order to take advantage of price-based promotions.

As shown in Figure 29-2, although brand-building investments such as advertising do decay over time, those effects are long term and gradual and do not decay at the same rate or to the same degree.

Prestige Pricing

Another pricing strategy, appropriate for certain brands in certain product categories and for certain customers, prestige pricing, uses price as an indicator of quality, performance, and status. Quality and performance refer to the actual, physical quality of the product. Status refers to the use of products to seek or communicate social standing or *success*. Inferences about both quality/performance and status are drawn from a variety of product-related cues ranging from spokespeople, advertising content, and other consumers of the product to its places of distribution, packaging, and price.

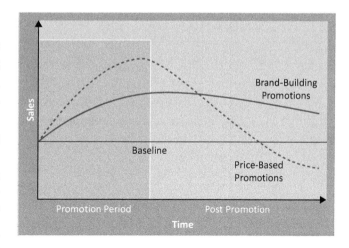

FIGURE 29-2 Short-Term and Long-Term Effects of Price Promotions

Consumers are frequently unable to judge the actual quality of various products due to a lack of expertise or the inability to inspect or try a product in advance of purchase. Wine is a good example; most consumers neither understand France's traditional *Appellation d'origine contrôlée* (AOC) wine certification and quality system, nor are familiar with the innumerable varieties, vintages, and brands produced across the many wine-making regions of the world. By necessity, many consumers rely on a small set of familiar brands, on point-of-purchase merchandising and in-store information, and on price. In this case, rather than reviewing price with simple minimization criteria, wine shoppers use price as an indicator of quality. This is true across a variety of other product categories as well.

An illustrative case of prestige pricing combined with packaging and selective distribution to create an exclusive status image is grappa. Grappa is a brandy made from grape pomace—the dregs of wine making, including grape skins, seeds, and stems—drunk by Italian peasants since the 12th century. In the late 1980s, producers softened grappa a little to make it more palatable to upscale tastes, packaged it in elegant designer bottles (including some in handblown Murano glass), and put outlandish prices on it (often more than $150 per bottle in the United States). One grappa, Marolo, was packaged in a Baccarat crystal decanter decorated with 18-karat gold and sold for as much as $2,800 a bottle (Buchalter & Levine, 1991). Grappa quickly became a fashionable and trendy drink in New York and Hollywood high society. As one restaurateur observed, grappa was transformed from a "hard liquor for strong, poor, earthbound people to an elegant, fruity and pricey spirit of considerable appeal to the affluent, urbane international consumer" (Bassano, 2005, para. 1). Prestige pricing is about understanding when and how consumers use price as a cue for quality, scarcity, and prestige, and then using price along with the other elements of the marketing mix to achieve that premium positioning.

SETTING AND ADJUSTING THE PRICE

The final price must be consistent with the core strategy and with the pricing objectives. Competitive reactions, changes in consumer and buyer behavior, variations in demand and in costs, and other changes, however, require that a company adapt prices to changing circumstances. There are a number of tactics that can be used to respond to such challenges, such as the following (Kotler & Armstrong, 2005):

- *price discounts and allowances* (e.g., quantity discounts, seasonal discounts)
- *promotional pricing* (e.g., cash rebates, low-interest financing, longer payment terms)
- *price differentiation* (e.g., customer segment, channel, location, or time differentiation)
- *price bundling* and complementary pricing (e.g., low price for inkjet printers, high price for ink cartridges)
- *yield management* (e.g., setting prices depending on the booking situation of an airline, i.e., low prices for travelers who buy the ticket well in advance and high prices for those who book later)

The short-term versus long-term implications of discounts and price-based promotions were discussed above; in general, discounting is very persuasive with regard to motivating purchase behavior, but it can damage the long-term health of the brand and the firm. When price adjustments are applied, it is of utmost importance that the effects on demand and profits are estimated. Depending on the contribution margin, it may well be that a 10% discount requires a 50% increase of sales volume if overall profits are to be maintained (see CVP analysis, above).

SUMMARY

Pricing is too often an afterthought to strategic planning. Managers routinely rely on their cost structure or market norms to set prices, but pricing can be a powerful element of a coherent strategy. Prices can accelerate cash flow or hasten the benefits of scale. Price can attract customers, and price can engage customers in long-term and profitable relationships. Price can signal quality, and price-based promotions can signal mediocrity and teach customers to shop by price rather than for benefits. As this Note has reviewed, effective pricing strategies consider costs, customers, competitors, and positioning objectives to maximize profits within long-term relationships.

REFERENCES

Bassano, A. (2005). *Grappa: Italian 'White Lightning' goes upscale*. Beverage Network. http://www.bevnetwork.com/pdf/mar05_grappa.pdf

Buchalter, G., & Levine, J. (1991). Italian white lightning. *Forbes*, 147(4), 94–95.

Cravens, D., & Nigel, P. (2006). *Strategic marketing* (8 (ed.). McGraw Hill.

Dolan, R., & Simon, H. (1996). *Power pricing*. Simon & Schuster.

Downie, M. (1977). Pinto madness. *Mother Jones* 2, 18–22.

"Economist." (2008). Shop-worn arguments. *The Economist, 386*(8561).

Guidry, F., Horrigan, J., & Craycraft, C. (1998). CVP analysis—A new look. *Journal of Managerial Issues, 10*(1), 74–85.

Hinterhuber, A. (2004). Towards value-based pricing—An integrative framework for decision making. *Industrial Marketing Management, 33*, 765–778.

Kotler, P., & Armstrong, G. (2005). *Principles of marketing.* Prentice Hall.

Kotler, P., & Keller, K. (2009). *Marketing management* (13th ed.). Pearson Education.

"LawSchool." (2007). Leegin Creative Leather Prods. v. PSKS, Inc. - 551 U.S. 877, 127 S. Ct. 2705. *Law School Case Brief.* https://www.lexisnexis.com/community/casebrief/p/casebrief-leegin-creative-leather-prods-v-psks-inc

Lee, M. T. (1998). The Ford Pinto case and the development of auto safety regulations, 1893–1978. *Business and Economic History*, 390–401.

McKibben, G. (1998). *Cutting edge: Gillette's journey to global leadership.* Harvard Business Press.

Stone, B., & Rosenbloom, S. (2009). Price war brews between Amazon and Wal-Mart. *The New York Times.*

Surowiecki, J. (2009). Priced to go. *The New Yorker, 85*(36).

PLACE—DISTRIBUTION

Channels of distribution involve how a product is delivered from the producer to the customer and all the functions that add value within that process. Traditionally, the marketing management literature has emphasized the distribution of goods (physically tangible products) to end consumers via wholesalers, distributors, agents, brokers, and retailers. Advances in technology and logistics, as evidenced by Amazon, along with the increased importance of services (intangible products) in modern economies have reshaped and, in particular, shortened many channels. Multiple distribution channels, in which the same product is made available through different and sometimes competing distribution paths, have proliferated, as have hybrid channels in which different paths deliver different parts of the overall bundle of value-adding functions.

The Internet has revolutionized distribution systems by not only lowering costs, allowing for more effective direct marketing and addressing new customers segments, but also increasing market transparency and reducing customer's switching costs. In the airline industry, for instance, the Internet has saved airlines roughly $10 to $15 per booking by allowing tickets to be easily purchased directly from the airline, rather than through intermediaries such as travel agents or travel sites. The increased price transparency, however, also means that airlines often have to sell a ticket on the Internet an estimated $50 to $100 lower than tickets purchased through other channels (Myers et al., 2004).

Distribution issues are often considered mundane, and the literature commonly treats *place* as a one-way, producer-toward-the-consumer flow, usually adopting the producer's downstream perspective. These viewpoints overlook important aspects of distribution and opportunities in distribution that are part of contemporary marketing strategy. Precipitating or at least anticipating changes in distribution systems has created substantial competitive advantages for many firms. For example, being the first mover into valuable distribution space can fashion a barrier to entry for later movers. Coca-Cola's early move into vending-machine distribution in Japan created a long-lived advantage—Coke quickly established more than a million vending machines in Japan and captured a 50% market share (Yoffie, 2002).

Many firms' core business models and strategies center on their own roles in distribution and the manner in which they add value within larger channel systems. Dell Computers' Dell Direct model is a noteworthy example of a strategy based on the firm's role within a larger supply chain. As the personal computer (PC) market evolved, Michael Dell recognized that consumers no longer required *hand-holding*; as the PC product life cycle evolved, customers were willing and able to buy direct but they wanted customized machines. In addition to selling customized products directly to consumers, the Dell Direct model also involves partnering closely with vendors to accelerate inventory. Michael Dell described that model:

> The supplier effectively becomes our partner. They assign their engineers to our design team, and we start to treat them as if they were part of the company. For example,

when we launch a new product, their engineers are stationed right in our plants ... So it's not, "Well, every two weeks deliver 5,000 to this warehouse, and we'll put them on the shelf, and then we'll take them off the shelf." It's, "Tomorrow morning we need 8,562 and deliver them to door number seven by 7 AM" (Magretta, 1998, p. 75).

The Dell Direct model was so efficient that Dell made money on the "float"; customers' payments are received almost immediately (via credit card payments and transfers) while vendors are paid on terms. To customers, Dell looked like the customized/direct alternative in the PC market—and from the customers' perspective that's what they are—but the company's overall strategy was as an efficient value-adding player within the channel from manufacturer to customer.

In summary, many strategists have found advantage by challenging assumptions about and anticipating changes in the manner via which products are distributed. Marketers continue to face challenges and find opportunities in getting the product to the customer. A foundation to understanding how channels work and identifying opportunities and threats in distribution is an understanding of the basic functions of value-adding activities that channels perform. This Note reviews those basic value-adding functions and how technology and other dynamics are changing the way those functions are performed, and then it outlines strategic considerations and alternatives in channels of distribution.

CHANNEL FUNCTIONS

Certain things have to happen in order to get a product from the manufacturer to the customer, regardless of the length of the channel, the number of entities in the channel, the type of product, or the type of customer. Somewhere in the channel these things have to occur for an efficient and effective delivery of the product to occur. For example, the product must be physically moved to the customer; it must be transported to the location where the customer needs it, when the customer needs it. The customer must pay for the product, either in advance, on delivery, or on terms. Also, the assortment of complementary products and services required to use and derive value from the product must be made available. All of these elements and more are the essential *channel functions*; valuable benefits that a channel of distribution as a whole provides to the customer and the marketer. Some of these functions are not relevant to some products or for some customers, and a single channel member does not necessarily even often provide all of these functions—but these things need to be done somewhere in most channels.

Different channel members may provide different channel functions, depending on the product category and even the brand within a product category. For example, Dell customizes and ships PCs directly to customers using delivery services such as UPS to physically move its computers from the manufacturer to the customer. Dell's logistics partners even assort various components of the order from vendors for Dell, such as workstations and screens. Dell also uses direct communications, including the Internet and toll-free telephone services, to provide customer support. Hewlett Packard (HP) competes directly with Dell in the PC market, but unlike Dell, HP distributes its computers through retail stores, delivering computers in bulk to distribution centers from which they are shipped to individual stores and using retail sales personnel and the retailers' customer-service staff for selling and support. Both of these strategies are viable and have been successful, but they approach distribution and service in different ways that create very different value propositions for the PC customer.

Understanding the strategic issues involved in channels of distribution begins with an understanding of the functions that channels provide or can provide. There have been many comprehensive lists and frameworks of channel functions proposed in the marketing literature that emphasize the breadth and diversity of value-added activities between the manufacturer or marketer and the customer. Table 30-1 shows an inclusive list of channel functions performed by intermediaries across three overarching categories: transactional functions, logistical functions, and facilitating functions. Some of these functions overlap—for example, financing is often a part of selling and involves risk-taking—but this extensive inventory provides a thorough conceptual perspective on the sorts of value-adding activities the channels provide.

TABLE 30-1 Distribution Functions Performed by Intermediaries (adapted from: from Rangan, 1994, Armstrong and Kotler, Roger et al., 2005.)

Transactional Functions
- *Buying*—Purchasing products for resale and making payments to manufacturer/vendor
- *Selling*—Connecting customers to buyers, promoting products, and managing accounting and receivables
- *Risk-Taking*—Assuming ownership risks of inventory to include obsolescence, spoilage, shrinkage, etc. as well as other risks associated with other functions below (e.g., credit risks associated with financing)

Logistical Functions
- *Sorting* or "breaking bulk"—making product available in desired quantities or volume
- *Assorting*—Bringing together diverse products (creating assortments) to meet simultaneous or related needs
- *Storing*—Holding products until needed (time convenience)
- *Transporting*—Physically moving products to the customer or place of need

Facilitating Functions
- *Financing*—Providing and managing credit and assuming credit risk
- *Grading*—Inspecting products and assigning them quality grades
- *Assuring*—Honoring warranties, guarantees, promised repairs and replacements, etc.
- *Maintaining and Repairing*—Regular or scheduled maintenance and exceptional repair
- *Installing and Tailoring*—Installation, customization, fitting, etc.
- *Promoting*—Marketing communications, including advertising, personal selling, and promotions and provision of required customer information to persuade customers to buy and rebuy
- *Negotiating*—Creating dialogue and bargaining to identify interests and reach agreement
- *Matching*—Fitting diverse customers with diverse product alternatives in conditions of scarcity
- *Training*—Technical training for customers and staff, help-desk support, etc.
- *Marketing Research*—Understanding the customers, competition, and market and communicating that information to manufacturers, suppliers, and other channel partners

Transactional Functions

Taking possession and then selling goods involves managing numerous specific transactions that impact capital and cash flow. Having layers of distributors is valuable for the manufacturer because it reduces the number of transactions (and therefore the bookkeeping and overhead) and it accelerates cash flow; the manufacturer usually receives payment before the ultimate customer buys the product. Taking possession of goods also involves inherent possession-related risks including spoilage, obsolesce/changes in tastes, and shrinkage (theft).

Logistical Functions

A fundamental function of channels is the physical distribution of the product. Logistical functions (i.e., logistics) encompass the following:

- getting the product to the place the customer experiences or meets the need,
- providing service at the time the customer experiences the need,
- providing the right size or quantity of the product that meets the customer's needs, and
- providing other products and accessories required to meet the need or set of needs.

Facilitating Functions

Although transactional and logistical functions may be the traditional core functions of distributors—the *nuts and bolts* of channels—facilitating functions such as financing, promoting, and servicing and supporting the installed base can be the most valuable and the most indispensable functions that channel members perform. Many distributors and retailers *own the relationship* with the customer via these value-added activities.

DISTRIBUTION DYNAMICS

Although sometimes disparaged as redundant or noncontributing profiteers, channel intermediaries (i.e., middlemen) invariably provide valuable functions or they are circumvented or replaced by market dynamics. If manufacturers find that they can provide a function or bundle of functions on their own and no longer require a distributor or agent, they integrate forward. If a retailer finds that it can deal directly with manufacturers and therefore does not need distributors, it deals directly with manufacturers. Farmers, for example, have organized into cooperatives to integrate forward into distribution, and they have enjoyed increased margins while also assuming the increased headaches of assorting, selling and promoting, facilitating logistics, dealing with spoilage, and providing customer service.

Changes in the competitive environment, especially in technology, have caused channel structures to change, and some channel members have become obsolete or redundant. Modern computational and database power, the proliferation of consumer credit cards and electronic banking, the wide availability of rapid-delivery services such as UPS and FedEx, along with the emergence of the Internet as a widely available two-way tool for marketing and communications have allowed many organizations to sell directly to their customers and to manage numerous accounts themselves.

At the same time, the emergence of huge retailers such as Aldi and Walmart has consolidated channel *power* at the retail level and increased the importance of key account management—that is, the emphasis on a few large retail accounts that comprise the vast majority of sales. This has decreased the ability of small retailers to compete and superseded the "jobbers," small distributors who called on individual retail accounts and assisted in the management of inventory and merchandising. While these changes threaten small players, such shifts also create opportunities, especially for firms that consolidate across a level of the channel (horizontal integration, i.e., taking over or merging with another firm in the same industry) or integrate backwards and/or forwards (vertical integration, i.e., owning its upstream suppliers or its downstream buyers).

Channel structures continue to evolve due to technological and competitive forces. Channel structures are also influenced by factors like the emergence of large, efficient third-party logistics suppliers, the maturation of many consumer products (e.g., consumer electronics and personal computers) toward life cycle stages at which consumers are comfortable with lower and less hands-on service and with purchasing items without personal inspection. These changes have led certain channel entities to lose share and profitability—their basic business models have been challenged—but others have grown and profited. Thus, the creative marketing strategist may find opportunities as well as hazards in the changing dynamics of marketing channels. Three related forces underlie channel dynamics and distribution outcomes for firms: channel power, channel control, and channel conflict. Each of these will be explored below.

Channel Power

Channel power is "the ability of a particular channel member to control or influence the decision-making and behavior of another channel member, or one channel member's potential for influence with another channel member" (American Marketing Association, Channel Power, 2021). There are several types of, or sources of, channel power:

- reward, that is, offering positive outcomes such as payment, margins, or traffic,
- coercive, that is, punishments such as withdrawal of products or of support,
- expert, that is, the ability to provide scarce and valuable expertise,
- legitimate, that is, ownership, legal/contractual, etc., and
- referent, that is, offering benefits via affiliation such as prestige.

In consumer goods, large manufacturers once had channel power over their retail partners (the "trade")—every grocer needed to have Coca-Cola in its assortment to meet their consumers' needs, so Coke had power over those retailers and could set the terms of trade. Consolidation in the grocery trade and the emergence of Walmart, Target, and others as retailing behemoths has shifted that power toward those fewer retail "key accounts." Understanding where power resides in a channel *and why* is important to managing distribution and identifying opportunities for shifts in channel structure.

Channel Control

Channel control, "the actual impact that a channel member achieves on an associated channel member's beliefs, attitudes, and behavior" (American Marketing Association, Channel Control, 2021) varies as an outcome of channel power and as a function of prices and margins for the product and the length of the channels. Many firms that require close control forge direct or exclusive channels, but others distribute through arms-length channels while providing control through intensive, company-owned services. Frito-Lay, for example, sells through groceries, discounters, and convenience stores but controls product quality, merchandising, and inventories via its intensive network of 10,000 route salespeople who call directly on stores on a daily basis.

Channel Conflict

Channel conflict, "disagreement among marketing channel members on goals and roles—who should do what and for what rewards" (Armstrong & Kotler, 2009, p. 297), can occur between levels of the channel (e.g., between manufacturer and distributor), between members at the same level in a channel (amongst distributors), or between different channels. Conflict can arise from different objectives. For example, in fast-food franchise systems conflict arises because of conflicting goals: the franchisor (the brand) wants to maintain and grow market share and absolute sales levels—franchisor revenues are tied to franchisee's gross sales and royalty rates—but franchisees need to maintain margins rather than top-line revenues. Conflict can also arise from perceived competition. When Nike opened its Niketown retail outlets, motivated as much by its interest in building the brand through consumer experience, retailers carrying Nike branded products perceived Niketown as competition (Collinger, 1998). Channel conflict can be expensive in terms of lost support and goodwill as well as in lost sales and reduced channel coverage.

STRATEGIC CHANNEL CONSIDERATIONS

There are a variety of issues to be considered in establishing and managing channels of distribution, including especially customer needs as well as the desired brand position, and costs and margin structures. An explanation of each follows:

Customer Needs and Behaviors

One essential driver of the channels required by a firm, a product, or a brand is the *target customer needs*, especially (a) needs for information, guidance, customization, and installation at the time of the purchase, (b) needs for the provision of or availability of service and support after the purchase, and (c) needs for convenience and extensive availability. Needs for selling and service support correspond with more limited, exclusive distribution. Needs for convenience and availability drive broader, intensive distribution.

Brand Positioning

Just as people are known by the company they keep, brands are known by the company *they* keep, and choosing channel partners connects the brand with channel partners (distributors and retailers) and with the other brands in the channel partners' assortments. Premium hair care products, for example, often choose to distribute only through salons to affiliate with the salons' perceived expertise, exclusivity, and style. Those same brands might decline to distribute through discounters to avoid being perceived as ordinary or cheap.

Choosing channel partners also links the brand, the firm, and the firm's business model to the channel partner and its business model. Firms selling through Walmart, for instance, often claim that Walmart forces a continued emphasis on cost reduction at the expense of quality.

Costs and Margin Structures

Consideration of the costs of distribution—and deliberation of possible savings in distribution—should begin with consideration of *the functions that are performed in the channel*, where they are performed, how well they are performed, and how well they meet customer needs. The marketing organization *pays* for distribution in two ways: directly in the actual expenses associated with managing and maintaining distribution, and indirectly in the form of margins retained by the entities in the channel (such as wholesalers, distributors, and retailers) as they resell and mark up the marketing organization's products. Direct channel management costs include selling expenses, logistics expenses, and promotions to channel members' sales forces and service personnel. Prominent costs incurred by channel members in delivering value-adding functions include transportation and handling, order processing and account management, accounts receivable management, and inventory management and carrying costs. These considerations influence choices across distribution alternatives, as will be discussed next.

STRATEGIC CHANNEL ALTERNATIVES

Decisions about structuring channels may be constrained for a number of reasons, such as being late to market (preferred channels are "taken") or not having available resources. These decisions are also shaped by the considerations outlined above: customer needs and behaviors, desired brand positioning, and cost structures, as well as channel power, control, and conflict. Aside from all those elements, structuring channels within any given marketing strategy entails consideration of at least two parameters: distribution intensity and channel structure and ownership.

Distribution Intensity

Channel coverage can vary from exclusive distribution systems in which only selected stores carry a product, such as that for Rolex watches, to intensive distribution that can approach being iniquitous (seeming to be available everywhere), such as Coca-Cola's objective of having every consumer be "within arm's reach of desire" (i.e., within an arm's reach of a Coca-Cola product) (Pendergrast, 2000, p. 9). Generally, four factors drive greater exclusivity in distribution: (a) the amount of effort buyers will expend in shopping for a product, (b) the required service and support from channel members required by customers, (c) the degree of prestige positioning sought, and (d) the desire to maintain price points and margins.

Channel Structure/Ownership

A marketer can forge several sorts of relationships and bases for cooperation with channel partners, ranging from fully independent (arm's length) to full ownership. In traditional arm's length channels, the various channel members act independently, motivated by self-interest (profits, margins, etc.), and do not coordinate activities other than as mutual interests and transactions dictate. These channels require investment in selling and account management, but they do not require large capital investments and are generally cheaper to establish. At the other extreme are company-owned channels. Control is highest in company-owned channels; in fact, control is *absolute* within parameters of organizational control. Systems owned by a company, such as Starbucks' cafés, enjoy greater control than franchised competitors, such as McDonald's and Dunkin' Donuts, and far greater control and market presence than firms selling through independent channels. On the other hand, operating company-owned channels requires much greater capital investments and has generally higher costs and constrained flexibility.

Multiple Channels

An alternative to designing a single distribution system that is becoming more common, given changes in competition and technology, is for firms to distribute through more than one channel at the same time. In a multiple channel arrangement, customers may choose their channel, but, at least in theory, they source all of the value-adding channel functions from that specific channel (which is the distinction between *multiple* and *hybrid* channels, discussed below). In practice, many consumers use higher-service channel members for shopping (to benefit from sales advisory service) and then resort to low-service discount channels for purchase, leading to predictable channel conflict and inescapable channel modifications.

Channel conflict is a significant problem with multiple channel distribution. Partners who add value see discount and direct channels as unfair competition. To deal with this conflict, some brands have created different products for different channels. Levi's, for example, has created lower-quality jeans for sale through discounters like Walmart, while continuing to offer higher-quality jeans through department and clothing stores. Of course, that tactic introduces a real threat of brand dilution and consumer confusion.

Hybrid Channels

Multiple-channel systems (as described above) are sometimes referred to as "Hybrid," but there are also emerging channel structures in which different, complementary functions are delivered to the same customers through different, parallel channels. This differs conceptually and strategically from delivering all functions through alternative channels to different customers. We use *hybrid* to refer to the latter, that is to the structuring of distribution so that the same customers receive different channel functions—which add up to the complete bundle of customer requirements—via different channels.

For example, high-end consumer electronics firms such as Bose (consumer audio equipment), Lexmark (printers), and Linksys (computer peripherals) distribute through the U.S. Army and Air Force Exchange Service (AAFES, the post exchange or "PX" stores), but those stores do not provide adequate selling or service support at the point of purchase. Customers require information and support to understand the product benefits, to make informed choices across alternatives, and to use the products once purchased. These brands contract with Military Sales and Service (MSS) to provide point-of-sale support. Therefore, the clerks working with the customers on the floor are not AAFES employees; they are MSS staff working on behalf of Bose, Lexmark, Linksys or other contracted brands (Anderson et al., 1997; Rangan, 1994; Rangan & Kastiri, 1995).

STRATEGIC DISTRIBUTION DECISIONS

Making strategic channel decisions—including designing new channels and reorienting existing channels—begins with a thorough analysis of customer needs with regard to the functions that channels provide. What do customers need and want from the product's distribution system? Thus, the first step in this process is to describe the firm's target segments with regard to their channel-function needs. Because needs are an essential descriptor in any segmentation classification, it is likely that differences related to channel-function needs influenced the segmentation scheme adopted in the firm's strategy development. However, in designing channels, those segments' specific needs related to channel function should be analyzed or reanalyzed in detail, and each segment's priorities, or rank-ordered needs, should be spelled out.

TABLE 30-2 Hypothetical Needs and Importance for Two Segments

REPAIR TRADE (MOM & POP PLUMBERS)	
Availability	1
Assortment (Breadth of inventory)	2
Location	3
Customer Service	4
Price	5
DO-IT-YOURSELF (DIY) CUSTOMERS	
Price	1
Customer Service	2
Assortment (Complementary products)	3
Location	4
Availability	5

A "big-box" home improvement retailer might, for example, have identified two key plumbing supply segments: small plumbing repair contractors ("Mom & Pop Plumbers") and Do-It-Yourself (DIY) customers. These segments' needs are different (see Table 30-2). Small plumbing repair contractors need the *exact* part for a problem *quickly*—their time is money to them and to their customers. Many of their customers are in emergency situations requiring immediate remedy; they cannot wait for a part to come in. In addition, when a plumber is charging $100 an hour (or more) and passing parts costs through to the customer (who has a leaking toilet or water all over the kitchen floor), the price of a part or fixture is not a prominent consideration.

On the other hand, DIY customers are less likely to be repairing urgent plumbing problems, but they are, almost by definition, price conscious; they are doing this job themselves and often to save the money. The DIY segment also needs and expects customer service and informative sales assistance. DIY customers are not "on the clock" and, although convenience matters, plumbing supplies are shopping goods to them; location and immediate availability are less important. These priorities are shown in Table 30-2 as rank orderings for both segments.

The next step in designing or modifying distribution systems is to benchmark both the firm's and its competitors' capabilities at delivering those salient customer needs. The big-box retailer might well determine that it delivers superior customer service—especially vis-à-vis plumbing supply houses that are not geared toward consumer retail merchandising, and the big box likely offers lower prices. Nevertheless, the big-box retailer's assortment and availability—the breadth of parts available and on-site—are inferior to those specialized plumbing supply houses and its locations are only slightly more convenient than those of the plumbing supply houses. Figure 30-3

REPAIR TRADE (MOM & POP PLUMBERS)		
Availibility	1	High← 7 – 6̄ – 5 – 4 – ③ – 2 – 1 →Low
Assortment (Breadth of inventory)	2	High← 7 – 6̄ – 5 – 4 – ③ – 2 – 1 →Low
Location	3	High← 7 – 6 – 5̄ – 4 – ③ – 2 – 1 →Low
Customer Service	4	High← 7 – 6 – ⑤ – 4 – 3̄ – 2 – 1 →Low
Price	5	High← 7 – ⑥ – 5 – 4̄ – 3 – 2 – 1 →Low
DO-IT-YOURSELF (DIY) CUSTOMERS		
Price	1	High← 7 – ⑥ – 5 – 4̄ – 3 – 2 – 1 →Low
Customer Service	2	High← 7 – 6 – ⑤ – 4 – 3̄ – 2 – 1 →Low
Assortment (Complementary products)	3	High← 7 – 6̄ – 5 – 4 – ③ – 2 – 1 →Low
Location	4	High← 7 – 6 – 5̄ – 4 – ③ – 2 – 1 →Low
Availability	5	High← 7 – 6̄ – 5 – 4 – ③ – 2 – 1 →Low

○ = "Big Box" Discount Home Improvement Retailer
□ = Plumbing Supply Houses

FIGURE 30-3 Firm and Competitor Capabilities on Functions by Segment and Priorities

shows a format for making these comparisons graphically. The big-box retailer's capabilities are shown in circles, plumbing supply houses' capabilities in squares.

The next step is to generate alternatives. Looking at the Mom & Pop requirements, for example, it is clear that inventory and convenience are the driving forces. Possible solutions could center on improving the availability of parts in a product category that can involve numerous low-priced SKUs (stock keeping units i.e., distinct items in the inventory). Investments in increased inventory, inventory management/warehousing technology, and logistics, as well as innovations such as single parts that can be adapted to fit many repair needs, might all be viable alternatives to consider. These alternatives may well include both multiple-and hybrid-channel configurations. This step should begin with the segment-by-segment analysis of customer needs vis-à-vis channel functions and generate as wide-ranging and inclusive a set of alternatives as possible.

Next, those various and numerous alternatives should be analyzed against their expected costs and benefits. What do the various options cost in financial terms, in terms of managerial resources and attention, and in terms of channel conflict and motivation? For example, investments in broader availability (stocking more parts in each store) are mostly about space and inventory carrying costs—things that can be readily quantified. Offering express/dedicated checkout and special contractor pricing may, on the other hand, have both monetary and consumer-goodwill costs; customers who are *not* offered discounts or special services may resent that lack of consideration. Channel conflict may be a greater threat in channels where members previously enjoyed exclusive rights to sell a product in certain markets; they will resent new programs that create multiple-channels targeting customers they had invested in and believed were theirs.

Of course, cost–benefit analyses also require careful quantification of the benefits of each alternative. Benefits may include greater customer satisfaction and loyalty, enhanced reputation and value, and increased sales, but all those benefits should, in the final analysis, be quantified as increased margins and profits. Finally, decisions can be made based on those cost–benefit analyses. That is, this process should facilitate informed and systematic choices across feasible distribution alternatives and should lead to systems that optimally meet customers' real needs for the values created by channel functions.

SUMMARY

Channels of distribution are rapidly changing due to competitive and customer considerations, as well as changes in technology. Understanding those changes and the strategic opportunities they present begins with an understanding of the value-adding functions performed by channels—the entities that don't provide real value and irreplaceable value are likely to be bypassed and eliminated. Channel dynamics include issues of power, control, and conflict—understanding who has power and control and anticipating and managing conflict are important to effective distribution. Finally, managing channels and making choices across channel alternatives should begin with careful assessment of customer needs in relation to channel functions and analysis of alternative mechanisms for delivering those value-adding functions to various segments.

REFERENCES

American Marketing Association. (2021). Channel Control. *AMA Dictionary.* https://marketing-dictionary.org/c/channel-control/

Anderson, E., Day, G. S., & Rangan, K. (1997). Strategic channel design. *MIT Sloan Management Review, 38*(4), 59–69.

Armstrong, G., & Kotler, P. (2009). *Marketing: An introduction* (9th ed.). Pearson Prentice Hall.

Collinger, T. (1998). Lines separating sales channels blur: Manufacturers, direct sellers, retailers invade each other's turf. *Advertising Age.*

Magretta, J. (1998). The power of virtual integration: An interview with Dell computer's Michael Dell. *Harvard Business Review, 76*(2), 72–84.

Myers, J., Pickersgill, A., & Van Metre, E. (2004). Steering customers to the right channels. *McKinsey Quarterly, 4*, 36–47.

Pendergrast, M. (2000). *For God, country and Coca-Cola.* Basic Books.

Rangan, K. (1994). *Reorienting channels of distribution.* Harvard Business School Press.

Rangan, K., & Kastiri, V. (1995). Designing channels of distribution. *Harvard Business School*, 1–12.

Yoffie, D. B. (2002). *Cola wars continue: Coke and Pepsi in the twenty-first century* (Vols. 9–702–442). Harvard Business School Press.

PROMOTION—INTEGRATED MARKETING COMMUNICATIONS

Integrated marketing communications—how the firm communicates its value proposition in a coordinated manner across all marketing channels—are essential to strategic success. The integrated characterization emphasizes the fact that customers have many points of contact with a firm across a variety of occasions and a variety of media. Each of those occasions is an opportunity to build brand equity with the customer. In an effective strategy, all points of contact provide an opportunity to deliver consistent, even synergistic, messages and experiences that build on each other to reinforce a singular position for the brand. This Note highlights the range of tools and basic strategic frameworks of integrated marketing communications.

THE COMMUNICATIONS MIX

In a fragmented media environment, marketers can no longer rely on traditional advertising to reach mass audiences efficiently; instead, they utilize a diverse set of tools appropriately mixed to develop a truly integrated marketing communication program. The communications mix has traditionally been defined as comprising advertising, sales promotions, direct marketing, public relations, and personal selling. Since people are such a critical element to personal selling and strategic marketing, Note 32 is dedicated to this topic.

Advertising entails communicating messages via paid media in which the sponsor is identified or known. Because advertising includes everything from multimillion-dollar television commercials shown on the Super Bowl to search engine marketing, it is a very broad category and difficult to treat as one. In general, it is effective at building awareness and interest and ineffective at communicating extensive information. As the proliferation of advertising continues to grow, such tactics often suffer from significant waste, clutter, and consumer skepticism.

Direct marketing such as direct mail, telemarketing, and email can offer a targeted and personalized approach to advertising. Specifically, direct marketing takes advantage of advances in computer and database power to target customers with communications that are personalized (but usually not truly personal) and to track customer responses to those communications. Marketers have the ability to collect, maintain, and analyze large databases of customer contact information and to buy similar customer data from a variety of vendors. Using those data to target customers with messages, as well as to customize offerings, is a powerful tool, but it has also spawned overwhelming clutter and increasing resentment (Post & Edmiston, 2014). Direct marketing communications—and especially email marketing messages—are unique in their ability to track responses and to connect directly with order taking and fulfillment.

Sales or *personal selling* (the focus of Note 32) involves communications targeted to the individual customer or account. Sales programs are capable of communicating and customizing large amounts of information (from the marketer to target customer, and from the customer to the marketer and firm). Personal selling is effective at moving customers to trial and adoption—that is, personal selling is capable of *closing the deal* and follow-up support. Personal selling is poorly suited to creating broad awareness or interest because the cost per exposure (the cost of each sales call or contact) is generally high, although absolute costs of sales programs can be modest, especially compared with those for advertising. The structure of sales relationships for many business-to-business products has deepened toward consultative partnerships, with sales engineers working closely with customers to create customized solutions to their problems and sometimes even maintaining offices in the customers' facilities.

Sales promotions are short-term incentives intended to move customers to *action*. Sales promotions include offers to consumers and to retail or trade partners. Price-based consumer sales promotions (coupons, deals, and volume deals such as bonus packs) are effective at increasing sales in the short term but have shortcomings in the longer term. These shortcomings include foregone revenue, degradation of brand image (due to price–quality inferences), and *training* customers to expect deals and to hasten or delay purchases (i.e., to buy earlier or later to take advantage of promotions). The trade-offs between brand building and price-based promotions will be discussed further below.

Public relations entails the management of the firm's complex relationships with its many *publics* or constituencies, including regulators, public interest groups, the media, and customers. Public relations is often referred to as *publicity*, which specifically entails efforts to gain media coverage, especially by journalists (i.e., press coverage) that appears as articles or segments in unpaid-for space (in newspapers or electronic media) rather than in paid-for (advertising) space. Publicity has greater credibility than advertising because of its mediated quality, but there is an intractable loss of brand control with that mediation; journalists can report negative stories as easily as they can positive stories, and the advent of social media allows such stories to be quickly shared with mass audiences (Edmiston, 2016).

OWNED–PAID–EARNED MEDIA FRAMEWORK

With the advent of digital marketing over the past decade, creative tactics are being devised every day that do not necessarily fit neatly into a single category in the traditional communications mix framework, but nevertheless they are persuasive and effective. Thus, a new framework has evolved to describe the communications mix relative to owned, paid and earned media, as shown in Figure 31-1. Owned media refers to those media channels and opportunities that are controlled directly by the organization. Paid media includes all paid placement opportunities across media channels. Earned media entails those media mentions about your brand, products and services that are not directly controlled by the organization. Ultimately, paid and earned media should drive toward owned media, and owned media should reinforce paid and earned media opportunities.

Today, few if any communications programs rely on only one or two tools in the communications mix. The most effective programs are truly integrated campaigns in which myriad tools are used and

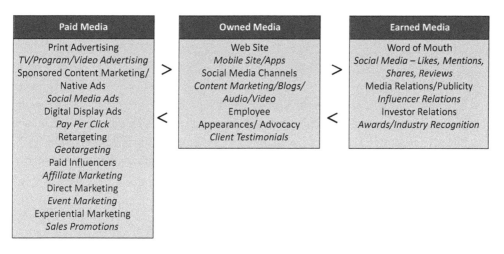

FIGURE 31-1   Owned–Paid–Earned Media Framework

coordinated so that customer contacts with the firm are consistent and *on strategy*. Such programs create and reinforce a compelling message that claims a singular position in consumer perceptions.

THE COMMUNICATIONS MANAGEMENT PROCESS

In order to create, manage, and evaluate a successful integrated marketing campaign, the manager should proceed through a process of specifying the target markets, gauging those customers' current relationship with the product or brand, establishing strategic objectives, setting the campaign budget, implementing the program, and finally evaluating the effort. Even ongoing, continuous communications programs, such as routine sales activities, will benefit from periodically going through these steps.

1. Specifying the Target Market

Targeting is the matching of a segment of customers and their specific needs with the firm and its sustainable competitive advantages. The crucial question in targeting is, "What specific needs of which specific customers can the firm meet better than the competition at a profit?" Determining the target market is the essential first step in any communications program. A number of basic characteristics of the target market, buyer behavior, and the product itself dictate fundamental differences in appropriate and effective communication mixes available to the marketer.

Type of Market

Businesses buy differently than consumers, and, as a result, we need to communicate in a different manner with B2B markets vs. B2C markets. Businesses use purchasing agents and buying centers (teams of users and experts to make large, generally more expensive purchases, often based on technical specifications and explicit procurement procedures). Thus, B2B communications are dominated by personal selling.

Target Market Concentration and Addressability

The more concentrated a market is and the more easily addressed the entities in the market are, the more likely it is that personal selling can be used to engage the market. *Addressability* refers to the ability of the marketer to identify and list or catalogue the members of a target market segment. For example, a pharmaceutical marketer can easily obtain a list of medical practices and doctors, complete with contact information and specialization such as pediatrics or geriatrics. On the other hand, it would be nearly impossible to create a similar database of all mothers of ill toddlers or all senior citizens. The physician's market is highly addressable while the patient's market is not easily addressed.

Order Size/Cost

Within both business and consumer markets, the size of a typical order and especially the total cost and margin of orders drive differences in the way buyers behave and the sorts of communications that can be used to connect with consumers. Expensive goods and orders with high total cost often require personal sales, and their margins justify and support sales efforts. Lower-cost goods are less well-suited to personal selling but do respond to wide reach, low-cost-per-exposure communications such as advertising and sales promotions.

Type of Product

Not only do the cost, typical order size, and typical margin influence the types of communications programs that can and should be used effectively, so do other characteristics of the product such as technological sophistication or complexity, required customer support and installation, and the need for customization. Complex products require more information and significant training, and information and training are best delivered via personal selling. Products that require customization or tailoring are also a good fit with personal selling and less well-suited to mass communications. Marketers of low-cost, low-tech, low-risk, and low-involvement products, on the other hand, may well use mass forms of communications to remind consumers of the brand and give emotional or social meaning to the brand.

Stage in the Product Life Cycle

Innovations in the early stages of the product life cycle often require greater information about the product and technical support. As the product life cycle evolves, customers gain experience and expertise and need less sales and service support. At the same time, in the introductory stage, innovations may command greater attention from customers who will more readily share testimonials or product reviews and from the media, making the use of publicity viable. Later in the life cycle, core benefits become widely available across product alternatives, peripheral benefits and attributes, including brand image, become more important, and advertising can serve to build brand image and remind customers of the brand, as highlighted in the video located here: https://bit.ly/prolifecycle.

Available Commercial Infrastructure and Cultural Differences

In adapting communications to the international markets or in developing global campaigns, it is important to recognize that many economies lack the communications infrastructure enjoyed in the developed world. In the developing world, mass media are gaining penetration, but that reach is still far lower than it is in the developed world. Similarly, direct communications that rely on the Internet or postal services are less reliable and have lower reach in the developing world. Even across developed, industrialized economies, customers respond differently to different promotion mix elements and certainly to different copywriting or arguments in persuasive messages, and those cultural differences will also drive differences in effective communication programs.

2. Determining Customers' Current Relationships with the Product/Brand

Shaping integrated communications programs within the context of the overarching marketing strategy, setting appropriate objectives, and evaluating results all require gauging the consumers' current (preprogram) relationships with the product/brand and the purchase decision (consumer *readiness to buy*). Table 31-1 presents some hierarchical or process models of consumer decision-making for both business-to-business and consumer markets. Although many such models have been proposed in the literature, they all break down the customer–product relationship into phases or steps, from unaware of the product or the need through awareness and evaluation toward purchase and, ultimately, adoption and loyalty.

Some strategies and associated communications programs will involve reinforcing or changing a brand's position in consumers' perceptions. In those cases, objectives should be specified in terms of consumers' perceptions and changes in those perceptions, often captured within perceptual maps. Positioning combines several factors, including the targeted customers and their needs, the firm's value proposition, and the intended brand definition—what the brand will promise to deliver better than the competition, as outlined in Note 24.

It is also important to gauge the customers' psychological relationship with the need, the product or brand, and the purchase. What are the customers' *motives* for making purchases? How

TABLE 31-1 Customer Readiness/Response Hierarchy Models

BUSINESS TO BUSINESS		BUSINESS TO CONSUMER		
DECISION PROCESS (ROBINSON ET AL., 1967)	**SALES FUNNEL (DALRYMPLE ET AL., 2004)**	**HIERARCHY OF EFFECTS (LAVIDGE & STEINER, 1961)**	**CONSUMER DECISION-MAKING PROCESS (NICOSIA, 1966)**	**ADOPTION PROCESS (ROGERS, 1962)**
Problem Recognition		Awareness	Need/Problem Recognition	Awareness
	Leads			
General Need Description		Knowledge	Information Search	Interest
Product Specification	Suspects	Liking	Evaluation of Alternatives	Evaluation
Supplier Search	Prospects	Preference		
Proposal Solicitation		Conviction		Trial
Supplier selection	Customers	Purchase	Decision	Adoption
Order Routine Specification				
Performance Review			Post-Purchase Behaviors	

do consumers go about making decisions in this product category? A variety of frameworks for categorizing customer motives and linking those motives to communications efforts have been proposed, most of which address, in one way or another, differences in consumer *involvement* with the product and the decision and distinguish elements of both *thinking* and *feeling* in the way consumers relate to the need and the product. One of the best known, the FCB Grid, will be presented in greater detail in Figure 31-2.

3. Setting Objectives

Any integrated marketing campaign should specify objectives in SMART (specific, measurable, actionable, relevant and time-bound) terms. As a core objective, many communications programs will have customers moving from their *current* readiness or relationship with the decision, established above, toward a *desired* state of readiness, whether that is greater awareness, heightened interest, more inquiries, greater preference, or simply increased sales. Objectives may also include the desired position in customer perceptions that the product or brand will claim or "own."

4. Setting the Budget

There are a few basic approaches to setting communications budgets. Many of these are reactive approaches—spending all the firm can afford, spending a stipulated percentage of sales, or matching the competition (competitive parity). Another approach, objective-based or task-oriented budgeting, is more proactive, although the resulting budgets are usually modified by the reality of scarce resources and competing priorities within the firm. Task-oriented budgeting begins with a set of tasks or objectives that the strategy seeks to accomplish, such as increasing consumer awareness, generating sales leads, or simply boosting sales, and then examines the costs associated with the communications activities necessary to accomplish those tasks. Those activities might include things like sending advertising messages, using direct mailings, or cold calling by the sales force. Once objectives have been translated into specific tasks, it is relatively straightforward to calculate the total budget. Task-oriented budgeting is preferable to reactive methods such as percentage of sales because it begins with strategic-related objectives and works its way to the required resources via costing out specific activities.

   A second set of budgeting considerations is across tools or elements of the promotion mix (for example, between sales and advertising or between price promotions and brand-building activities) and between customer acquisition and customer retention. Both of these allocations can be informed by comparing expected returns against costs. Specifically, if the strategist understands the lifetime value of its customers and can estimate the number of customers acquired by each tool under consideration, it is relatively straightforward to compute the expected return on investment (ROI) for each tool (advertisements, promotions, etc.) and to make informed choices about investments in those activities. Similarly, if those returns are known for elements of an integrated communications program, they can be easily compared with increased profits from enhanced customer retention.

5. Implementing the Program

From a strategic perspective, the critical tasks in integrated communications management focus on specifying the target markets/segments, determining where the target customers are in relationship to the decision and the purchase, and establishing the strategic objectives and budgets. Implementing a communications program is tactical—and complex. Whole industries are devoted to providing communications services, including advertising and public relations firms, direct marketing agencies, media brokers, and agents and distributors who will handle sales as well as distribution functions. It is, nevertheless, important for the strategist to understand the whole communications process and to oversee the tactical implementation of the campaign with emphasis on staying on strategy.

6. Evaluating the Communications Effort

Measuring the effectiveness and return on a communications program is essential for adjusting and improving communications, as well as justifying such investments. One of the most difficult arguments to make within a firm is for long-term brand-building investments. Although brand-building tactics may not be directly attributable to immediate sales or profits, that does not mean brand building does not impact sales and financial results, especially long-term results. And, it also does not mean that the long-term and short-term effectiveness of communications programs cannot be measured or linked to financial contributions.

Evaluating the effectiveness of a communications effort is predicated on specifically describing the target markets and segments and the precampaign relationship of those customers with the product or brand (the first and second steps, above) and setting detailed, measurable objectives for the campaign (the third step, above). Establishing customers' pre- and post-campaign relationship with the product generally requires marketing research and, specifically, survey research.

Marketing return on investment (MROI), or return on marketing is a powerful tool for marketing strategists. ROI is a ratio—the profit earned divided by the investment made to achieve that profit:

$$\text{Marketing ROI} = \frac{\text{Profits}}{\text{Investment (Costs)}}$$

Profits are *not* simply sales or gross revenues—profits are net contribution or units sold multiplied by average margins (margin being price minus unit costs). From a strategic perspective, these computations should consider the lifetime value of the customer—how much does each acquired customer provide for the firm across the lifetime of their relationship with the brand? This computation—the lifetime value of a customer—can be done for different levels of *readiness* (such as awareness, liking, or commitment; See Table 31-1 above). How much is a percentage gain in awareness worth in increased sales and in increased margins? Knowing what a percentage change in a level of readiness is worth in sales across time (the lifetime value of those customers) allows communications campaigns to be expressed in ROI or MROI. If the firm invests $10 million in a campaign that increases awareness by 1%, which might, for example, equal 10,000 customers becoming aware of the brand, and each customer who is aware of the brand has a lifetime value of $150, then the campaign would have a ROI or MROI of 1.5 (15 million divided by 10 million). This ROI can be compared to alternative uses of the resources (the $10 million), including other communications campaigns or alternative tactics.

STRATEGIC COMMUNICATIONS CHALLENGES

The following sections detail four specific strategic communications challenges, including (a) push versus pull, (b) brand building versus promotions, (c) customer motives and B2C decision making, and (d) B2B motives and buyer behavior.

Push Versus Pull

A basic distinction in marketing communications is between *push* and *pull* strategies. When the focus of a communications program is on building demand at the consumer level it is a *pull* strategy; the consumer demand pulls the product through the channel of distribution. That is, distributors, wholesalers, and retailers are motivated to stock and sell the product because of the downstream demand. Sometimes that demand will manifest itself in actual requests from consumers to retailers to stock a product; retailers would then ask their wholesalers for the product, wholesalers would ask their distributors or brokers, and so forth. While the idea that consumers literally request the product may help illustrate the idea underlying a *pull* strategy, actual consumer requests aren't necessary or even typical. Usually a pull campaign builds demand at the level of the ultimate consumer using mass communications tools like advertising while also selling to distributors, wholesalers, and retailers to persuade them to stock and sell the product, often using evidence from research and other markets to show that consumers will buy the product once it's on the shelves. It is the relative emphasis on generating demand at the consumer level that distinguishes a *pull* strategy.

A *push* strategy, on the other hand, emphasizes building demand in the channel of distribution, especially at the next level down the channel. The manufacturer emphasizes sales efforts directed toward distributors; distributors then sell to wholesalers who sell to customers or retailers (who sell to consumers). Those selling efforts persuade the channel members to stock and sell the product and then the channel members' sales force works to sell the product to the next channel entities. Push strategies emphasize direct selling and trade promotions and are typically found in B2B markets.

Although *push versus pull* makes for a neat dichotomy, most marketing communications campaigns include elements of *both*, and the real distinction is a matter of degree. For example, Coca-Cola, an iconic global consumer brand famous for massive advertising and consumer-marketing programs, also has an elaborate and highly regarded sales organization working closely with channel members, from bottlers to distributors, retailers, and restaurateurs, to build distribution and facilitate consumption. Similarly, although selling military planes is a long, intensive *push* process of lobbying and bidding to governments, Northrop Grumman, Boeing, and other large defense contractors in the United States also use mass media, including advertising in major national newspapers, to reinforce the brand and to build goodwill amongst opinion leaders, lawmakers, and the general public.

Brand Building Versus Promotions

Another basic distinction can be drawn between brand-building efforts (including advertising) and price-based promotions. Price promotions such as special deals (price discounts), coupons, and bonus packs tend to have an immediate and marked impact on sales—there is no question that consumers do buy products when considered a *good deal*. However, price-based promotions can have serious negative effects in the long term.

The first and most obvious negative effect is the inherent loss of revenue—price promotions, by lowering the price, lower the revenue realized for the product. Other possible negative effects are more subtle and less immediate. Lowering the price for a specific period of time may shift sales forward in time; that is, some customers who buy on deal would have bought later (when the product would be offered at full price). As price promotions become more common and predictable, consumers may also shift purchases out in time to wait for the next deal rather than buy at full price. This purchase shifting may compound the loss of revenue, distort demand, and disrupt production planning. Additionally, price is an important signal of quality—especially in some product categories where consumers lack the ability or expertise to judge substantive quality. By lowering the effective price, price promotions can diminish consumers' perceptions of the product's quality in the long term.

Another set of long-term and undesirable effects of price promotions relates to trade promotions, or deals offered to channel partners, especially retailers. These trade promotions can include price reductions (such as case allowances and extra product deals), as well as cooperative advertising, contests, and slotting or shelving fees (direct payments for stocking consideration). Trade promotions can quickly become expected, a necessary part of doing business with the retailers, and are hard to control. Often retailers drop incentives directly to their own bottom line, and some channel members divert promotions to other retailers and to other markets. In fact, an entire industry called *diverting* has emerged in which one retailer will take advantage of a trade promotion offered to it, such as discounts for volume orders, and then resell inventory via intermediates who then resell to other retailers and to other geographic markets for whom the promotion was never intended.

The fact that trade promotions become expected rather than exceptional, and the additional reality that many customers misdirect trade promotions, does not make it easy for manufacturers to decline to participate—trade promotions have become a necessary prerequisite of doing business with certain retailers. However, certain retailers such as Walmart have recognized that trade promotions distort their business model and may distract energies from core value propositions. Thus, Walmart accepts no trade promotions (and does not allow its buyers to accept gifts or other consideration from its vendors). Thus, the largest retailer in the world has been able to own the position of *everyday low prices* in the marketplace.

Customer Motives and B2C Decision-Making

Customers are motivated by different things to different degrees, depending on the product category and occasion as well as on the customers themselves. Certain consumers react more to emotional messages while others respond to rational appeals (i.e., facts and figures). Similarly, customers do not bring the same level of interest or attention to all purchases or to all product categories. Some products, such as laundry detergent, are inherently uninteresting—marketers call that level of interest or enthusiasm for a purchase or a product *involvement*—while others are inherently engaging, such as cars and movies. Even though some products may be more engaging, customers also vary in their degree of involvement within product categories; some people are movie junkies or car enthusiasts while others far less engaged and perhaps even uninvolved with these products.

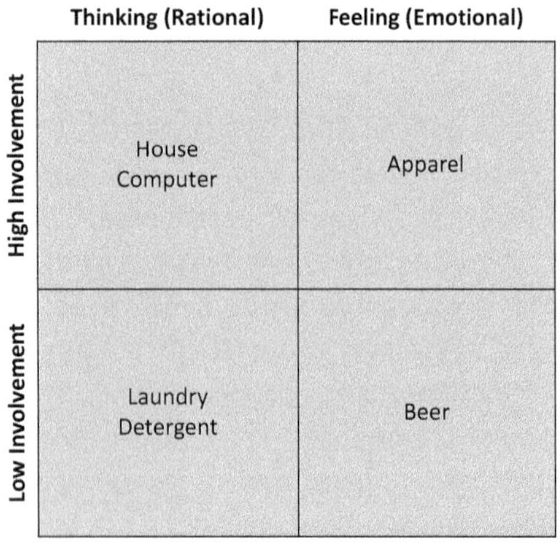

	Thinking (Rational)	Feeling (Emotional)
High Involvement	House Computer	Apparel
Low Involvement	Laundry Detergent	Beer

FIGURE 31-2 FCB Grid

Many frameworks have been proposed to gauge consumers' purchase and consumption motives in order to develop appropriate communications messages. One of the best known is the FCB Grid, developed by the Foote Cone & Belding advertising agency, which makes basic distinctions between thinking and feeling products on one axes and high versus low involvement products on the other, as shown in Figure 31-2.

Richard Vaughn (1980; 1986) introduced this now-well-known framework while a director of research at Foote Cone & Belding advertising agency. In the FCB Grid, products like computers and life insurance are high-involvement/thinking products; customers generally learn (think) about these products, form a preference (feel), and then buy or *act*. Perfume and apparel are examples of high-involvement/feeling products; the purchase process for these affective product categories usually follows a *feel-learn-act* flow in which customers' emotions are the primary and most influential factor. Low-involvement/thinking products, or habitual purchases, include mundane household consumables (such as detergent and groceries) that follow a *do-learn-feel* process in which trial may precede evaluation and feelings (and feelings are low-intensity preferences). Finally, low-involvement/feeling products are items such as beer and candy that involve a *do-feel-think* consumer decision process; rational evaluations come after the act and the feelings (which often involve satisfaction or self-indulgent pleasure).

The FCB Grid is just one prominent framework for classifying and understanding customer motivations and tying those motives to differences in suitable and effective communications programs. Many other frameworks have been proposed (Rossiter et al., 1991), but the basic implication of these tools is that customers are motivated by different things for different products. It is also true that different customers on different occasions are going to be motivated by different things; for example, there are certainly some occasions where customers will purchase candy in a very rational (thinking) and highly involved manner. These motives are generally consumer motives—they apply less well to B2B products, most of which are fairly rational or *thinking* products and are purchased initially in a highly analytic fashion even if they later become "straight rebuys" (or habitual purchases); B2B motives are discussed below.

Understanding customer needs, customer motives, and the customer purchase decision process informs the development of the integrated marketing communications program. Vaughn linked the FCB Grid to advertising copy (messages and creative content): Messages focus on the decision process (e.g., thinking-feeling-doing) and persuasive content expected to influence the relevant processes. Understanding the motives and decision-making process can also influence decisions about the overall promotions mix; for example, sales are effective in influencing rational, thinking purchases but are usually less persuasive with regard to feeling decisions or low-involvement purchases.

B2B Motives and Buyer Behavior

Most industrial or B2B purchases are approached in a relatively high-involvement (at least for the initial purchase) and highly rational/thinking manner; however, there are important distinctions in the B2B sector just as there are in consumer products and purchase decisions. Understanding how B2B customers make decisions, how they fashion specifications and proceed through the buying process, and what motivates or drives B2B purchases is important. Buying processes and motives will be different by product category and by firm (or segment of firms). For example, when purchasing the same products, some firms will use a purchasing agent from the outset, and those purchases will, therefore, be driven by price and efficiencies such as delivery time and quantity. Other firms will begin with buying centers to determine requirements, set specifications, issue requests for proposals (RFPs), and ultimately to make the purchase decision. Buying centers are teams working, either formally or informally, to make purchase decisions for an organization. There are many roles in buying centers from (a) users (the people who will ultimately make use of the purchased good or service and who influence the purchase through that application role), (b) influencers (experts in some aspect of the purchase), (c) gatekeepers (people who control the flow of information in the organization), and (d) buyers (the people who will ultimately commit the organization to the purchase). In order to communicate with organizational buyers effectively, it is necessary to understand the buying criteria, the buying process, and the various roles in that buying process.

SUMMARY

Managing the communications mix is an essential part of marketing strategy, and the marketing manager must address integrated marketing communications at the strategic level. This includes understanding a broad range of owned, paid and earned media, the integration of these tools, and basic processes for managing and evaluating communications programs that build on and reinforce a unique value proposition in the mindset of consumers. Integrated marketing communications require deep and broad understandings of consumer motives, buying behaviors, and relationships with the product and the brand.

REFERENCES

Dalrymple, D., Cron, W., & DeCarlo, T. (2004). *Sales management.* John Wiley & Sons.

Edmiston, D. (2016). Developing the perfect pitch: Creating a positive first impression through social media. *Marketing Education Review, 26*(1), 3–7.

Lavidge, R. J., & Steiner, G. A. (1961). A model for predictive measurements of advertising effectiveness. *Journal of Marketing, 25*(6), 59–62.

Nicosia, F. (1966). *Consumer decision processes.* Prentice Hall.

Post, R., & Edmiston, D. (2014). Challenging big data preconceptions: New ways of thinking about data and integrated marketing communication. *International Journal of Integrated Marketing Communications, 6*(1), 18–24.

Robinson, P., Faris, C., & Wind, Y. (1967). *Industrial buying behavior and creative marketing.* Allyn & Bacon.

Rogers, E. (1962). *Diffusion of innovation.* Free Press.

Rossiter, J., Percy, L., & Donovan, R. J. (1991). A better advertising planning grid. *Journal of Advertising Research*, 31(5), 11–21.

Vaughn, R. (1980). How advertising works: A planning model ... Putting it all together. *Journal of Advertising Research*, 20(5), 27–33.

Vaughn, R. (1986). How advertising works: A planning model revisited. *Journal of Advertising Research*, 26(1), 57–66.

Selling—and the management of it—is one of the critical decision areas of the marketing mix. Manufacturers, retailers, and service suppliers must carefully consider how much personal selling to use relative to other marketing mix elements, particularly advertising and sales promotion. This balance reflects our assumptions about the relative effectiveness and efficiency of the mix elements in reaching our targeted consumers. The impact of personal selling certainly extends beyond the promotional mix decision; however, it will depend to a great extent on how well we manage the sales function. Experience tells us that salesforces are not created equal and that the quality of sales management will determine the value returned for selling dollar expended. In this respect it is like advertising, where competitors can spend identical sums for ads but have vastly different results because of the relative effectiveness of those ads.

As *New York Times* best-selling author Daniel Pink emphasized in his book *To Sell Is Human*, everybody is selling something (Pink, 2012). Most marketing programs include a selling component, and the people delivering that component are critical to its success. In fact, personal selling tends to be the most expensive promotion tool, costing industrial companies an average of almost $275 per sales call (Zabanga, 2021). Still, to many organizations, selling is fundamental to their marketing mix and the basis of their competitive edge. In the broadest sense, every person in an organization has a role to play relative to sales and as a brand advocate for their employer. However, for purposes of this Note, the focus will be primarily on the sales management function and how best to support personal selling within an organization.

To determine the role of personal selling in the marketing mix, firms start by analyzing buying behavior, in effect the buying processes of their target consumers. Companies look at how they can interject themselves into these processes, asking question after question, such as the following: How should our message be carried to these people? How many are there? How often should they be visited? What kind of salesperson would best interact with these customers? How can advertising help the sale? How does service fit with the selling situation? How much does the sales call cost relative to other avenues to the consumer such as media advertising, digital advertising, social media, telemarketing, or direct mail? We could—and should—go on with the questions, but the process should be clear: we start with the marketplace, our consumers, and work back to our personal selling decisions.

This Note was adapted from Ring, Newton, Borden, and Farris (1989), and highlights both the consultative nature of modern selling behavior as well as the complexity of the tasks that salespeople may perform. So, let us examine the evolution of the four stages of selling behavior to help us gain this understanding.

STAGE I: THE MUSIC MAN

The concept of what constitutes good selling behavior has changed over the years. Back in the days before World War I (these dates are approximate and vary widely with the sophistication of individual firms), success in personal selling was regarded as a function of a salesperson's personality and ability to charm customers. The prevalent mythology was that "Good salesmen are born, not made." Consequently, few firms gave salespeople any training or supervision. Little attention was given to performance evaluation, as straight commission weeded out the unfit. Many of the general public's notions about salespeople stem from the sales practices of this era, as dramatized by several playwrights. Willie Loman of Arthur Miller's *Death of a Salesman* is a failure because he can no longer impress his customers; Harold Hill of *The Music Man* is so popular and entertaining that he can persuade anyone to buy almost anything.

STAGE II: THE ANIMATED CATALOG

After World War I, increased industrialization and competition caused many prospective buyers to pay closer attention to product performance. In response, sellers began to train their salesforces in product features. The prevalent mythology was that "A good salesman is someone who knows his product." Although this stage was a vast improvement over reliance on sheer personality, sales presentations tended to become mechanical repetitions of product information that could have been easily transmitted through a good product brochure. The *canned presentation* or *product pitch* produced a generation of salespeople who were little more than animated catalogs.

STAGE III: THE MAGIC FORMULA

During the 1930s, as competition became more intense and salesforces got larger with influxes of young inexperienced salespeople, sellers' training activities began to include attention to buyer's needs. Salespeople were trained to make canned sales presentations designed to (a) manipulate buyers' reactions, and (b) give salespeople confidence in their ability to sell by providing them with a *road map of the sale*—a series of steps through which they were to lead the customer. A prime example of this approach was AIDA: Attention–Interest–Desire–Action. Success in personal selling was considered a function of how well a salesperson could communicate the benefits of their product line, as opposed to the characteristics of the product line; in effect, the tactic was to "sell the sizzle instead of the steak."

The prevalent mythology was that *a good salesman controls the sale*. Again, this stage was a vast improvement over the animated catalog. It acknowledged the presence of a customer and the legitimacy of customer needs. But it produced a generation of salespeople who equated selling with outwitting the customer through the use of a magic formula.

STAGE IV: THE PROBLEM SOLVER

During the 1950s, it became apparent to many sales executives that not only were sophisticated buyers becoming familiar with all these probing and closing techniques, but also customers' thought processes seldom followed the salesperson's *road map*. Furthermore, buyers were demanding more professionalism from salespeople, asking them to take more of an advisory role. "Let me make up my own mind" was becoming a common buyers' plea. In response, sellers' training activities began to stress the salesperson's role as a consultant. The sale became a two-step process: (a) to determine and articulate for the customer the real problem he or she faced; and (b) to present the product's benefits as a partial or complete solution to that problem.

This responsive kind of selling forced the salesperson to become more analytical and more sensitive to the wide range of factors affecting the buyer's decision. Thus, success in personal selling was considered a function of how well a salesperson could help customers determine the criteria for choosing among alternative products, as well as how skillful they were in demonstrating how their products satisfied these criteria. In this fashion, a good salesperson literally *allowed the customer to buy*. By helping the customer to define their own needs, the salesperson entered the sale at the very beginning and, in this way, could often place their products at a considerable advantage, which is now referred to as *consultative selling*. Customers are more receptive to this new sales approach, and salespeople themselves feel prouder about what they do for a living.

Obviously, these four stages did not fully replace one another but have evolved to complement one another. It takes personal acceptability, technical competence, and creative flair to be an effective problem solver. However, a salesperson who cannot handle the last stage, a role similar to that of a management consultant, will find customers have come to expect this kind of professional activity. Increases in the efficiency of alternative methods of delivering a sales message—advertising, mobile, social media, etc.—and a tendency to automate and digitize purchasing decisions—may sound the death knell for all but the most sophisticated professional salesforces.

TASKS OF CONSULTATIVE SELLING

Having seen the consultative nature of modern personal selling, we are now in a better position to examine the activities salespeople perform, activities that vary according to the firm's customers and its overall marketing strategy. We will briefly describe several main types of selling tasks including trade, missionary, technical, and entrepreneurial. However, these categories are not exclusive or exhaustive. For example, retail selling (behind-the-counter) and delivery (route) selling have not been included in this Note. Even the attributes and skills required to carry out the four main types of selling tasks vary considerably; the managerial policies and the amount and kinds of supervision appropriate to each of these tasks also differ.

The primary responsibility of *trade selling* is to build sales volume by providing the firm's customers with promotional assistance, thereby making the firm's resellers more effective. The trade salesforce, therefore, sells *through* rather than *to* its customers. Trade selling is common in many industries, but it predominates in consumer durables and nondurables such as furniture, apparel,

318 | Marketing Management: A Strategic Framework and Tools for Success

textiles, and food, as well as in wholesale firms. Since many consumer products tend to be mature and are promoted directly to the user, a firm's trade selling is often less critical to marketing success than are its advertising and promotion.

Missionary selling builds volume by persuading second-order or indirect consumers to order from the firm's direct customers, which are its wholesalers and other channels of distribution. Thus, the missionary salesforce *sells for* its direct customers, whereas the trade salesforce *sells through* them. Missionary selling is common in the chemical, transportation, wholesaling, and pharmaceutical industries.

The primary role of *technical selling* is to increase sales volume by providing the firm's customers with technical advice and assistance. Unlike trade or missionary sales, the technical salesperson sells directly *to* the user or buyer. Technical selling is common in the industries of chemical, machinery, office products and technology, and heavy machinery.

The primary role of *entrepreneurial selling* is to obtain new accounts for its company. Converting a total stranger into a customer is the critical task. This kind of selling is also called *canvassing* and *cold calling*. Like technical selling, it is selling to customers. Unlike technical selling, it may require a great deal of aggressiveness and the capacity to withstand feelings of rejection when customers say "no." Entrepreneurial selling is common in almost all industries.

HYBRID SALESFORCES

Almost every sales organization is a hybrid of two or more of these four types of salesforces. Many sales jobs require new business development in addition to trade, missionary, or technical selling. Many sales jobs require missionary work in addition to trade or technical selling. Top managers must recognize that no two selling jobs are alike, even in firms competing in the same industry. Each firm will have a different marketing strategy, with each strategy requiring different behavior from the salesforce.

THE SALES MANAGER

The primary responsibility of the sales manager is to encourage conformity between actual behavior (what the salesperson does) and desired behavior (what the company wants them to do). But this important position is often the Achilles' heel of the salesforce. Good sales management is made up of (a) a properly defined job which permits the manager to spend enough time performing appropriate field supervisory activities, and (b) personal behaviors that meet the needs of subordinates and encourage them to high performance.

The lack of adequate field supervision is a common complaint among salespeople, their customers, and even senior managers. One reason for the lack of adequate supervision is managers' belief that experienced salespeople do not need supervision or will not stand for it. "Salespeople should be treated as if they were in business for themselves," many managers assume. According to this view, mature salespeople—particularly those paid on straight commission—when left alone will act in their own self-interest and maximize their own and the company's sales volume. This view found its genesis in the Music Man stage of selling behavior, and it is still fairly widespread.

Today, however, marketing strategies are too dynamic and complex to permit salespeople to act merely in their own self-interest. Most sales organizations require their personnel to perform many activities that fall outside a salesperson's definition of self-interest. Salespeople are seldom in business for themselves. They are hired to implement marketing strategy. Furthermore, lack of supervision is particularly damaging to high-performance salespeople, who often want to do even better and whose efforts are all too often taken for granted.

A second reason for inadequate field supervision is that companies often fail to properly define the sales manager's job. Field managers and senior managers alike often do not recognize that the field manager's key tasks are observing actual salesforce behavior and working to improve it in the field. Instead of giving highest priority to supervisory tasks, some companies assign field sales managers customers of their own to handle, either because "It's good for them to keep engaged in the sales process" or because the size or importance of the accounts seems to warrant a manager's attention. This practice can cause managers to overemphasize selling at the expense of developing the skills of their salesforce—particularly if the managers' incomes and performance appraisals depend on their success with their own accounts.

Other firms, rather than seeing their managers as primarily salespeople, see them as primarily administrators. This attitude causes field sales managers to become bogged down with paperwork, report writing, and other duties often better left to staff specialists—such activities as recruiting and hiring new salespeople, reconciling expense accounts, or conducting customer surveys. Assigning any administrative task to a field manager should always be considered a trade-off. Is this administrative task worth depriving a manager of time in the field to work with their salespeople?

Often newly promoted sales managers understand field supervision should be their priority. Yet they may be uncertain how to supervise. One reason for such uncertainty is a lack of training. Many firms routinely promote their best salespeople without preparing them adequately for their new responsibilities. But success as a salesperson does not guarantee success as a manager. Unless the selling job had a great deal of managerial content—such as a job in which planning, coordinating, and integrating the tasks of many people were critical to consummating the sale—most salespeople find that managing other people's activities requires different skills from asking a customer for an order. In many sales organizations, the super salesperson is often the least likely to be a good planner, a good organizer, and a good delegator. Furthermore, the super salesperson is often unaware of the reasons for their success and thus is unable to coach and direct the behavior of others.

Another reason for new managers' uncertainty is that senior managers may fail to communicate their objectives for the salesforce. Not only must senior managers define for field sales managers the precise role of the salesforce in the firm's marketing strategy, but they must also update that definition every time changes in the competitive environment force changes in marketing strategy. If current desired behavior is not understood, sales managers have no recourse but to direct their salespeople to perform as they always have—or even worse, to perform as the managers performed when *they* were salespeople. Unless the activities of the salesforce correspond to the desired behavior as determined by marketing strategy, the salesforce will be doing one thing while senior executives expect another. Once the sales manager understands the salesforce's role in the firm's marketing strategy, they can determine the kind of supervision appropriate to this role and to the needs of individual salespeople.

Coaching

The manager's most important task is teaching salespeople how to sell efficiently and effectively. Most coaching takes place one-on-one in the field; some takes place in small group-training sessions. Working in the field allows the manager to make calls with a salesperson and to observe, participate in, demonstrate, or take over the sale. *Observation* is the most common practice when making calls with experienced salespeople. *Sidewalk critiques* give the field sales manager the opportunity to compliment professional behavior and to correct unprofessional behavior. *Participation* in the sale can be an effective method of training salespeople in the finer points of such activities as answering questions, handling objections, and asking for the order. *Demonstration* is a tool for helping salespeople learn how to handle a module of the sale; for instance, how to make a new product introduction. *Taking over* is a technique usually reserved for rescuing an important sale when it is obvious that the selling situation is beyond the salesperson's control.

Counseling

Counseling requires a great deal of judgment on the part of the field sales manager. On the one hand, giving advice and direction in response to a salesperson's request for career guidance is an important aspect of the manager's job. On the other hand, helping a salesperson iron out marital or financial problems is seldom wise, and ales managers cannot be expected to act as priests or psychiatrists. Nevertheless, listening in a nondirective, nonjudgmental fashion to a salesperson's personal problems can be supportive and morale-building when the personal problems begin to affect job performance. Most experienced sales managers, however, confine their prescriptive advice to pointing out the job-related consequences of a salesperson's personal situation.

Controlling

The responsibility for the performance of the salesforce ultimately rests with the sales manager. An organizational climate that encourages high performance will be created largely through the sales manager's personal style, but it will also be affected by the pressures and expectations of superiors and subordinates. Handling such pressures require a clear understanding of the job's authorities and responsibilities, as well as considerable insight into the motivations of other people. The appropriate amount of control is usually determined by the competence of the salespeople and the risks inherent in the selling situations. *Delegation* ("You take care of it") is usually a safe course with competent salespeople. *Direction* ("Take care of it *this* way") is more often required for less-competent salespeople or in high-risk selling situations. *Doing* ("Let me take care of it") may be necessary when salespeople are unable or ill-equipped to take charge themselves.

Evaluating

Not only must the field sales manager monitor and evaluate performance, they must communicate this evaluation to the individual salesperson. How to measure performance, how to identify areas for individual improvement, and how to communicate the evaluation in such a way as to improve a salesperson's performance are among the most demanding of the field sales manager's tasks. Experienced field sales managers find that performance appraisals can be powerful tools for improving results when they adhere to the following rules: (a) appraise performance along dimensions relevant to the job, (b) avoid appraising personal attributes, (c) appraise frequently, and (d) focus appraisals on future action plans, not on past experiences.

Administrating

A certain number of administrative duties are required of most sales managers. Assigning sales territories and administering sales quotas are two of the more frequent ones. Many sales managers are required to assign accounts to their salespeople. This activity involves making judgments about workload, matching characteristics of salespeople to those of key customers, estimating sales potential, and, above all, trying to balance fairly an individual's workload against the potential sales volume within their territory. Sales managers must effectively communicate objectives to salespeople. Many companies use personal sales quotas to make these objectives clear. Quotas can be based on historical sales performance, others on estimates of sales potential, and still others attempt to tailor the quota to the strengths and weaknesses of the individual salesperson. Some companies view quotas as forecasts—they expect quotas to be met. Other companies view quotas as targets—they expect only the best salespeople to meet them. Still other companies use quotas as a basis for compensation.

To administer quotas effectively, the field sales manager must understand their purpose and understand the influence that they exert on salespeople in various situations. For instance, quotas based on historical sales (often called *ratchets* when they are based on percentage increases over the previous year's sales) tend to give the better salesperson the harder challenge as they must get more and more sales from the same territory. And quotas based on potential sales tend to give the weaker salespeople the harder challenge because the potential in their territories grows faster than their abilities. Quotas can be personalized to challenge strong and weak performers equally. However, personalized quotas do not provide the sales forecasting given by historical quotas, nor the comparative evaluation possibilities of quotas based on potential.

THE SALES EXECUTIVE

The sales executive's major responsibilities are (a) to determine the precise role that the salesforce is to play in the firm's marketing strategy, and (b) to design and implement a sales management system that encourages the salesperson to enact that role.

Determining the Role of the Salesforce

Anyone who has spent time observing salespeople from different companies as they make their sales calls will appreciate that defining these activities as "selling" is a vast oversimplification. Selling is much more than merely asking for the order. The activities can range from "hand-holding" to pressuring the customer to buy; from long involved negotiations with numerous customer "influentials" to door-to-door canvassing; from making highly technical presentations to sophisticated customers to haggling over price on bulk items that are purchased repeatedly. Within the same industry, salespeople who are selling practically identical products to similar classes of customers will exhibit different behavior. This variety of activity is, or ought to be, a function of the role assigned to the salesforce within the firm's marketing strategy, not a function of how salespeople think they ought to behave. Experienced sales executives, therefore, begin with a clear understanding of the specific desired behavior and do not sidestep this necessary analytical task by describing salesforce activities in generalizations, such as "They are paid to sell." Overgeneralization may cause executives to ignore salesforce activities that are vital to the marketing strategy.

The first step in determining desired behavior is understanding the firm's marketing strategy, which is often more difficult than it sounds. Sometimes the sales executive's ignorance of marketing strategy arises from their failure to participate with marketing executives in formulating marketing strategy. The sales executive's nonparticipation can lead to a lack of understanding of how the firm has chosen to compete, lack of commitment to marketing objectives, and improper direction of field sales activities.

Sometimes the sales executive's lack of participation is caused by the formal organization itself. Reporting relationships often do not require communications between sales and marketing. Furthermore, sales and marketing personnel often have different backgrounds and personalities. Marketing executives tend to be analytical, tend to have formal education in business administration, and tend to talk in a language of their own, using such terms as *positioning, segmentation, gross rating points*, and so on. Many sales executives, on the other hand, are people who have made their marks in the field of sales, have less formal business training, and are more at ease taking a customer to lunch than analyzing quantitative data. Most firms' methods of evaluating performance reinforce these differences: Marketing executives are frequently evaluated in terms of profitability and return on investment; sales executives are more frequently evaluated in terms of sales volume.

Sales executives who make the more useful contributions to strategy formulation are the ones who are familiar with marketing concepts and terminology. Some companies help sales executives achieve this familiarity through management development programs; other firms use a career path that gives promising salespeople positions in marketing early in their careers. By the same token, some companies insist on sales experience before giving marketing executives positions of greater responsibility. It is just as important for the marketing strategist to understand the realities of the marketplace as seen through the eyes of a salesperson as it is for the sales executive to understand how the firm has chosen to compete.

The sales executive must also keep up with subtle shifts in marketing strategy that may affect desired salesforce behavior. Nearly all companies modify their marketing strategy from year to year. Prices are changed, dealers are added or dropped, new products are featured, new advertising campaigns are started, and so on. Every time a company modifies its strategy, it inexorably modifies the desired behavior or the salesforce. Even though these modifications are minor, over time they add up. If most marketing and sales executives were to examine their marketing plans of 5 years earlier, they would be surprised at the difference between those plans and their plans for this year. Similarly, if these executives were to examine in detail the specific activities required of the sales staff 5 years earlier, they would be surprised at the differences in today's activities.

For example, one company that made some subtle changes in its product line several years ago ended up reducing its volume with smaller, less profitable customers and increasing its volume with more profitable, larger customers. As marketing's efforts toward the larger customers intensified, sales executives found themselves with obsolete call standards, badly aligned sales territories, and a salesforce largely ill-equipped to explain new product benefits to more sophisticated purchasers. Furthermore, many field sales managers were uncertain about the company's new sales emphasis and were continuing to coach and direct salespeople to call on the older, smaller accounts, instead of training them to be more effective with the purchasing agents of the more profitable larger accounts. Before any policies can be instituted to encourage desired behavior, before any supervision can help the salesforce perform desired behavior, the sales executive must know what that desired behavior is.

Designing the Sales Management System

The sales management system is that collection of policies, procedures, and practices that encourage salespeople to carry out their role in the firm's marketing strategy. Experienced sales executives are cautious about accepting advice from outsiders on how to design a system or how to change one. What competitors do, what prestigious firms do, what is suggested in journal articles may not be relevant. What may be good practice for one salesforce may be wrong for another. Thus, thoughtful sales executives continually ask themselves questions such as these: Are the salespeople deployed correctly? Are selection and training procedures effective? Are controls sufficient? Are salespeople being paid too little or too much? Are they adequately supervised? In short, are management policies and practices still appropriate to the selling task as we define it today?

Of course, a company's management policies and practices will not constitute all the influences on salesforce behavior. Common sense suggests that *how well* a firm's executives implement their policies has a greater impact on personnel performance than *what* policies these executives choose to implement. And the effects of a firm's practices are often influenced by outside factors, such as industry norms or competitive situations.

Nevertheless, sales executives are responsible for deciding the most appropriate form or organization for their salesforce, the most appropriate selection criteria, compensation plan, span of control, and so forth. A major set of sales management myths hold that certain sales management practices are associated with high performance and others with low turnover. While certain practices may have validity in the context of the situation within which they originated, the theorems do not necessarily remain valid when they are applied to other, quite different situations. The point is that "best practice" needs to be highly particularized right down to the individual company. Mythology is no substitute for a good, hard, close look at reality.

Given a clear understanding of the firm's marketing strategy and expectations regarding the behavior of its salesforce, sales executives can favorably influence performance by employing a judicious combination of policies and practices. To choose these policies, the executive must consider the following factors:

- The organizational approach that best encourages the kind of salesforce behavior that the marketing strategy calls for.
- The territory assignments that provide the best strategic support—that is, the most efficient and effective market coverage.
- The kind of salesperson best suited to the company's selling unit.
- The amount and kind of initial and subsequent training that best prepare the salesforce to fulfill its role in the marketing strategy.
- The level and method of compensation that best rewards the salesforce for performing its required tasks well.
- The measures and controls that best serve to direct and monitor the desired salesforce behavior.
- The system for evaluating salesforce performance that best encourages the desired performance.

It is the combination of polices that is important. To rely too heavily on one element of the sales management system is to depend on mythology. For example, experienced sales executives avoid placing a disproportionate emphasis on compensation plans. In effect, these sales executives have overcome the notion that "I can rely on my pay plan to get better performance." Most experienced sales executives agree that there are no magic wands. Compensation will influence sales behavior. But compensation decisions will also have an impact on selection and training decisions. Sales executives who accept the fact that all these decisions are highly interrelated recognize that the proper combination of policies and practices, each designed to encourage the desired behavior, produces a total effect greater than the sum of the parts.

A CONCEPTUAL FRAMEWORK

The complexities of salesforce management problems require the ability to understand the consequences of one's decisions on several organizational layers. To diagram these relationships and to provide the reader with a conceptual framework for improving skills in building and maintaining an effective salesforce, we will use a baseball diamond model as shown in Figure 32-1.

Home plate is the alpha and omega of baseball. No runs are scored unless all four bases are touched. The behavior of the customer is the alpha and omega of business. For the marketer, no sale is made until all four bases are touched. Beginning with an analysis of customer behavior, the marketing executive attempts to match their available resources to the risks, opportunities, and constraints in the competitive environment. This matching process results in a marketing strategy, a decision to create customers in a way unique to that company. The firm gets to first base when the marketing executive has developed a sound marketing strategy.

Working within the marketing strategy developed for the firm, the sales executive defines the role to be played by the salesforce and creates a management system to support that role. The role

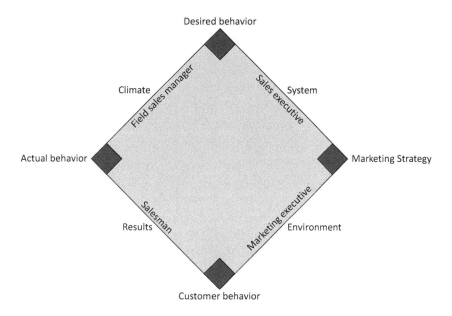

FIGURE 32-1 Analogy for Building an Effective Salesforce

is the desired behavior (what the executive would do if they were the *sole* salesperson); the system is the combination of policies and practices selected to encourage the salespeople to behave in a particular manner (as the executive would behave if he or she were the sole salesperson). The firm gets to second base when the sales executive has clearly defined the desired behavior of the salesforce and has chosen that combination of policies and practices (selection, training, compensation, and so forth) that best encourages that behavior.

Working from an understanding of the desired salesforce behavior, the sales manager creates that supervisory climate that best encourages conformity between actual behavior (what the salesperson does) and desired behavior (what the company wants them to do). The firm gets to third base if the sales manager ensures that the actual behavior of the salesforce is congruent with the desired behavior.

In baseball, only runs count, and the only way to score runs is to cross home plate. Similarly, the old cliché in business is, "Nothing happens until the sale is made." The firm crosses home plate as often as the actual behavior of the salesperson produces the desired customer behavior.

Clearly, the most effective organizations touch all the bases. To achieve this goal, many people must perform their jobs well. The salesperson must be good at persuading the customer to buy. The sales manager must be good at teaching and encouraging the salespeople to perform well. The sales executive must be good at defining the role of the salesforce in the company's marketing mix and good at creating a set of management policies and practices to encourage fulfillment of that role. Ultimately, the marketing manager must create an effective overall strategy within which the salesforce operates.

SUMMARY

It is rare to find a business that does not depend on a selling component, and the people delivering that component are critical to its success. To determine the optimal role of personal selling in the marketing mix, firms start by analyzing the buying processes of their target consumers. To fully appreciate the strengths that selling can bring to marketing programs, it is important to consider both the consultative nature of modern selling behavior and the complexity of sales tasks. The various types of selling tasks can include trade, missionary, technical, and entrepreneurial; almost every sales organization is a hybrid of two or more of these four types.

Today, marketing strategies are too dynamic and complex to permit salespeople to act merely in their self-interest, and managers need to actively guide the sales efforts. Once a sales manager understands the salesforce's role in the firm's marketing strategy, they can determine the kind of support (coaching, counseling, controlling, evaluating, and/or administrating) appropriate to this role and to the needs of the individual salesperson. Given a clear understanding of the firm's marketing strategy and expectations regarding the behavior of its salesforce, sales managers can influence performance favorably by designing a sales management system that employs a thoughtful combination of policies and practices.

REFERENCES

Pink, D. H. (2012). *To sell is human: The surprising truth about moving others*. Riverhead Books.

Ring, L., Newton, D., Borden Jr., N., & Farris, P. (1989). *Decisions in marketing: Cases and text*. Irwin.

Zabanga Marketing. (2021, July 9). *Setting the total promotion budget and mix*. https://www.zabanga.us/sales-promotion/setting-the-total-promotion-budget-and-mix.html

Executing a marketing strategy and implementing a marketing mix requires resources. The strategy and mix are, of course, expected to generate revenues that more than offset the associated expenditures, but they will nevertheless also necessitate investments. Therefore, a strategy and marketing mix plan must be translated into the projected revenues expected to result from those activities (sales forecasts) and specific expenses expected to be associated with the activities (budgets). Once those plans have been established, they should be translated into desired outcomes and measures of those outcomes (objectives and metrics). Whereas *goals* are the general, long-term desired conditions (often part of or implicit in corporate mission and visions), *objectives* are the more specific and desired results tied to specific time frames. While these two words are synonyms in the common English dictionary, they are typically used to denote this *general* versus *specific* distinction in the strategy literature.

MARKETING PLANNING AS AN ITERATIVE PROCESS

The relationships of strategy to marketing mix implementation, forecasts, budgets, and objectives underlie the Strategic Marketing Framework that organizes this book. The organization's missions, vision, and goals shape its strategies, which, in turn, shape general objectives that drive the development of the marketing mix (i.e., specific tactics, including products, prices, place or distribution, promotions and people). The marketing mix must be developed based on forecasts and supported with an appropriate budget. At the same time that the objectives shape the development of the marketing mix, they are themselves related to the mission, vision, goals, and to the strategy. This Note focuses on forecasting, budgeting, and establishing specific objectives and metrics for moving forward to effectively implement and to facilitate subsequent assessment and adjustment.

Planning the marketing mix, forecasting, budgeting and objective setting are *inseparable* and *iterative processes*. The iterative nature of these processes is important to emphasize. Effective planning will link specific activities and investments—for example, the commitment of 10 salespeople costing $1,000,000, or four quarterly coupon/price promotions at $1,000,000—to specific expected benefits or forecasted outcomes (e.g., a number of new retail accounts or a specific level of increased sales and new customers). That is, various activities and their associated costs should be linked to their forecast effects as closely as possible.

Such links between inputs and outputs may be based on assumption—certain assumptions are inevitable in developing forecasts—but they may also be based on observations of past effects and on marketing research. Then, marketing mix and budget decisions can be adjusted to *optimize* their forecasted effectiveness. Budget level and allocation questions can be posed and tested based on understandings of their forecasted impacts: *Is an investment in new salespeople worthwhile? Are 10 new salespeople more effective than four quarterly coupon promotions? Should we commit or request the resources to do both?* The resolution of those iterative, maximization analyses should be incorporated into resulting plans.

Thus, marketing mix development, forecasting, and budgeting are inextricably linked and should be done iteratively within pro forma analyses to develop and optimize investments and to arrive at effective objectives and metrics. The first step is to outline a preliminary marketing mix derived from strategic planning and forecasts, including an estimation of the costs for those marketing activities (a budget). That mix is then adjusted or optimized within pro forma models, including forecasts, budget implications, and resource constraints. Once an optimal mix is determined, forecasts and budgets can be finalized and a set of objectives established, as shown in Figure 33-1.

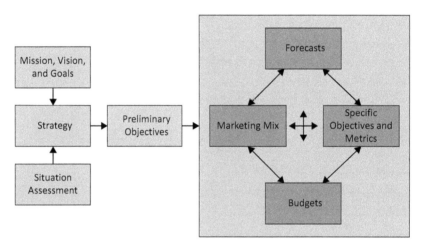

FIGURE 33-1   Planning the Marketing Mix, Forecasts, Budgets, and Objectives

FORECASTING

A sales forecast usually contains two parts: the *market forecast*, which estimates future sales for the entire market or industry, and the *sales forecast*, which estimates the sales and the market share of the particular company and its products. There are two ways to obtain those forecasts: primary research and secondary research. In primary research the firm develops its own forecast based on customer surveys, expert opinions, estimates of sales force, and the like. In secondary research, forecasts are acquired from specialized vendors (market research firms and industry experts) that regularly estimate sales trends in the industry. Companies use many methods to forecast sales: They can be based on customer data (e.g., assessment of buying intention), expert opinions (e.g., sales force estimates), or historical data (e.g., time-series analysis). Table 33-1 gives an overview of these sales forecasting methods with their strengths and weaknesses.

TABLE 33-1 Sales Forecast Methods

METHOD	DESCRIPTION	STRENGTH	WEAKNESS
1. Assessment of buyer's intentions	In a representative survey, customers are asked to indicate their intention to buy a specific product in the next period of time	• Works well for products for which purchases are planned in advance (e.g., industrial products, consumer durables) or for new products • Forecasts are directly derived from customers' buying intentions	• Requires representative and reliable market research • Can be costly and time consuming
2. Sales force estimates	Salespeople estimate the future sales they can make	• Sales people usually have important insights into their markets, competition etc. • Estimates available for individual sales territories • Easy to do	• Estimates might be biased as salespeople want to have the objectives set low enough
3. Expert opinions (such as "Delphi surveys" in which estimates are aggregated, sent back, refined in several iterative rounds)	Experts (e.g., dealers, distributors, trade associations, consultants) are asked to estimate future sales	• Utilizes "collective" wisdom of experts • Relatively easy and quick	• Can be costly • Difficult to find and motivate experts
4. Market tests	The company chooses representative markets (e.g., cities, regions) where the product is introduced with the full marketing plan (or variations to test the effect of single activities) and tests the market reaction	• Works well for new products • Effectiveness of marketing activities can be tested	• Expensive and time consuming • Competitors get to know your strategy
5. Time-series analysis and predictive analytics	Statistical methods (e.g., exponential smoothing, econometric models, data mining, predictive modeling, machine learning) are used to predict future sales from historical data	• Less subjective • Can use massive amounts of data and variables to uncover unknown correlations and make predictions	• Not suitable for innovations (no historical data) • Volume, variety, and velocity of big data pose challenges in data capture and storage • Accuracy depends on reliability and data comprehensiveness, skills in data analysis, and assumptions • Requires sophisticated statistical skills

Note. Table source: Piercy, N. F., Cravens, D. W., & Lane, N. (2010). Marketing out of the recession: Recovery is coming, but things will never be the same again. *The Marketing Review, 10*(1), 3–23.

Sales forecasts are an essential input to the formulation of marketing objectives and setting objectives, but objectives and budgets also impact forecasts. Without realistic assumptions about market size and trends, it is impossible to set realistic sales targets. The results of a sales forecast predict future sales given a specific marketing mix or effort. Forecasts usually begin by estimating how sales will evolve without changing the marketing mix or committing additional resources, or with a specific proposition about marketing mix effort based on strategic considerations. Subsequently, if sales forecasts are short of the strategic objectives, the manager will consider additional and new marketing initiatives and, therefore, revise the budget, which will in turn influence sales forecasts. Thus, forecasting, setting objectives, and budgeting are dynamic and iterative, rather than sequential activities.

It is also invaluable to develop, as specifically as possible, estimates of the effects of specific mix elements and allocated resources on sales. For example, historic data, managerial judgment, and/or marketing research can be used to develop an estimate of the relationship between advertising expenditures and sales, sales-force effort and sales, price promotions and sales, and the like. In this way, specific marketing mixes and expenditures (budgets) can be forecast onto future sales, revenues, and profits at a more detailed level. Such forecasts of return on marketing investments by marketing mix elements are not always possible and are not always precise, but these are the basis for modeling the effects of different marketing mix combinations and permutations and for thereby performing pro forma analyses to optimize the effectiveness of the marketing mix expenditures.

BUDGETING

As noted, forecasting results, establishing budgets, and setting marketing objectives go hand in hand; these activities make up the heart of the marketing plan. The marketing plan specifies what the objectives are and how they should be achieved and estimates the costs for each marketing task. The marketing budget depends on the strategies, the strategic objectives of the business unit and, unavoidably, on the financial constraints of the company. Basically, there are four ways to determine the marketing budget, including extrapolation, percentage of sales, target costing, and bottom-up budgeting.

1. *Extrapolation*: Building upon the previous year's budget as a base, those allocations are either increased or decreased by a certain amount or are left unchanged. This approach is problematic as it does not explicitly consider marketing objectives, changes in strategies, costs, or adjustments to the competition or evolving opportunities.
2. *Percentage of sales*: The marketing budget is determined as a percentage of the projected sales or profits. This is a simple method, but it reverses *cause* and *effect*. Sales are a result of marketing activities, not vice versa.
3. *Target costing*: The company determines the target sales volume and determines the target profit. The remaining resources—after profits are taken from projected sales—are the *de facto* marketing budget. This approach applies the *all-you-can-afford method* and, similar to the percentage of sales approach, it does not consider the causal relationship between the marketing budget and the target sales or profits.
4. *Bottom-up budgeting*: This approach derives the required marketing budget from the objectives of the business unit. The objectives determine all marketing activities that are needed, the costs for each, and the total marketing budget. The bottom-up approach requires breaking

down of all the specific expenses for the marketing department, including expenses of the sales force, market research, advertising, public relations, promotions, and marketing overhead. Bottom-up budgeting is the most effective but also the most complex. It highlights the need to integrate objective setting, to develop the marketing mix, and to establish the budget based on those drivers.

Costs for all marketing activities can be divided into direct marketing costs (e.g., promotions, discounts, folders), semi-fixed marketing costs (such as media advertising, public relations), and fixed marketing costs (including marketing department overhead, sales force management expenses, marketing research and the like). Once all tasks and activities are determined, the costs are estimated. Table 33-2 contains the marketing budget of a business unit, broken down to marketing budgets for the single segments and an estimation of segment profitability. Segment four produces a loss while all other segments are profitable. Overall, the business unit targets are met. Marketing budgets usually are established for 1 year. However, market developments should be monitored in shorter time intervals (e.g., on a monthly or quarterly basis), so that marketing managers can react if changes in a competitor's actions, changes in market demand, etc., require immediate action and a change in marketing plans.

TABLE 33-2 Sample Marketing Budget

BUSINESS UNIT 1: NET MARKETING CONTRIBUTION					
	SEGMENT 1	**SEGMENT 2**	**SEGMENT 3**	**SEGMENT 4**	**TOTAL**
Total market					
Volume (units)	480,000	1,300,000	250,000	860,000	2,890,000
Average unit price ($)	120	145	120	125	133
Dollar sales (millions)	57,600,000	188,500,000	30,000,000	107,500,000	383,600,000
Company Sales					
Average unit price ($)	125	138	118	126	130
Units sold	101,376	218,551	82,627	68,254	470,808
Market share (% units)	21.1	16.8	33.1	7.9	16.3
Sales revenue (millions)	12,672,000	30,160,000	9,750,000	8,600,000	61,182,000
Market share (% dollar sales)	22.0	16.0	32.5	8.0	15.9
Cost of Goods sold (millions)	8,236,800	19,604,000	6,337,500	5,590,000	39,768,300
Gross profit (millions)	4,435,200	10,556,000	3,412,500	3,010,000	21,413,700
Direct marketing costs					
Promotions	120,000	350,000	60,000	120,000	650,000
Discounts	60,000	160,000	35,000	50,000	305,000
Folders and mailing	40,000	110,000	20,000	50,000	220,000
Misc.	50,000	100,000	25,000	45,000	220,000

TABLE 33-2 Sample Marketing Budget (Continued)

BUSINESS UNIT 1: NET MARKETING CONTRIBUTION					
	SEGMENT 1	SEGMENT 2	SEGMENT 3	SEGMENT 4	TOTAL
Semi-fixed Marketing Costs					
Media advertising	450,000	1,200,000	200,000	400,000	2,250,000
POS	100,000	250,000	60,000	95,000	505,000
Public relations	20,000	50,000	10,000	20,000	100,000
Fixed marketing costs					
Marketing department	120,000	240,000	60,000	120,000	540,000
Salesforce	240,000	480,000	120,000	240,000	1,080,000
Market research	50,000	125,000	25,000	45,000	245,000
Misc.	10,000	30,000	5,000	10,000	55,000
Total marketing expenses	1,260,000	3,095,000	620,000	1,195,000	6,170,000
in % of sales sale revenue	9.94	10.26	6.36	13.90	10.08
Net Marketing Contribution	**3,175,200**	**7,461,000**	**2,792,500**	**1,815,000**	**15243,700**
Other operating expenses	2,150,000	6,900,000	1,450,000	1,900,000	12,400,000
Net profit (before taxes)	**1,025,200**	**561,000**	**1,342,500**	**−85,000**	**2,843,700**
Assets	11,200,000	19,800,000	5,200,000	10,900,000	47,100,000
Return on assets (%)	**9.15**	**2.83**	**25.82**	**−0.78**	**6.04**
Return on sales (%)	8.09	1.86	13.77	−0.99	4.65

OBJECTIVES

To be effective, objectives should be Specific, Measureable, Achievable, Relevant, and Time-specific, or "SMART." That is, the more specific, measurable, achievable, relevant, and time-specific an objective is, the better it guides action and investment, motivates the team, and facilitates assessment and adjustment. Vague objectives lead to confused and ineffective effort, discourage initiative, and complicate diagnosis and remedial action.

The marketing function must contribute to the overarching objectives of the business unit; the business unit in turn contributes to the overall vision and mission of the company. This hierarchy of goals is important because only marketing objectives that are consistent with the business unit strategy and the overall company mission and vision contribute to the long-term success of the firm. Well-managed companies translate visionary goals into long-term strategic objectives of the business units and then systematically derive objectives for the various business functions, including marketing, from those business unit objectives (see Figure 33-2).

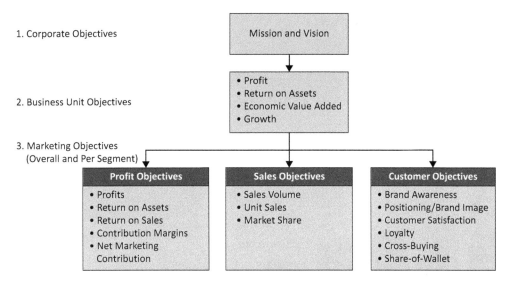

FIGURE 33-2   Hierarchy of Objectives

Three types of marketing objectives should be specified at the overall level and at the segment level (Lambin et al., 2012):

- profit objectives (e.g., profits, return on assets, return on sales, contribution margin, net marketing contribution);
- sales objectives (e.g., sales volume, unit sales, market share); and
- customer objectives (e.g., brand awareness, positioning, customer satisfaction, loyalty, cross-buying, share of wallet).

The marketing manager now must specify how the single market segments, or customers, contribute to the overall objective. This requires three basic steps:

1. Set profit objectives per segment.
2. Determine sales volume and market share needed to achieve that target profit.
3. Specify levels of brand awareness, brand image, purchase rates, customer satisfaction, and customer loyalty needed to achieve the target market share.

Staircase analysis is a useful framework for step number three, specifying levels of hierarchical customer "readiness." Staircase analysis estimates the hierarchical components that influence future sales volume (illustrated in Figure 33-3):

- market potential: the maximum of all customers who could possibly purchase in the product category
- actual market: the number of customers who actually buy the product category
- brand awareness: the percentage of customers of the actual market that are aware of the brand
- brand image: the percentage of customers that know the brand and also find it attractive

- purchase rate: the number of customers that actually bought the product
- share of wallet: the company's share of the customer's annual purchase volume
- repurchase rate: the number of customers who buy again
- cross-buying rate: the number of customers that buy more than one product category from a specific supplier

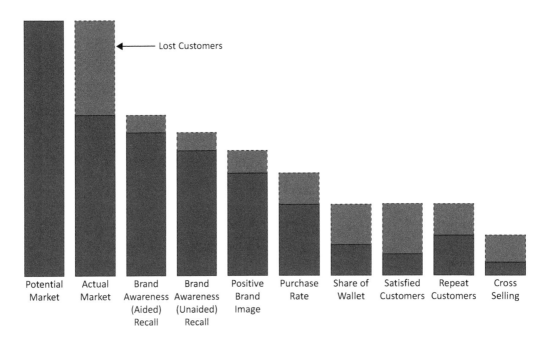

FIGURE 33-3   Staircase Analysis

Another systematic method for developing specific objectives is the Net Marketing Contribution (NMC) approach (Best, 2005). The NMC measures how marketing strategies contribute to the overall profits of a business unit and helps to identify the necessary marketing activities:

$$\textbf{NMC = Gross profit — marketing expenses}$$

$$\textbf{= [(unit volume · unit price) — Costs of goods sold] — marketing expenses}$$

The NMC can be further broken down to identify the universe of feasible strategies to increase profits (see Figure 33-4). Each cell in this tree represents an opportunity to increase overall profitability:

- Overall profitability can be increased by increasing net marketing contribution or decreasing operating expenses (expenses that do not vary with the marketing strategy, e.g., R&D, corporate overhead).
- Net marketing contribution can be increased by increasing sales volume or lowering cost of goods sold (COGS, i.e., total cost or producing a product that varies with the volume sold, e.g., materials, direct labor, transportation, manufacturing overhead based on usage of the

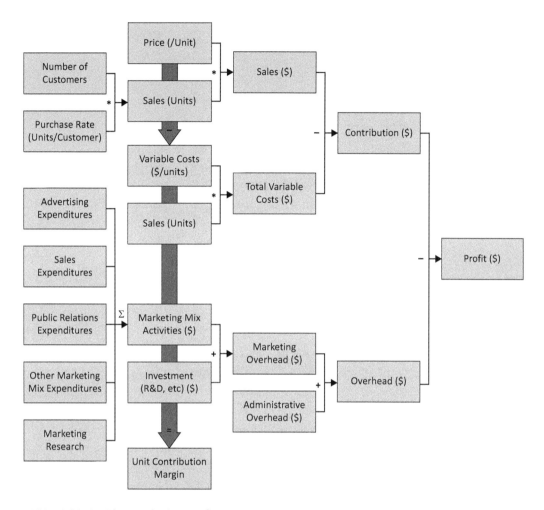

FIGURE 33-4 The Marketing Profit Tree

fixed manufacturing plant) or by increasing marketing efficiency (and as a consequence lowering marketing expenses).

- Sales volume can be increased by increasing market demand or market share.
- Market share can be increased by increasing the number of units sold or by increasing unit price.
- The number of units sold can be increased by increasing the number of customers or by increasing the average purchase volume.
- Average purchase volume can be increased by increasing the rate (frequency per period) or average individual purchase volume.
- The number of customers can be increased by acquiring new customers and keeping existing customers.
- New customers can be acquired as they leave competitors or as nonusers convert.
- The number of lost customers can be decreased by increasing loyalty, reducing customer switching to competitors, or preventing customers from becoming inactive.

Hence, for each cell, specific marketing objectives can be formulated. Keep in mind the importance of objectives being specific, measurable, achievable, relevant, and time-specific.

FINALIZING THE MARKETING MIX

Once specific objectives are formulated, the marketing mix can be finalized. Note that the process of creating a budget, making forecasts, and setting SMART marketing objectives *began* with an understanding of strategic business objectives and the establishment of a preliminary marketing mix. Initial forecasts were then based on that draft marketing mix and on an understanding of the effects of each tactic on resulting sales revenues and profits. With the budget, forecasts, and objectives refined and adjusted, a final marketing mix emerges. That final marketing mix, by the way, then solidifies the final budget, final forecasts, and specific objectives.

SUMMARY

The strategic marketing process ties situation analysis—including scrutiny of the organization's mission, vision, and goals—to strategy formulation, and that strategy drives the development and execution of a marketing mix. Diligent and effective strategic management requires that the implementation plan be linked with forecast results and detailed budgets, and then those plans, forecasts, and budgets be tied to specific and measurable objectives. These various deliverables—a detailed implementation plan, a set of related forecasts, an associated budget, and specific and measurable objectives—need to be generated through iterative and interconnected analyses that optimize the expected impact of the investments. Comparing realized results against objectives using the specific metrics, identifying gaps, and formulating improvement plans is the essence of assessment and adjustment; however, such assessment is simply impossible if SMART objectives were not derived from the marketing mix plan in advance.

REFERENCES

Best, R. (2005). *Market-based management: Strategies for growing customer value and profitability.*

Lambin, J.-J., Chumpitaz, R., & Schuiling, I. (2012). *Market-driven management* (3rd ed.). Macmillan Education.

Piercy, N. F., Cravens, D. W., & Lane, N. (2010). Marketing out of the recession: Recovery is coming, but things will never be the same again. *The Marketing Review, 10*(1), 3–23.

Appendix A: Basic Financial Math for Marketing

Developing a solid foundation in financial metrics and basic financial math is critical to effective marketing management. The ability to collect, analyze, and apply data, and to extract actionable insights from those analyses is fundamental to strategic thinking and tactical decision-making. This appendix will review concepts such as cost–volume–profit logic, breakeven analysis, the time value of money, and customer lifetime value to provide an understanding of important metrics that guide and support marketing decisions.

PART ONE: COST–VOLUME–PROFIT LOGIC

Certain fundamental relationships among prices, volume, and costs define the income statement and drive profitability. These relationships are logical—you can deduce them by thinking about the way a business works and the way its accounts are defined and relate to one another. In fact, understanding their interrelationships can illuminate important aspects of business plans and differentiate alternatives in strategic planning.

The basic definition of profit is that Profit = Revenue – Costs. Individuals not as familiar with financial metrics will often use the terms *profit* and *revenue* interchangeably. Of course, that is certainly not appropriate as marketers must consider costs as much as revenue when determining the most effective strategies and tactics. Understanding the drivers of both revenue and costs is a critical foundation for identifying opportunities to maximize profit.

Definition of Terms and Their Interrelationships

Total revenue: (R; the total amount of money taken in) equals average price ($\bar{P}$; the average amount received for each individual unit sold) multiplied by quantity sold (Q; the number of units sold):

$$R = \bar{P} * Q$$

"Selling prices" are generally stated for each level of distribution. So there may be a manufacturer's selling price, a distributor's selling price, and a retail selling price. In that respect, the selling prices may be viewed as codifying "outbound logistics" to channel members and customers.

For example, when Perdue Farms was considering whether to enter the chicken hot dog business, their analysts estimated they could sell 200,000 pounds of this product each week at a manufacturer's selling price of $0.75 per pound. This level of sales would have resulted in total revenue of 200,000*$0.75, or $150,000 per week (which, when multiplied by 52, equates to $7.8 million per year in total revenue). In that same example, the distributor's selling price was expected to be $0.80 per pound and the retail selling price was expected to be $1.23 per pound.

Total variable costs: (TVC; the cost of goods sold) equals variable costs per unit (VC/u; the cost of each unit sold) multiplied by quantity sold (Q):

$$TVC = VC/u * Q$$

Variable costs represent the costs of material and labor coming into the firm—its "inbound logistics" in its value chain. Variable costs are costs that vary with volume. To return to the previous example, Perdue Farms' analysts estimated that the variable costs per unit for chicken hot dogs would be $0.582 per pound (including processing and packaging), and $0.582 multiplied by 200,000 pounds per week would yield a total variable cost of $116,400 per week (or $6,052,800 per year).

Total costs: (C; the overall total paid out to operate the business which is often referred to as "total expenses") equal total variable costs (TVC) plus total fixed costs (FC or "overhead"; costs that don't vary with production or change across levels of sales):

$$C = TVC + FC$$

Fixed costs do not vary with volume. As more units are manufactured and sold, fixed costs remain the same. Fixed costs represent the value chain "operations" of the firm. In Perdue's case, total fixed costs related to the chicken hot dogs amounted to $1.2 million for marketing, $60,000 in salaried expenses, and $22,500 in depreciation, for a total of $1.2825 million in total fixed costs. Therefore, the total costs were equal to $6,052,800 (TVC) plus $1.285 million (FC), for a total of $7,335,300.

Profit: Total revenue (R; money in) minus total costs (C; money out) equals profit (π; the money the firm can keep):

$$R - C = \pi$$

In the Perdue example, the profit is therefore equal to $7.8 million (in total revenue) minus $7,337,800 (in total costs), for a final value of $462,200.

These relationships are fairly straightforward, and they make sense if we think about what goes into each variable or "account" and how revenue and costs are incurred. Despite its apparent simplicity, this cost–volume–profit logic (presented graphically in Figure A-1) and its application to marketing strategy can be extremely informative. In fact, cost–volume–profit logic facilitates sensitivity analysis and underlies breakeven analysis—two basic ways of evaluating investments, including capital outlays and marketing expenditures and alternatives.

As Figure A-1 illustrates, several of the basic components involved in cost–volume–profit logic (shown as nodes in the graphic) can be broken out even further. For example, as stated earlier, revenue equals average price times quantity sold (R = $\overline{P} * Q$), and quantity sold itself can be broken down to the number of customers (C) multiplied by the average purchase quantity (PQ):

$$Q = C * \overline{P}Q$$

This greater detail underscores two basic ways to grow sales: either attract more customers or sell more products per customer (increase use). For instance, in the aforementioned example, Perdue debated whether to market its chicken hot dogs to heavy users (who might consume as much as one pound per week) or to light users (who might only use one pound per month). Clearly, fewer heavy users would be needed to reach estimated revenue than if the target were light users.

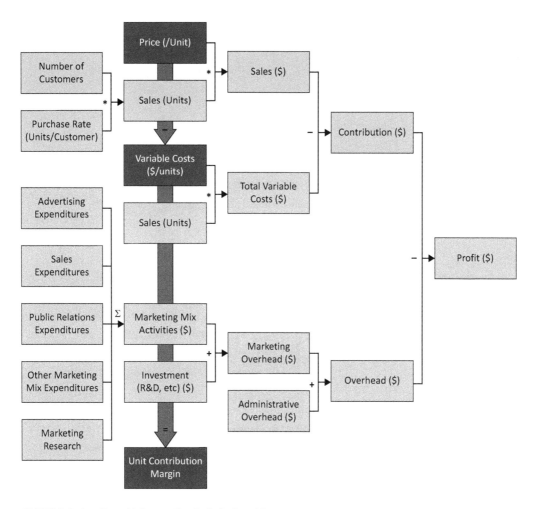

FIGURE A-1   Cost–Volume–Profit Relationships

It is useful here to think about the revenue per pound and per user as well as the total revenue that might be expected. In other words, there is valuable information in both aggregate and unit-level analyses. Figure A-1 shows both. At the aggregate level, unit-level price is multiplied times quantity sold and unit-level variable costs are also multiplied times quantity sold to arrive at sales (total revenue) and total variable costs. This allows for dynamic modeling. For example, if price changes, quantity sold changes. As a result, revenue and costs change in concert. Typically, as price is increased, quantity sold decreases In Perdue's case, one alternative possibility that was considered was to market to light users at a much higher price, say $0.90 per pound instead of $0.75. The company expected that at the higher price, demand would be much lower but that the higher price would compensate with increased revenue per pound sold.

It is also helpful to understand that unit-level revenue (price) minus variable costs per unit yields a value known as the "contribution margin"—or the contribution of each unit to covering overhead. Contribution margin per unit is a key measure; it almost always varies across the firm's assortment of products and product bundles, and it is invaluable information for understanding which products make more money and which make less and what roles each product plays within the overall assortment and strategy. In the Perdue example, the contribution was equal to the manufacturer's selling price ($0.75 per pound) minus the variable costs ($0.582 per pound) for a value of $0.168 per pound.

Cost Structures

Costs or expenses can be thought of as falling into two categories: variable and fixed. Variable costs are costs directly associated with a unit of product sold. For example, if a store sells a dress, it incurs the cost of that dress. If it does not sell the dress, the dress stays in inventory and the costs are not incurred (leaving out the cash flow implications of buying and storing the dress to have at the ready). However, salaries and rent are fixed costs—in other words they do not change with every unit sold—because the store had to have clerks available, as well as the store facility itself, whether or not a customer came in to buy the dress.

Of course, some costs are neither perfectly variable nor completely fixed; costs can also be mixed, semi-variable, step-function, and so forth. These variants are not hard to incorporate into cost–volume–profit thinking. For example, if the store can sell 20 dresses per clerk and it must schedule another clerk when sales are expected to exceed 20 (and yet another clerk on very busy days when sales will exceed 40, and so forth), then fixed costs become a step function.

Sensitivity Analyses

The relationships spelled out in the previous sections allow us to create dynamic models—models in which changes in one variable or assumption change the whole system—and also to perform sensitivity analyses. Sensitivity analyses are "what-if" analyses in which changes in specific variables are modeled out to determine their impact on other variables and, ultimately, their effects on profits. In this regard, it is worth noting that quantity sold (Q, or "Sales" in Figure A-1) appears twice in the model: both revenue ($R = \bar{P} * Q$) and total variable costs ($TVC = VC * Q$) are a function of Q. This makes sense because both revenue and costs are direct functions of the number of units that are sold. Also, in the real world, the quantity sold is typically related to price; in most cases (but not all), if the price is lowered, then the quantity sold will increase. Similarly, there is a relationship between another variable—one not expressly included in these models—and quantity sold. That variable is quality. In general, the higher the quality of a product (at a given price), the higher the quantity sold and, most likely, the higher the variable costs per unit.

Thus, these basic formulas allow us to perform "what-if" analyses. What if we lower the price (and keep quality constant) and assume sales increase by some certain percentage? What if we raise the quality 20% (and assume variable costs also go up exactly 20%), raise the price 10%, and assume sales increase 8% (after all, we're increasing quality by more than we're increasing price)? Of course, we often have good marketing research data regarding how much sales will increase or decrease given specific changes in price, quality, and marketing expenditures, but sometimes we must live with informed assumptions. If these assumptions are sensible and ranges of possible outcomes are considered (via sensitivity analyses), then the possible outcomes are likely well covered. Still, it is important to understand the interrelationships in cost–volume–profit thinking and to "surface" (i.e., state clearly) and test all related underlying assumptions.

Elasticity

Elasticity refers to responsiveness of demand. In other words, elasticity is a measure of changes in demand/sales due to changes in any marketer input, including things like advertising, sales effort, and so forth. In economics, the term "price elasticity of demand" relates the demand for a commodity, such as gasoline, to changes in the price of that commodity. Gasoline demand, for example, is not terribly elastic because consumption is partly discretionary, partly a function of long-term decisions (such as the length of one's commute), and partly tied to ongoing commercial activities that are not easily adjusted. In contrast, demand for wine is more elastic because a large portion of this demand is discretionary and, when price goes up, consumers can quickly adjust their wine consumption and find substitutes.

A firm often must make assumptions about or perform research to determine the elasticity of demand for its particular products (as compared to broad categories of commodities). There are also other change–effect relationships very similar to price elasticity that the marketing strategist will want to estimate or measure as well. For instance, how much do sales (demand) increase given a change in advertising? How much do sales drop given a cut in personal selling efforts? How much will demand fall if quality or service is pared back? In each of these cases, elasticity is defined by the general formula:

$$E = \frac{\Delta Q}{\Delta P} \text{ or } E = \frac{\Delta Q}{\Delta I},$$

where E is elasticity, Δ ("delta") is change, Q is quantity demanded, P is price, and I is the more general variable "input"—in other words, the input that the firm changes, whether it be the price, advertising, sales, quality, or something else. Drawing on basic algebra, this same equation can be reformulated by multiplying each side by ΔI:

$$\Delta Q = E \times \Delta I$$

Thus, if a firm has a series of observations about quantities sold at different levels of the input, it can estimate E by running regressions; here, E is simply the beta (β) for I regressed on Q.

Even if the strategic marketer is unfamiliar with the underlying math of regression, the logic of these relationships remains straightforward: How does Q change when some input I is changed? For example, in the chicken hot dog example, the question might be "How does the quantity purchased change as the price per pound of chicken hot dogs is either raised or lowered?" Estimating these relationships and understanding the effects of changes in the various components of the cost–volume–profit relationship is fundamental to sensitivity analysis.

Breakeven Analysis

Earlier in this appendix, we recognized a simple cost structure, distinguishing costs as purely variable costs and purely fixed costs. (Again, variable costs change with each unit sold, whereas fixed costs do not change across any level of sales.) Although costs can behave differently than these two simple classifications, use of these two categories allows us to determine the point in sales at which total revenue is equal to total costs (variable costs times quantity sold plus total fixed costs)—that is, the point at which the firm does not make a profit but also does not take a loss. This is also known as the breakeven point, and it can be calculated as follows:

$$R = C \ (\pi = 0)$$

We know that revenue equals average price times quantity sold, that total cost equals total variable costs (TVC) plus total fixed costs (FC), and that total variable costs equals variable costs per unit times quantity sold:

$$R = \bar{P} * Q$$

$$C = TVC + FC$$

$$TVC = VC/u * Q$$

Using basic algebraic principles, we can combine these equations as follows:

$$C = VC/u * Q + FC$$

Therefore, at breakeven, revenue is equal to total variable costs (TVC) plus total fixed costs (FC):

$$(\bar{P} * Q) = (VC/u * Q) + FC$$

and profit (π) is zero. We can solve this equation for Q (the breakeven quantity in units) by subtracting (VC/u * Q) from both sides and then dividing by (P – VC/u):

$$Q_{be} = \frac{FC}{(\bar{P} - VC/u)}$$

Figure A-2 shows breakeven graphically. Breakeven (in units) is an important sales level to determine. Strategic marketers want to understand breakeven because it represents the point at which capital investments (such as new plants or equipment) and program investments (such as advertising or research and development) are paid back without a profit, but without a loss either.

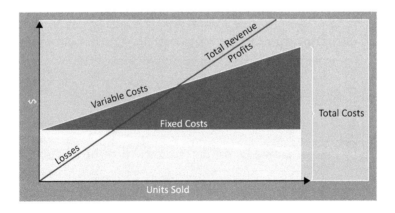

FIGURE A-2 Breakeven Analysis

Marketers will also want to know how changes in price affect payback. An increase in price will steepen the total revenue line because each incremental unit of sales brings in more. However, the price increase may also reduce the likelihood of achieving a given level of sales in units.

Margins and Markups

Above we defined a margin—in particular, the "contribution margin"—as the difference between the sales price per unit and the total variable costs per unit (CM = P – VC/u). In other words, the contribution margin is the difference between what a reseller, such as a retailer, pays for a product and the sales price (e.g., if a store sells a dress for $100 and its cost for the dress was $50, its contribution margin is $50). Still, it is worthwhile to clarify some particular uses of the term *margin* and to distinguish it from the term *markup*, if only because these terms are often confused and do have specific and different meanings.

A margin, as stated, is the difference between sales price and total variable costs. If margin is expressed as a percentage, it is always the difference divided by the total selling price. Remember, margin is *not* the difference divided by the costs. In comparison, markup is the amount over costs that a firm, usually an entity in the channel of distribution (such as a retailer), adds onto what they paid for a product to arrive at the selling price. Markup can be attributed to the value created by particular operations. Thus, the retailer's margin and its markup are the same amount of money in dollars *and* in percentage terms. Usually, markup is expressed as a percentage; it is the amount of profit divided by the selling price of the unit sold. This is often confusing because it seems logical that markup would be in the cost, as in the cost plus the markup. *It is not.* In retailing in particular, markup is always expressed as a percentage of selling price—and thereby related as a percentage of selling price. Because both markup on selling price and markup on cost are conventionally expressed as percentages, the result of using the wrong reference point (denominator) would be dramatic and would cause confusion.

Gross margins and changes in gross margin can be readily graphed in a two-dimensional space defined by average price and quantity sold because gross margin (the total contribution of sales toward fixed costs) is equal to average price ($\bar{P}$) multiplied by quantity sold (Q). Figure A-3 shows such a graph comparing gross margins for sales of a product with costs of $100, comparing sales at a price of $200 (where quantity sold is estimated to be 1,000) with sales at a price of $150 (in which case the contribution margin has been cut from $100 to $50 and quantity sold is estimated to be 1,500). The graph highlights the reality that, at the reduced price (and reduced contribution margin), the firm realizes increased sales in

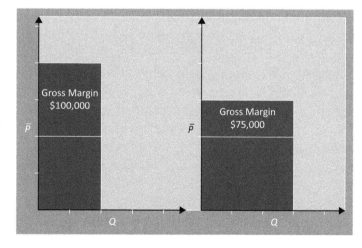

FIGURE A-3 Comparison of Gross Margins

units (from 1,000 to 1,500) and increased sales in dollars (from $200,000 to $225,000), but the gross contribution margin drops from $100,000 to $75,000.

Summary: Cost–Volume–Profit Logic

As illustrated in the preceding sections, cost–volume–profit logic—the relationships among revenue, costs, volume (sales), and profits—is fundamental to analyzing marketing programs, comparing alternatives, and formulating marketing strategies. This logic does not involve complicated math, but it usually involves making well-founded assumptions, surfacing those assumptions (i.e., articulating the assumptions and testing them against reality as far as possible), and relating known parameters, links, and plans to these fundamental business relationships. This process allows marketers to consider a wide variety of scenarios, such as how a drop or raise in price would affect sales. Or another scenario might explore the relationship between spending a particular amount on a marketing communications program. Having a solid, even intuitive, understanding of the logical relationships integrated in the cost–volume–profit framework is therefore an invaluable tool for analyzing alternatives and thinking strategically.

PART TWO: THE TIME VALUE OF MONEY

Money changes value across time—in fact, it is almost always true that any amount today will be worth more in the future. For example, if a business takes out a loan today for some amount of money, say $100,000, it must repay *more than $100,000* in the future. If the company were only going to pay back an identical amount ($100,000), there would be no incentive for the lender to make the loan. In fact, given the reality of inflation—the fact that things generally become more expensive across time—the lender would actually lose money if they loaned money today and only received that same amount back later. Because of these concerns, lenders must charge some additional interest rate (on top of inflation) that represents the *profit* on a loan. (After all, if a lender only charges the rate of inflation, it will still have no incentive to commit its money and take on the risks of the loan to get back essentially exactly what it lent). Thus, a loan's interest rate over and above inflation can be thought of as the "price" the lender charges for the loan.

As previously mentioned, money changes value across time, and, as a rule, it takes more money in the future ("future value") to equal a given amount of money today ("present value"). It is not difficult to understand the basic logic of this "time value of money" and to translate these ideas into simple formulas. In fact, these formulas are programmed into most spreadsheet applications and are easy to apply. The following sections explain the logic of the underlying algorithms because it is useful to understand this logic before applying the spreadsheet tools.

The Basic Logic and Formula

If a bank loans a company $100 today and the simple interest rate is 10%, then in one year, the repayment amount will be $110—that is, $100 today equals $110 in one year at 10% interest. In this situation, the present value (PV) is $100; the interest rate (i) is 10%; and the future value (C) is $110.

If we express this as an equation, the future value equals the present value itself plus interest (i.e., the present value multiplied times the interest rate):

$$C_1 = (PV_0 * 1) + (PV_0 * i)$$

Basic algebra (specifically the distributive property) allows us to reformulate this equation as follows:

$$C_1 = PV_0 * (1 + i)$$

It is similarly uncomplicated to work out a formula for present value—or the amount some future payment is worth today—by dividing each side of the future value equation by $(1 + i)$ (i.e., multiplying both sides by $\frac{1}{(1+i)}$) to arrive at the following:

$$PV_0 = \frac{C_1}{(1 + i)}$$

These straightforward formulas are for future value *after just one year* and for present value of an amount that will occur in *one year*. The subscript indicates the point in time or "period." Here, zero (0) is the present (zero periods have passed so far), so PV_0 is actually redundant, and C_1 indicates future value after one period.

Multiple Years

Of course, people are frequently interested in thinking about the value of money received in *more than one year*. What if we wanted to calculate the present value of money received in two years, for example? In this situation, we can use C_2 to denote the future value after two periods—here two years because we're defining each period as equal to one year in our analysis. (Note that such analyses can also be done with months as the unit of time.) Similarly, C_3 would denote a lapse of three periods; and so on.

We can figure out how much some amount today would be worth in *two* periods by remembering that if we invested an amount today in, say, a bank, we'd want to have the bank add the interest after one period—or "compound" our investment—and then compute the second-period interest using our original investment amount *plus* the amount we earned in period one. So if we invest $100 and the interest rate is 10%, after one year we have $110. Then, after the second year, we earn 10% on the entire $110 (not only on the original $100). Our total amount after both years can therefore be calculated using the following formula:

$$C_2 = [PV_0 \times (1 + i) \times 1] + [PV_0 \times (1 + i) \times i]$$

Here we're computing the end of the *first* year balance $(PV_0 * (1 + i))$ times one (which gives us the original amount back) and also multiplying the end-of-the-*first*-year balance times the interest rate (i) to get the increase in value. Again, we can use basic algebra to pull out the common term $PV_0 * (1 + i)$, which leaves $(1 + i)$ and we'd get $[PV_0 * (1 + i)] \times (1 + i)$ which equals $[PV_0 * (1 + i)^2]$. So:

$$C_2 = PV_0 * (1 + i)^2$$

and therefore:

$$PV_0 = \frac{C_2}{(1 + i)^2}$$

We can now create a general formula by recognizing that the key to compounding interest is simply multiplying by $(1 + i)$. Compounding across two periods was achieved by multiplying times $(1 + i)^2$; thus, compounding across three periods would be achieved by multiplying $(1 + i) \times (1 + i) \times (1 + i)$ or $(1 + i)^3$, and compounding across n periods would be achieved by multiplying times $(1 + i)^n$. So, the general forms of the relationship between present value and future value are:

$$C_n = PV_0 * (1 + i)^n$$

and:

$$PV_0 = \frac{C_n}{(1 + i)^n}$$

These equations use the subscript n to indicate some indeterminate number of periods, n, so C_n is the generic "future value after some number of periods n."

Annuities

Often in business and certainly in marketing, the manager is not just analyzing the present value of a single future amount received (or paid) in time period n. Instead, the issue is valuing some stream of revenue that recur across n periods of time—that is, the concern is for valuing a series of payments or profitable sales on a recurring basis. For example, banks make loans and expect to be paid back with a series of regularly recurring loan payments. Similarly, a marketer who wins a customer's loyalty—his or her repeated patronage across time—has a recurring stream of margins with some specific present value. These recurring streams of revenue are called annuities, and the present value of an annuity is referred to as the "net present value" (NPV), which is simply *the sum of the present values of each payment*. Thus, if a marketer knows that a customer will buy one unit every year for 3 years and the margin or profit on each sale is $10 at a 5% interest rate, the net present value of that 3-year annuity could be computed using the formulas above. In fact, the NPV is simply the sum of three present value computations:

$$NPV_0 = \frac{C_1}{(1 + i)^1} + \frac{C_2}{(1 + i)^2} + \frac{C_3}{(1 + i)^3}$$

which, in our example, yields the following:

$$NPV_0 = \frac{10}{(1+.05)} + \frac{10}{(1+.05)^2} + \frac{10}{(1+.05)^3} = \$27.23 \,(not \; \$30!).$$

Thus, the general formula for net present value is simply:

$$NPV_0 = \sum_1^T \frac{C_n}{(1+i)^n},$$

where sigma (Σ) denotes *sum* (add these terms all together) and the whole formula denotes "the sum of the values of this formula from $n = 1$ to $n = T$," with T representing the number of periods. It is now a bit clearer why we use C for what's been labeled "future value"—C denotes a future cash flow. It is important to remember that, if the period for analysis is *months* instead of years, then the interest rate (i) should be the annual interest rate divided by 12. Similarly, if you're using quarters, the interest rate is the annual interest rate divided by 4, and so on.

If an annuity is going to involve some initial investment—as annuities usually do—than an extension of this logic and formula is to include the initial investment as C_0 (value today), which is usually negative (i.e., it is a cost, not a revenue):

$$NPV_0 = -C_0 + \sum_1^T \frac{C_n}{(1+i)^n} \; or \; NPV_0 = \sum_1^T \frac{C_n}{(1+i)^n} - C_0$$

This calculation is because C_0 would normally be negative (i.e., an investment or cost, not an inflow of cash). For example, if the initial investment to achieve a 3-period annuity of $10 per period at 5% interest is $15, the formula would be:

$$NPV_0 = C_0 + \frac{C_1}{(1+i)^1} + \frac{C_2}{(1+i)^2} + \frac{C_3}{(1+i)^3}$$

and the calculation would be:

$$NPV_0 = \frac{10}{(1+.05)} + \frac{10}{(1+.05)^2} + \frac{10}{(1+.05)^3} - \$15$$

which equals $12.23.

Summary: Time Value of Money

The relationships above and the corresponding formulas are really all it takes to understand the logic and the underlying the concepts of future value, present value, and net present value (the present value of an annuity). This logic and these formulas are the very basis for thinking about "the time value of money." As stated previously, money changes value across time, and the time value of money is an essential concept in business—especially for marketers, who must think strategically about pricing, future prices and future costs, delayed payments (financing), and recurring streams of revenue, such as rents and customer lifetime value (CLV). Of course, the time value of money is also important when thinking about borrowing for cash flow and for capital budgeting tasks. This value is easily computed in any spreadsheet application, but it is still useful to understand the time value of money conceptually before running those computations.

PART THREE: CUSTOMER LIFETIME VALUE (CLV)

Decisions regarding how much to spend on retaining existing customers, how much to spend on customer acquisition, and how to balance and make trade-offs between those investments cannot be made strategically without a well-grounded and thorough understanding of *how much a customer is worth to the firm*. Similarly, targeting decisions—deciding which segments to focus on and which to ignore or avoid—are better made when they are informed by a sound estimation of the value of the customers in each segment. The value of the customer to the firm is not complicated, especially from a strategic thinking perspective, but it is also not as simple as it might appear at first.

What Is the Value of a Customer?

If a firm focuses on the sale of a single item on a single occasion, the *value* might be thought of as the dollar amount the customer purchases from the firm. For example, if a customer would have purchased an item (i) for $1,000, but a salesperson lost the customer due to a service failure of some sort, a manager might reprimand them, *"That was a thousand-dollar customer you lost for us!"* The manager would be basically correct because if a customer had purchased that single item for a thousand dollars, they would have generated $1,000 in gross sales revenue. In this simplistic and incomplete analysis, the formula for considering this narrow construct of customer value would be:

$$CV_i = Gross\ Sales\ Revenue_i$$

$$CV_i = R_i$$

However, that formula would still be incomplete, missing important considerations, and such an understanding would likely lead to flawed decision-making.

Consider Contribution Margin

With regard to customer value, the strategist should usually care less about gross sales and more about *gross margin*—the profit after the cost of goods sold and direct expenses. Every company has expenses associated with every sale. If the cost of goods sold for one unit of a product is $900, then the *contribution margin* from that sale of $1,000 is $100 (10%), as shown in Table A-1. Contribution margin is usually understood as the difference (or *margin between*) revenue and costs. Managers often focus on the contribution margin of one unit of a single product sold (contribution margin is also often considered as the percentage of sales revenue minus costs).

When the cost of goods sold is considered, the value of the customer in the example for that single transaction is $100 (10% of gross revenue). If gross sales were considered instead of contribution margin, some very profitable customers might be overlooked, while some marginally profitable or even unprofitable customers might be overvalued. So the manager might have been more correct to assert, "*That was a hundred dollars in margin you just lost for us!*"

TABLE A-1 Calculating Contribution Margin

Gross Sale	$1,000	100%
Cost of Goods Sold	$900	90%
Contribution Margin	$100	10%

$$CV_i = Contribution\ Margin_i$$

Or because contribution margin is sales revenue (R) minus costs (C):

$$CV = (R_i - C_i)$$

Consider Acquisition Costs

Another thing missing from the simplistic understanding of value as gross sales or even value as gross margin is that a certain amount of money and effort was spent on acquiring the customer. Subtracting the acquisition cost for a customer c is simple, at least arithmetically:

$$CV = (R_i - C_i) - AC$$

In this example, the contribution margin is for a single transaction of one unit of a single product (item i). That is consistent with the way many managers think about contribution margin for a single unit of a specific product or SKU. However, as a marketing strategist thinking about CLV, that is usually too narrow of an understanding of "the value of a customer". The value of a customer is better understood by aggregating all the unit-level margins associated with the customer; that is, as the sum of the margins across all of the items purchased by that customer. Every item in a shopping basket has a certain margin (price minus cost of goods sold and direct variable costs) and the margin in a customer's overall shopping basket is the total margin across all the items they purchase at that time.

Analyzing the whole shopping basket for the transaction is relatively simple. Customers are likely to purchase multiple items and/or several services at once, and a strategic marketer—even if they're focused on just the one occasion—would be wise to consider the overall margin in the shopping basket. For example, the customer who purchased one item worth $1,000 is likely to also purchase two or three other items. In the table below, the shopping basket recognizes the customer is "worth" $200 for just this single occasion because they purchased four items with total margin of $200, as shown in Table A-2. So, thinking about the whole shopping basket, the manager might have chastised the salesperson by noting, "*That was $200 in total margin you just lost for us.*"

TABLE A-2 Calculating Contribution Margin Across Multiple Products

	ITEM #1	ITEM #2	ITEM #3	ITEM #4	TOTAL
Gross Sale	$1,000	$250	$100	$650	$2,000
Cost of Goods Sold	$900	$225	$90	$585	$1,800
Contribution Margin	$100	$25	$10	$65	$200

At this point, the formula for customer value would be the sum of the margins for all items in the shopping basket (b) on one occasion:

$$CV = (R_b - C_b) - AC$$

Consider the Customer Lifetime

While including the gross margin on the whole shopping basket is a more complete analysis than focusing on just one item in the basket, it is not the *lifetime* value of the customer; it's just the value of that specific assortment or basket of goods on that single occasion. Thus, a strategic marketing manager should consider the *Customer Lifetime Value (CLV)*. That is, the more important strategic understanding of CLV would be the summed contribution margin not on a single transaction or visit but across the expected or forecasted lifetime of that customer's relationship with the company. Understanding CLV will guide strategic decisions about how much to invest in acquiring the customer and how much to spend retaining the customer—for example, in service recovery—and it will be more informative as a way to compare segments when making targeting decisions or establishing priorities across segments.

If the average customer purchases from the company for 8 years, for example, at a rate of once per year, then the CLV would not be the value of one transaction; it would be more complete and more strategic to consider all 8 years of transactions. That is, it is better to consider the complete relationship with the customer across time, not a single occasion or single transaction. A customer who purchases $2,000 of product once per year for 8 years might be thought of as being "worth" 8 X $200, or $1,600, as shown in Table A-3.

TABLE A-3 Calculating Customer Lifetime Value

	YEAR 1	YEAR 2	YEAR 3	YEAR 4	YEAR 5	YEAR 6	YEAR 7	YEAR 8
Gross Sales	$2,000	$2,000	$2,000	$2,000	$2,000	$2,000	$2,000	$2,000
Costs of Goods Sold	$1,800	$1,800	$1,800	$1,800	$1,800	$1,800	$1,800	$1,800
Contribution Margin	$200	$200	$200	$200	$200	$200	$200	$200
Cumulative "Value"	$200	$400	$600	$800	$1,000	$1,200	$1,400	$1,600

So if the manager understands the stream of revenue and the stream of contribution margins the customer represents, they would tell the salesperson, "*You just lost us $1,600 in total contribution margin—money to the bottom line we'd have gotten over the lifetime of that customer's relationship with our firm—when you lost us that customer.*" That is, in this CLV equation, if the customer's lifetime with the firm is considered, it would be the sum of all the margins across all the transactions with the customer *c* across the lifetime of that customer's relationship with the firm (N periods) minus the acquisition costs (A).

$$CLV = \sum_{n=0}^{N} (R_t - C_t) - AC$$

Decay

In reality, if the average customer does business with the firm for 8 years, some of those customers will do business with the firm for 1 year, others will remain with the firm for 20 years. A few customers will, in fact, stay with the firm for exactly 8 years, but only a few. That observation may complicate the analyses, but it also offers more accurate and more granular understanding of customer behavior and the strategic implications of that behavior.

It is not so difficult to model this decay phenomenon. If, for example, 7.5% of customers defect every year (the rate of defection is termed the "churn rate"), it turns out the average tenure of a customer with the firm is almost exactly 8 years; however, it obviously does not mean that 100% of the customers stay 8 years and then, all at once, defect to other brands or leave the market. Customers leave across time.

Regardless of how good the firm is or how wonderful its products and services are, some percentage of customers will defect in year one. If that defection or *churn rate* is 7.5%, then the inverse, the *retention rate*, is 92.5%. The retention rate is logically and computationally the inverse of the defection rate. If the firm started the year with 1,000 customers, the firm will lose 75 customers and have 925 customers at the end of the first year. The next year, 7.5% of the customers will leave again (if the 7.5% estimation is correct across the range of customers' time with the brand). Thus, 7.5% of the remaining 925 customers equates to a loss of approximately 69 customers, as shown in Table A-4.

After year eight, half of the customers have stopped doing business with the firm, but half still remain. Depending on the relevant time horizon adopted for the analysis, it is possible to estimate that some customers will remain with the brand after 20 years (in fact, if the annual defection rate is a constant 7.5%, more than 200 customers will remain after 20 years). Graphically, this exponential decay function looks like a flattening negative curve, as shown in Figure A-4.

Adding the decay function to the formula for CLV, our formula for Customer Lifetime Value is finally complete. It considers margin, not gross sales, it considers the whole shopping basket of products or services the customer purchases from the firm, it considers the time value of money, and it considers a constant rate (not amount) of decay across the customer lifetime.

$$CLV = \sum_{n=0}^{N} ((R_n - C_n) * r_n) - AC$$

TABLE A-4 Calculating Total Contribution Margin of Customers Across 20 Years

YEAR	NUMBER STARTING THE PERIOD	TOTAL CONTRIBUTION MARGIN ($200)	NUMBER DEFECTED THIS PERIOD	NUMBER REMAINING
1	1,000	$200,000	75	925
2	925	$185,000	69	856
3	856	$171,200	64	792
4	791	$158,200	59	732
5	732	$146,400	55	677
6	677	$135,400	51	626
7	626	$125,200	47	579
8	579	$115,800	43	536
9	536	$107,200	40	496
10	496	$99,200	37	459
11	459	$91,800	34	425
12	424	$84,800	32	392
13	392	$78,400	29	363
14	363	$72,600	27	336
15	336	$67,200	25	311
16	311	$62,208	23	287
17	287	$57,400	22	265
18	266	$53,142	20	246
19	246	$49,200	18	228
20	228	$45,400	17	210

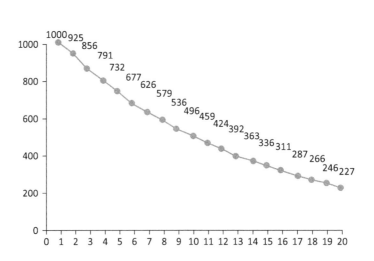

FIGURE A-4   7.5% Decay of 1,000 Initial Customers Across 20 Years

CLV and the Time Value of Money

Even after adding in these logical considerations—margin instead of revenue, the cost of customer acquisition, the entire market basket purchased, the lifetime of the customer, and the decay or churn rate of customers—summing the simple stream of revenue and stream of contribution margins for the customer ignores *the time-value of money*. Money is more or less valuable based on time and on when it is to be received or paid. Revenue is worth more now than if it is a future revenue. In the example developed here, the $200 that will be earned in year eight is not worth $200 today—it needs to be discounted to a net present value (NPV). Future revenue should be discounted at prevailing interest rates or *discount rate*.

In the example, if the customer's purchase behavior is expected to be constant across the years, rather than discount each year's contribution margin from a particular customer, as developed above in this Appendix, the manager can compute the NPV of the stream of revenue—$200 per year for 8 years. If prevailing interest rates and inflation dictate a discount rate of 5%, that stream of $2,000 from sales, each carrying a $200 margin, is worth $1,292 today, as shown in Table A-5.

TABLE A-5 Calculating Net Present Value

	YEAR 1	YEAR 2	YEAR 3	YEAR 4	YEAR 5	YEAR 6	YEAR 7	YEAR 8
Gross Sales	$2,000	$2,000	$2,000	$2,000	$2,000	$2,000	$2,000	$2,000
Costs of Goods Sold	$1,800	$1,800	$1,800	$1,800	$1,800	$1,800	$1,800	$1,800
Contribution Margin	$200	$200	$200	$200	$200	$200	$200	$200
NPV	$1,292							

As developed above, a future stream of revenue is adjusted for the time value of money by dividing by $(1 + d)$ where d is the discount rate and n is the period. Summing across all periods N computes the net present value, NPV, of the stream of revenue across the lifetime. Therefore, the formula developed for the lifetime stream of revenue minus costs adjusted for the retention rate r, that is the summation of the gross margin for the customer's market basket discounted by the retention rate, is the future stream of contributions to the firm. Then that term can be divided by $(1 + d)^n$ to compute the current value of that contribution—the net present value—and summing those is the positive portion of the equation. Then integrating the acquisition costs, AC, complete the formula and the logic for Customer Lifetime Value:

$$CLV = \sum_{n=0}^{N} \frac{((R_n - C_n) * r_n)}{(1+d)^n} - AC$$

Where:
CLV = Customer Lifetime Value
N = the number of periods
R = Revenue
C = Costs

r = Retention rate (the inverse of decay or churn)

d = Discount rate

AC = Acquisition Costs

This is the complete formula for Customer Lifetime Value!

Summary: Customer Lifetime Value

Customer Lifetime Value (CLV) is the net present value (NPV) of a stream of recurring margins (not gross sales revenue) on all products purchased across the expected lifetime of the customer. That expected lifetime of a customer is best modeled by including a retention rate, which is in effect the number of customers who remain from period to period (the inverse of the decay or churn rate). This computed NPV of a stream of margins then needs to be reduced by the acquisition costs, the money spent to initially acquire the customer, and discounted by a discount rate that reflects the time value of money. Understanding CLV is essential to making strategic decisions about budgets for customer acquisition, retention, and targeting. The use of CLV enhances the marketing manager's knowledge of the firm's or brand's relationship with its customers and ultimately leads to better informed decisions.

Appendix B: Building a Strategic Marketing Plan Exercise

A major objective of this book is to provide you with the process, concepts, and tools needed to develop a strategic marketing plan. All strategic marketing plans are fundamentally similar, varying in the degree of specificity required as a function of the planner's predilections and corporate policy. What follows in this Appendix is a set of worksheets that will assist you in developing a strategic marketing plan for a specific product or market. The worksheets provide an overview of planning considerations and tentative decisions for a particular line of business.

There is no expectation that you will have all of the specific data and information necessary to make your planning precise. You may have to make estimates and judgments. However, this exercise will reveal the areas in which you need particular kinds of data or information. For example, you may be able to give only nominal estimates of your competitive advantages here (using a plus or minus to indicate whether you are in a better or worse position than specific competitors), but you could gather more precise ordinal data via marketing research in your actual planning process.

STRATEGIC MARKETING PLAN FOUNDATION

All strategic marketing plans pose and answer three fundamental questions: (a) Where are we now? (b) Where do we want to go? (c) How do we get there? In fact, these three questions form the basic structure of this exercise. You could use the worksheets to help prepare a strategic marketing plan for any business unit, line of business, product, or market.

A. Situation Assessment: Where Are We Now?

The exercise begins by asking you to consider the question "Where are we now?" This exercise is called the "Situation Assessment." **Worksheet A-1** asks you to provide a business definition describing the business in which your company wants to be involved. You should refer to the particular line of business here, not the company as a total organization. Your business definition should be specific; it is not enough to simply say the company will "provide solutions." You must specify the kinds of solutions it will provide to different types of people or organizations and the ways in which these will differ from the competition.

Next, you will provide a market profile with **Worksheet A-2**. This profile must assess the overall market and define it in terms of the relevant or served market. For example, at the broadest level, Federal Express serves the "rush" market with its overnight delivery services. However, the more precise market that Federal Express wishes to serve is the time- and reliability-sensitive market for small packages (under 70 pounds) and documents.

In the market profile, it is important to *estimate* market size, share, and growth and give an indication of the life cycle stage for the product market. You should also designate your company's largest competitor and its share relative to that competitor.

Worksheet A-3 requires you to segment the overall market that you have identified. This is often the most time-consuming task in the exercise, but it is a critical one. The worksheet includes some basic instructions to refresh your memory about approaches to market segmentation and gets you started by asking you to list specific differences across the total market.

You will then assess differences in the benefits sought by each market segment with **Worksheet A-4**. If there are no differences, then your segmentation approach is flawed. On the other hand, all segments may benefit the most from a single attribute but vary in terms of the other attributes. The cell entries on the worksheet are rank orders of the benefits for each segment.

Worksheet A-5 continues the "Where are we now?" exercise by asking you to describe buyer behavior and determine what the decision-making process is for each segment. It may be similar across segments, but you should still examine the decision-making unit (DMU) and the decision-making process (DMP). In many products or markets, the chooser (i.e., the person or persons responsible for the decision to buy from you versus another vendor) may be different from the user (i.e., the individual who will actually use or consume your services). It is sufficient to indicate job titles to characterize the DMUs. You may wish to characterize the DMP in terms of time (long or short term), complexity, or qualitative factors (routine or modified rebuy, new task, political, performance, etc.).

Worksheet A-6 asks you to assess the individual market segments that you have identified and define them in terms of the relevant market. This is similar to the process in Worksheet A-2, and it may be helpful for you to refer to the information about the total served market in that worksheet and break it down by market segment.

Next, you will develop an overview of the environment in **Worksheet A-7** based on three analyses:

- Market trends: What are the crucial current and potential trends in the overall market?
- Competitive trends: What are the crucial elements of competitors' strategies and where are they heading?
- Segment/customer trends: What crucial trends best describe segment and customer trends that affect your marketing planning in the product or market?

Worksheet A-8 asks you to provide a relative assessment of how your company stacks up against its major competitors. First, you will list the competitors in the product or market. Then, for each competitor, you will indicate with pluses and minuses whether your company is better (+) or worse (-) on each benefit (from **Worksheet A-4**) and give brief examples when possible. Note that specific, ordinal data could be gathered to provide a more precise determination of your relative ranking on each benefit.

Worksheet A-9 continues the assessment of your company versus its competitors by asking for your overall judgment about the company's relative strength against each competitor in the market segments in which you compete. You will use pluses and minuses in your assessment again, and your judgments may heavily reflect those made in Worksheet A-8. Once again, give brief examples to illustrate your points when possible. Note that market research could be used to more precisely describe the nature and extent of your relative position in this grid.

Worksheet A-10 continues the situation assessment by asking you to construct one or more perceptual maps and indicate your company's relative position on each map versus competitors. Each map is, in effect, a cross section of a customer's mindset and should reflect how customers perceive the company relative to the competition. This will require you to choose dimensions. For example, individual customers may perceive various competitive options in terms of size (so the dimension might be "large to small") and in terms of focus (so the other dimension might be "general purpose to specialized purpose"). You may have multiple perceptual maps for each segment if you have many significant dimensions or characteristics.

Worksheet A-11 completes the situation assessment with a SWOT (Strengths, Weaknesses, Opportunities, and Threats) analysis by segment and for the overall market. To a large extent, this exercise will provide a quick summary of the analyses you have completed to this point.

Worksheet A-12 extends the situation assessment to portfolio analysis and establishes a transition from "Where are we now?" to "Where do we want to go?" This worksheet consists of five pages:

1. Market Attractiveness/Competitive Position Portfolio Model Development Process (this page lists the steps involved in the process).
2. Market Attractiveness/Competitive Position Criteria Examples (this page lists ideas for increasing the attractiveness and strength of your company).
3. Market Attractiveness/Competitive Position Model Input Criteria Evaluation Development (this page asks you to establish which of the criteria from page 2 you will use to improve the market attractiveness and competitive position of your company and to complete steps 2 and 3 from page 1).
4. Market Attractiveness/Competitive Position Graph (this page asks you to determine the relative position of strategies for improving market attractiveness and competitive position and to complete steps 4 and 5 from page 1).
5. Market Attractiveness/Competitive Position Graph Prescriptions (this page provides an example of strategies and their likely positions in each of the nine portfolio matrix boxes).

B. Proposed Strategy: Where Do We Want to Go?

Once you have fully assessed your company's market and position in the market, you are ready to propose a strategy (**Worksheet B-1**). The term "strategy" refers to your company's overall plan of action. It should be distinguished from "tactics," which are expedients for carrying out strategies, and "objectives," which are near-term, measurable, desired end results. Objectives may be qualitative (e.g., increases in customer satisfaction), but they should always be measurable (e.g., a 20% increase in satisfaction measures).

Typically, marketing strategies involve detailed plans regarding products and services and/or markets. As discussed previously in this book, strategies designed to exploit current markets with current products or services are market penetration strategies; plans to develop new markets or focus on particular markets are market development or market segmentation strategies. Other examples of strategies include new product or product development strategies as well as diversification strategies, which involve simultaneous moves into new markets with new products or services.

Still other marketing strategies include market dominance, low cost, product differentiation, and control of supply or distribution. There are many other strategies too, and it is up to you to rationalize the strategy you choose based on the situation assessment to this point. The fourth and fifth pages of Worksheet A-12 should be very helpful in determining your company's strategy.

Once you have clearly stated your company's strategy, the next step is to make it more explicit by specifying objectives (also on Worksheet B-1). As discussed earlier, these are near-term (usually one year), measurable, desired end results, usually expressed in terms of market share, financial measures, and/or additional, qualitative measures. Note that strategies precede objectives here. Some individuals might believe that objectives should be set first and strategies then specified to achieve those objectives. This approach is perfectly acceptable—strategies and objectives are derived hand in hand in strategic market planning.

Finally, you will assess risks on **Worksheet B-2**. To do this, you must ask yourself what types of things might happen that would jeopardize the strategy and threaten your company's ability to achieve its objectives.

C. Marketing Tactics: How Do We Get There?

After your company's strategy is set, you must turn your attention to specifying the marketing tactics your company will use to carry out its strategy and achieve its objectives in the context of the situation. **Worksheet C-1** asks you to consider and describe what will be required in terms of the marketing mix and internal operations support. Note that internal operations support refers to "what will be done, when, and by whom," and the other elements parallel what we have described as the marketing mix.

The financial consequences described in **Worksheet C-2** require you to give preliminary thought to the costs of your company's marketing tactics by segment. Again, precision is not expected here, but you should have an idea of costs, margins, and expenses that will enable you to give reasonable estimates that describe your expectations.

GETTING STARTED

Remember, this is an exercise designed to get you started with building a strategic marketing plan. By the time you have completed all of the worksheets, you will have used many of the major concepts and tools from this book and applied them to a specific business. This exercise should also help you understand the kinds of information required for sound strategic marketing planning and get you started on your way toward completing a preliminary strategic marketing plan. You may be somewhat uncomfortable making estimates instead of using actual data; however, you will learn where in the process you need precise data, what kinds of data would be most helpful, and how these data are used in decision-making related to strategic marketing.

STRATEGIC MARKETING PLAN

BUSINESS DEFINITION (PRODUCT, LINE OF BUSINESS, INDUSTRY SEGMENT)

STRATEGIC MARKETING PLAN

TOTAL MARKET PROFILE

a. Size (Units and/or $)

b. Share:

   i. Now:

   ii. In Three Years:

c. Growth

   Trend

   APGR, 3 years

d. Life Cycle Stage

e. Largest Competitor

   Your Company's Relative Share

STRATEGIC MARKETING PLAN

SEGMENTING THE MARKET

Now that you have described the total relevant or "served" market, your task is to subdivide the market into the most appropriate and useful segments. This is a difficult task and demands careful analysis from all team members. You should start by listing the areas of differences across the total market. For example, the market may vary by size of firms, nature of business, decision-making units, decision criteria, and so on. Next, you should evaluate these market differences by the criteria for segmentation, including the following:

- Are the segments reachable, differentially responsive to some element(s) of the marketing mix, and likely to be profitable given different costs that may be associated with starting each of them with different mixes?

....

....

- Are the segments reasonably exclusive, yet mutually exhaustive? Are excluded segments ones that your company is just as happy to walk away from?

....

....

....

....

....

- Which segmentation approach presents the greatest "product–company–market fit?" In other words, which approach makes the most sense in terms of how your company is set up now, how well established it is (compared to its competitors) in each segment, and what barriers to competitive entry are in each segmentation approach?

....

....

- Which segmentation approach fits with your company's LOB mission, goals, and resources? For example, you might define segments that your company has not traditionally served but may choose to serve given their growth potential, possibilities for add-on business later, fit with other corporate business, etc.

. . . .

. . . .

. . . .

. . . .

. . . .

Try sequential segmentation: start with broad industry descriptors, proceed through company characteristics, and try uncovering some differences due to desired benefits of needs. The result may well be a multidimensional segmentation. Note that you will complete **Worksheets A-4** through **A-6** using your segmentation approach. You might look at these forms now to help you get started.

STRATEGIC MARKETING PLAN

WORKSHEET A-4

CUSTOMER BENEFITS SOUGHT (rank the order of benefits *for each segment*)	SEGMENT A	SEGMENT B	SEGMENT C	SEGMENT D	SEGMENT E

STRATEGIC MARKETING PLAN

ANALYSIS OF DECISION MAKERS IN EACH SEGMENT

	SEGMENT A	SEGMENT B	SEGMENT C	SEGMENT D	SEGMENT E
Decision-Making Unit (DMU) (Buyers, Influencers)					
Decision-Making Process (DMP)					

STRATEGIC MARKETING PLAN

	TOTAL	SEGMENT A	SEGMENT B	SEGMENT C	SEGMENT D	SEGMENT E
Size (Units and/or $)						
Share Now Sought in Three Years						
Growth Trend APGR, 3 years						
Life Cycle Stage						
Largest Competitor Today/Future Your Relative Share						

ENVIRONMENT: OUR RELATIVE POSITION VIS-À-VIS MARKETS, COMPETITORS, SEGMENTS, AND CUSTOMERS

- Market Trends

....
....
....

- Competitive Trends

....
....

- Segment/Customer Trends

....
....
....

COMPETITIVE ANALYSIS

MAJOR COMPETITORS	MAJOR BENEFITS				
	BENEFIT 1	BENEFIT 2	BENEFIT 3	BENEFIT 4	BENEFIT 5

WORKSHEET A-9

STRATEGIC MARKETING PLAN

STRENGTH OF COMPETITORS BY SEGMENT (+ WE ARE BETTER THAN COMPETITORS; – WE ARE WORSE THAN COMPETITORS)

MAJOR COMPETITOR	SEGMENT A	SEGMENT B	SEGMENT C	SEGMENT D	SEGMENT E

WORKSHEET A-10

STRATEGIC MARKETING PLAN

COMPETITIVE POSITIONING (AXIS RELATES TO BENEFITS VALUED BY SEGMENT)

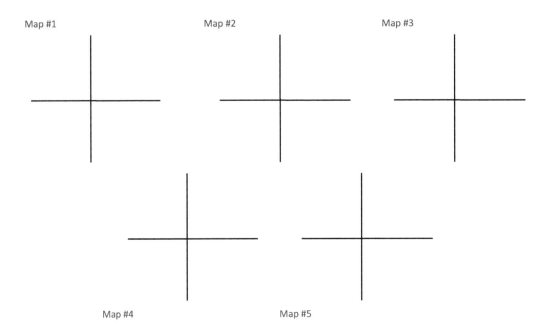

Map #1

Map #2

Map #3

Map #4

Map #5

STRATEGIC MARKETING PLAN

SWOT ANALYSIS: STRENGTHS, WEAKNESSES, OPPORTUNITIES, THREATS

	STRENGTHS	WEAKNESSES	OPPORTUNITIES	THREATS
Segment A				
Segment B				
Segment C				
Segment D				
Segment E				

STRATEGIC MARKETING PLAN

MARKET ATTRACTIVENESS/COMPETITIVE POSITION PORTFOLIO

Model Development Process

STEP 1 Establish the level and units of analysis (business units, segments, or product markets).

. . . .

. . . .

. . . .

. . . .

STEP 2   Identify the factors underlying the market attractiveness and competitive position dimensions.

. . . .

. . . .

. . . .

. . . .

STEP 3   Assign weights to factors to reflect their relative importance.

. . . .

. . . .

. . . .

. . . .

STEP 4   Assess the *current* position of each business or product on each factor, and aggregate the factor judgments into an overall score reflecting the position on the two classification dimensions.

. . . .

. . . .

. . . .

. . . .

STEP 5   Project the future position of each unit, based on forecasts of environmental trends and a continuation of the present strategy.

. . . .

. . . .

. . . .

. . . .

STEP 6   Explore possible changes in the position of each of the units and the implications of these changes for strategies and resource requirements.

. . . .

. . . .

. . . .

. . . .

MARKET ATTRACTIVENESS/COMPETITIVE POSITION CRITERIA

Examples

ATTRACTIVENESS OF YOUR BUSINESS	STRENGTH OF YOUR COMPETITIVE POSITION
A. MARKET FACTORS • Size (Dollars, Units) • Size of Product Market • Market Growth Rate • Stage in Life Cycle • Diversity of Market (Potential for Differentiation) • Price Elasticity • Bargaining Power of Customers • Cyclicality/Seasonality of Demand **B. ECONOMIC AND TECHNOLOGICAL FACTORS** • Investment Intensity • Nature of Investment (Facilities, Working Capital, Leases) • Ability to Pass Through Effects of Inflation • Industry Capacity • Level and Maturity of Technology Utilization • Barriers to Entry/Exit • Access to Raw Materials **C. COMPETITIVE FACTORS** • Types of Competitors • Structure of Competition • Substitution Threats • Perceived Differentiation Among Competitors **D. ENVIRONMENTAL FACTORS** • Regulatory Climate • Degree of Social Acceptance • Human Factors Such as Unionization	**A. MARKET POSITION** • Relative Share of Market • Rate of Change of Share • Variability of Share Across Segments • Perceived Differentiation of Quality, Price and Service • Breadth of Product • Company Image **B. ECONOMIC AND TECHNOLOGICAL POSITION** • Relative Cost Position • Capacity Utilization • Technological Position • Patented Technology, Product or Process **C. CAPABILITIES** • Management Strength and Depth • Marketing Strength • Distribution System • Labor Relations • Relationships with Regulators

MARKET ATTRACTIVENESS/COMPETITIVE POSITION MODEL

Input Criteria Evaluation Development

MARKET ATTRACTIVENESS	X AXIS	CRITERIA	HIGH	MEDIUM	LOW
		Opportunity Size			
		Opportunity Growth			

POSITIONS CAPABILITIES	Y AXIS	CRITERIA	HIGH	MEDIUM	LOW
		Skills To Support Segment			

STRATEGIC MARKETING PLAN

MARKET ATTRACTIVENESS/COMPETITIVE POSITION GRAPH

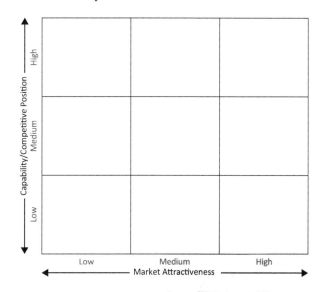

PRESCRIPTIONS

Protect & Refocus	**Build Selectively**	**Reinforce**
• Manage for Current Earnings • Concentrate on Attractive Segments • Defend Strengths	• Invest Heavily in Most Attractive Segments • Build up Ability to Counter Competition • Emphasize Profitability by Raising Productivity	• Invest to Grow at Maximum Digestible Rate • Concentrate Effort on Maintaining Strength
Preserve Cash Flow	**Manage for Earnings**	**Invest to Build**
• Protect Position in Most Profitable Segment • Upgrade Product Line • Minimize Investment	• Protect Existing Program • Concentrate Investments in Segments where Profitability is Good and Risk is Relatively Low	• Challenge for Leadership • Build Selectively on Strengths • Reinforce Vulnerable Areas
Divest	**Limited Expansion or Harvest**	**Exploit Industry Attractiveness**
• Sell at time that will Maximize Cash Value • Cut Fixed Costs and Avoid Investment Meanwhile	• Look for Ways to Expand without High Risk; Otherwise Minimize Investment and Rationalize Operations	• Specialize Around Limited Strengths • Seek Ways to Overcome Weaknessess • Withdraw if Indication of Sustainable Growth are Lacking

Capability/Competitive Position: High / Medium / Low

Market Attractiveness: Low / Medium / High

STRATEGIC MARKETING PLAN

1. **Strategic Statement (overall and/or by segment):** "Strategy" refers to the overall plan of action, e.g., penetration, segmentation, new products, diversification defense, flanker, etc. "Tactics," to be specified later, refers to near-term specific actions or maneuvers that you will employ to carry out your strategy.

. . . .

. . . .

2. **Objectives (overall and/or by segment):** "Objectives" are near-term, measurable, desired end results; they may be qualitative, but some objectives must be quantitative.

. . . .

. . . .

STRATEGIC MARKETING PLAN

RISK ANALYSIS

EVENT OR ASSUMPTION	LIKELIHOOD OF OCCURRENCE	POSSIBLE IMPACT	CONTINGENCY PLAN

RISK ASSESSMENT

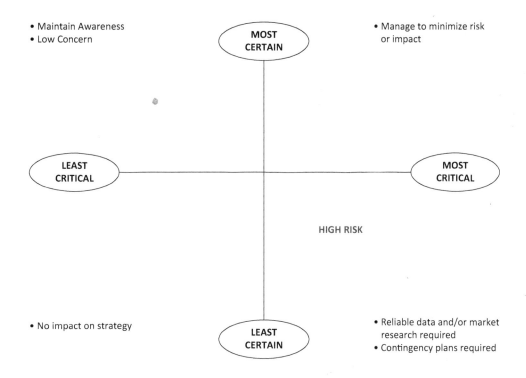

- Maintain Awareness
- Low Concern

- Manage to minimize risk or impact

MOST CERTAIN

LEAST CRITICAL

MOST CRITICAL

HIGH RISK

- No impact on strategy

LEAST CERTAIN

- Reliable data and/or market research required
- Contingency plans required

STRATEGIC MARKETING PLAN

	SEGMENT A		SEGMENT B		SEGMENT C	
	CURRENT POSITION	PLAN	CURRENT POSITION	PLAN	CURRENT POSITION	PLAN
Product						
Service Maintenance/Customer Support						
Distribution/Channel Design						
Communications						
Pricing Strategy						
Internal/Operations Support						

WORKSHEET C-1

STRATEGIC MARKETING PLAN

	SEGMENT D		SEGMENT E	
	CURRENT POSITION	PLAN	CURRENT POSITION	PLAN
Product				
Service Maintenance/Customer Support				
Distribution/Channel Design				
Communications				
Pricing Strategy				
Internal/Operations Support				

WORKSHEET C-2

STRATEGIC MARKETING PLAN

FINANCIAL CONSEQUENCES (ENTER ACTUAL NUMBERS OR ESTIMATES)

	SEGMENT A	SEGMENT B	SEGMENT C	SEGMENT D	SEGMENT E
Share of Market					
Relative Share of Market					
Sales					
Margins (%)					
Marketing Expenses					
Contribution after Marketing Expenses					

Appendix C: One-Page Memo

Tom Peters and Robert Waterman, in their now classic book *In Search of Excellence*, included a section on the value of a "bias for action," and highlighted the value of the one-page memo as a tool for effective, action-oriented communications and for clarifying thinking:

> John Steinbeck once said that the first step toward writing a novel is to write a one-page statement of purpose. If you can't get the one page clear, it isn't likely you'll get far with the novel … It's little wonder that key assumptions get lost in a 100-page investment proposal. The logic probably is loose. The writing most likely is padded. The thinking is almost by definition shoddy. And, worse, the ensuing debate about the proposal among senior executives and reviewers is apt to be similarly unfocused. (Peters & Waterman, 1982, p. 151)

One-page memos are *required* at Procter & Gamble, one of the world's preeminent consumer marketing companies (Bloom, 2016), and they are invaluable for any company and any marketing strategist. Distilling the essential ideas of an analysis or arguments for a proposal down to one-page is not easy. It often takes more time than writing longer reports, but the exercise greatly enhances communication and persuasion. Additionally, the process frequently leads to better underlying ideas as managers are forced to clarify their thinking, surface and examine their assumptions, and test their own decision-making criteria and processes.

WHAT TO INCLUDE/USE OF APPENDICES

Creating a one-page memo does not require that all the relevant information be included on that one page. Important data can be appended to the memo, but any data that are attached should be clearly cited and explained. The writer should not just point the reader to an appendix (for example, "financial statements are attached") but, rather, should summarize and interpret the attachments (for example, "The impact on financial performance, shown in the Appendix A, will be lower per-unit margins but higher net contribution and profitability"). The one-page memo will point the reader to the important information and tell them what it means. Of course, those appended materials should also be relevant, readable, and succinct.

COMMUNICATING AND SELLING YOUR IDEA

The process of writing a one-page memo is interwoven with the process of making decisions and thinking about persuading others to endorse the ideas the memo conveys. The "others" being persuaded are usually busy themselves and often have jobs higher in the organization than the writer. In fact, thinking about who exactly the memo is targeting and exactly what action is being proposed—*Who do you want to do what?*—is an important first step in framing the task of creating a one-page memo. Other initial considerations should include determining exactly what is being recommended—*What changes does the memo want to effect?*—and what the most compelling arguments are for the proposal. This analysis—who the intended decision makers are, what it is the memo recommends they do or approve, and what are the essential arguments for accepting your proposal—leads to considerations of persuasive strategy. What do those readers care about? That is, what are the readers' needs and motivations? What does the reader need to know? What reactions might the reader have, and how can undesirable reactions be anticipated and cut off?

CREATING THE ONE-PAGE MEMO

The first steps in drafting a one-page memo—steps which precede any writing—are preparation and organization. Marketers will be able to plan the memo as they answer the following questions:

- Who are your readers?
- What are the readers' needs and motivations? What drives this audience to act or not act?
- What is the objective? What does the memo recommend (specific actions, approvals, etc.)?
- What do the readers need to know?
- What will persuade/motivate the reader to take desired action?
- What are some possible reader reactions—questions, concerns, and reservations?

Once this context has been fleshed out in some detail, then the writer can begin to gather specific elements of the memo. The next step is to organize, analyze, summarize, and prioritize the information. Organizing is part of the preparation for writing because writers must be confident that they have all of the facts and that those facts supported by data are on hand. An important step in the persuasion process should include sorting facts as supportive or contrary and by importance and power to persuade the intended audience. This should produce an ordered summary of the key pieces of information—or "key points" for the memo.

When the information and key points have been organized, analyzed, summarized, and prioritized, the memo writer should outline the memo *in detail*. Any good piece of communication has an underlying, organizing outline. This outline may be in the memo writer's head, but that invites negligence. Explicit outlines are most useful when they are written and available for reference in the next writing stages, the drafting and review and rewriting of the memo itself. Outlines are not set in stone, but maintaining an explicit outline while writing is an important practice for producing clear, concise, and persuasive memos.

In summary, the writing process includes, in order:

1. Organize, analyze, and summarize information without putting it into a memo or worrying about how it will appear in the memo.
2. Prioritize the information—what is important and what is less important?

3. Create a detailed outline of the memo.
4. Draft the memo.
5. Review the memo. Step back and review the memo for form and substance, adopting the intended reader's perspective in at least one early reading.
6. Rewrite—and rewrite and rewrite.

A generic outline of every one-page memo is not really possible because each memo has a particular purpose, and the outline will change depending on that purpose. However, one outline that can be adapted to many strategic business settings includes the following:

1. The Idea: What are you proposing?
2. Background: What facts and events have led to this being important?
3. Details: How will it work?
4. Motivate the Audience: Who will benefit, and how will they benefit?
5. Next Steps: Who has to do what and by when for this to happen?

A more detailed version of this generic outline is included as Table C-1 below.

TABLE C-1 Detailed Outline of a One-Page Memo

1. **Opening/"The Whole Idea"**
   "I recommend ..."; "This memo recommends ..."

   Succinct statement of:

   - what you're recommending and when;
   - why you're recommending it—what you expect it to accomplish;
   - expected impact;
   - actionability;
   - *action/decision expected of reader* (*assuming agreement*); and
   - key next step and timing if reader agrees.

   Concurrences of others, as required (1 sentence).

2. **Background**
   Briefly explain what the issue is about to help the reader understand and put the recommendation into perspective. If appropriate, include the following:

   - project description;
   - past History/experience;
   - current situation;
   - definition of the problem, opportunity, need, issue, and cause;
   - solution requirements: performance—cost—timing—other; and
   - any pertinent statements of strategy, principles, or objectives.

3. **Recommendation/How it works/How it will work**
   Briefly outline entire recommendation. Cover all important elements. Define the Solution. Include the following:

   - objectives
   - strategic focus
   - implementation plan
   - financial implications
   - impact on other functions/brands/businesses
   - evaluation/measurement—criteria of success

4. **Basis for Recommendation/Key Benefits**

   Concise statement of most important rationale for the recommendation.

   "The most important reasons for this recommendation are …" (typically 2–3, in priority order)

   Advantages–Benefits–Positives–Pros–Urgency

5. **Discussion**
   Briefly identify, if appropriate, and address the following:

   - reasons for not accepting the recommendation
   - arguments against
   - major disadvantages—cons
   - major risks/concerns and how to plan to manage those risks
   - important (and obvious) alternatives to recommendation—"Alternative options considered include …"
   - implications of rejection of recommendation—consequences of *not* accepting the proposal
   - key issues—key factors for success and problems expected
   - all basic assumptions
   - any feasibility issues

6. **Next Steps and Timing**
   Briefly identify *what happens next*, when, and who is responsible.

SUMMARY

Marketing managers usually influence the broader organization and make things happen, not by claiming resources or commanding action—in most organizations they do not have that sort of authority—but rather by *persuading* the organization to commit resources and people to support proposals and programs. Learning to communicate persuasively in concise memos can be a powerful tool in that process. It can also be invaluable in organizing and directing the marketing effort; senior executives do not have time to read lengthy missives, but must be managed, informed, and motivated, all of which require effective communications from the marketing manager. This Appendix presents basic guidelines with regard to creating a one-page memo. The keys to creating an effective memo are careful preparation, consideration of the audience, the audience's motivation to read/respond to the memo, and concise composition.

REFERENCES

Bloom, M. (2016, April 20). What marketers can learn from P & G's one-page memo. *The Marketing Journal.* https://www.marketingjournal.org/what-marketers-can-learn-from-pgs-one-page-memo-madison-bloom/

Peters, T. J. & Waterman, Jr., R. H. (1982). *In search of excellence: Lessons from America's best-run companies.* Harper & Row.

Printed in the USA
CPSIA information can be obtained
at www.ICGtesting.com
LVHW080802120224
771366LV00004B/4